THE TAVISTOCK CENTURY

THE TAVISTOCK CENTURY

2020 Vision

Edited by

**Margot Waddell and
Sebastian Kraemer**

PHOENIX
PUBLISHING HOUSE
firing the mind

First published in 2021 by
Phoenix Publishing House Ltd
62 Bucknell Road
Bicester
Oxfordshire OX26 2DS

British Library Cataloguing in Publication Data

A C.I.P. for this book is available from the British Library

Paperback ISBN-13: 978-1-912691-71-5
Hardback ISBN-13: 978-1-80013-099-9

Typeset by Medlar Publishing Solutions Pvt Ltd, India

www.firingthemind.com

Contents

Preface   xi
Margot Waddell

Foreword: The Tavistock enigma   xv
Anton Obholzer

Part I
The Tavistock legacy

1. Challenge, change, and sabotage   3
   Anton Obholzer

2. What lies beneath   11
   James Astor

3. Psychoanalysis, social science, and the Tavistock tradition   15
   David Armstrong and Michael Rustin

4. Research at the Tavistock   29
   Michael Rustin and David Armstrong

5. *"Mummy's gone away and left me behind"*
   James Robertson at the Tavistock Clinic   47
   Mary Lindsay

6. The Tavistock Institute of Medical Psychology, 1920–2020   61
   Brett Kahr

7. John Bowlby at the Tavistock   67
   Margaret Rustin

8. Balint groups   73
   Andrew Elder

9. Alexis Brook: the contribution of a psychotherapist in primary care   85
   Andrew Elder

10. Extending the reach of the "talking cure"   95
    Margaret Rustin

Part II
Pregnancy and under-fives

11. The psychopathology of publications concerning reactions
    to stillbirths and neonatal deaths   105
    Sandy Bourne

12. Parent–infant psychotherapy at a baby clinic and at the Tavistock Clinic   109
    Dilys Daws

13. Service for under-fives in the child and family department at the Tavistock:
    short-term applications of psychoanalytic practice and infant observation 117
    Lisa Miller

Part III
Children and adolescents

14. The Child Guidance Training Centre 1929–1984   123
    Juliet Hopkins
    with additional material from Marcus Johns, Judith Trowell, and Gillian Miles

15. Gloucester House: a story of endurance, inspiration, and innovation   131
    Nell Nicholson
    with added material from Gillian Miles and Marcus Johns, together with his addendum

16. A foothold in paediatrics   143
    Sebastian Kraemer

17. Early psychoanalytic approaches to autism at the Tavistock   151
    Maria Rhode

18. Eating Disorders Workshop—Tavistock Adolescent Department   155
    Gianna Williams

19. The creation of a service for children and adolescents facing
    gender identity issues   159
    Domenico Di Ceglie

20. The establishment of the Young People's Counselling Service   165
    Fred Balfour

21. Facing it out: the Adolescent Department   169
    Margot Waddell

Part IV
Couples and families

22. A brief history of Tavistock Relationships   175
    Andrew Balfour

23. Tavistock Relationships and the growth of couple
    psychoanalysis 1988–2019: a personal memoir   183
    Mary Morgan

24. Family therapy across the decades: evolution and discontinuous change 187
    Sarah Helps, Sara Barratt, and Gwyn Daniel

Part V
Working with adults

25. Brief psychotherapy: practice and research   199
    David Malan

26. The Tavistock Adult Depression Study (TADS)   205
    David Taylor

27. Working at the Tavistock Clinic Adult Department 1972–1997   209
    John Steiner

28. The Adult Department   213
    Julian Lousada

29. The Adult Department: a group at work   219
    Caroline Garland

30. The Fitzjohn's Unit   229
    David Bell

Part VI
Psychology, social work, and nursing

31. The psychology discipline   233
    Louise Lyon and Emilia Dowling

32. Holding tensions: social work and the Tavistock   241
    Andrew Cooper

33. Nursing at the Tavistock Clinic   247
    Peter Griffiths

Part VII
Consultation, court, and organisations

34. Child protection and the courts   257
    Judith Trowell

35. Autonomic countertransference: the psychopathic mind and the institution   265
    Rob Hale

36. The Tavistock legacy in America: making sense of society   277
    Edward R. Shapiro and James Krantz

37. Psychoanalytic thinking in organisational settings and the therapeutic community tradition   281
    Jenny Sprince

38. Group relations and religion   285
    Wesley Carr

39. The new landscape of leadership: living in radical uncertainty   289
    Jon Stokes

Part VIII
Performance, publications, and policy

40. *"Give them time"*
    Pigeon holes and pasta—the making of a Tavistock TV programme   299
    Beth Holgate

41. The *Tavistock Gazette*, pantomimes, and books   303
    Valerie Sinason

42. Tavistock pantomimes   309
    Jenny Sprince and Paul Pengelly

43. The Tavistock Clinic Series   313
    Margot Waddell

44. Tavistock policy seminars: a contained and disruptive space   319
    Andrew Cooper

Afterword

Soldiering on   329
Sebastian Kraemer

References   341
Index   371

Preface

Margot Waddell

A spirit of hope permeates this book; hope that we might succeed in communicating something of the spirit, passion even, with which the whole Tavistock staff, that is receptionists, secretaries, porters, psychiatrists, psychotherapists, psychoanalysts, psychologists, social workers and nurses, trainees and consultants alike, have been able, over the years, to bring about a cohesive working relationship—one that could embrace the changing post-war social and political conditions, and also to embrace a new world within the NHS structure of 1948.

In the following pages, we have sought to unite a multiplicity of our own voices—each speaking, and in our own idiom, about what it has been like to be a part of the formation and sustaining of an institution dedicated to taking in, bearing and working with the intensity, for so many, of the pain of being alive, who could—despite all—hold onto the decency, thoughtfulness, and non-judgemental reality of what that work required.

Some have written at length, some very briefly, about the spirit of innovation that was involved; about the capacity to sustain contradictions and to risk change. In the early days, work in the NHS attracted people who found it worthwhile to struggle with issues of "insight and responsibility", an aspect of Erik Erikson's work that had so struck Anton Obholzer, whose conception this book is, when Erikson visited South Africa to think and write about the work of Gandhi.

A favoured metaphor that, implicitly or explicitly, runs through these pages is a horticultural one, a reference point for Anton—that of the relationship between the "rootstock" and the capacity to grow into, and to share, a common orchard. The rootstock, may, with time, bear quantities of varieties of, say, apples, but the basic tree remains at the core. The disparate and, in a creative sense, maverick contributions that follow epitomise something of the daring and dedication of this Tavistock institution to do things differently, to be able to trust in some kind of central graft while yielding so many and such distinct fruits.

To trace the history of a single institution over 100 years is no mean undertaking. We have chosen to concentrate on the later years of the Tavistock's being—the years leading up to, and expressed by, its place in the NHS, a history based in the personal memories recounted by those who have contributed to this volume. The early years have been formally and beautifully recorded by Henry Dicks in his "Fifty Years of the Tavistock Clinic" (1970). Many of those who were involved in these Second World War years speak of their lasting respect for the men and women who led the way, and we can celebrate, in this volume, what that legacy really amounted to. For example, the choice of publisher for this book, Phoenix Publishing House, evokes for us the band of war psychiatrists—Jock Sutherland, Wilfred Bion, John Rickman, John Bowlby, Eric Trist, and others—who carrying forward certain beliefs about what constituted mental health and how to work with that on the traumatic battles lines, were the same psychiatrists and social scientists who formed "Operation Phoenix", as the founding characters of what became the NHS model of Tavistock thinking.

One of the most lasting aspects of the thinking of this group had been characterised by Wilfred Bion, an army psychiatrist who had fought as an adolescent tank commander in the First World War, and had worked for the pre-NHS Tavistock during the 1930s until he was called up. Bion made the crucially important distinction between something he called the "work group" by contrast with the "basic assumption group". This distinction is central to our story. What was it that allowed, indeed fostered and nurtured the capacity for a disparate body of workers genuinely to cooperate together for the good of all? What was the nature of the forces that undermined that capacity, the ones that favoured some fantasy of an "ideal" saviour and an "ideal" couple who would produce a solution, or who would flee from responsibility? This was by contrast with those who could work with contradictions, with splitting, negation, denial—in other words, the stuff of group processes, either as staff or as general group members.

To take full account of the extensive and diffuse undertakings and innovations of this group, as it extended over the years, would require many volumes and we have had to limit ourselves, painfully, to an indicative selection. In general, the book traces a developmental path from the wartime psychiatric forces that played such a formative part in the thinking of Operation Phoenix. This group of thinkers drew on the societal and psychological changes of the following years, and took the original thinking forward into the post-war territory of the new NHS. As will become evident in the following pages, that progressive tradition was a powerful, even inspirational one.

We begin with some fairly lengthy pieces which cover aspects of the early history. There are two in particular: on the one hand, the legacy of the innovative thinking that shaped insight into the nature of leadership and group participation that was so fundamental to the clinic's formative thinking, and, on the other, the inspiring work of John Bowlby and James Robertson in relation to the preconditions for the psychic development of children who needed medical care, or were separated from their parental base. Those longer contributions also include accounts of post-war developments in psychiatric, social, psychoanalytic, systemic, and group thinking and the central importance of combining aspects of all such areas in order, collectively, to develop a new institutional base. It soon became clear that such a base required the emotional watershed steps that need to be understood in the course of making one's way across the life cycle.

If we started this book now it would no doubt be rather different. We would have given more space to current social injustices which, while always present, have rapidly become mainstream in possibly hopeful ways. Following its long tradition of working with the effects of personal trauma, abuse and neglect, the Tavistock's increasing concern during the twenty-first century with people disadvantaged by migration, racism and sexual prejudice could be the starting point for a second volume.

* * *

Margot Waddell

Biographical details are hard for those, like me, who need to go back to the very beginning. My external biographical story is relatively simple, but the inside story is not. In terms of my adult life and the strength of my commitment to the Tavistock, something of the background story does need to be told.

From an early age, I wanted to be a clever and effective person, like my wonderful father (a working-class scholarship boy from Edinburgh whose own father had fought in the trenches and whose grandfather had regularly driven the Flying Scotsman in four hours from London to Edinburgh). My mother had been brought up, much like Bion, under the Indian Raj. It was she who taught me how to speak and to engage with the literary qualities of life.

She was, however, slow to realise the extent to which I suffered at the ghastly girls' day schools to which I was consigned (while the boys went to posh boarding schools) and I desperately wanted to go to a local state high school. Finally, I prevailed, was properly taught, and ended up at Cambridge, loving the experience and going on to do a PhD on George Eliot and her intellectual history background.

Halfway through my research, however, I suffered a crisis of conscience: what was I doing in academe when some of my close and talented friends were in the local psychiatric hospital and two of them had committed suicide? I wanted to leave and become a psychiatrist, but my parents couldn't afford that. A good friend suggested that I ask her godfather for advice: "His name is John Bowlby and he works in London at a clinic called the Tavistock." That was the beginning of the rest of my life.

Much later, at Anton Obholzer's suggestion, I applied, soon after qualifying, for a job in the Adolescent Department at the Tavistock, where, I had, effectively, grown up. I was not even shortlisted and it was only thanks to the intervention of Lydia Tischler who, not knowingly at the time, had insisted that I be put on the shortlist, "out of principle", as she told me at a chance encounter with her recently. This was the key that opened the door to my future.

Not surprisingly, then, all the seeds of my lifelong devotion to the work of the Tavistock were sown very early on. In brief, my birth in 1946 meant that my already traumatised brother, having lived with his equally traumatised mother through the London Blitz, then suffered the experience, so vividly described in Mary Lindsay's chapter on Bowlby and the Robertsons' work, in this book, of being effectively banished and abandoned during my mother's "confinement". He never really recovered. Yet at eight years old he was sent to boarding school, as was the custom at the time.

In the post-war years, the boys tended to be sent to boarding school and the girls hung around hoping to be air hostesses or to marry and settle down after attending a finishing school. My own trajectory, however, was different. Fresh from academe, two things immediately mentally and emotionally knocked me over. I asked my then tutor, Martha Harris, what I should read before embarking on two years of infant observation, as a prelude, possibly, to training. She paused before saying: "Don't read anything. Preconception blocks observation." Shortly after that I met Wilfred Bion at a summer seminar at the Tavistock. He was talking about the plethora of theories involved in any kind of psychoanalytic training—so much so, he said, "that sometimes one cannot tell the wisdom for the knowledge". My "real" learning, as opposed to my academic aspirations, began here.

For it was "here" that I started to have the courage to learn from my own experience and not from any excessive ambitions of an academic kind. Despite knowing that my research was closely related to George Eliot's perception of precisely that skewed picture of what "success" looks like, I had not taken it in, personally. The rest of the story is short and simple. I worked my way, devotedly, through the adolescent training. I learned from my students in our many deeply reciprocal encounters. I became head of Child and Adolescent Psychotherapy in the Department and tried my best to extend what I was learning in the many published works and lectures that I managed to produce. In 1978 I took on, together with Nick Temple, editing what became known as the Tavistock Clinic Book Series. We have just published the fifty-sixth book. These, along with the Tavistock's other accomplishments, extended across the world. What I felt that I had learned from the quality of the Tavistock's attitudes was fundamentality informative.

So, for now, my legacy is the three books (1998, 2004, 2018) and many journal articles and book chapters, that I believe to be reaching readers far and wide and in many different translations. There were some truly inspirational figures in my background to whom I shall be forever grateful, my parents above all. My mother offered me a crucial gift, alongside her emotional generosity and selfless care for others. As alluded to earlier, she taught me how to communicate, how to speak, how to love literature and to express that in my own idiom. This legacy is one that the Tavistock continually fostered and, hopefully, will be passing on. As these few details attest, both personally, politically, and professionally, "growing up" is a central issue and one with which we all need, urgently, to engage.

Inside Lives: Psychoanalysis and the Growth of Personality, Duckworth, 1998 (Karnac, 2002).
Understanding 12–14-Year-Olds, Rosendale Press, 2004 (Jessica Kingsley, 2005).
On Adolescence: Inside Stories, Routledge, 2018.

Foreword: The Tavistock enigma

Anton Obholzer

Dedication: To all members of Tavi families, not only the so-called "stars" but everyone who has contributed to our existence—thank you.

This book could easily be mistaken for a Festschrift of a pop group instead of what it really is. The idea of celebration is very much on the mark because the contents cover the first 100 years of the work of the Tavi. The fan club element is, however, far off the mark because little could be a more serious contribution to our present-day society's personal and work practice than the narratives detailed in these pages.

The Tavi is a worldwide community of people with states of mind that have in common a wish to be in touch with what really goes on in the actual world as opposed to the make-believe one that is so commercially peddled in the media and elsewhere. It is devotedly multidisciplinary in its membership. There are many differences, but they all have the same intellectual "bone marrow" of believing in observation and subsequent hypothesis building, rather than the usual, reflex "flight into action".

What the book sets out to do is to record societal and psychological change, growth, and development over the past century from a Tavistock perspective. A process led, in part, by the Tavistock taking up social and psychological ideas that were already present in the wider society, and ripe for application (see Stokes, Chapter 39).

A constant in the field of individual, group, and institutional dynamics is to ensure that the work undertaken by both client and consultant does not fail on account of our falling into states of hopelessness and despair, or of omnipotence and dishonesty. To achieve this balance requires regular monitoring, as well as thought and humility. These same principles apply in specific industries and tasks. Under "personal industries" we might place family and child rearing, from infancy, through childhood, adolescence, parenthood; education; workplace roles; midlife; retirement; and death.

There are many forefathers and some foremothers of the Tavi who need to be retrieved. The mothers are nowadays coming to the fore again, given the greater awareness of women's contributions in society. Melanie Klein and Anna Freud always had key places in the front rows of analytic institutes, but there were many others. Inevitably there are many men to be mentioned, premier, of course, being Freud and Jung. A further one is Erik Erikson, a Danish-American who described the life cycle in which a series of emotional watershed steps need to be mastered in the move from birth to death. Many of these steps are there in the various sections of the book (though Erikson was never knowingly connected with the Tavistock).

By contrast, Wilfred Bion, one of the "Tavi greats", made crucial observations about groups and the adult workplace, in particular the existence of work and basic assumption groups. In the latter the individual "gave up" their personal identity and operated as part of the unconscious "slipstream" and thought of the group and its direction of travel. These were the basic assumption "fellow travellers" of whom there always are many. By contrast the "workplace state of mind" members mostly retained their individual identity and functioned accordingly, whatever setting and application they were in. These two states of mind—basic assumption and work group—obviously play a key role in organisations, particularly in the public sector and in the workplace. Bion began to conceive this distinction when working with other army psychiatrists and psychologists in the War Office Selection Boards (WOSB) during the Second World War. These colleagues went on to create the revived Tavistock—Operation Phoenix—after the war was over.

Basic assumptions are associated with all of human activity, creating a social defensive system that protects us from the "fallout" of anxieties in groups of any kind. So the health system is there to shield us from death, the army from uncontrolled violence, the education system has its own defensive role, and so on. The names of Eric Miller, Isabel Menzies Lyth, Elizabeth Bott Spillius, Pierre Turquet, Bob Gosling—all key Tavistock senior staff—come to mind. As has often been said by philosophers, "mankind can but little cope with emotional pain". We therefore create the above-mentioned social systems—the "unbearable detritus" being handed to the office bearers of these systems, to doctors, teachers, police, and so on.

The Tavistock approach is strongly anchored in observation and thought, as opposed to flight and denial. Only a few decades ago young hospitalised children in long-term orthopaedic wards were allowed one parental visit a week, if that. Nowadays it would be hard to find a paediatric ward that does not cater for the mother or carer to stay overnight, if the child is admitted as a patient (see Lindsay, Chapter 5). What we now know from research and observation is that, besides protection from psychological harm, the time taken for post-operative healing is reduced when children in hospital have mothers or carers with them. Not surprisingly there are many other conditions which "lurked underground" without their disturbing effects on everyday life being noted. For example, abortion or stillborn babies were not often acknowledged as significant emotional triggers affecting family and personal dynamics, sometimes for life (see Bourne, Chapter 11). These changes in our understanding of our basic, evolutionary human need for protection are due to the research work of the other "Tavi great" John Bowlby, and his co-workers at the Clinic, James and Joyce Robertson, Mary Ainsworth, and their successors.

Until the later part of the last century, little attention was paid to the unconscious dynamics of group and institutional processes. Disturbances were either seen as "individual issues" and sometimes treated as an individual, or else dealt with by attempting to "manage them away". These approaches still have a considerable ideological hold in psychology and in business schools. They are presented as the one and only way of diagnosing and treating problems rather than one of a handful of possible approaches. The danger, then, is to stick to one's theory about the problem and pursue its pseudo-solution without considering other options; in fact to pursue the pseudo-solution with more and greater energy until one finally hits the ultimate brick wall. Wilfred Bion encouraged the consultant/coach to be "free of memory and desire", a useful reminder when entering a foreign system to keep an open mind without a preconception as to what might be going on. The response to be avoided is to be stampeded into a solution which precisely parallels the problem brought for discussion. The result being that coaches are pushed into the role of "snake-oil salesmen".

So what is this book about? Not surprisingly, a question is what should be included and discussed and what not; where are the boundaries of the various Tavi "tribal" units? What is true Tavi and what is, as a colleague pithily put it "the wrong side of the blanket"? I am often struck by the parallels that happen in religious organisations—Shia or Sunni, Catholic or Protestant. The Afghans annually hold a Durga (meeting) which invites all tribal subgroups to attend. The first day is all friendship and help, the second work, on the third day it is all fight, difference, and AK47s. And so it often is with Tavi-style meetings. The narcissism of small differences and the wish to convert others to one's own way of thinking by contrast with listening, and agreeing that *there are many different ways of seeing things*. We fully recognise that we cannot satisfy and acknowledge everyone and their perspective, and, in fact, might please no one. But that is the reality of the everyday Tavi in the world today, so it is no surprise that in writing about the phenomenon, we are also re-enacting the various behaviours we are writing about.

The Tavistock was founded in 1920 in Tavistock Square, London as the Tavistock Institute of Medical Psychology. This organisation still exists and is the rootstock and original trunk of the structures that exist today. To continue with the horticultural image, it is the trunk from which all the so-called Tavis branch off. The original trunk, when the NHS was created after WWII, led to the development of the *Tavistock and Portman NHS Foundation Trust*, a UK National Health Service (NHS) public sector structure. A main branch leading from the original trunk is the Tavistock Institute of Human Relations—the Tavistock institute which deals with socially concerned organisations, government policy, research, and consulting. The Tavistock Institute of Medical Psychology continues to exist and remains as sponsor of the marital institute now known as Tavistock Relationships. There are many other related family saplings, some called "Tavistock", others by their original names, for example the Portman Clinic.

What in all of this can be specifically identified in the emotional and professional DNA of the Tavi? Respect, careful observation, co-workership, the risk and avoidance of hubris, omnipotence, and burnout issues.

How does one preside over and lead a creative organisation with all its difficulties, rivalries, and prima donna type behaviour? To quote from a chapter on the role of the administrator in a recent book, *Turning the Tide*, about the Tavistock Fitzjohn's Unit, "You can tell immediately it's a Fitzjohn's patient by the expression on their face—they quickly want to pass it on" (Lane & Nicholls, 2018, p. 38). Receptionists in GP surgeries—and any GP will readily concede how valuable their receptionist is to their practice—frequently have to contend with people whose behaviour may become distorted under the pressure of pain and anxiety. The role of their receptionist, known as "Ibi", rightly occupies the whole of Lane and Nicholls' chapter in the Fitzjohn's Unit book (Meyerowitz & Bell, 2018). As acknowledged in the dedication to that book, it is the administrative staff who make for the fertile and rich soil in which the Tavistock tree can flourish. If the soil and tree are neglected, the crop will be small, ordinary, and not distinguishable from the bland, tasteless commercial crop which meets the requirements of auditors and accountants. If that happens creativity is lost, as is learning and innovation. The product becomes indistinguishable from everyday routine products. This, in turn, puts creative institutions at risk of becoming as sterile as the industrial products they produce. As Oscar Wilde said, "they know the price of everything and the value of nothing".

What follows are chapters on inducing and fostering professional technical creativity which include warmth, pleasure, fun, and a degree of delinquency.

* * *

Anton Meinhard Obholzer

I was born in 1938 of Austrian parents in Stellenbosch, Cape Province, South Africa. My father had been recruited by the University of Stellenbosch to head the Department of Physical Education which was in its early stage of development. His tenure was short lived, as was his early role of father, since all "enemy aliens" were interned by the South African regime. After some time, he was repatriated to Austria, leaving his wife and child to cope as best we could in South Africa. He was not able to return until 1948.

I grew up in the care of my mother who struggled with her abandoned situation and also by my aunt who, I later realised, did most of the missing parenting role and loving of me as a child. We spoke German at home, English at school, Afrikaans with the neighbours, and my nanny was Xhosa. After many years of reflection and analysis I've come, not surprisingly, to the conclusion that this early dynamic "stew" I grew up in provided the raw material for much, if not all, of my adult life and career.

I matriculated from St Patrick's, the Christian Brothers College in Kimberley (the diamond mining town) and after that took a gap year in Europe. This was my first contact with my extended family about whom I had heard so much from my mother but had actually never met on account of the war. Returning to South Africa I enrolled at Stellenbosch University for a degree in forestry. It did not take long for me to realise that I was more interested in people than in trees and I managed to switch to Cape Town University Medical School where I qualified in medicine in 1963.

After a hectic period in casualty departments in the Cape slums and in general practice, I felt the need to have more contact and insight into people's emotional/social lives and embarked on training as a specialist psychiatrist. The then head of department, Professor Lynn Gillis, to whom I owe a lifelong debt, encouraged all trainees to follow their own bent, so when at the height of political troubles in the mid- to late 1960s Erik Erikson passed through the Cape to research his book on Gandhi (1969), I was blown away by his "Insight and Freedom"[1] lecture that he gave to the University (Erikson, 1968). A combination of this, and some time spent in a mix of farming and antique dealing on the side, led to a bursary to explore the European roots of some aspects of Cape culture.

In retrospect it's not hard to make links between my early life and a subsequent search for my identity.

So we, my wife, Annabel, an artist, and our three young children arrived in England in the early 1970s. Instead of returning to the Cape as originally planned, we found our way into the rich opportunities for life and work in London. When the bursary money ran out, my first job was in a psychiatric "bin" on night duty and on call to the elderly demented patients who had fallen out of bed. From then onwards I had a foot on the more compelling psychiatric/psychoanalytic ladder and trained at the Royal College of Psychiatrists, the Tavistock Clinic, and the Institute of Psychoanalysis.

It is likely that it was my early experience, living in a complex societal system, that allowed me to enter and appreciate complicated systems of interaction, particularly in the mental health field. I had learnt not to take denial and repression as a given, but that it was quite possible to turn such matters on their head and, more likely, to thrive. This quality became particularly necessary at certain key points of the Tavistock's history, for example when the Tavistock was part of the same management group as neighbouring NHS units that were determined to asset strip our resources for their own benefit. With the collective efforts of colleagues and with the positive attitude of the members of the Tavistock and Portman Trust, we managed to achieve our independence and to preserve an atmosphere of research and adventure which was sadly lacking in much of the rest of the NHS. The pressure to conform to standards that are laid down for solely financial and political purposes remains a threat to our future to this day, yet it needs to be robustly defended against in confirming our ongoing work and existence. Conforming to measures of uniformity and survival are likely to lead to the death of the organisation, but as ever, the battle continues.

Note

1. Based on Erikson's *Insight and Responsibility: Lectures on the Ethical Implications of Psychoanalytical Insight* (1964)

Part I

The Tavistock legacy

CHAPTER ONE

Challenge, change, and sabotage

Anton Obholzer

There has been no shortage of inquiries, working parties, recommendations, reports, and executive letters from on high as to what is to be done about improving the mental health of the nation. Yet, despite all our best efforts, progress has been painfully slow and disappointing. This chapter [from a conference presentation given in 1997] is an attempt to look at some of the issues that in my view slow down and, at some times, completely sabotage the process of change and, in the case of mental health, ensure that we continue to be trapped in the present day mix of swamps and logjams.

I do not believe that the fundamental problem is shortage of staff or lack of money. This might come as a surprise to some of my colleagues and a pleasant relief to the NHS Executive. I believe that we have more than enough staff engaged in the mental health field in the widest sense, but that the vast majority of them are poorly trained and ill-supported in their work. This covers both the formal and voluntary sectors. Until we make better use of our existing staff we cannot tell whether there is enough money in the system or not.

So if we have enough reports, executive letters, staff, and money why is the system not working? I believe that many of the reports and recommendations to managers and workers alike are no better than telling someone who is distressed to "pull themselves together". This form of treatment, whether applied to a child, an adolescent, an adult, a professional, or mental health workers in the broadest sense, does not work. Even if it takes the form of action paragraphs, deadlines, or penalties of how, and by when, one has to pull oneself together, it does not work.

In order to improve the situation one has to understand it not only in its conscious manifestation (as most reports do) but also in its unconscious manifestation in terms of the underlying and unspoken nature of the problem. I am not talking about some mysterious or esoteric approach peddled on behalf of one or other sectarian point of view, be it psychiatry,

3

psychoanalysis, or whatever. I'm talking about what we all know but don't, and often dare not, speak about, about: the fact that working with the mentally ill drives us to despair and into dark and seemingly hopeless places; that making progress, or even just maintaining one's sanity and morale, can be a full-time occupation; and that taking flight from the pain of the work accounts for much of the difficulty experienced in the field.

I am not saying that it is hopeless, or that nothing can be done: I am saying it makes us feel hopeless and despairing. This can often not be spoken about. We then fall into denial of the very existence of the problem, and in that state of mind we then find it difficult to help ourselves, our colleagues, and our organisation. The process can go one step further by what, in my field, is called projective identification, a technical way of describing the mote in one's brother's eye when one does not see the beam in one's own. It is at this stage that the mechanism of blame enters the equation; blaming lack of money, lack of workers, the government, the profession, and so on. It makes for a state of self-righteous comfort but does nothing towards making progress in improving mental health.

But is it true that working in the mental health field is more painful than other work? I think it is. Occupational health teaches us that there are occupational hazards to all forms of work. "Mad as a hatter" is a good example from the past. Silicosis, farmer's lung, for example, are well known. Radiographers carry a disk on their lapel that measures the degree of radiation that they have been exposed to. There is similar risk of "radiation" in the mental health field. Working with mental distress causes the distress to be communicated to the workers and for the workers to become stressed and distressed in turn.

In the past—in recognition of the stress of the work—psychiatrists were allowed to retire at fifty-five (instead of sixty-five) and draw their pension. Of all medical workers psychiatrists have the highest suicide rate. You may think that this is because the profession draws the most unstable doctors, but that instability—if it is true—may also be an asset for doing the work. As the Baptist minister John Martin proclaimed of his contemporary William Blake's alleged madness, "If Blake is cracked, his is a crack that lets in the Light." The real reason is the stress arising from the work. I have been speaking about psychiatrists, but it must be understood that they should be seen as only one of the many professions that work with the mentally disturbed and ill, and that the processes (and the historic retirement rights) I describe apply equally to all professionals in the field.

Why does this process matter? It is a minor problem affecting some individuals, so what! But I would say that far from being a minor problem it is a major problem, and addressing it holds the key to shifting the mental health logjam. In spite of our best efforts there is severe bias and fear in the public's mind about mental illness. All of us present at any of our conferences will know that this is irrational, but for all that, it is a fearsome reality in how our society functions.

All "threats" in our society have been "allocated" office bearers and institutions whose task it is to deal with these threats and to remove them from society and from our conscious concerns.

The same applies whether we are talking about physical, medical, or emotional threats.

It is no coincidence that the mentally ill were incarcerated in institutions on green field sites away from the centres of population. "Out of sight, out of mind" was the policy. That policy has now been changed, and we have "care in the community", but the state of "out of sight, out of mind" is still with us, exactly as before, only it takes a different form. The most pernicious form is now the state of mind of the workers in their approach to the patients. Because repeated daily exposure to the mentally ill is draining, the workers fall into a state of mind of not being in touch with their patients. This can take a variety of forms. At its most concrete it can mean that workers lose contact with patients. You have all seen the statistics and read the multiple recommendations about how this is to be avoided. But, whatever the recommendations, if you want to "lose" a patient you will.

I need to make quite clear what I am saying. I am not saying that workers consciously and wilfully lose patients. Far from it. The vast majority of workers are dedicated and hard working, and would rightly protest at such an outrageous suggestion. And yet a great many patients are lost—I believe for unconscious reasons. Just as one is inclined to "forget" unpleasant appointments and deadlines, so workers forget patients. And if they are working in a system in which there is little training and no awareness of these processes, *they themselves feel forgotten*. When that happens, the likelihood of patients—particularly the most troubling ones—being forgotten is ever higher.

Another equally concrete way of losing contact with patients is either to become ill yourself as a worker (illness rates in care in the community workers are high) or to leave (staff loss and turnover is equally high and, of course, expensive). But these are only the most visible manifestations of the process of distancing yourself from the work. There are more subtle and thus pernicious ways of distancing yourself from patients. For example by not having your mind on the job, by being distracted, taking flight into other activities that fall into the orbit of the work but enable escape from the discomfort of the work at the emotional "coalface". Keeping the patient and his or her needs in mind in the context of their family and social systems means being in touch with all the distressing and, at times, hopeless aspects of being mentally ill in often very unsatisfactory personal, social, economic, and housing conditions. Working with other agencies and other workers, in social, housing, finance, and the like, only compounds the experience of difficulty. And so it is understandable that liaison does not happen and people fall into the gaps between the various professionals and institutions that are supposed to look after them.

I am not justifying this state of mind in workers, nor their professional conduct, but I believe that what they are doing in everyday layman's language is turning a blind eye to discomfort, pain, and threats, and that executive letters and their ilk make no difference to the situation whatsoever. You can turn a blind eye to an executive letter and bin it, just as you can to any other painful situation. If bombarded by deadlines and threats you will feel persecuted and find ways around them, or have a breakdown or leave, but you are unlikely to comply with the injunction to face something that is unbearable. I should reassure you that I am not by character depressive, negative, or cynical in my approach. I believe that a lot can be done to change the situation, but before we change it we need to understand what the problem is. In many instances we have attempted to address the symptoms without understanding the underlying problems.

I should also say that the foregoing ideas about how workers relate to stress and how it affects their work and the institutions in which they work comes from a long and honourable tradition of research that by and large has had very little influence in the health and mental health fields. This is because the message is unwelcome and defended against, a case of "shooting the messenger" if he brings unwelcome news or brings ways of understanding that do not fit into the "regulation" way of seeing things. In this regard I, too, as messenger run a risk, not of being shot, but of being politely welcomed and then completely forgotten, for the message I bring is a disturbing one.

Why is working with the mentally ill so upsetting?

There are several interrelated factors. If one is to work with an open mind in this field one has to ask oneself about the causes of mental illness. In doing so it is clear that there are many genetic, biological, psychological, sociological, and economic factors that affect human development and mental health and the onset of mental illness. It is hard to think about these issues "out there"—as affecting only others or patients. It is natural that one should also have thoughts about one's own upbringing and about how our behaviour affects our own children. At that level the situation becomes a lot more difficult and close to the bone.

This, in part, explains why all concerned seem to make so little connection between child and adolescent development and adult behaviour. Quite understandably, we fall into a state of mind of "it did me no harm, so why should it affect my children?", failing to take into account that perhaps we are least best placed to judge whether or not "it" has done no harm. Parenthood, in any case, is about a degree of regret. How much more so if our child has become mentally ill. At times like that we may well fall into finding an explanation that makes sense to us, often one that helps us move away from our own unspoken and unacknowledged sense of guilt. Sometimes this generates a "crusading" state of mind that can be very helpful in raising money and providing support, but at the price of pursuing a particular approach. Nothing gives a better boost to one's identity than having an enemy, preferably an unreasonable and hateful one. This may explain why mental health—unlike, say, surgery, paediatrics, or professions outside the health sector—is riven with strife and factionalism. There is a greater "personal invasiveness" factor in working with mental states than there is with other treatment "products" that are processed as part of the work.

Additionally, we grow up in a culture where we are supposed to be able to deal with everything that life throws at us with "a stiff upper lip". While that culture is undoubtedly changing, the fallout from it is still with us. Then there is the peculiar situation where the expertise that goes with working with the mentally ill is not recognised. No one would claim to know as much of their field as an engineer or a scientist or a lawyer. But when it comes to mental health we're all "experts". This is partly for the reasons mentioned above—the divisions and "enemy" states in the mental health professions—but also because we have all been children and have grown up and thus have a degree of expertise, simply from our own experience. Besides mental health the only other fields where this applies are education and social services, for similar reasons. We are in the grip of flight and defensive processes from painful work and are divided amongst ourselves.

I haven't told you anything that you don't know, though perhaps I have cast some light on why it is happening. And I've repeatedly said that I don't believe that change by fiat or injunction works.

What is to be done?

The first is that the splitting process that creates gaps between departments and budgets—the gaps into which patients fall—needs to be narrowed and closed if at all possible. We need the best possible conditions for human development. Today's patients are a generation ago's babies. We need a better integration of health, social, educational, and fiscal policy. At present we have separate empires with their office bearers who pay lip service to cooperation, but jealously guard their power and their budgets. We need to address this fragmentation which not only serves to maintain the status quo, but embodies a denial of the importance of people as the world's and nation's most important asset. The present arrangement also embodies a sense of "no can do" which is based on a sense of hopelessness about ever making improvements in mental health.

The present green paper on cooperation between health and social services and the appointment of a minister for public health[1] give some hope, but the risk of these developments being caught up and bound in the process of hopelessness mentioned above are enormous. The social process of change is inexorably geared in favour of no change *unless we build "addressing resistance to change" in as an integral part of the process.* The risk of the round of conferences to which we go is that, having serviced our sense of guilt by attending and giving views, we all go our separate ways. Acknowledgement of the difficulty of mental health work should be addressed in both mental health training programmes and in staff support (see, for example, Hale, Chapter 35) and continuing education systems, which too many workers don't have. Around half the workers in the mental health field have had either no training at all, or no adequate training. Staff development systems (see many other chapters in this volume) are either completely absent or else unclear in what they are trying to achieve, and by what means. It is for these reasons that what is required is not more staff but better trained and better supported staff. And that does not necessarily mean more money—it is too early to say—but it surely requires a change in training—in training organisations, and in the commissioning of training. The present system of commissioning training in the mental health field is in desperate trouble, partly because it is caught up in a doctrinaire policy designed by the previous government [in the mid-1990s[2]]. While on paper the policy makes sense, in practice it is so out of touch with reality that I sometimes wonder whether it is not an unconscious attack on both the patients and the workers in the mental health field. This is not as bizarre an idea as it might seem to be at first glance. It is not uncommon for people to be resentful of, and hostile towards, those that drive one into despair. And what is the despair about? In spite of the civil servants' best intentions, it is about our frustratingly slow rate of change in the field. Doctors get angry and frustrated with patients that don't respond to their therapeutic ministrations and turn away from them, or fall into punitive therapeutic regimes. It would be surprising if civil servants did not fall into a similar state of mind.

Be that as it may, the way mental health training is supposed to proceed is as follows: there are separate systems for medics and non-medics—so much for multidisciplinary work—and these are then to come together at some stage in the future. So much for history. And training is supposed to be commissioned by consortia. The fact that these consortia have hardly got their act together as regards basic nurse training, never mind mental health work, is not mentioned. And then mental health training is to be commissioned by these mechanisms. It may be a brave attempt to empower purchasers (now known as commissioners) and to wrest the baton from crusty training organisations that keep on producing what suits them. But it takes no account of the fact that mental health has always been a Cinderella area, for reasons of personal and social discomfort. The chances of success following this approach to commissioning training I believe are nil, because the commissioners are quite out of touch with the needs of mental health professionals.

Summary

Even within existing staff resources, there are great opportunities for improving mental health services. But we have to have a service that is based on a developmental backbone, coordinates policy and finance between different departments and budgets, and does not make an artificial and defensive differentiation between mental health, mental illness, and, the latest department preoccupation, serious mental health. Staff training and support systems need to be *multidisciplinary and be funded in a multidisciplinary way*. That means addressing entrenched financial fiefdoms that hold out against the many recommendations for multidisciplinary work. Management structures in multidisciplinary work need to be clarified—no private sector organisation would survive for long if it were saddled with the structures the NHS has to suffer. Training has to be geared to the needs of the patients, not the prejudices of the trainers.

So, am I not just producing another report with edicts and injunctions? I believe not, for an integral part of change should be time-limited, audited, and researched pilot projects with management consultancy and staff support groups focused on issues of change and resistance to change. Such pilots would cost very little compared to the massive expenditure and waste we are experiencing at present in our attempts to change the situation, and I believe would produce a realistic way ahead, then to be applied on a wider scale.

Anton Obholzer
Chief executive
Tavistock and Portman NHS Trust, 120 Belsize Lane, NW3 5BA

July 1997

Anton Obholzer led the Tavistock Clinic, and then the Tavistock and Portman Trust, between 1985 and 2002, while at the same time building on decades of group relations and management programmes to develop consultancy around the world.

He is co-editor of the bestselling *Unconscious at Work* (second edition, 2019) and the author of *Workplace Intelligence: Unconscious Forces and How to Manage Them* (Routledge 2021).

[Anton Obholzer's biography appears on p. xviii]

Notes

1. Tessa Jowell (1947–2018) was the first minister of public health, appointed by Prime Minister Tony Blair in May 1997. A little known fact about her time as an elected councillor in the Tavistock's local council (Camden) is that she joined the family systems training at the Tavistock Clinic in the late 1970s. Tessa later took a lead role in the setting up of Labour's flagship Sure Start based in children's centres. Despite the indifference of later governments it achieved many of its goals, particularly in support of the most disadvantaged children (Cattan, Conti, Farquharson, & Ginja, 2019).
2. This chapter was given as a talk at a conference in 1997, less than three months after Labour's victory in the general election, after eighteen years of Conservative rule. To prove its good management of the economy, the new government announced it would maintain the previous chancellor's pledge to "freeze public expenditure for two years" (Larry Elliott, *The Guardian*, March 12, 2007).

CHAPTER TWO

What lies beneath

James Astor

When Stephen Spender wrote, "I think continually of those who were truly great," he wasn't thinking of Bion, Klein, or Fordham. He was writing about those who in the past had courageously done something that changed our world. The characteristic of these people was that they had in mind what had gone before. There are echoes here of Freud's thought that those who cannot remember are condemned to repeat past behaviours, which they are unable to change. Auden, famously, did remember Freud in his poem "In Memory of Sigmund Freud" (1939) in which he wrote, "to us he is no more a person but a whole climate of opinion under whom we conduct our different lives". These poets and this expression identifies the underlying elements that made the Tavistock distinctive. The education of the spirit, the awareness and acknowledgement of the essential qualities of living in the depressive position underpinned the psychodynamic departments of the Tavistock. This provided the shared base for the recognition that whether you are a Jungian, a Kleinian, a Freudian, or a systemic, couple or family therapist you will meet on common ground, even if therapeutic approaches to that ground are varied.

This Tavistock, where I studied, offered Bowlby on attachment theory, Turquet on group behaviours, detailed Freud reading seminars, and essential Kleinian concepts, including Bion's post-Kleinian developments. Jung was not read and only Frances Tustin, by then established in Buckinghamshire, acknowledged Fordham's contribution to studies in autism. Away from Fitzjohn's Avenue—wittily referred to by Jonathan Miller on the occasion of the installation of Sigmund Freud's statue next to the Tavistock Centre as "the gateway to the avenue of the unconscious"—was, amid so much else, the Tavistock of organisational consultancy led by Eric Miller. This part of the organisation played a huge role internally as we were encouraged to take part in its Leicester conferences. Smaller conferences, but just as powerful, were conducted regularly on site for the staff within the Tavistock Centre itself. Leicester conferences were occasions when the staff created conditions for the participants that were intended to generate anxiety and confusion in group task situations, which, provided the participants did not go crazy, revealed the unconscious dynamics of the groups and organisations created within the conference structure, and our active role in promoting, or undermining, the work of groups.

Those of us who worked or taught there experienced the enjoyment of being in this atmosphere; to go back to Auden's "In Memory of Sigmund Freud" (1939), it is a matter for rejoicing "to serve enlightenment like him".

The Tavistock, primarily a teaching and treating institution, has been an organisation that has had different associations and a range of professional groups. What has changed is that the word "Tavistock" is now often used as a soubriquet appropriated by any and all who have crossed its threshold to confer stature on themselves. When I first encountered this organisation, it was to see Martha Harris who ran the child psychotherapy training. I was about to go to university. I wanted to train to work psychotherapeutically with children and was considering degree courses. I thought that the University College London Psychology Department would be the most appropriate, not least because it had a psychoanalyst on the staff, Cecily de Monchaux. Mattie Harris, in our meeting, surprised me by suggesting that I would be as well equipped for working in this field with an English degree as with a psychology degree. Her reason was that learning to think about people, their motivations, behaviours, compulsions, their self-destructive tendencies, and entrapment in the effects of childhood trauma was nowhere better explored than in English literature. This was before literature courses at universities were treated as social or political artefacts; before, too, the Balkanisation of such studies into feminist, black, or gay groupings had taken hold.

The diverse elements of the various departments of the Tavistock Clinic, while underpinned by acceptance of our common values and aspirations to tolerate "Negative Capability", (Keats, 1817[1]) needed leadership. The leader who could sustain the creativity of the organisation had to be familiar with the dynamics of these different groups of therapists, social workers, and teachers and also to have the presence to impose organisational constraints and unpopular decisions. It required a leader able to encourage the various teams to peek over the barriers that they had put round their territories and acknowledge the value of the other's point of view.

This was the Tavistock that I knew. For many of those years it was led by Anton Obholzer, a clinician and organisational consultant with a sense of the purpose of the institution and the skill to manage the funders. Anton's "Consulting to Institutions" workshop (Obholzer & Roberts, 2019), in which I participated, exemplified the ethos of passionate enquiry and good humoured acknowledgement of divergent views, conducted in an atmosphere of respectful debate. This workshop was enlivened by Anton inviting others to join in, others who were not part of the Tavistock—grist to the mill. I used to sit next to Ruth Levitt, an academic and organisational consultant, whose ability to cut through the dissemblance and diversionary behaviours of the clients being reported on, to reveal the essence of a problem hidden from all the parties to the process, was a resource used by Anton, sometimes sparingly, sometimes not. Ruth's analysis had something of the surgeon's precision and sharpness of insight, always delivered diffidently. But there was no mistaking the clarity of thought that structured her analysis. The point was to learn and to understand, to experiment, partially to succeed, to examine our failures and take responsibility. This was what was life enhancing about these collaborations and that atmosphere, stimulated by the wider context of teaching and being challenged by our students.

But the climate of opinion, even then, was moving away from what Auden referred to. If the psychoanalytic had been the metric we adhered to, now societal pressures, such as diversity, educational disadvantage, and contemporary problems that educational institutions had to address were beginning to emerge. Occasionally I found myself caught between the institutional and personal points of view. When I was marking students' dissertations for their master's degree course (linked to the University of East London) I recommended that students who could not write grammatical English be awarded a diploma not a master's degree. The exam board, however, felt that this did not give sufficient recognition to their circumstances; for example if the candidate had come to education late in life and had experienced what is now described as historical economic and social disadvantage. Contained in the board's response was the idea, still debated today, that the institution might have to make allowances for past societal failures.

Pressure on sought-after places in centres of further education has kept alive the difficult subject of whether educational decisions should or should not be decided principally on a meritocratic basis. If so what does this actually mean? Not least because standardised tests, usually cited as suitable instruments for maintaining a meritocratic system, favour the advantaged student from a supportive and economically stable background. From my small sample, I noticed that reverse discrimination had become an element in the debate. Now that there is an increased need for the services of the Tavistock, combined with a reduction in funding, the focus for the managers has been to find money to survive. When this is driven by results, top–down directives to see patients within a few days of an enquiry, then time to reflect, to confer, to craft individual treatments to suit the circumstances are in danger of going out of the window, hasty formulaic responses predominating. This should be a concern for all of us who know the Tavistock from earlier times.

The Tavistock that I knew encouraged us to explore knowledge and reflect on its essence and instrumentality, to learn from our mistakes and to listen to other points of view. To value the dark, or as Auden (1939) wrote of Freud:

> but he would have us remember most of all
> to be enthusiastic over the night,
> not only for the sense of wonder
> it alone has to offer, but also
> because it needs our love.

This culture is difficult to nurture and easy to destroy, especially when governments do not recognise that anticipating a problem and providing a resource is more effective in the long term than treating the problem when it arises.

Note

1. "I had not a dispute but a disquisition with Dilke, on various subjects; several things dovetailed in my mind, & at once it struck me, what quality went to form a Man of Achievement especially in literature & which Shakespeare possessed so enormously—I mean Negative Capability, that is when man is capable of being in uncertainties, Mysteries, doubts, without any irritable reaching after fact & reason" (John Keats in a letter to his brothers dated Sunday, December 21, 1817).

* * *

James Astor studied at the Tavistock and trained at the Society of Analytical Psychology in adult and child analysis. He worked in child guidance, in a hospital child psychiatry department, and as a training analyst in private practice, before joining Anton Obholzer's Consulting to Institutions workshop. There followed from this, consultancy work with organisations as diverse as social work departments, drug rehabilitation centres, and hospital Accident and Emergency departments. While doing this he also taught on the Organisational Consultancy module (D10) at the Tavistock and at the University of East London.

While teaching and engaging with the trainings at the SAP he worked closely with Michael Fordham, and published *Michael Fordham: Innovations in Analytical Psychology* (Routledge, 1995) and papers on analytical psychology and its relation to psychoanalysis, the self, transference, and interpretation. He is a chartered psychologist and was a member of the Association of Child Psychotherapists, the Society of Analytical Psychology, the British Association of Psychotherapists, and the Tavistock Society of Psychotherapists.

CHAPTER THREE

Psychoanalysis, social science, and the Tavistock tradition

David Armstrong and Michael Rustin

This chapter describes the development of the Tavistock Clinic and the Tavistock Institute of Human Relations (TIHR), with particular reference to their formation during the Second World War and the early post-war period, and to their expansion and development until the end of the last century. TIHR emerged from the Tavistock Clinic in the immediate post-war years. However, the two organisations' close association means that, throughout the chapter, we often refer to them as a single entity, "the Tavistock", distinguishing them as and when it is helpful to do so.

Our particular focus is on the integration between psychoanalytic and social- and community-oriented perspectives. We believe that the Tavistock was an exemplary context in which this integration was attempted, and to a degree accomplished. This happened within the Tavistock's work in both clinical practices and in research, both of which were significantly shaped by the commitments to democracy and social justice in post-war Britain, exemplified in the development of its health, welfare, and education services. We argue that in this early context there was a firm commitment at the Tavistock to integrate both research and practice, and bring together psychological and social understandings. From a present-day perspective, this is a promise that has remained incompletely fulfilled, although one hopes to see its renewal. In another chapter in this volume, we will give particular attention to the generation of knowledge at the Tavistock, to what should be understood in inclusive terms as its research tradition.

Although psychoanalytic ideas and methods were the most fundamental influence on its practices, the Tavistock's orientation was always broader than that of psychoanalysis itself. Where the Institute of Psychoanalysis, the training body of the British Psychoanalytical Society, was mainly committed to the preservation and development of the psychoanalytic work of Freud and his successors, the Tavistock took as its field the improvement of the mental health and well-being of society itself. Its founding figures, Hugh Crichton-Miller and J. R. Rees, were psychiatrists who were influenced by various strands of psychoanalytic thinking, but who were not themselves psychoanalysts. Moreover, the preferred description of the Tavistock's orientation in the inter-war years was psychodynamic rather than psychoanalytic.

Meanwhile, the links between the Tavistock and academic social sciences such as sociology and anthropology have been somewhat indirect, in part because the Tavistock for most of its history existed outside the university system, and has upheld the distinctive idea that research and practice should always be reciprocally connected to one another. In many sociology teaching departments, focused mainly on sociological theory and empirical research, one would have heard little of "the Tavistock tradition", although in the contexts of more "applied" social sciences, such as social policy, social work, and business studies, and in the sociology of the family and of organisations, its ideas were more present. In a related article (Rustin & Armstrong, 2019) we have given specific attention to the connections between the fields of sociology and psychoanalysis which developed within the Tavistock tradition. We describe this as a "double dissonance", since neither psychoanalysis nor sociology have taken an "orthodox" form in this relationship, although both have been influenced by the Tavistock's contributions.[1]

To understand how the Tavistock's ideas evolved, one needs to say something about the history of the institution, and in particular about a dynamic phase of its development just after the Second World War that brought psychoanalytic and social scientific perspectives into close juxtaposition.

Tavistock initiatives during the Second World War

The origins of this dynamic phase of development lay in the work of a group of psychiatrists, psychoanalysts, psychologists, and social scientists who were recruited into the British Army during the Second World War to work in military psychiatry. They undertook a number of initiatives that anticipated what was later to develop at the Tavistock, through the work of what became known as the Tavistock group. One such initiative was the "Northfield Experiments" (Bridger, 1990; Harrison, 2000; Trist, 1985). In the first of these, Wilfred Bion and John Rickman set up a therapeutic community within a military hospital for soldiers with long-standing psychiatric problems (see Harrison, 2000, p. 184). Bion's idea was that soldier-patients would be left free to organise their own lives within the community, with Bion's role primarily an interpretative one. The "enemy", as Bion defined it, was the neurosis from which the soldier-patients were suffering. The idea was that they needed to learn to take responsibility for their own states of mind to be able to resume their identities as functioning soldiers. This initial experiment lasted for only six weeks before it was closed down by the authorities as a setting of and for, as they saw it, chaos and indiscipline.[2] It is notable that an experiment that lasted for such a short time remains so prominent in the Tavistock's folk memory.

Bion had begun a training psychoanalysis with Rickman in 1938, which was interrupted by the war. Around 1946, he began a further analysis with Melanie Klein. His *Experiences in Groups*

(1961) is the classic text in which he set out the principles of group relations as this approach later developed, drawing on both his war and post-war experiences at the Tavistock. Bion, working as a military psychiatrist, was responsible for a second important initiative in the army, a then radical approach to officer recruitment. He proposed that the lack of sufficient candidates being sent forward for officer training from the regiments should be remedied by allowing nomination from all ranks. This increased the number of candidates coming forward, and was found to bring no decline in their quality. Bion had sought understanding and support for this initiative from military officers, rather than the psychiatric establishment in the army, which he no doubt won in part because he was himself a soldier of high reputation, having been awarded the Distinguished Service Order for his bravery in the First World War. The idea of regimental nomination was terminated by the authorities (the military were overruled on this by civilian officials), as a democratic step too far, but the other elements of the new officer selection system, established as the War Office Selection Board (WOSB), proved effective, and were widely followed, first in the army and other armed services, and later in many civil institutions. The system dispensed with the idea that effective selection could be achieved solely through interviews of candidates by senior officers. Psychologists were introduced to devise and conduct more complex tests, and these procedures were complemented by practical exercises in which candidates were observed addressing practical tasks relevant to officer responsibilities, and in their behaviour in the "leaderless groups" whose purpose was to identify capacities to work constructively with others. An entire programme for the selection and optimum deployment of human resources evolved from these initiatives (Trist & Murray, 1990a). This was a pioneering instance of the practical engagement of the social sciences, as the Tavistock psychiatrists saw this.

One thing that is striking about these initiatives is their democratic, anti-authoritarian nature, and the idea that people's capabilities do not necessarily coincide with their social status and can be best revealed through being put to the test in shared individual and collective tasks. They are one of many instances of class barriers being broken down in the context of the war and also reveal underlying resistances to these moves towards democratisation. Thus, we see Bion's own initiatives being terminated by instruction from above, although their crucial discoveries were later to become recognised and adopted under more diplomatic leadership than his own (Bridger, 1990). A similar pattern was to emerge later on in the action research projects of TIHR, where even democratic innovations—for example, in self-managing work-groups in factories or coal mines—brought benefits in morale and productivity, yet they met resistance and often failed to take wider root in their institutional environment. Eric Trist (1985) writes of the Tavistock group's wartime experience that they had found relevant, in reflecting on their perplexity at the abrupt setbacks they were experiencing, in Fairbairn's concept of the "internal saboteur", linking Freud's concept of unconscious resistance to understanding to a broader social field (see Obholzer, Chapter 1).

A third early Tavistock initiative was the post-war civilian resettlement programme, which dealt in particular with the problems of returning prisoners of war. Bion and Rickman understood that the critical source of anxiety for resettled soldiers lay in the domain of their "object relationships". (This idea derives from a development by Klein, Bowlby, and Winnicott of object relations theory in psychoanalysis, which held that relationships between infants and their mothers or primary carers were fundamental to development.) These relationships to loved objects, Bion and Rickman argued, were of profound importance to the soldiers' identities and self-respect—matters that were particularly acute for former prisoners of war. Here we see a close connection between understandings of interpersonal life being developed within psychoanalysis at this time and an important social intervention by the Tavistock.

Trist was later to describe this emerging wartime "cluster" of practitioner-researchers as foreshadowing the idea of a "composite work group" sharing each others' skills, and with a rotating rather than fixed leadership (Armstrong, 2012, p. 108). What linked its members was their involvement in a series of "inventions", in which they worked alongside military personnel on a variety of problems.

In retrospect, there seem to have been four main elements which were to characterise the approach of the Tavistock group to its presenting problem areas. These were:

- A freedom from prior professional preconceptions, either conceptual or methodological
- An approach that saw the presenting problem in terms of the wider social field in which it was located and of which the Tavistock group was itself a part: a citizenry at war and men who were soldiers
- A focus on the group as the primary vehicle of intervention, and
- An implicit belief in human resourcefulness and agency, across or beyond differences of station or class.

To these should be added one further element that didn't so much define an approach, at least initially, as shape its outcome, namely,

- The presence and evocation of "resistance", both external and internal, as a fact of life that needed to be recognised. One might think of this as an acceptance of the frequent necessity to tolerate and understand conflict, if difficult things were to be done.

Each of these elements was to be mirrored in the experience of the post-war reconfiguration of the Tavistock group, both within the Clinic and in the newly incorporated Institute. In each, both theory and method were consequent on the evolution of a collaborative practice that acknowledged the interdependence of social and psychological factors operating within a defined structural, organisational, and cultural wider field.

The Tavistock project after the war

At the end of the war, the entire group who had worked together in military psychiatry—Bion, Rickman, Trist, Jock Sutherland, John Bowlby, Tommy Wilson, Hugh Murray, Harold Bridger, and Isabel Menzies—either rejoined or were invited to join the Tavistock, and began a period of considerable transformation known as "Operation Phoenix". In a complicated and difficult process, the pre-war leadership of J. R. Rees was replaced and a staff group was established that was committed both to psychoanalysis and its integration within broader social contexts. Pre-war, the Tavistock Clinic had existed under the governance of the Tavistock Institute for Medical Psychology. A grant from the Rockefeller Foundation in 1946 enabled the foundation of the Tavistock Institute of Human Relations, initially as a division of the Clinic. When the Clinic decided to join the newly established National Health Service in 1947, the TIHR retained its independent status. At this time, the links between the two institutions were close in terms of people and orientations, but also because training and teaching functions (later to grow substantially) remained the responsibility of TIHR (Dicks, 1970; Trist, 1985; Trist & Murray, 1990a). In 1994, TIHR moved from the Tavistock Centre in Hampstead to its own offices in central London. At this time the Clinic set up its own dedicated consultancy service (formerly the Tavistock Consultancy Service, now Tavistock Consulting) led by Jon Stokes (see Chapter 39), who carried forward and re-established internally the Tavistock's social and organisational tradition.

The innovative Tavistock group had gathered together during the general mobilisation of human resources that had taken place during the Second World War. In many spheres of society, an old hierarchical order had been shaken up. The setting-up of a conscript army with the opportunities this created for advancement for people from outside the upper classes, the necessity and opportunity for women to work outside the home, and a reforming spirit that came about in a struggle, defined as one of democracy against fascism, influenced this development. Exposure in the wartime alliance to the example of American innovation and energy was another factor, as ideas from American social science became influential for the Tavistock group and in the social sciences in Britain more generally.

An important influence on the Tavistock—particularly on the TIHR's model of research—was the American social scientist Kurt Lewin, who had been a refugee from Nazi Germany. His development of "field theory" provided a crucial theoretical link for the Tavistock between individual and social perspectives (Lewin, 1952). The interaction between figure and ground, person and environment—individuals-in-their-world—became the source of the Tavistock's "unit of attention" and its intellectual DNA. From this grew its multidisciplinary approach and the diversity of its fields of work. This was distinct from the Institute of Psychoanalysis, whose main commitment was to the training of psychoanalysts, and whose unit of attention was the "inner world of the individual".[3] The two bodies formed an unusual institutional couple, the Institute looking mainly inwards to the development of the psychoanalytic profession and its domain of knowledge, while the Tavistock looked mainly outwards to the mental health needs of the community. Their contributions supported one another, although not without some tensions.

Lewin (1952) was a pioneering advocate of "action research". This is the idea that knowledge of social processes is gained through practical engagement, with interventions functioning as social experiments designed to enhance the understanding of participants and testing hypotheses through actions. Lewin had also been influential in developing a theory of democratic leadership (Armstrong & Rustin, 2012) with a model contrasting laissez-faire, authoritarian, and democratic forms that demonstrated the greater effectiveness of the third of these. This theory was consonant with the Tavistock's commitment to democratic forms of organisation, already evident in its wartime projects and central to its later research and practice. In 1947, Lewin contributed to the founding of the journal *Human Relations*, in which much of the Tavistock's early socio-psychoanalytical and socio-technical work was published. He was to have spent a period in England on scholarly leave, but died in February 1947 before this visit could begin. Although important connections with work in the United States continued (Trist and A. K. Rice later took up posts in the USA, see Shapiro & Krantz, Chapter 36), it seems likely that Lewin's early death limited what this transatlantic connection could accomplish.

In the years between 1945 and 1946, the Tavistock embarked on a radical reorientation of its fields of clinical and research practice, and their organisational embodiments (Dicks, 1970, p. 121ff.). At the heart of this reorientation was a concept of social and community psychiatry that sought to link and integrate "Social Sciences with Dynamic Psychology" (Trist & Murray, 1990b, p. 5). This was the first of the "chief needs" stated in a planning programme drawn up by an Interim Medical Committee elected by the Clinic's staff and chaired by Bion in October 1945. This programme found expression in a reconceptualisation of the Clinic's medical mission as it was built up to enter the NHS, and in the separate incorporation of an "Institute of Human Relations for the study of wider social problems not accepted as in the area of mental health" (p. 5).

This moment was radical and anti-establishment in its spirit. The idea of "engagement" in the description of the Tavistock's original mission was a deliberate invocation of the ethos of Jean-Paul Sartre and Albert Camus (Trist & Murray, 1990a, p. xi). (This idea was reformulated as "commitment" in the politics of the New Left a little later.) Similarly, Bion's (1948) scarcely remembered presidential address to the Medical Section of the British Psychological Society in 1947, "Psychiatry at a time of crisis", challenged any conventional separating out of societal and psychiatric domains. So, for example, speculating on the nature of a society's collective discontents and their emotional sources, he comments:

> We also have to bear in mind those organisations which in themselves produce problems for the majority of those living in that organisation. It is possible for a society to be organised in such a way that the majority of its members are psychiatrically disinherited. (p. 84)

In the 1950s, 1960s and 1970s, the TIHR engaged in a number of research studies to understand and improve work organisation within what it named the "socio-technical perspective". These studies both drew on and confirmed the wartime emphasis on resourcefulness and agency and the resistances to which it could be subject. Distinctive to this approach was a commitment to action research and democratic self-organisation in the workplace. Trist insisted that the initiative for the development of self-managed groups in the Tavistock's coal mining study came in the first instance from a group of miners themselves, as an initiative "from below" (Trist & Bamforth, 1951; Trist, Higgin, Murray, & Pollock, 1963). This idea that knowledge often emerges best from practice also has its origin in the psychoanalytic and therapeutic milieu in which TIHR had begun its life. Psychoanalytic understanding has been largely sought in the British tradition within the context of the clinical setting (M. J. Rustin, 2019). Here, the primary focus is the psychological difficulties of individual patients and their resolution through understandings shared with them. The TIHR broadened this approach into the idea of "socio-analysis", defining its subject—or one might say its quasi-patient—in broader social terms. The object of study might thus be difficulties within an organisation or an institution, or the social relationships within them.

From the 1950s onwards, a considerable number of publications emanated from the Tavistock. Some of these aimed to set out the principles and theoretical ideas underpinning the Tavistock's work (e.g., Bion, 1961; Emery & Trist, 1973; Miller & Rice, 1967; Trist & Sofer, 1959). Others were specific reports of mainly action research (e.g., Bott, 1957; Emery, 1970; Herbst, 1976; Jaques, 1953, 1955; Menzies, 1960; Miller, 1993; Miller & Gwynne, 1972; Rice, 1958; Trist & Bamforth, 1951).

The three volume anthology *The Social Engagement of Social Science* (Trist & Murray, 1990a, 1993, 1997) describes research undertaken between 1946 and 1989. The subtitles of the volumes (*The Socio-Psychological Perspective, The Socio-Technical Perspective, and The Socio-Ecological Perspective*) convey both the Tavistock's commitment to integration in the social sciences and the changing focus of its work during this period. Research publications from the Tavistock community have continued to appear, but those earlier years were exceptionally productive. (For more recent work, see, for example, Armstrong, 2005; T. Dartington, 2010; Huffington, Armstrong, Halton, Hoyle, & Pooley, 2004; Obholzer & Roberts, 2019; Sher, 2012.)

The Tavistock researchers thought of themselves as working in social science, understood in a broad and inclusive way. They were averse to disciplinary demarcations and drew on wide sources and currents in social science—for example those of cybernetics and open systems theory, ecological ideas, anthropology, economics, and psychology. They were insistent on the need to integrate psychological and social perspectives, linked through practice and problem-solving, which most psychologists and sociologists, concerned with building their own academic disciplines, were disinclined to do. Another factor in their cross-disciplinary orientation was the fact that the Tavistock was at this point largely independent of the university system, although some of its members later took up senior academic posts.

Some TIHR research studies made explicit use of psychoanalytic ideas to understand social practices within institutions. Two of the most influential were by Jaques (1951, 1955) and Isabel Menzies (1960; Menzies Lyth, 1988). Their key psychoanalytic ideas were those of unconscious anxieties and defences against anxiety, first developed in a clinical context by Melanie Klein. Both were research projects undertaken as consultancy and were concerned with anxieties generated within work settings. Jaques' 1951 study was a "socio-analysis" of a factory engaged at the time in an extensive organisational change. This study foreshadowed what was later to emerge as a major conceptual breakthrough: the formulation of social systems as a defence against anxiety, one of the foremost examples in the Tavistock tradition that links psychoanalytic and sociological ideas (Armstrong & Rustin, 2015). In Jaques' study, anxieties were located in the relations between managers, workers, and their trade union representatives, and were of both paranoid-schizoid and depressive kinds. His formulation was to highlight a recurring tension between explanations which focused on the internal dynamics of individuals and their social effects, and those which were based on psychoanalytically linked understandings of group and organisational behaviour. For Jaques, the defences against persecutory and depressive anxiety were seen as the result of projections of internal conflicts onto the social and cultural organisational structure. Thus, the source of these conflicts lay in the inner worlds of individuals.

Menzies' study was of a nursing system, in particular its mode of training, in a general hospital. She saw the primary source of anxiety as linked to the mental pain evoked by the actual tasks of nursing, arising from proximity to the suffering bodies and minds of patients, though she was less specific about whether these anxieties were paranoid-schizoid or depressive. It seems they were of both kinds—depressive anxieties aroused by contact with the patients and paranoid-schizoid (persecutory) anxieties aroused by the authoritarian managerial style of the hospital.[4] She thought these anxieties impacted on the entire social system exposed to them. The defences resorted to—the avoidance of emotional contact with patients, disavowal of mental pain, ritualised behaviours—became institutionalised as behaviour patterns that new entrants to the organisation found themselves constrained to adopt, thereby reinforcing their anxieties.

A tension between "internal" and "external" forces is built into any practice that seeks to relate psychological and social domains. In their historical overview, Trist and Murray (1990b) distinguish social-psychological (emphasising "external" forces) and psycho-social (emphasising "internal" forces) perspectives, located in the TIHR and the Tavistock Clinic respectively (p. 6). However, the focus in each case was less on integration and more on operationalising a dialogue. This dialectical view prefigured the agency-structure relation later theorised in the field of sociology by Anthony Giddens (1984) in his concept of structuration, although the Tavistock's work gave specific attention to dynamic unconscious processes largely unrecognised by Giddens. This two-way or bi-directional patterning of this interaction and its ubiquity in organisational life has been extended through the concept of "Organization in the Mind" developed by David Armstrong and colleagues at Tavistock Consulting since 1994 (Armstrong, 2005).

In the early post-war years, this conception of a socio-psychological dialogue was to influence the recruitment and training of staff across both the Clinic and the TIHR. According to Trist and Murray (1990b, p. 6), the criteria for recruitment included a "willingness to participate in the redefined social mission and to undergo psychoanalysis". It was agreed that "training would be in the hands of the British Psychoanalytical Society and social applications in the hands of the Institute" and that "the Society agreed to provide training analysts for acceptable candidates, whether they were to become full-time analysts, to combine psychoanalysis with broader endeavours in the health field, or use psychoanalytic understanding outside the health area in organisational and social projects" (p. 6). Simultaneously, Bion was to run study groups for staff, and meetings and seminars were to be held that were open to all staff, regardless of their particular departmental membership.

For Trist and Murray, these provisions were seen as "part of the enterprise of building the new Tavistock", a "major experiment" seeking to build on and learn from the wartime experience in addressing the personal, organisational, and social challenges of post-war reconstruction, and reconstituting the organisational and cultural structure of the "composite work group" (p. 6). Not all were fated to survive. By the time one of us (Armstrong) joined the TIHR in the late 1950s, the requirement of psychoanalytic experience was no longer operative nor, following Bion's departure, had there been any formal continuation of the staff study groups. The open culture of dialogue and exchange across the patch still flourished, though without the potential advantages of a fully shared "formation".

An advance crucial for the future development of the Tavistock's entire project was the invention of the group relations conference. The first of these—"the Leicester conference"—was directed by Eric Trist in 1957. We discuss these in Chapter 4.

It remains an open question just how far this "experiment" realised its founding vision of building bridges between social and psychological fields within the whole range of its practices, clinical and organisational, and between socio- and psycho-analysis. In the three volumes of the Tavistock anthology, for example, the more psychoanalytic perspective becomes progressively weaker, as attention focuses more on larger-scale "socio-technical" or "socio-ecological" dilemmas. One can recognise the remarkable synthesis of social and psychoanalytic perspectives that was achieved between the wartime experiments of Bion, Rickman, and others, and the innovative action research projects reported in the Tavistock anthology, yet note that the momentum of this development somewhat stalled from the 1990s onwards in a changed political climate and with the dispersal abroad of some of its principal actors.

Nevertheless, despite this less favourable context, significant work in this tradition has continued, in part in a "Tavistock" practice of organisational consultancy informed by both psychoanalytic and open-systems theory (Armstrong, 2005; Huffington, Armstrong, Halton, Hoyle, & Pooley, 2004; Obholzer & Roberts, 2019). Although Bion left the field of group work after the 1960s, his idea of unconscious "basic assumptions" as drivers of organisational behaviour has remained influential. His later psychoanalytical theory concerning the dispositions to know and "not-know" (parallel to those of love and hate) added a new dimension to the understanding of social phenomena of denial and disavowal (S. Cohen, 2001; Cooper, 2005; Cooper & Lousada, 2005; M. E. Rustin, 2005; Steiner, 1993). Jaques' and Menzies Lyth's paradigm of unconscious defences against anxiety also continues to be of interest (Armstrong & Rustin, 2015). However, some of the most generative concepts in the Tavistock's later work, such as that of the "turbulent environment" (Emery & Trist, 1965) have a psychoanalytic resonance which is yet to be fully elaborated.

The Tavistock Clinic

In the last section we focused mainly on the work of the TIHR and Tavistock Consulting. Here, we offer some reflections on the Tavistock Clinic. In what ways has its work connected psychological and psychoanalytic thinking focused on individuals, to wider understandings and practices oriented towards social needs?

From its beginning the Clinic had a conception of mental needs which referred not to individuals in isolation, but to individuals understood in their many relationships, within families, institutions, and the wider society. It embodied this conception in its clinical practices. Most influential among its psychological perspectives has been the psychoanalytic, but qualified by the fact that this conception has not usually been of an "inner" world separate from the "external" relationships of the self. Indeed, the need to recognise outside as well as internal realities has been a point of difference between the Tavistock's approach and psychoanalytic orthodoxy.

This dimension has been present in most of the Clinic's work, including that of John Bowlby (1969, 1973, 1980) and later attachment theorists, the psychoanalytic object relations tradition, and systemic family therapy (Burck, Barratt, & Kavner, 2013) (whose approach is different from psychoanalysis, but whose clinical ethos shares much with it; see Helps, Barratt, and Daniel, Chapter 24), and the critical approach to mental health of R. D. Laing (1960, 1961).

Within its specific field of socio-psychoanalytic knowledge and practice, the Tavistock Clinic evolved a range of complementary kinds of social intervention over many years. These lie within the fields of clinical and allied practices, professional training, and distinctive forms of learning. There has been a strong research dimension to this work, mainly taking the form of practice-based research. Many of the fifty-plus volumes in the Tavistock Clinic series report such work, for example, Armstrong (2005), Cooper and Lousada (2005), and Rustin and Rustin (2019).

The Tavistock's clinical interventions have encompassed virtually every phase of the life cycle, from birth to extreme old age. It has brought psychosocial understanding to many services and institutions in the community, for example, to medical general practice (see Elder, Chapter 9); neonatal units and children's wards in hospitals (M. Cohen, 2003, and Kraemer, Chapter 16); day nurseries and schools (see Lyon & Dowling, Chapter 31); families (see Helps, Barratt, & Daniel, Chapter 24); adolescent peer groups; and care homes for the old. It has developed specialisms in couple therapy, now located in Tavistock Relationships (see A. Balfour, Chapter 22, and Morgan, Chapter 23), and in forensic psychotherapy within the Portman Clinic (see Hale, Chapter 35), now part of the Tavistock and Portman NHS Trust. The growth of these services at the Clinic, and thus within the NHS, was an element in the larger development of the welfare system in post-war Britain.

The Trust trains members of several mental health and related professions, including adult and child psychotherapy, family therapy, clinical and educational psychology, mental health nursing, social work, psychiatry, and organisational consultancy. It defines its practice as multidisciplinary, each of whose perspectives has usually been distinct from the mainstream.

Multidisciplinary team-working was a key aspect of its work. When John Bowlby was in dispute with fellow members of the Institute of Psychoanalysis, he was chair of the Department for Children and Parents and presided over the development of the profession of psychoanalytic child psychotherapy, while himself being a pioneering practitioner in what in Britain was the new field of family therapy (Bowlby, 1949). What has been shared throughout the Clinic has been its commitment to the idea of "talking cures" and of preventive interventions, such as the support of family ties.

Related to its clinical practices, the Clinic developed various forms of learning, consistent with its "training mission" (M. J. Rustin, 2003). The distinctive focus of these is, following Bion's (1962) expression, "learning from experience". Among them are infant observation, young child observation, psychoanalytically informed "work discussion" (a kind of reflective practice), institutional observation,[5] group relations, personal analysis, supervision of therapy, theoretical teaching, and in recent years research methods. The common intention of these forms of learning (one could describe them as necessarily "slow learning") is to shape understandings at a deeper level. This means to equip learners with a "habitus" (Bourdieu, 1980)—that is, a sensibility and internalised understanding of ideas—that enables them to act with patients, clients, and in other working contexts in response to situations as they evolve in the moment.

We should mention that, in its early post-war years, the Tavistock sought to configure its own organisation in a way that embodied its conception of creative practice. Having been set up through the collective decision of its senior staff members, the post-war Clinic adopted a democratic constitution, with its senior officers elected by the permanent professional staff. The conventional hierarchy in a mental health clinic, in which authority was held by psychiatrists, was thus qualified by the idea of a shared responsibility between professionals. In the 1980s the Child and Family Department pioneered the practice of "senior member responsible" for clinical cases, which up to then had all been under psychiatric authority (an innovation anticipated twenty years earlier by the pathbreaking non-medical counselling service for adolescents; see F. Balfour, Chapter 20).

The internal structure was conceived as a "matrix", as defined by Eric Miller (1993, p. 193), with two complementary lines of authority to which staff were accountable. In one, authority lay within the professional disciplines of the Clinic, while the other lay in the management of the clinical departments. A Professional Committee, by which these different functions were represented, was for many years the key decision-making entity, working primarily by consensus arrived at through discussion and argument. The concept of the creative, self-organising work group developed in industrial contexts by TIHR action-researchers had an affinity to the form of organisation adopted within the Clinic. This system facilitated, for a period, considerable creative development.

In later decades, the social environment that had facilitated the "democratic" aspects of the Tavistock project became less favourable. Research focused on democratic forms of organisation in the workplace became unfashionable in Britain in the 1980s, ironically just as Japanese car manufacturers' adoption of methods which involved fuller workforce participation—"Total

Quality Control", "Quality Circles", and "Just-in-Time" production systems—(Ishikawa, 1985) gave them a competitive advantage in the motor industry. At the Tavistock Clinic, closer incorporation within the NHS required the adoption of a more standardised, budget-driven, managerialist model of organisation, and the election by staff of their managers was brought to an end in 1994. There was pressure for the Clinic to become a more eclectic institution and to adopt "evidence-based" treatments in place of those informed by professional knowledge and experience. Debates about these issues continue as the 100th anniversary of the Tavistock's foundation approaches in 2020. How to reconcile the creativity of its tradition with the organisational constraints of a reconstituted NHS continues to be, as it always has been, the challenge of its engagement.

Notes

1. Rustin and Rustin (2016) contains broader reflections on the relations between sociology and psychoanalysis.
2. The second Northfield Experiment initiated by Harold Bridger in 1944 when the outcome of the war was no longer uncertain, and supported later by Tom Main, established a more durable relationship with the military authorities and was to offer an early blueprint for the "discovery of the therapeutic community" (Bridger, 1990; Harrison, 2018). Bridger (1990, p. 86) wrote that they had created there a society that was both reparative and democratic.
3. We are indebted to William Halton for these formulations.
4. William Halton (2015) has suggested that the obsessional nature of the nursing system reflected an element of unconscious hatred of the patients.
5. See Hinshelwood and Skogstad (2000). Institutional observation developed from the Tavistock's method of infant observation, and was introduced as a form of learning by Anton Obholzer and the late Branka Pecotic at the Tavistock, and the late Ross Lazar in Germany. Institutional observation has been an essential form of learning in the organisational consultancy programmes at the Tavistock.

* * *

David Armstrong is an associate consultant at Tavistock Consulting. He trained as a social psychologist at the Tavistock Institute of Human Relations and worked in action research and organisational consultancy at the University of London and the Grubb Institute before returning to the Tavistock in 1994 to join a newly established consultancy service at the Tavistock Clinic. A distinguished member of the International Society for the Psychoanalytic Study of Organisations, he is the author of *Organization in the Mind: Psychoanalysis, Group Relations and Organizational Consultancy* (2005) and editor (with Michael Rustin) of *Social Defences against Anxiety: Explorations in a Paradigm* (2015).

Michael Rustin is a professor of sociology at the University of East London, a visiting professor at the Tavistock and Portman NHS Trust, and an associate of the British Psychoanalytical Society. He had a significant role in the development of the academic partnership between the University of East London and the Tavistock Clinic. He has published widely on the interrelations between psychoanalysis and society. His recent books include *Researching the Unconscious: Principles of Psychoanalytic Method* (2019), *New Discoveries in Child Psychotherapy: Findings from Qualitative Research* (edited with Margaret Rustin, 2019) and *Reading Klein* (with Margaret Rustin, 2016).

CHAPTER FOUR

Research at the Tavistock

Michael Rustin and David Armstrong

I n this chapter we put forward the view that the Tavistock, in all of its various historical branches, has been engaged, since its foundation in 1920, in the systematic generation of new knowledge. Most Tavistock researchers have been "practitioner researchers", engaged in work whose purpose has been to inform and enhance professional activities. Their investigations have been about *doing* as well as knowing, about making, designing, and performing, and about the conditions which make innovative work possible. We shall argue that the Tavistock's invention of institutional, therapeutic, and educational practices should be understood as research of a distinctive and valuable kind.

This claim contradicts the dominant view of the nature of science and scientific knowledge, which privileges an ideal of objectivity, inquiries which are value-free, and knowledge as a field of universal truths, believed to advance inexorably over time. As a philosophical presupposition this has worked well for the natural sciences, with physics as its exemplary field, and has seen vast progress in the applications of the sciences for human benefit, for example in medicine and in many other technologies.

However, as a programme for the human and social sciences, where the Tavistock's work lies, this has proved less satisfactory. In those fields, "subjectivity" and attention to emotions, both among subjects and researchers, has often been an essential source of knowledge and understanding, and not a contamination of them. The goal of these fields of knowledge is often to understand differences and developments, rather than to discover universal truths and uniformities. Specificities and cases, among individuals and societies, have been of intrinsic interest. Knowledge of these kinds has been often obtained by methodologies—participatory, observational, and imaginative—other than those of experimental and laboratory science.

There are alternative philosophical traditions which help us to understand the ways in which knowledge has been shaped by human interests. Aristotle's investigation of the diversity of human practices and of the values implicit in them is one foundation of this view. He wrote books on physics, rhetoric, politics, poetics, metaphysics, ethics, and the history of animals. He proposed that poetry and drama as well as science were a source of understanding. This is a conception of understanding rooted in human experience rather than in the idea of pure reason. The American pragmatist tradition (Legg, 2019; Moore, 1961), whose leading figures have been William James, John Dewey, and C. S. Pierce, proposed that knowledge had evolved, consistent with Darwinian evolutionary theory, as a human adaptation to its environments. Dewey criticised "the tendency of traditional philosophies to abstract and reify concepts derived from living contexts" … "Human thinking is not a phenomenon which is radically outside of (or external to) the world its seeks to know … Rather, human knowing is *among* the ways organisms with evolved capacities for thought and language cope with problems. Minds, then, are not passively observing the world; rather, they are actively adapting, experimenting, and innovating" (Hildebrand, 2018).

Science and social purpose

Thomas Kuhn's (1962) rewriting of the history of the sciences as one of changing paradigms, each bringing changes in the objects and methods of inquiry, has brought a recognition of the diversity of the sciences, liberating for example for the fields of psychoanalysis and sociology (M. J. Rustin, 2019). Of great value for the understanding of the practice-based conception of knowledge which is the essence of the Tavistock's tradition is Stephen Toulmin's account (1990, 2001) of the development of scientific knowledge as having been essentially shaped by human and social purposes. He argued that scientific discovery had mostly been conducted not in a sphere separate from practical human purposes, but on the contrary in ways closely linked to and motivated by them. He noted that the starting point for Darwin's study of biological evolution was his knowledge of the selective breeding of plants and animals, "natural selection" in his paradigm taking the place of deliberate and calculated selection. Researches into human bodies have been motivated by medical concerns regarding the causes of illness and health. Chemistry arose from the desire to make use of the materials of the Earth for human purposes—its origin was in alchemy—and retains close links with industrial interests. Even the development of physics, from Leonardo, has been motivated by the wish to control the forces of nature to serve human purposes, whether military or economic.

Nevertheless, scientific fields have established a significant distance from the practical applications of their findings, and the sciences and the technologies are themselves distinct practices in their own right. Toulmin's purpose was not to question the value of the "objectivist" sciences, but rather to restore a balance between these different spheres of knowledge. One of these he saw as intellectualist, theoretical, and universalist in its aspirations, and the other practical, professionally based, and responsive to the diversity of human purposes.

Research at the Tavistock[1]

We cannot here set out an extensive philosophical rationale for the Tavistock's research tradition. Let us merely note that this has been focused principally on problems and practices intended to enhance its subjects' self-understanding. This is contrary to a critical view of the dominant human sciences held by Adorno and Horkheimer (1997) and Foucault (Gutting & Oksala, 2019) which held that their implicit mission has been to classify, discipline, and control subjects, rather than to liberate them. The Tavistock's humanist and democratic orientation may have been one factor contributing to its relative isolation in relation both to the scientific academy, and to the larger systems of health, education, and welfare services.[2]

The Tavistock's contribution to knowledge has evolved in different subgenres, to some degree related to its organisational subdivisions. These have included the Tavistock Clinic; the Tavistock Institute of Human Relations (TIHR); the Portman Clinic (engaged in forensic therapeutic practice, which became part of the Tavistock and Portman NHS Trust in 1994); the organisation successively named the Family Discussion Bureau, the Tavistock Marital Studies Institute, and now Tavistock Relationships, whose practice is psychotherapy with couples; and institutions conducting work in organisational consultancy and group relations, which now includes both TIHR and, within the Tavistock NHS Trust, Tavistock Consulting.

Now follows a review of the Tavistock's research achievements in several of its fields of practice.

Practical institutional design

From its beginning, the Tavistock has been committed to the design of institutions which can contribute to the enhancement of community mental health (Dicks, 1970; Trist & Murray, 1990). Throughout its history it has been the inventor and incubator of different organisational forms, many of which have been emulated elsewhere. For example:

1. The invention of the Tavistock

The Tavistock's own design and operation, especially as it evolved through Operation Phoenix after the war, can itself be understood as a work of practical research. The idea of bringing together different professional disciplines to study and treat mental illnesses in the context of families, institutions, and communities, and the interdisciplinary and by conventional standards the non-hierarchical practice of this work was a creative discovery. This larger concept and the institutional design which followed from it was the precondition for the forms of learning through practice which have taken place.

2. Attachment research at the Clinic

One of the most important research programmes instituted and carried out at the Tavistock was that of attachment theory (Holmes, 1993). This was developed by John Bowlby and colleagues, who included James and Joyce Robertson, Colin Murray Parkes, and Mary Ainsworth, before her return to Canada to continue her research while still in collaboration with Bowlby in London. Bowlby had been one of the psychiatrists and psychoanalysts who joined the Tavistock after the war, to work not in the Institute of Psychoanalysis but as founder of the Department for Children and Parents which he chaired for twenty-two years (Kraemer, Steele, & Holmes, 2007). However, although he had an important role in supporting the development of the department and its clinical services (as Margaret Rustin describes in Chapter 7) his best-known achievement was in research, in his responsibility for initiating the new paradigm of attachment theory, a scientific project whose influence has extended across the world. In some respects this paradigm was the most traditionally "scientific" of all the Tavistock's research programmes. Bowlby was inspired by Darwin, and drew in his work on ethological studies of infant–mother relationships among primates, and on evolutionary theory, with collaborators such as Mary Ainsworth and Robert Hinde. Bowlby valued experimentation and quantitative evidence. The Strange Situation Test, which identified several different patterns of attachment between small children and parents, and the Adult Attachment Interview which identified these patterns in adult subjects, were instruments of great diagnostic value. The prediction of attachment behaviour in small children from the data of a life-story interview, conducted with parents even prior to children's birth, gave a remarkable empirical corroboration of the postulates of attachment theory. Like much Tavistock research and practice, some of the inspiration for Bowlby's research lay in his experience of the war, in particular of the consequences of the early separation of children from parents in wartime conditions.[3]

Although Bowlby believed firmly in the objective methods of the natural sciences, his paradigm converged in important ways with the theories of psychoanalysts of the contemporary "object relations" school, such as Klein and Winnicott. He had been broadly a supporter of Klein's positions against Anna Freud and her allies in the British Psychoanalytical Society's (BPAS) Controversial Discussions of 1941–45 (King & Steiner, 1991). He later disagreed with what he believed was Klein's excessive emphasis on the internal or intrapsychic causes of childhood mental disturbance, in contrast to the qualities of maternal care which his research was revealing to be decisive. His early papers on attachment research were received mostly with indifference or hostility at the BPAS where he first presented them, and where his position was regarded by some as inconsistent with psychoanalytic principles. In reality, one of the core ideas of attachment theory, the "internal working model", is a formulation related to the object relations concepts of internalisation and introjections.[4] It is interesting to note that in the Controversial Discussions Bowlby was among the four "wartime psychiatrists" who had been attacked by Edward Glover, Klein's leading opponent, and spoken of with disdain: "Ex-Army members will undoubtedly get Beveridge (i.e., future NHS) jobs if they want them" (King & Steiner, 1991, p. 893). It seems that bad blood may have gone back a long way. These bitter arguments did not damage Bowlby's constructive relationships with his psychoanalyst colleagues at the Tavistock, and he remained a lifelong member of the BPAS.

The attachment theorists sought to follow standard scientific procedures in their research, and for the most part to keep researcher and practitioner roles distinct. The fact that the Anna Freud Centre was so strongly committed to canonical scientific norms, while the Tavistock gave greater emphasis to clinical practice and to practice-based investigation, is one reason why in later years research in attachment theory was pursued more actively at the Anna Freud Centre, for example by Howard and Miriam Steele, and by Peter Fonagy and Mary Target, than at the Tavistock. But in some influential attachment studies, such as in the making of James Robertson's (1952) film *A Two-Year-Old Goes to Hospital* (see Lindsay, Chapter 5), the dimensions of practice and investigation were closely linked, in what became a classic of action research, based in its first crucial instance on a single case study. Recent work at the Tavistock has linked attachment perspectives to developments in neurobiology and evolutionary theory (Music, 2017, 2019).

While Bowlby and his colleagues sought scientific objectivity, their commitment to the avoidance of emotional suffering and damage to children in their family environment was intense. A similar commitment to alleviate suffering was present in Colin Murray Parkes' work on experiences of loss and mourning at the other end of the life cycle (Parkes, Stevenson-Hinde, & Marris, 1993). A valuable volume *The Politics of Attachment* (Kraemer & Roberts, 1996) set out the implications for society and social policy of these ideas. Like other major new scientific paradigms, attachment theory aroused considerable opposition, for example in Michael Rutter's critique of Bowlby's early thesis of "maternal deprivation", from psychoanalytic fundamentalists, and from feminists, perturbed at Bowlby's insistence on the importance of the maternal role. But these arguments were examples of the resistances which powerful new ideas and discoveries often provoke when they challenge accepted thinking, and they testify to their significance (Armstrong, 2017). Such challenges also helped to refine the theory, so that it became clearer that the maternal role was not exclusively mother's.

More recent systematic research from the Tavistock Clinic are the studies by Peter Hobson and Matthew Patrick using the Adult Attachment Interview (Patrick, Hobson, Castle, Howard, & Maughan, 1994) and the Strange Situation Test (Hobson, Patrick, Crandell, & García-Pérez, 2005; Hobson et al., 2009) on mothers with borderline personality disorder. They showed that the communication of a high proportion of these women with their infants was disrupted, disoriented, and fearful.

TIHR's research programme

Formally speaking, the research activities of the Tavistock were located between 1948 and 1994 in TIHR. The *Tavistock Anthology: The Social Engagement of Social Science* (Trist & Murray, 1990a, 1993, 1997) provides an account of the research undertaken by TIHR and its members from 1941 until 1993. These three remarkable volumes are subtitled *The Socio-Psychological*, the *Socio-Technical*, and the *Socio-Ecological*, each reflecting a phase in the Institute's work. This development reflects an increasing distance between the clinical and psychoanalytical approaches of the Clinic, which were closest to TIHR's research during its socio-psychological phase, and the more social scientific perspectives of the Institute, which become predominant later.

The Institute's work has been characterised by its commitment to the methods of action research, concerned with the conduct and evaluation of practical interventions and their outcomes (Lewin, 1947). This has been the case both for research conducted in the course of their practice by psychotherapists at the Clinic, and for the more institutionally oriented investigations undertaken at the Institute, by researchers often in the role of organisational consultants. Professions, for example those of medicine, the law, or the military are characterised by a commitment to shared values, rather than merely material interests. The distinctive value-commitment of the different professions which make up the Tavistock has been to the idea of understandings which are developed and shared between researchers and their subjects. This is the case both for the psychotherapies, whether psychoanalytic or family systemic, and for the practice of "action research" conducted with the members of institutions and groups.

The volume of work accomplished at the Institute has been immense. Here we can only identify some of its central themes and arguments. One of these is the idea of democratic organisation, as a practice which stimulates commitment and creativity. This was the lesson learned from Kurt Lewin and his colleagues' study in the 1930s of authoritarian, laissez-faire, and democratic forms of leadership in the USA (Lewin, 1939), whose findings he shared with Tavistock researchers when he worked briefly with them after the Second World War. The Tavistock psychiatrists' innovations during the war, in officer selection at the War Office Selection Board (White, 2015), and in the Northfield Experiments with psychologically injured soldiers, were based on the idea that groups of individuals should be invited to take responsibility for themselves. The ideas of study groups, group relations, group therapy, and therapeutic communities emerged from this matrix of ideas and practices.

The Tavistock's own form of organisation after the war was collegial, rather than hierarchical, until decades later when the NHS demanded a reversion to managerial hierarchy, and to a mainly corporate model of governance. The largest of TIHR's action research programmes were devoted to experiments in self-managed forms of work organisation in many different industrial contexts. These included coal mines, weaving mills in India, and merchant ships. Although democratic organisation was hardly feasible in conditions of imprisonment, Tavistock researchers (Emery, 1970) demonstrated that prisons were better institutions when they were designed to allow greater autonomy and association for prisoners. The method of pursuing these researches was usually to observe existing practices, to identify desirable improvements in them, and to study the outcomes of changes made in interaction with workforce participants. These interventions were linked in the 1970s with a wider industrial movement concerned with the quality of working life, active for example in the Japanese and Swedish car industries. These innovations involved giving employees greater autonomy and more active and creative roles within their workplaces, for the benefit both of the firms and their workers. It was a challenge to the mechanistic divisions of labour of scientific Taylorism, of which Lewin had been specifically critical as early as the 1920s (Lewin, 1920). These developments were part of wider attempts to achieve a new settlement of class antagonisms within the workplace, during a period of increased industrial conflict. It seems however that Margaret Thatcher's election victory in 1979 brought an end to consensus-seeking initiatives of these kinds. From then on, an alternative laissez-faire philosophy which asserted the virtues of markets and which attacked "collectivist" values took command.

A second crucial area of TIHR's focus was on the unconscious dimensions of and impediments to the functioning of institutions. The seminal researches were studies of unconscious defences against anxiety, by Elliott Jaques (1955) and Isabel Menzies (1960). Menzies' study of the nursing system of a general hospital has been widely cited since it was first published sixty years ago. Her study revealed the destructive ways in which mental pain arising from trainee nurses' experiences with patients was managed in the nursing system. Instead of nurses being helped to be made aware of these unconscious anxieties, so that they could become better able to cope with them, their anxieties were denied and repressed. Meaningless rituals of task performance and uncaring hierarchies of authority were placed in the way of the personal care of patients. The outcome was many nurse trainees' disillusionment, sickness, and withdrawal from their training.

This was a classic example of a single institutional study, carefully reported, which brought a new understanding to a large field of practice, even though the specific hospital which commissioned the research was unable to implement its recommendations. *Social Defences against Anxiety: Explorations in a Paradigm* (Armstrong & Rustin, 2015) revisited that research programme, showing its continuing relevance.

The idea that there are unconscious dimensions of group and institutional life has been a consistent theme of Tavistock research. Its organisational consultancy service has undertaken many studies in which this has been a central focus, usually conducted as action research projects. Their findings were designed to be shared with the subjects of research, who were to be supported in bringing about relevant changes. Two important volumes of papers, *The Unconscious at Work* (Obholzer & Roberts, 1994, second edition, 2019) and *Working Below the Surface* (Huffington, Armstrong, Halton, Hoyle, & Pooley, 2004) reported examples of this work. Armstrong's *Organization in the Mind* (2005) provided insights, based on consultancy experience, on the interactions between organisations' structures and processes and the unconscious engagements of their members.

Most but not all research in TIHR was conducted making use of action research methods. Among projects which were more conventionally sociological or anthropological, in which the researcher role was not as a participant or consultant, were Elizabeth Bott Spillius' classic study *Family and Social Network* (Bott, 1957), and Robert and Rhona Rapoport's research on "The Dual Career Family" (1969). Each reflected the Tavistock's interest in patterns of family relationship as central to well-being. Bott Spillius, who later became a leading psychoanalyst, identified a major change which was then taking place in family relationships. Families were becoming smaller, with conjugal partnerships becoming more important, and separate-sex relationships with female kin and male workmates less so. This study insightfully demonstrated the connections between a changing class structure and its effects on families and their networks. The Rapoports' study identified another important social change, where both male and female members of a marital partnership had major commitments to their careers.

Significant developments in organisational theory were made by Tavistock researchers to underpin and to show the wider relevance of researches often initially based on case studies. One was the theory of unconscious defences against anxiety. Another was the development of socio-technical systems theory. This set out a model of the relations (Miller & Rice, 1967) between organisations and their environment which has become valuable for the understandings of institutions of many kinds (see Shapiro & Krantz, Chapter 36; Stokes, Chapter 39). In later years, this perspective was broadened still further within an "ecological perspective" to examine the impact of the wider environment of organisations and working lives. The crisis of climate change has now shown the prescience of this approach. TIHR researchers developed an illuminating typology of organisational environments, referring each of them to case examples. They termed these, in order of their increasing complexity, (1) placid, randomised, (2) placid, clustered, (3) disturbed reactive, (4) turbulent, highly unpredictable, and needing coordination based on shared values, (5) vortical—a further level of turbulence to characterise "vortices" to which no rational adaptation is possible (Babüroğlu, 1988; Emery & Trist, 1965). TIHR research became increasingly sophisticated as it developed links to academic networks in different nations, especially in interdisciplinary departments of business and management, where there was more sympathy for participative action research and for case-study methods than there was within most academic social science disciplines.

The generation of knowledge at the Tavistock Clinic

We will now review the innovative therapeutic and educational practices which have been developed at the Tavistock Clinic. We understand these as forms of research, existing long before their academic recognition within doctoral programmes during the last two decades. This corpus of clinical findings and of developments in theory and technique has influenced an entire field of practice, and has been disseminated through substantial publication and in professional networks. This is also the case for the Tavistock's innovations in the fields of learning and teaching, and in psychoanalytic and systemic family therapy. These forms of knowledge can be described as "human technologies", which like many material technologies emerge from practice-based research. We will set out some examples of this achievement. They are too numerous, over this long period of 100 years, for a comprehensive survey to be possible.

Methods of learning from emotional experience

From the 1940s onwards, psychoanalysts and child psychotherapists at the Tavistock Clinic devised a portfolio of learning and teaching methods, intended to develop students' understanding of the unconscious dimensions of relationships in infancy and childhood. This began with Esther Bick's invention of psychoanalytic infant observation, a procedure in which students observed infants (taking the role of a passive observer) for one hour per week in their family setting, ideally from the time of their birth until their second birthday (Briggs, 2002; Harris, Bick, & Williams, 2018; Miller, Rustin, Rustin, & Shuttleworth, 1989; Reid, 1997; Salzberger-Wittenberg, 1997, 1999; Waddell, 2006). The observations reported from these visits were and are discussed with an experienced supervisor, in a small group of observers. This has been found to be an effective means of developing students' capacities to observe mother–baby interactions, to become aware of the unconscious feelings evoked in this setting, including those of observers, and to learn the relevance to these experiences of psychoanalytic forms of understanding. This method of infant observation has become widely (and internationally) employed in contexts of education for many professionals who work with children and families including trainee psychoanalysts, child psychotherapists, and social workers. Its method has generated knowledge of mother–infant behaviours, which has been reported over many years in a specialist journal (*Infant Observation*) and in several books. This approach to learning has been extended to the observation of under-fives as "young child observation" (Adamo & Rustin, 2014), and to the practice of observation in settings concerned with children and adolescents in which the observer occupies an active working role, and is not merely a passive observer. This practice is called "work discussion" (Rustin & Bradley, 2008). The active working role of the observer in these settings enables attention to be given to a wider range of phenomena, for example the institutional dynamics which may be observed in a school. Another important development was the integration of thinking about group process, characteristic of the group relations world, and approaches to small group teaching within the Tavistock (Gosling, Miller, Woodhouse, & Turquet, 1967). This was of particular interest to Isca Wittenberg, who was also responsible for the influence of group relations approaches on the events which were created to mark students' introduction to the Tavistock and to the ending of their studies there (Salzberger-Wittenberg, 2013).

A further enlargement of the scope of the observational method has come with the development of a therapeutic form of infant observation, designed to throw light on and to alleviate difficulties occurring in relationships between mothers and infants, but distinct from more intensive therapeutic interventions. This approach was first developed by practitioners of infant observation in France, but has been emulated and developed in England, for example by Jenifer Wakelyn (2019).

Distinctive of the Tavistock's approach to learning and research through observation is its attention to the unconscious dimensions of relationships, studied, in part, through attention to transference and countertransference phenomena. These methods are related to and indeed originally derive from the practices of clinical psychoanalytic supervision (Esther Bick was a psychoanalyst). Such clinical supervision has been widely practised at the Tavistock, but its origin lies in psychoanalytic practice beyond it. These extended learning methods have been a practical research achievement in themselves, but have also become a resource for research into, for example, mother–infant relationships. There are affinities between these methods and those of cultural anthropology, even though their theoretical frames of reference are different.

Therapeutic innovations

A second important sphere of "research as practice" which we will review is the different forms of therapeutic intervention. There have been many of these. Among them are:

- The model of short-term psychoanalytic psychotherapy for adults designed in the 1970s by David Malan (1979; see also Chapter 25).
- The four-session model of adolescent psychotherapy designed as the Young People's Consultation Service by Fred Balfour (see Chapter 20).
- The practice of short-term consultation designed to understand and resolve relationship difficulties between infants and children under five, and their mothers or primary carers. This model of short-term consultation was first devised by Martha Harris, and has been developed into an established model of intervention for mothers and infants (see Miller, Chapter 13).

Another influential practice was Michael Balint's group work with GPs, which aimed to enhance their sensitivity to the emotional needs of patients and the demands these made on doctors (see Elder, Chapter 8).

The above are examples of interventions which are distinctive of a community mental health clinic such as the Tavistock, where priority has been given to developing resource-efficient responses to a diversity of mental health needs.

Many different kinds of psychotherapy, designed to meet the needs of different patient and client categories, have been designed and practised over the years. Some examples of these are work with people with eating disorders (see Williams, Chapter 18), patients with borderline states of mind (Steiner, Chapter 27), children with autism or Asperger's syndrome (Rhode, Chapter 17), forensic patients (Hale, Chapter 35), severely deprived children, sexually abused children (Trowell, Chapter 34), dysfunctional families (Helps, Barratt, & Daniel, Chapter 24), patients who have been refugees, and those suffering from trauma (Garland, Chapter 29), and from gender dysphoria (Di Ceglie, Chapter 19), the last of which has now become a major field of work at the Tavistock. A specific kind of connection between clinical practice, research, and professional training has been made through the institution of the Clinical Research Workshop (M. E. Rustin, 1991). These, in different areas of specialism, have involved the detailed consideration of sequences of clinical cases, often over many years, with the purpose of developing theories and therapeutic techniques arising from them. Considerable publication has arisen from these workshops, for example, Alvarez and Reid (1999), Boston and Szur (1983), Hopkins (2004), Steiner (1993, 2004), Whyte (2004), and Williams, Williams, Desmarais, and

Ravenscroft (2004). The idea of narcissistic or borderline states of mind was given a broader social application by Cooper and Lousada in *Borderline Welfare* (2005). A valuable theoretical contribution from a child psychotherapist was by Meira Likierman (2001), who in her book on Melanie Klein drew attention to Ferenczi's influence on her work.

It is difficult to summarise the full range of innovative clinical work with many kinds of client that has taken place at the Tavistock, given its mission to support mental well-being over the entire life-course. Many professional disciplines have been responsible for the design of these therapeutic modalities. In most of its units and departments, clinical supervision and discussion have contributed to professional knowledge, and to the development of the capabilities of trainees.

In recent years, the practice and therapeutic outcomes of these kinds of intervention have been described in the volumes produced in the Tavistock Clinic Series of books (these are now more than fifty in number; see Waddell, Chapter 43), but also in many other publications, including books produced by the Tavistock's systemic family therapists, and in articles in many journals, including several in which Tavistock staff have taken editorial roles.

Group relations and group relations conferences

Another important invention of the Tavistock over many years has been the group relations conference, pioneered in 1957 as the Leicester conference (Miller 1990a, 1990b) and continued since by TIHR, while the Tavistock Clinic maintains its in-house version. This is an instrument designed for learning about unconscious processes as they arise in small and large groups and in inter-group relations. The beginnings of this work lay in the form of experiential learning initiated by Kurt Lewin and his colleagues at the National Training Laboratories in Bethel, Maine, who invented the T-Groups (training groups) (Bradford, Gibb, & Benne, 1964). Lewin's holistic conception, linked to Gestalt theory, of the crucial relations between parts and wholes, the individual and the social, was of great significance for the development of TIHR, even though Lewin himself died in 1947.[5] The Tavistock's group relations programmes, with an important additional psychoanalytic dimension added by Wilfred Bion (1961) following wartime innovations with groups of soldiers, evolved into a significant method of management and professional education, extending to the study of large-group phenomena and also into a form of group psychotherapy. Its development is discussed in Miller (1990a, 1990b), Rice (1965), and Trist and Sofer (1959), and its therapeutic forms in Garland (2010). "Social Dreaming" is a further learning practice which has evolved from group relations (Lawrence, 1988).

Large-scale studies of the outcomes of psychotherapies

Since 1990 the Tavistock Clinic has been engaged in systematic research into therapeutic outcomes, pressed to do this in part because of the demands from NHS commissioners to provide an evidence base for its modes of treatment, superior (from some points of view) to what could be provided by the intensive studies of small numbers of cases. Examples of these investigations are:

- Research into sexually abused girls, directed by Judith Trowell (Trowell et al., 2002).
- The Childhood Depression Study (Trowell et al., 2007; Trowell & Miles, 2011) which compared the treatment of a sample of seventy-two depressed children and young adolescents in programmes of one year's once-weekly psychoanalytic psychotherapy, with a parallel programme of systemic family therapy, conducted in three locations, London, Athens, and Helsinki. This study was directed by Judith Trowell and David Campbell, significantly bringing together different clinical and theoretical perspectives. It showed remarkably positive outcomes from both modalities of treatment, in which a large majority of the patients improved substantially, especially when the post-treatment follow-up was taken into account.
- The IMPACT Study into severe adolescent depression (Cregeen, Hughes, Midgley, Rhode, & Rustin, 2017; Goodyer et al., 2017). This was a randomised control trial of three treatment modalities, short-term psychoanalytic psychotherapy (STPP), cognitive behavioural therapy (CBT), and specialist clinical care (however in a significantly upgraded and manualised version led by child psychiatrists) of the treatment which patients with this diagnosis could normally expect to receive from the NHS. This study had a large randomised sample of 540 cases, divided equally between the three modalities and treated in Child and Adolescent Mental Health Services clinics in London, East Anglia, and north-west England. The project was led by Professor Ian Goodyer at Cambridge University, with important contributions to the research made by Peter Fonagy and Mary Target at University College London, and Jonathan Hill at Manchester University. The principal contribution of the Tavistock was in the organisation and supervision of the clinical work in both child psychotherapy (Margaret Rustin) and specialist clinical care (Rob Senior).

This study came about because the findings of the preceding Child Depression Study had been unexpectedly positive, in the view of those with authority in NHS mental health research. Its modes of treatment were thus deemed to justify a more decisive investigation, with a larger sample size (540 cases) to determine whether their outcomes justified inclusion as recommended treatments in the NICE (National Institute for Clinical Excellence) guidelines. (Unfortunately the systemic family therapy mode of treatment was not included in the STPP study, even though it had been intended to replicate the previous study.) The IMPACT findings demonstrated that the three treatment modalities had each produced positive outcomes for the treatment sample. The equivalence, in clinical and cost-effectiveness terms, of the child psychotherapy and CBT interventions was an important counter to the frequent assertions of the superiority of CBT to psychoanalytic psychotherapy. Those claims had been widely made to justify the adoption of CBT as the dominant treatment modality in the IAPT (Improving Access to Psychological Therapies) programme which has been "rolled out" in NHS mental health services (Layard, 2005a, 2005b; Layard & Clark, 2014). While IMPACT's findings, and their representation in NICE guidelines, were welcome, there was disappointment among child psychotherapists that their treatment method had been shown to be merely equal in its outcomes to the others being tested.

- The Tavistock Adult Depression Study (TADS, see Taylor, Chapter 26) is a fourth recent example of clinical outcome research (Fonagy et al., 2015; Rost, Luyten, Fearon, & Fonagy, 2019; Taylor et al., 2012). In this, with a sample of 129 patients "with long-standing major depression who had failed at least two different treatments and were considered to have treatment-resistant depression" (Fonagy et al., p. 312), the outcome of treatment in eighteen months of once-weekly psychoanalytic psychotherapy as an adjunct to treatment-as-usual (TAU) was compared with an equivalent-sized control group receiving treatment-as-usual alone. TAU consisted of a wide range of short-term therapies recommended by the National Institute for Health and Clinical Excellence in 2009 (NICE[6]), including CBT, counselling, and other brief psychotherapies. In line with other psychoanalytic psychotherapy studies significant differences between the two groups emerged over the long-term follow-up. At the two-year follow-up 30% of those who received the psychoanalytic treatment were in partial remission compared with only 4% who received TAU. Rost and colleagues (2019) found important differential treatment effects revealing the importance of pre-treatment personality features on treatment outcome. Given the chronicity and substantial co-morbidity of this sample, findings are promising that psychoanalytic psychotherapy can be beneficial to this patient group over the long term.

The updated version of the current draft NICE guidelines on the recognition of and management for depression in adults has included the study in their review, but ignored the significance of long-term follow-up data on the treatment outcomes. A stakeholder coalition group has been calling on NICE to attend to various methodological flaws in this update, stating that "This guideline is not fit for purpose and if published will seriously impede the care of millions of people in the UK suffering from depression, potentially even causing clinical harm." It argues "that NICE should conduct a proper analysis of 1 and 2-year follow-up data from trials and prioritise treatment recommendations made on the basis of these data over and above recommendations which are made on the basis of short term outcomes (less than 1 year)."[7]

These randomised clinical trials are distinctive, among the Tavistock's research activities, for having followed standard research protocols in clearly separating the functions of researchers from those of the clinicians whose practice they are investigating. Even so, in an unexpected way this separation was found not to be complete. Interviews with research subjects showed that, in the process of data collection, the regular interactions of research staff with patients may well have had a supplementary therapeutic benefit.[8] The standard scientific norm of separating "action" from "research" functions is different from the situation of a practitioner who conducts, reports on, and evaluates her own work. In that situation maintaining an objective stance may depend on the self-scrutiny of the clinician-researcher, on supervision, and on post-facto analysis of clinical reports.

In the study of autism (see Rhode, Chapter 17), Tavistock staff members were engaged in both case-based research in clinical settings (Alvarez & Reid 1999; Meltzer, Bremner, Hoxter, Weddell, & Wittenberg, 1975), and in more classically scientific experimental research in a university context, with a substantial psychoanalytic and philosophical underpinning, in Peter Hobson's work (Hobson, 2002).

There is a prevailing orthodoxy which defines as "scientific" only those forms of investigation in which the functions of "research" are wholly separated from other practices, in other words where the exclusive commitment is to the practice of research itself. We do not question the value of investigations which take that classical form. But we hold that the practice-based research of the Tavistock has made its own substantial and original contribution to knowledge, and that much of this knowledge could not have been obtained by any other methods.

The Tavistock's professional doctoral research programmes

We now turn to researches conducted within the Professional Doctorate Programmes which have been validated since 1990 by the University of East London, and in the last four years by the University of Essex. These have developed within the professional disciplines of child and adolescent psychotherapy, social work, systemic family therapy, psychoanalytic and systemic consultancy to organisations, and clinical psychology. By intention, and by virtue of their being professional doctorates rather than PhDs, these programmes have most often accredited research related to professional practice, and have thus been consistent with this Tavistock tradition. A decision was made at their outset that these programmes were to be designated as "research doctorates", and not as doctoral programmes based on advanced learning and skill-enhancement alone. Word limits for these professional doctorate theses, criteria for the approval of research proposals, and assessment of completed theses were all deliberately aligned with PhD regulations. The principal differences from the PhD lay in the slightly shorter maximum length of written theses required, and the expectation that their original contribution should be to "professional knowledge", in contrast to knowledge mainly located within an academic discipline. The format adopted for theses within the first period of thirty years of these programmes remained close to the PhD's, regarding the requirement to situate an investigation within its relevant research literature, to specify and justify its research methods, and to give a systematic report of research findings and the evidence which supports them.

The purpose of these programmes was to enable professionals to make an original contribution to the knowledge base of their professions at a relatively early stage of their careers, and to equip them with the skills and confidence to undertake further research in the future. There was also the aim of ensuring that the professional and academic status of those trained at the Tavistock kept up with that of those trained elsewhere. More than 150 doctoral awards in all these disciplines have been made since the programme began, nearly ninety of them in child psychotherapy alone. Some of these have led to further research, have influenced NHS practice, and have found additional forms of publication and dissemination. The requirements of doctoral study have encouraged researchers and their supervisors to address deficiencies in their fields, for example in regard to research methodologies. A rigorous approach to qualitative methods of data analysis, such as interpretive phenomenological analysis, and grounded theory, has been an achievement of this programme. In some professional doctoral programmes, for example in child psychotherapy, social work, and organisational consultancy, the scope of established qualitative research methods has been extended to take account of unconscious dimensions of relationships and social processes. Examples of the findings of research in one of these programmes are reported in the edited collection of papers, *New Discoveries in Child Psychotherapy: Findings from Qualitative Research* (Rustin & Rustin, 2019).

In the course of the development of these doctoral programmes, the Tavistock was also able to gain academic recognition through the award of PhD degrees to sixteen members, or former members, of its teaching staff on the basis of their published clinical studies.

Current research at the Tavistock

The Trust today continues to be actively engaged in research and is involved in a broad range of externally funded research studies with a particular emphasis on children and young people's mental health and development. Here are summaries of five of these projects.

Longitudinal Outcomes of Gender Identity in Children (LOGIC)

This longitudinal study looks at the development of gender identity in children and young people aged between three and thirteen years. Conducted in the UK, the study began in 2019 and is following participating families at three time points over a two-year period. Dr Eilis Kennedy is the chief investigator on the LOGIC study and Dr Rob Senior is a co-investigator. The study is funded by the National Institute for Health Research (NIHR). More information is at https://logicstudy.uk/

Personalised Programmes for Children (PPC)

This study is looking at personalised approaches to the treatment of behavioural difficulties in children. In this project we work with families to develop a programme that is tailored to both parents' and children's needs, and to find out whether this approach works better than current parent training programmes. Dr Senior is chief investigator and Dr Kennedy is a co-investigator on the PPC study, which is also funded by the NIHR. More information is at https://tavistockandportman.nhs.uk/research-and-innovation/our-research/research-projects/personalised-programmes-children-ppc/

Personalised psychological intervention for individuals with Primary Sclerosing Cholangitis Wellbeing Study (PSC) and their families

This research aims to investigate the impact of primary sclerosing cholangitis, a rare but serious liver condition that increases the chances of developing cancer, on mental health and wellbeing. The aim is to develop a framework that will help people affected by PSC to get the psychological support they need. Dr Kennedy is the chief investigator on the PSC Wellbeing Study, which is run in partnership with and funded by the UK-based charity PSC Support. More information is at the study's website https://pscsupport.org.uk/the-psc-wellbeing-study/

Clinical study of intergenerational trauma

This study, funded by a generous donation to the Tavistock Clinic Foundation, is of six complex clinical cases of children and adolescents treated by child psychotherapists in different NHS settings in conjunction with work with parents. The study is conducted as a clinical research workshop, convened by Margaret Rustin at the Tavistock, which is analysing and comparing the presented case material. The purpose is to gain understanding of the transmission of traumatic experiences between generations within families.

Research collaborations

Nurturing change: VIPP foster care study

This project aims to evaluate a new form of support, called Video-feedback Intervention to promote Positive Parenting (VIPP), which is designed to help foster and kinship carers better understand and respond to their child's emotions and behaviour. It is led by Professor Pasco Fearon at the Research Department of Clinical, Educational and Health Psychology, University College London, in partnership with several other universities and five NHS trusts. Drs Kennedy and Senior are co-investigators on this study. More information is at https://ucl.ac.uk/pals/research/clinical-educational-and-health-psychology/research-groups/nurturing-change-vipp-foster

Evaluating the real-world implementation of the Family Nurse Partnership

The Family Nurse Partnership (FNP) is a home-visiting programme designed to improve the outcomes of teenage pregnancies in terms of child health and development. This study aims to improve our understanding of the context in which FNP is currently delivered in the UK, and the factors that influence results, to find out who might benefit most from FNP and how service delivery may be improved. This project, funded by the NIHR, is led by Dr Katie Harron who is based at the UCL Great Ormond Street Institute of Child Health. Dr Kennedy is a co-investigator on this study. More information is accessible at https://ucl.ac.uk/child-health/people/harron-katie

Mentalization for Offending Adult Males

A randomised controlled trial known as Mentalization for Offending Adult Males (MOAM), led by Professor Peter Fonagy at University College London is being implemented across thirteen sites. The research trial is a five year project which started in January 2016 and is funded by the National Institute for Health Research. Dr Jessica Yakeley at the Portman Clinic is a co-investigator. Further information is at https://ucl.ac.uk/psychoanalysis/research/mentalization-offending-adult-males-moam

Conclusion

We hope that in this chapter we have been able to demonstrate, by reference to a limited portion of its work, how substantial the Tavistock's contribution to the generation of new knowledge has been and continues to be.

[David Armstrong's biography appears on p. 26 and Michael Rustin's on p. 27]

Notes

1. The Tavistock and Portman NHS Foundation Trust website provides a valuable history of the Tavistock's work at https://tavistockandportman.nhs.uk/about-us/who-we-are/history/
2. It is not without significance that some of the Tavistock's methods of practice and understanding occupy a space somewhere between the arts and the sciences, as these are usually understood.
3. Yet Bowlby was already primed, partly from his own early life experience, but also from personal and clinical contact with children in the 1920s and 30s who had become disturbed as a result of prolonged separation from their parents (Van Dijken, 1998).
4. Alan Shuttleworth (1999, 2002) drew valuable attention to the important convergences between these perspectives, concerning a shared idea of relatedness.
5. We are grateful for advice from William Halton on the Tavistock's group relations work.
6. https://nice.org.uk/guidance/cg90
7. Stakeholder position statement on the NICE guideline for depression in adults (2019) https://cdn.ymaws.com/www.psychotherapyresearch.org/resource/resmgr/docs/downloads/StakeholderPositionStatement.pdf
8. A similar effect is found in infant observation (Rhode, 2012).

CHAPTER FIVE

"Mummy's gone away and left me behind"
James Robertson at the Tavistock Clinic

Mary Lindsay

J ames Robertson (1911–1988) would have fully recognised the despair, desolation, and panic of a small child taken to hospital, or residential home, and left there without his mother. He observed and described with concern and compassion how the child felt at this time.

With little understanding of language, no understanding of time, and with no one person to look after him or her, the child could not be comforted. It was James Robertson's tireless research and campaigning, in the face of ignorance and prejudice, that did much to ensure that mothers[1] were eventually able to come into hospital and look after their small children, and that residential care for children under five was closed.

Born and brought up in Glasgow, Robertson had gone to WEA (Workers' Educational Association) classes after work, and by the age of twenty-eight had finally got to college. He was there less than a year, but when war broke out, by now a Quaker and conscientious objector who wanted to help the community, he went to London to join the Pacifist Service Unit.[2] There he helped with the evacuation of the children from where the bombs were about to fall. Coming from a close-knit, working-class family, Robertson had been deeply concerned about the distress of the small children being separated from their parents, but could do nothing about it. In any case, the Blitz was about to start—all seventy-nine nights of it—and each day he was dealing with the ensuing chaos and carnage. Joyce, a friend from college, who had come down to visit him, saw it was "not her scene", but heard that a woman in Hampstead was looking for people to care for small children.

This woman was Anna Freud, setting up the Hampstead War Nurseries for children who had lost homes, and sometimes families, in the Blitz. Joyce was the first to join her. Robertson became a regular visitor and was appointed by Miss Freud to look after the boiler, carry out general maintenance, and fire watching. "Unlike the typical residential nurseries at that time, the Hampstead War Nurseries aimed to involve absent parents as much as possible. The London house was open to visiting at all hours. Mothers who wanted to breastfeed their infants were offered employment in the household" (Kennedy, 1996, p. 206).

All those working at the Hampstead Nurseries were expected to observe and record the children's behaviour on cards available. Anna Freud used these in her weekly talks to the staff about emotional development and also published them in 1942 and 1944, the first of their kind, later published together as Volume 3 of *The Writings of Anna Freud* (A. Freud, 1973). There had been little or no clinical interest in the subject of separation of small children from their mothers. Should the staff be upset by the children's distress, Miss Freud was always available. One of her sayings was "We are all learning, all the time".

By the end of the war, James and Joyce had married and their first child, Katherine, was born. When she fell ill her parents had an experience which was to animate their joint enterprise for the rest of their lives:

> In 1945, our 13-month-old Katherine was admitted to Great Ormond Street hospital late one night, dangerously ill with gastro-enteritis and an unidentified secondary infection. We had to leave her at the door, no visiting was allowed although we could occasionally peep through a window in the door. A week later we were allowed her home, a little girl who would not let me out of her sight. I am eternally grateful for the medical care, which saved her life. Katherine recovered physically but was perhaps left vulnerable to anxiety which can still surface today. We heard later that the ward sister gave her special attention, carried her around, perhaps because she was so desperately ill but also because she had been taken to the hospital ward by an eminent London paediatrician. The vision of 13-month-old Katherine in a hospital cot sustained James Robertson years later when he was subjected to many attacks as he campaigned to change conditions for children in hospital with his film *A Two-Year-Old Goes to Hospital*. (Joyce Robertson, 2011)

The Separation Research Unit

At the Hampstead Nurseries, James Robertson gradually became the social worker to the children and their parents and took a wartime social science diploma. After the war he went to the London School of Economics, qualifying as a psychiatric social worker. In February 1948 Robertson was the first person to join John Bowlby in his newly set up Separation Research Unit at the Tavistock Clinic. Bowlby had long been interested in the effect of separation on children. Having chosen medicine over the navy "to improve the community as a whole" (Van Dijken, 1998, p. 46), he had worked in a special school for maladjusted children. Here, following the "new psychology", it was generally accepted that these children had suffered emotional adversity during their early years. A few years later, in training as an adult psychiatrist, he learned that loss and disappointment could lead to psychotic illness, then as a child psychiatrist he realised from the histories of two children in particular that early separation from the mother could lead to emotional damage. Separation was not necessarily the most frequent or most damaging experience, but it was a definite fact that had happened and could thus be used for scientific investigation. Bowlby also saw that children in an institution needed one person caring for them.[3] He was greatly concerned about the effects of evacuation of young children under five, away from their mothers, and persuaded two eminent physicians of childhood to sign a letter to the *British Medical Journal* about it (Bowlby, Miller, & Winnicott, 1939). A copy was sent to *The Times*, but never published, much to Bowlby's annoyance.

At the time, all studies about separation had been retrospective, including Bowlby's own papers on "Forty-four Juvenile Thieves" (Bowlby, 1944a, 1944b). He now wanted to do a prospective study, for which he needed Robertson. As Bowlby later explained to Milton Senn in 1977, "… [Robertson] had got a lot of experience with problems I was interested in … and seemed to me to have other great merits" (also cited in Van der Horst & Van de Veer, 2009). At the time of his appointment to the Separation Research Unit, Robertson had just started his training analysis with encouragement and financial support sourced by Miss Freud.[4]

Children separated from their parents needed to be found. After some discussion with Robertson, Bowlby decided that children in hospital might be appropriate, because they had little or no contact with their parents—once a week, once a month, or not at all. Thus, it was on February 11, 1948 that Robertson went "in all innocence" to a local children's ward. He was told by the consultant paediatrician and the ward sister that it was a "happy children's ward" (Robertson & Robertson, 1989, pp. 10–11). But he saw that though the older children understood why they were there, and might be said to be fairly happy, it was the little ones under five, and particularly those under three, who were distraught at being abandoned; their mothers had gone away and left them behind. After their initial distress at being admitted—crying, shaking the cot, throwing themselves about—they had stopped. Medical and nursing staff saw this behaviour as "settling", whereas Robertson realised that they were now in despair at having been abandoned and felt they would never see their mothers again. If a nurse stopped by one of these silent toddlers the child would often start crying. She would be reprimanded for making the child unhappy, but what she was doing was revealing the child's distress. It was this difference in the interpretation of the children's behaviour that caused the rift between Robertson and medical and nursing staff. Unlike the Robertsons and their colleagues in the Hampstead Nurseries a few years earlier, these staff did not have anyone like Anna Freud to discuss their observations and experiences with.

Medical and nursing staff were not taught about the emotional and developmental needs of small children. In those days nurses had not had their own children, and many of the doctors had gone to boarding school at eight and "had never really returned home". They all had to learn about physical illness—not always comfortable—and their job in the hospital was to deal with it and to detach from the distress in order to get on with their work. There was a general reluctance to have more visiting times because the children became so distressed. But the visits were not creating the distress, they were uncovering it.

As there were no first-hand observations on what happened to separated children, Bowlby appointed Robertson as a field worker to observe and describe the behaviour of young children during and after separation from the mother (Robertson & Robertson, 1989, p. 10). Over the next four years Robertson made and recorded objective observations on the behaviour of children of between eighteen and thirty months before, during, and after their time in hospital.

Bowlby later wrote "[Robertson's] early observations first impressed me with the great potential of naturalistic studies of how young children behave when temporarily out of mother's care" (Bowlby, 1969, p. xvii). Mary Ainsworth, who joined Bowlby's research group in 1950, was inspired by Robertson's great talent for observation. "Although he himself was very modest about his data—transcriptions of his observational notes—I was deeply impressed with their value. I was entranced with the prospect of a future study of my own in which I would employ simple, direct, naturalistic observation, and use simple descriptive statistics to deal with its findings" (Ainsworth, 1983).

Robertson's descriptions of the child's behaviour on returning home from hospital were quite new. He found that as soon as they returned home their seemingly settled state in hospital "gave way to difficult behaviour—clinging to the mother, temper tantrums, and disturbed sleep, bedwetting, regression and aggression against the mother" … as if blaming her for leaving them behind (Robertson & Robertson, 1989, p. 13). This behaviour usually lasted for a week or two, but could be longer, occasionally even for years. After discussion with Bowlby and the rest of the research team, Robertson formulated three stages through which separated children went. At first they protest at the loss of the mother, distraught at being abandoned and cry, often shaking the cot, a reaction which would normally bring their mother running. Despair gradually follows protest, characterised by an increasing hopelessness that they would ever see her again. If the young child stays longer he enters the third stage, denial (later called detachment) in which, although he appears happy and interested in his surroundings, he has given up on his mother. Although detachment may not take long in a separated child, Robertson gives a harrowing description of it in a long-stay patient, Mary, aged two. Her mother had brought her "an expensive 'indestructible' doll. After the visit, Mary, using hands and teeth, rent it apart" (Robertson & Robertson, 1989, p. 16).

In 1950 Bowlby was asked by the World Health Organization to advise on the mental health of homeless children, and on the first of January he left the Tavistock Clinic for five months. Travelling to Europe and America, he read the literature, met with child psychiatrists and other workers in the field, and formulated the well-known description: "The infant and young child should experience a warm, intimate and continuous relationship with his mother (or permanent mother-substitute) in which both find satisfaction and enjoyment" (Bowlby, 1951, p. 67). He realised that the damage done to personality development by separation needed further investigation.

While Bowlby was away, Alan Moncrieff, professor of paediatrics at the Hospital for Sick Children, Great Ormond Street, invited Robertson to come and give a paper about his research findings to the annual meeting of the British Paediatric Association at Windemere, which was in April of that year, 1950.[5] Robertson was apprehensive but hoped that the distinguished pae-diatrician Sir James Spence, who had mothers admitted with their young children at his Babies Hospital in Newcastle (thirty beds for a population of several million), would support him. In his presentation, Robertson stressed the importance of a continuous relationship, how separation in hospital can lead to difficulties in relationships later on. He described the three stages of protest, despair, and denial/detachment. Then Spence got up and was scathing about emotional upset—"What is wrong with emotional upset? This year we are celebrating the centenary of the death of Wordsworth, the great Lakeland poet. He suffered from emotional upset, yet look at the poems he produced" (Robertson & Robertson, 1989, p. 20; see also Brandon, Lindsay, Lovell-Davis, & Kraemer, 2009). Spence, a chain-smoker, was probably suffering from post-traumatic stress disorder following action in a frightening First World War. Robertson, some-one only a step away from the tenements, inexperienced and as yet without status in this realm, felt much diminished by the unexpected attitude of a professor whom he had expected to be an ally. He also felt that the paediatricians themselves, although considerate to him, were not "lit up" by his talk.

Returning to London from Glasgow at the end of April after visiting his family, he suddenly decided to get off at Newcastle and went to see Spence at the Babies Hospital. Spence greeted him, showed him round, and Robertson was very impressed with the way he talked to the mothers who were looking after their babies. Spence was scathing about psychiatry. When asked about the children he saw in the ward, Spence, patting Robertson's knee as if to comfort him, said, "I know how much these children need. Twice a week is enough" (Robertson & Robertson, 1989, p. 21). Robertson noted how well Spence understood the mother's need to be with the sick child, but Spence did not see the child's need to be with the mother. He idealised the mother's need to look after their children and "the babies got a spin off" (p. 22).

On the train back to London, he realised that if Spence could not understand the children's needs then no other paediatrician would. Over the years Robertson had tried to show how distressed the children were, but medical and nursing staff, unable to see it, had poured scorn on him and would not believe him. He had read somewhere that visual communication pierces defences as the spoken word cannot. And thus it was that he got the idea of making a film (maybe from his courses at WEA) and presented it to Bowlby, who had also been interested in photography in his earlier years. Bowlby, realising the film could be important, insisted that it be objective.

Laura

A child was chosen from a hospital waiting list by a secretary with a pin, so that she could be filmed before being admitted to hospital. When Robertson met Laura his heart sank—she was an unusual child, expected not to make a fuss and discouraged from crying—but she was the subject that had been randomly selected for this study. Her mother was four months pregnant. A camera was bought for the project with a loan from Tom Main of the Cassel Hospital.

Robertson learned to use it over the weekend and, with no prior experience, he made an outstanding film, *A Two-Year-Old Goes to Hospital* (1952).

Robertson filmed a short sequence sample at the same time each day with a clock next to the cot, along with the "main events"—parental visits, relations with staff, and medical examinations. In spite of efforts not to do so, Laura did cry when her mother left. But when she saw her parents the next day, she was inconsolable. Most of the time she managed to keep back her tears, but occasionally, as when visited by a nurse for a play session, she cried. Her attempts not to do so were poignant. During each of the four visits her failure to acknowledge her mother grew longer. She constantly asked for her mother. Even so, she refused to take mother's hand as they left the hospital.

On her return home Laura would not let her mother out of her sight but scratched and kicked her when she was there. She wet and soiled, refused to sleep alone, would not eat, and had temper tantrums—the usual behaviour of children on their return home, as Robertson had noted. She refused to talk about her stay in hospital. This lasted for less time than for most children.

A few months after Laura came home her mother was admitted to hospital for four weeks to have the baby, as was customary in those days. During this time Laura stayed with her grandmother and saw neither of her parents. When mother returned home with the baby she phoned Laura who was very excited about the thought of seeing her again. Laura was taken home by car and banged on the door shouting "Mummy, mummy!" When her mother opened the door, she said, "But I want my mummy!" She did not recognise her mother for two days, but was happy to see her father who was taking a week's holiday.

Six months later, Robertson brought the film to show the family one evening. Suddenly Laura was in the room and, after a short time, turned to her mother saying, "Where was you all that time mummy, where was you?" Then she sobbed, burying her head in her father's shoulder.

Nine months after she came back from hospital the family went to an exhibition leaving Laura in a crèche. Suddenly they heard her screaming. It turned out that an official photographer was coming round taking photographs and it took an hour to soothe her. At the age of sixteen she saw the film again and was only slightly upset; "That meant nothing to me," she said, reaching out and taking hold of her father's tie, just as she had done on the evening of her operation (Robertson & Robertson, 1989, p. 42).

When they first saw it, Bowlby and Robertson wondered if the film (which the Robertsons describe in detail in their book (pp. 26–42)) could be used at all. It was Joyce Robertson who said—as a loving mother she knew how exasperating tears could be—that Laura's restraint was much more poignant. So they decided to keep the film. "The struggle of a child aged two and a half to control her feelings proved very painful, possibly even more than a film about a continuously crying child" (p. 43).

In the spring of 1952 John Bowlby gave the paper, "A Two-Year-Old Goes to Hospital" at the British Psychoanalytical Society, following the screening by Robertson the week before (Bowlby, Robertson, & Rosenbluth, 1952). The paper was mainly concerned with the increased length of time that Laura takes to recognise her mother when she visits, and with theoretical hypotheses to explain that. Bowlby had not yet fully formulated the concept of attachment. There is no record of the discussion, but some evidence that the film had a lukewarm reception from the psychoanalysts. Some noted that Laura would have been more preoccupied with her mother's pregnancy than with being separated from her.

Then in the summer of 1952 Bowlby took Robertson to Chichester to the World Federation for Mental Health. The film was shown again and Robertson gave a paper on the Children Act 1948 (Robertson & Bowlby, 1952). He described the urgent need for deprived children, without family or home, to be properly managed and for the formation of the Children's Department under the auspices of the Home Office (later on this function became incorporated into local social services). He also reported how there was beginning to be a better understanding of children's needs. Based on his and Bowlby's findings, paediatricians at St Mary's Hospital in Paddington were soon to set up an entirely original project which kept mother and small child together by bringing the hospital into the home ("home care for sick children"; Lightwood, Brimblecombe, Reinhold, Burnard, & Davis, 1957).

Finally on November 28, 1952 the film was shown again, this time at a special meeting of the Section of Paediatrics of the Royal Society of Medicine under the chairmanship of Donald Winnicott, president of the Section. Bowlby began by saying the film was about fretting, a name then used for children in distress. His department was looking at the "psychological processes" which lead to the emotional damage caused by separation with the aim of improving methods of care. Robertson talked about the importance of recording objective data on initial "overt fretting" and subsequent "settling in" of young children in hospital. At issue was the behaviour of the children, about which he and the medical and nursing staff differed in interpretation (Bowlby & Robertson, 1953). The film aroused great anger. Although Winnicott was aware of Laura's distress, he commented that she had not got to the stage of being detached.[6] The anger of the audience was such that both the *British Medical Journal* and the *The Lancet* toned down their reports on the showing of the film. Those present said that Robertson had slandered paediatrics, that children in their wards were happy, and that parents had never complained (Robertson & Robertson, 1989, p. 44). Bowlby decided that Robertson's film should only be shown to medical and nursing staff, so that the professions could get used to the idea before the general public. It was feared that mothers might not allow their children to come into hospital when they saw they were so unhappy. While health professionals could not accept the message of the film, its quality was apparent early on to the National Film Archive (bfi.org.uk) where it is part of the collection.

In 1953 Robertson was made a temporary consultant to the World Health Organization and took the film of Laura to America. Although his audiences were not antagonistic to the film, they said that American children did not behave like this as they were less cossetted. But Robertson saw that, when separated, they were just as distressed as the children in the UK. He noted that in North America, if you had the money you could stay with your child; if not, you couldn't. There was hostility between the parents and the nurses. He then took the film to Europe, again encountering resistance from the older paediatricians and occasional support from the younger ones. He had the same dismissive and sometimes hostile reception in Belfast (where they were so antagonistic that they forgot to tell him where he was staying), and again in his home city, Glasgow. Finally the film was shown in Newcastle, where Robertson hoped that the impartiality of the film would allow Spence to understand it, but Spence was just as antagonistic as he had been at the British Paediatric Association three years earlier.[7]

In 1954 Robertson's second daughter Jean, then aged four, had to have her tonsils out and he arranged with paediatrician Dr Ronald MacKeith that this should be done at the Evelina Children's Hospital, part of Guy's. As a special concession her mother was admitted to a cubicle in the ward to be with Jean throughout her stay. Joyce Robertson wrote an excellent and moving description of what Jean said and did, which was written up with comments by Anna Freud (Robertson & Freud, 1956). Accompanied and so well understood by her mother, Jean was able to start nursery school a few weeks later, unlike another child of the same age who had been in hospital without her mother, who took several months to recover.

Shortly after the first showing of Robertson's film in Scotland, the child psychiatrist Dr (later Professor) Fred Stone—having recently returned from two years in Boston—was offered a research grant by his colleagues at Glasgow's Royal Hospital for Sick Children to "disprove all this Bowlby nonsense" (Karen, 1998, p. 80). Needless to say he did not accept this. Instead, he suggested that they should compare and contrast two similar wards in the children's hospital, one with unrestricted visiting, and the other continuing with its usual arrangements. Nursing staff protested that parents would get in the way of their work, and one report shows how there was also a fear of being judged harshly by parents when they saw what really went on in a paediatric ward. "You're really meaning to say that … no matter what we're doing, no matter what state of chaos we're in, a parent can just walk in and see how we're neglecting their poor kids" (Karen, 1988, p. 80[8]). Following Stone's proposed study there would be regular meetings to discuss progress. Though he waited, no meetings were requested. After a few months, he heard that the whole of the Royal Hospital for Sick Children in Glasgow had rather rapidly changed to unrestricted visiting.

Putting Robertson into practice: Dr Dermod MacCarthy

Of all the medical and nursing staff at the Royal Society of Medicine paediatric meeting in 1952, only the paediatrician Dermod MacCarthy, from Amersham General and Stoke Mandeville Hospitals, was initially moved by the film to think of changing his practice. This was because on their way home in his car his ward sister at Amersham, Sister Morris, pointed out to him the need that small children have for their mothers. Ivy Morris had been a nanny and was probably the only person in the audience who knew anything about the day-to-day lives of healthy, small children. When MacCarthy was not around she would have the mothers spend the day with them on the paediatric ward. MacCarthy was somewhat startled but he had great respect for Sister Morris. He himself had been very distressed and lonely after tonsillectomy in childhood. Having been brought up in the questioning world of the Bloomsbury set he always said that anyone dealing with children should remember their own childhood (MacCarthy, 1954).

The next day, on a relaxed Saturday morning ward round, he saw how distressed the young children on his ward were. "I was angry but after the film I really heard children crying for the first time." As Robertson later describes it, "Dr MacCarthy put his roused anxiety to good use. He had long been easy about visiting and occasionally had mothers to stay: but now he recognized the full implications of the young child's need of the mother. He quickly opened the ward to unrestricted visiting and encouraged all mothers of under-fives to stay. He did not pick and choose between them on grounds that some were more suitable than others; family doctors in the community could tell the mother of any young child they were sending to hospital that she could stay with him." (Robertson & Robertson, 1989, p. 54).

When I arrived at Amersham hospital as a paediatric registrar in 1954, mothers coming into the hospital was a going concern. This is something that requires tact and understanding. We all adored Sister Morris even when she was scolding us. She had an amazing capacity for making everyone in the ward feel it was a good place to be. I never heard of any problems that she had with the mothers, but she was not always there. Anxious mothers and worried nurses are not used to meeting at two in the morning and sometimes there would be disputes requiring many cups of tea and the presence of the registrar from fifteen miles away. By the time I got there the dispute had usually been sorted out and all I had to do was congratulate everybody.

In 1956 Robertson returned to Amersham to make the second film, *Going to Hospital with Mother* which was released in 1958 (Robertson, 1958a). By this time it had been routine for nearly three years at Amersham for all mothers of under-fives to come in with their children. As Robertson says, "Dr MacCarthy's relaxed ward was heart-warming to see" (Robertson & Robertson, 1989, p. 54). The film shows Sally at home, making a great fuss about having her face wiped, and then in hospital where she made an equal fuss about being examined. But her mother was there holding her and comforting her immediately afterwards. In the film Sally is happy throughout her stay, showing no signs of concern about being in hospital. Mother is able to talk with the surgeon and the medical staff at Amersham about any concerns that she has. The film was very well received. In the discussion following Robertson's lecture about the film at the Royal Society of Medicine, Dermod MacCarthy said: "One of the benefits of getting mothers into a general paediatric ward is to improve people's observation by throwing into sharp contrast the state of the child who is alone and anxious, and the security of the one who has his mother" (Robertson, 1959, p. 384).

Ten years later, Dermod MacCarthy, Ivy Morris, and I published a paper on our experience of 1,000 mothers using the ordinary cubicles of a children's ward. The purpose was the prevention of unhappiness in the child, the benefits of nursing by the mother, and the mother's need to do this nursing. These aims were "to a great extent … achieved, and the scheme [was] welcomed enthusiastically by local parents" (MacCarthy, Lindsay, & Morris, 1962).[9] Robertson followed the work closely from the beginning and we found his encouragement and our exchange of views invaluable.

MacCarthy went on to campaign not only to help encourage mothers to stay in hospital, but also to try to change the attitudes of both medical staff and the parents—he called it his "barrel organ". His paediatric ward, which was open to unrestricted visiting, became a model which Robertson later described in his book *Young Children in Hospital* (Robertson, 1958b).

The Platt Report and its aftermath: a damp squib

Returning to the beginning of the NHS in 1948, when medical care became free, middle-class parents, used to paying for their care by having nurses into the home or children in nursing homes, found that though all treatment was free, they were not able to visit the children as they had been used to. It may be this that contributed to the Ministry of Health sending out three memoranda in 1949, 1951, and 1956 advising that visiting in hospitals should be increased. But hospitals took little notice.

By 1956, the government had become exasperated by there being little or no increase in visiting times and set up a committee to look at the emotional needs of children in hospital. The Committee on the Welfare of Children in Hospital, later known as the Platt Report, had as its chairman Sir Harry Platt, then president of the Royal College of Surgeons. Many organisations concerned with children were asked to send in evidence. Robertson, representing the Tavistock, sent in his memorandum. Platt suggested that this was so helpful and comprehensive that he should make it into a book. In this book, *Young Children in Hospital* (1958b), which was translated into many different languages including Japanese, Robertson describes the distress of young children in hospital without their mothers and the sometimes prolonged emotional damage that followed. He compared that to the situation at Amersham where mothers were automatically invited to accompany children under five.

When Robertson gave his evidence to the Platt committee he showed his two films and brought MacCarthy with him.[10] Robertson presented the problem and MacCarthy's ward showed the solution. There is no record of what actually happened at the twenty committee meetings, except the following quote, "It was an absorbing experience to sit beside him [Platt] and watch the way in which he guided discussion while his own views crystallized" (Gledhill, 1987). The Platt Report (Ministry of Health, 1959) recommended that children and adolescents should not be admitted unless unavoidable and must not be nursed on adult wards, that parents should be allowed to visit whenever they want, consideration should be given to the admission of mothers (especially to those with under-fives), and that attention be given to how children should be emotionally cared for and also educated whilst in hospital. The Report also recommended that medical and nursing staff be better educated in the emotional needs and development of young children.

In 1958 the BBC asked Robertson to prepare a programme about his films. Although he had spent considerable amount of time on it, when he went to the BBC to discuss it further he was told they had taken medical advice that the programme should not take place. It was probably a government embargo—they knew a report on the subject was to be published in a few months and it was felt that government policy should be ahead of Robertson's films.

The Platt Report was published in 1959 and incorporated most of Robertson's recommendations. Over the following two years, it was sent round to hospital administrators and medical and nursing departments, and quietly put aside to gather dust.

1961—A turning point for children in hospital: mothers get together as a pressure group

In January 1961, Robertson wrote three articles for *The Observer* and one for *The Guardian* about the need that young children have for their mothers when they go to hospital. Lord Astor, who owned *The Observer* at the time, said that persuading the editor of his women's page to include the articles was one of the most important moments of his life. Mary Stott, the editor of the women's page of *The Guardian*, was always very supportive of Robertson's ideas. Robertson also gave a talk on the radio telling mothers that if they were not allowed to stay they should first talk to the ward sister, then to the consultant, and then to the medical administrator, and if they were still refused, they should get a chair and sit beside their child— this was perfectly legal.

It was in the spring of 1961 that, at last, Robertson was asked to talk on television and show sequences from his two films. He had on the programme with him his wife Joyce, Dermod MacCarthy, Sister Morris, and paediatrician Ronald MacKeith. He showed Laura's distress and Sally's happiness and talked about the need for facilities to be available for the mothers to come into hospital to help look after their young children. At the time, all programmes were live and, disobeying the orders of the producer, Robertson famously went to the microphone and asked anyone who had experience of being with or without their child in hospital to write to him. This brought in 400 letters, extracts of which were made into a book (Robertson, 1962), with a foreword by Sir Harry Platt in which he states that "Robertson's pioneer studies on the psychological trauma inflicted on young children during periods of stay in hospital" had brought the issue "vividly before the notice of a wide public" and "had a strong influence" on his own report, whilst also serving to "remind us that all is not yet well" (Robertson & Robertson, 1989, p. 60).

One of the letters Robertson received was from Jane Thomas, "the letter that that canny Scot had been waiting for" (Thomas, 1990). Thomas made many suggestions to publicise Robertson's work, and with some mothers from Battersea met him at the Tavistock Clinic. From the very beginning Robertson had had in mind the idea of a pressure group. He now told Jane Thomas and the other mothers to form such a group without mentioning his name, using the recommendations of the Platt Report as their *raison d'être*. Thus "Mother Care for Children in Hospital" was created. Several branches sprang up and these got together and started annual meetings as the organisation grew. Their first office opened in London. In 1965 the organisation was large enough to be called the National Association for the Welfare of Children in Hospital (NAWCH). Medical and nursing staff now joined. Dermod MacCarthy was the main speaker at the annual conferences for the first two or three years. A driving force behind this movement from the very start was Peg Belson, who lived in the same block of flats as Jane Thomas. Writing in 2004, Peg tells of the international movement they started, all from meetings "on a bench in Battersea Park with children underfoot" (Belson, 2004, p. 359).

At last the Platt Report had a reason to exist. The Platt Report had said that consideration should be given to the admission of mothers for the first few days for children under five. But NAWCH ignored this and said that all mothers must come into hospital to look after their small children. NAWCH needed the Platt Report and the Platt Report needed NAWCH. Had the mothers, who knew their children better than anyone, not been inspired by Robertson to create this movement, resistance to parental visiting would have been even greater. After all, doctors and nurses have a job to do, and there seemed in those days no good reason to have extra people getting in the way of this vital task. Though it may seem shocking now, we paediatricians did not notice the children's distress. At the time the priority for a child in hospital was simply that he or she should recover from illness, and not die, as many had in preceding decades. By promoting a child's right to parental presence in local and national meetings, and occasionally on TV, NAWCH encouraged public discussion of childhood separation. Doctors and nurses were part of this debate, but it was led by the fierce passion of mothers who did not want their children to suffer unnecessary and harmful separation on top of being ill. Only gradually did the work of Bowlby, Ainsworth, and Robertson show us all that being deprived of caregivers undermines children's health and development. This was a fundamental change in our understanding of human needs.

Robertson had much to be proud of. He had, in effect, persuaded medical and nursing staff to at least look at the children's needs, made two films that should encourage this, and had campaigned ceaselessly for over ten years to try to make doctors, nurses, and the public sufficiently concerned about the welfare of children in hospital to do something about it.

Children in substitute care

In 1969 the Robertsons made a film, *John*, financed by Kodak, showing a child of seventeen months who was admitted to a residential nursery for eight days. For the first day or so he coped but over the following days deteriorated gradually in front of the camera, ending up lying on the floor with a large teddy bear and refusing to eat. The film was devastating to watch and did much to end residential care for children under five. It won a number of awards and is still watched around the world.

In the 1960s James and Joyce Robertson fostered four children supported by grants for eleven years from the Grant Foundation in New York. A film was made of each child, *Young Children in Brief Separation* (Robertson & Robertson, 1971), showing how a substitute mother enabled the children to be able to cope with being away from parents. The four young children were often anxious and sometimes angry or upset, but none reacted with the acute distress and despair that had been described in young children alone in hospital. "When given a substitute mother who cared for them with concern and empathy, none of our fostered children were acutely distressed, as were the children Robertson had observed in hospitals and other institutions many years earlier" (Robertson & Robertson, 1989, p. 147). At the annual conference of NAWCH in 1973, James and Joyce Robertson discussed the idea of a foster mother looking after the child in hospital if the mother was unable to do so. It seemed at first that this might work, but, as June Jolly has said, it was found to be too complicated. This happens in Australia, but not elsewhere.

The Robertsons continued to have an office at the Tavistock Clinic until James retired in 1976. After they left the Tavistock, they set up the Robertson Centre and acted as expert witnesses in the children's courts and also held teaching sessions.

Conclusion

James Robertson's contribution to the improvement of the care of children, both in hospital and in residential homes, was immense. His courageous campaigning left us all with an understanding of the young child's urgent need for a mother or mother-substitute. Thus it became normal for mothers to take part in the care of their children in hospital, especially those aged under three, and in this, with the combination of the Platt Report and NAWCH, the UK led the world. Between them, Bowlby, Robertson, and Ainsworth initiated a paradigm shift in human consciousness such that old ways of looking at children now seem unimaginable. Robertson's other legacy is the films he made, which won many awards and which have done, and will do, so much to educate anyone who has to do with small children.

> James Robertson was a remarkable person who achieved great things. His sensitive observations and brilliant filming made history,[11] and the courage with which he disseminated— often in the face of ignorant and prejudiced criticism—what were then very unpopular findings, was legendary. He will always be remembered as the man who revolutionized children's hospitals, though he accomplished much else besides. I am personally deeply grateful for all that he did.
>
> (John Bowlby on the back cover of *Separation and the Very Young*,
> Robertson & Robertson, 1989)

Acknowledgement

My thanks to Katherine McGilly who provided the story, published by her mother Joyce Robertson, of her own stay in hospital as an infant in 1945.

Notes

1. And, of course, others with responsibility for the child.
2. Robertson was in fact blind in one eye and so would never have been called up.
3. As early as 1939 Bowlby wrote, "If a child needs to be in a hospital or other institution it is of paramount importance that one single person takes care of the child," because otherwise "the children

have no opportunity of forming solid emotional ties to any one person. This, more than any other single thing accounts, I believe, for the withdrawn impersonality of the institutional child" (Substitute homes, *Mother and Child*, April 3–7, p. 6, cited by Van Dijken, *John Bowlby: His Early Life*, 1998, p. 94).

4. There is no record of who the psychoanalyst was.

5. Not 1951, as is usually recorded.

6. Donald Winnicott's own delicate position on children in hospital is revealed in a letter written fifteen years earlier. As a newly appointed consultant paediatrician in the 1920s Winnicott had decided not to be responsible for inpatient children because, as he much later explained, "If I become an in-patient doctor I shall develop the capacity not to be disturbed by the distress of the children, otherwise I shall not be an effective doctor" (letter to Margaret Torrie, September 5, 1967 in *The Spontaneous Gesture: Selected Letters of D. W. Winnicott* (p. 168). London: Karnac, 1999.

7. In a letter to Dermod MacCarthy, Robertson describes how he later had "quite a close personal relationship" with Spence. Robertson wrote that Spence "knew much less about mothers and children than do you" and anticipated a "Dermod MacCarthy Medal" (alongside the James Spence Medal, "the highest honour bestowed by the Royal College of Paediatrics and Child Health") (unpublished letter from Robertson to MacCarthy, Tavistock Child Development Research Unit, October 15, 1974).

8. Citing Barbara Smuts' interview with Fred Stone, August 1, 1977, from an unpublished manuscript in the National Library of Medicine, Washington, DC. Other parts of this interview have since been published in Duschinsky & White (2019, chapter 11), sourced at the Wellcome Collection Archive.

9. Unfortunately our paper was published after the Platt Report and there was hardly any reaction to it.

10. As it happened, MacCarthy and Sheldon, the most senior person on the committee, knew each other, and Robertson and Harry Platt got on extremely well.

11. A full list of the Robertsons' ten films, and how to rent or buy them, is at www.concordmedia.org.uk/categories/robertson-films

* * *

Mary Lindsay FRCPsych, FRCP, FRCPCH(Hon), qualified in medicine in 1951 and, as a paediatric registrar, appeared in James Robertson's influential 1958 film *Going to Hospital with Mother*. Later, as a consultant child psychiatrist she was an early pioneer of mental health liaison in paediatrics, working again with Dr MacCarthy and his patients, and also with Professor David Baum in his diabetic clinic in Oxford. She presented the Oxford experience in her presidential address to the paediatric section of the Royal Society of Medicine in 1989, published in Lindsay (2017).

In 1974 Drs Lindsay and MacCarthy started the celebrated child psychiatry/paediatric meetings at the postgraduate centre at Stoke Mandeville Hospital which took place three times a year and continued for eighteen years. In 1976, although a child psychiatrist working in the home counties, Dr Lindsay was elected to the British Paediatric Association and in 2007 to an honorary fellowship of the Royal College of Paediatrics and Child Health, a rare distinction. In 1993 in recognition of her outstanding work in medicine, she was elected a fellow of the Royal College of Physicians of London.

CHAPTER SIX

The Tavistock Institute of Medical Psychology, 1920–2020

Brett Kahr

In December, 1919, not long after the Great War, a group of well-intentioned physicians and clergymen convened in the drawing room of Lady Margaret Nicholson on Pont Street, in South West London, to plan the opening of a specialist clinic for men, women, and children suffering from nervous illnesses, who would be treated by the newly popularised intervention known as psychotherapy. Spurred by the vision of Dr Hugh Crichton-Miller, a medical practitioner who had deployed depth psychology in his work with shell shock survivors, this forward-thinking band of social justice advocates decided that the new clinic should offer assistance to those members of the public who could not afford private fees.

The committee leapt into action and rented a four-storey building at 51 Tavistock Square, in Central London, a former Victory Club hostel for veterans. Tavistock Square proved a most favourable location as many of the physicians who would volunteer their clinical services already maintained private offices nearby in Harley Street.

On September 27, 1920, the Tavistock Clinic for Functional Nervous Disorders opened its doors, comprising, inter alia, four consulting rooms, a lecture hall, a large drawing room covered in grey and white Chinese wallpaper, and a stone staircase. Dr Edgar Alan Hamilton-Pearson, one of the staff physicians, treated the very first patient—a child. Not long thereafter, Dr Mary Hemingway (who subsequently married the clinic's second medical director, Dr John Rawlings Rees), consulted to the first adult patient. Delighted by this achievement, Crichton-Miller, the founding medical director, beamed, "My dream has come true".

During the first year of operation, between 1920 and 1921, the clinic welcomed 248 new patients and raised approximately £300 in order to pay for basic operating costs. Not only did the honorary physicians donate several hours per week but so, too, did Sylvia Leith-Ross, the clinic's secretary,[1] who lived in the top-floor flat of 51 Tavistock Square.

The name of this new institution proved, at times, to be somewhat confusing. Although most referred to this centre for psychological healing as the Tavistock Clinic for Functional Nervous Disorders, on certain documents and in certain publications the organisation would be known, instead, as the Tavistock Clinic for Functional Nerve Cases. Strikingly, the General Post Office would, at times, send letters intended for the Tavistock Clinic to the ancient market town of Tavistock in the county of Devon in the South West of England; consequently, the clinic eventually inserted the word "Square" into its moniker, and the organisation became restyled as the Tavistock Square Clinic for Functional Nervous Disorders, sometimes referred to simply as the Tavistock Square Clinic.

Spurred by Crichton-Miller's passionate vision and, moreover, by the desperate need to care for the emotional devastation of Britons ravaged by a World War, the Tavistock Square Clinic for Functional Nervous Disorders began to flourish, and, by 1927, the staff had welcomed some 489 new patients, mostly women. In the class-conscious climate of the 1920s, the clinic divided its patients into professionals and non-professionals, the former group consisting of teachers, social workers, clergymen, artists, and students, and the latter group comprised clerks, artisans, tradesmen, domestic servants, and, its largest constituency, namely, housewives. In due course, a Children's Department began to offer psychotherapy to youngsters with a wide range of presenting problems, including nervousness, stammering, masturbation, enuresis, nail-biting, stealing, lying, truancy, asthma, and cruelty.

Dr Thomas Walker Mitchell, a pioneering British psychoanalyst, donated many books and periodicals, as did a woman called Miss Reynolds. This small collection formed the basis of the clinic's library, which would continue to swell in size over time.

To complicate matters, the fast-growing clinic soon required a governing body to supervise its increasing load of clinical responsibilities and other activities, which included public lectures and fund-raising, as well as the right to accept "legacies and donations"; and on August 9, 1929, the clinic created a separate body, under the Companies Acts 1908 to 1917, called The Institute of Medical Psychology, with Dr Hugh Crichton-Miller as Honorary Director. The objectives of this new limited company included the promotion of the study of psychotherapy and the provision of treatment for those persons unable to pay specialist fees. The term "medical psychology" carries little meaning today in psychoanalytical circles. But, during the nineteenth century and the first part of the twentieth century, and, even for decades thereafter, this common phrase denoted the body of work practised by those physicians interested in the contribution of the human mind to the genesis of mental illness.

In its early days, the Institute of Medical Psychology worked tirelessly to raise monies for such essential items as sixty to seventy yards of carpet to cover the staircase, as the sound of clunking heels created too much noise and no doubt interrupted many early psychotherapy sessions; and the clinic also required a typewriter—then quite a luxury. Happily, charitable individuals such as Lady Margaret Nicholson donated £15; and the unpaid secretary, Sylvia Leith-Ross, generously bequeathed £40. In due course, the board of the Institute of Medical Psychology (rendered hereafter as IMP) even succeeded in obtaining a luxurious donation of

£3,000 from an anonymous source, while, in the 1929–1930 financial year, many members of the public offered smaller sums as an expression of thanks for the recovery of His Majesty King George V, who had survived a life-threatening septicaemia.

The leaders of the IMP—mostly aristocrats, retired military leaders, and members of government—worked effectively, not only to raise funds for the clinic, but, also, to elevate its public profile. For instance, in 1930, Eva Violet Mond Isaacs, the Viscountess Erleigh, hosted a special Guy Fawkes Ball on behalf of the clinic, which raised some £800. This extraordinary woman, granddaughter of the distinguished chemist Ludwig Mond (who discovered the compound nickel carbonyl), had maintained a long-standing interest in psychological matters and had previously chaired a series of talks on behalf of the National Society of Day Nurseries, which included a lecture by a young physician called Dr Donald Winnicott. The IMP enlisted the services not only of a viscountess, but, also, of Hollywood moguls. Even the wealthy American film studio, Warner Brothers, whose movies included *The Jazz Singer*—the first feature-length "talkie"—made a regular donation of £1 per week to the clinic. One cannot help but admire the industry and the initiative of the IMP to engage leaders from both "high culture" (i.e. aristocrats and government officials) and "popular culture" (i.e. film producers) in the work of psychotherapy and psychoanalysis. Unlike the more insular British Psycho-Analytical Society, founded only months previously in 1919, the Tavistock Square Clinic and its board, the IMP, embarked upon a series of huge outreach campaigns.

Although the clinic had, since 1920, traded under the name The Tavistock Square Clinic for Functional Nervous Disorders and other variants, by 1931, the organisation became officially known, not as the Tavistock Clinic, but, rather, as The Institute of Medical Psychology, because Dr John Rawlings Rees, its deputy medical director, and his colleagues, agreed that, in order to promote the organisation's training in psychotherapy, the notion of an institute would have to take precedence over that of a clinic. Indeed, this institution produced its annual reports under the IMP name with the words "Tavistock Square Clinic" relegated to brackets. Dr Rees eventually succeeded Dr Crichton-Miller as the chief physician and became appointed as Medical Director of the Institute of Medical Psychology.

In this same year, 1931, Beatrice, Lady Blackett, and her husband, Sir Basil Blackett, hosted a special meeting at their home to sign up supporters, and they collected cheques which amounted to £377 18s. This new offshoot, The Friends of the Institute of Medical Psychology, proved efficacious, and, in 1932, Lady Blackett ceded her role to Lady Cynthia Colville—a Woman of the Bedchamber to Her Majesty Queen Mary—who became the Chairman of this scheme, which, by the end of 1932, boasted some 116 members. The wealthy, well-connected, grandees who ran the IMP continued to have an impact and succeeded in enlisting the services of some of Great Britain's most significant cultural icons who would assist with publicity and fund-raising. For instance, on May 1, 1933, the Olympic champion sprinter, Harold Abrahams, spoke at the Annual Meeting of the IMP; and on December 9, 1933, A. P. Herbert [Alan Patrick Herbert], a hugely prominent and multi-talented journalist, humourist, and lyricist of West End light operas, opened the IMP's Christmas Fair.

Perhaps the most impressive achievement of the IMP during its early years may well be the appointment of His Royal Highness Prince George The Duke of Kent, son of King George V and Queen Mary, as the IMP's first President. On June 13, 1934, Prince George visited the organisation's headquarters which, by this point, had moved from Tavistock Square to Malet Street, not far from University College London. Although Prince George could not sit in on actual psychotherapy sessions, he did spend time in the children's playroom and he also watched the administration of certain intelligence tests. Nearly a fortnight later, His Royal Highness received his presidency and spoke at a special dinner, during which he paid tribute to the IMP: "Having visited this Institution a few days ago, and being much impressed by its organisation and the work it is doing, I am convinced it merits every support." Not long thereafter, the noted Hungarian sculptor, Professor Sigismund de Strobl, created a marble bust of the new President,[2] which would be placed in the IMP's entrance hall, unveiled on April 7, 1936, by none other than Lucy Baldwin, the wife of the Prime Minister, Stanley Baldwin.

Surrounded by royalty, by politicians, and by celebrities, the IMP continued to thrive. In 1935, the organisation received ratification from the University of London that the clinic would now be recognised as an official training institution for those physicians seeking the Diploma in Psychological Medicine—at that point an essential qualification for aspiring psychiatrists. Moreover, the IMP even acquired new premises, approximately 31,400 square feet, on Ridgmount Street, not far from its location on Malet Street. And, also in this year, two members of staff, Dr Mary Luff and Dr Marjorie Garrod, published an important piece of follow-up research on 500 cases, demonstrating that a large percentage of the clinic's patients improved over a period of three years (Luff & Garrod, 1935).

Although the organisation traded first and foremost as the IMP, the members of the general public knew it predominantly as the "Tavistock"; and hence, in 1936, the organisation switched the order of its public titles to The Tavistock Clinic (The Institute of Medical Psychology).

Sadly, with the outbreak of the Second World War, the IMP decided that it would not be safe to operate a psychotherapy clinic in Central London, and so the organisation relocated to the headquarters of Westfield College, part of the University of London, on Kidderpore Avenue in Hampstead, North West London. Tragically, in due course, the Nazis bombed both the IMP clinic premises on Malet Street and, also, the old location on Tavistock Square, which became reduced to "pavement level". The German airmen also destroyed the intended new home on Ridgmount Street.

As the war ended, the IMP moved into new headquarters on Beaumont Street in the heart of London's West End. Somehow, with its decades of history and vision, the organisation survived the war and began to reconstitute itself with visionary staff and board members, and, in the immediate aftermath, such iconic figures as Dr Wilfred Bion and Dr John Bowlby crafted a new vision for the clinic's future.

On July 5, 1948, Great Britain celebrated the creation of a National Health Service, providing free medical care for all, and the Tavistock Clinic became one of its component institutions, under the aegis of the North-West Metropolitan Hospital Region of the NHS. In view of this new organisational arrangement, the IMP could no longer function as the supervising body of the Tavistock Clinic. This now became the task of the British government. Hence, the IMP and the Tavistock Clinic had to part company in spite of their multi-decade history. However, on June 29, 1951, the Institute of Medical Psychology became rebranded by a Special Resolution pursuant to The Companies Act, 1948, as The Tavistock Institute of Medical Psychology (hereafter known as TIMP). Although no longer in charge of the clinic per se, TIMP received donations on behalf of the Tavistock Clinic; for instance, in 1959, the TIMP inherited a huge bequest of £37,000 from the will of Hugh Eric Robertson, a former Captain in the Indian Army.

Of greatest importance, in 1956, the TIMP became the governing body of the Family Discussion Bureau, an organisation founded in 1946 by the social worker Enid Eichholz (later Enid Balint), who, through her cunning, enlisted the services and support of leading Tavistock Clinic psychiatrists such as Dr John Bowlby and Dr A. T. M. ("Tommy") Wilson to support her pioneering work on the development of psychoanalytically orientated marital psychotherapy. The Family Discussion Bureau had, for many years, operated as part of the Family Welfare Association, but, through the collaboration between Enid Eichholz Balint and various sympathetic psychoanalysts, it eventually became incorporated into the Tavistock Clinic family and subsequently adopted the title the Institute of Marital Studies, and later, the Tavistock Institute of Marital Studies, and eventually, the Tavistock Marital Studies Institute, followed by the Tavistock Centre for Couple Relationships and, ultimately, Tavistock Relationships (see A. Balfour, Chapter 22). For over sixty years, TIMP has served as the governing body of these foundational couple psychotherapeutic clinical and training institutions.

The present-day interrelationship between the Tavistock Centre on Belsize Lane, North London, and Tavistock Relationships, now located on Hallam Street, in Central London, remains strong. Dr Anton Obholzer, former Chair of the Professional Committee of the Tavistock Clinic (and subsequently Chief Executive of the Tavistock and Portman NHS Trust), later served as Chair of the TIMP, eventually succeeded by the policy researcher and political advisor Professor Nick Pearce. TIMP continues to function not only as the supervisory body of Tavistock Relationships—the United Kingdom's leading couple psychoanalytical organisation—but it also promotes research and public relations through its group of Senior Fellows who have made, and continue to make, significant contributions to the promotion of couple mental health, both nationally and internationally.

Once but a small town in the county of Devon, the name "Tavistock" has grown into a massive mental health brand. I hope that I have offered some further clarity about the vital achievements of the IMP and its successor, the TIMP, which have worked tirelessly to integrate psychotherapy and couple psychotherapy into the public consciousness over nearly a century.

Editorial notes

1. Sylvia Leith-Ross (1884–1980) was a remarkable anthropologist and writer. In 1921 she published *Fulani Grammar*, translations of folk tales from Northern Nigeria. Hugh Crichton-Miller wrote of her work during the Tavistock's first five years: "without her the Clinic would never have seen the light of day". M. Crowder, 'Introduction', in S. Leith-Ross (1983) *Stepping Stones: Memoirs of Colonial Nigeria, 1907–1960*. [Oxford Dictionary of National Biography.]
2. This bust now stands in the ground floor lift hall of the Tavistock Centre in Belsize Lane, London.

* * *

Professor Brett Kahr has worked in the mental health profession for over forty years. He is Senior Fellow at the Tavistock Institute of Medical Psychology in London and, also, Visiting Professor of Psychoanalysis and Mental Health at the Regent's School of Psychotherapy and Psychology, Regent's University London. He is the author of fifteen books on a range of psychological topics. Virtually all of the information conveyed within this short essay derives from Brett Kahr's ongoing research in the archives of the Tavistock Clinic in London (now housed at the London Metropolitan Archives); in the Royal Society of Medicine; and, most especially, in the Archives and Manuscripts department at the Wellcome Library, part of the Wellcome Collection, also in London.

CHAPTER SEVEN

John Bowlby at the Tavistock*

Margaret Rustin

John Bowlby's role in building institutional structures which fostered clinical creativity is perhaps less well known than his research work which established the foundations of attachment theory. For those who grew up in the context he influenced he was a figure of major importance, and the international reputation of the Tavistock Clinic and of its child psychotherapy training owes him a great debt. His vision of the potential of the Department for Children and Parents at the Tavistock Clinic was pivotal. He had not only a conception of the necessity for work with both children and parents in a child mental health clinic, and imaginative ideas about different ways in which that could be done, but also a picture of multi-disciplinary collaboration which was exemplary. The pre-war child guidance model of parallel work with children and mothers was expanded in several ways. First, the wider context of the children's lives was to be taken account of through attention to the child's school experience and the involvement of fathers in the clinical work. Second, he was part of a small group of psychoanalysts and analytically minded child psychiatrists who believed that a new profession of child psychotherapy was needed. Their argument was that the number of children who required specialised treatment was far too large to be met by current professional resources. The understanding of the child's mind taking shape within child analysis was impressive, and the pool of experienced professionals who would be interested to undertake a further formal training as part of the development of a public health oriented child and family mental health service was of excellent calibre. Hitherto, training had only been available within the narrower context of child analytic training or on an individual ad hoc basis.

---

* Originally published as Rustin, M. (2007). John Bowlby at the Tavistock. *Attachment and Human Development*, 9(4): 355–359. Reprinted by permission of Taylor & Francis Ltd, http://www.tandfonline.com.

Bowlby invited Esther Bick, a formidably able child analyst with a strong background in child development, to set up training within the NHS, which the Tavistock Clinic had decided to join, in line with its commitment to a broad conception of the relevance of psychoanalytic ideas to community mental health. It soon became apparent that Bick and Bowlby did not get on at a personal level, and her emphasis on internal factors in children's emotional difficulties was too narrow for his taste. Before she moved on, Bick was able to establish training which combined naturalistic infant observation, the academic study of child development and of psychoanalytic theory, and closely supervised clinical work with children and adolescents alongside personal analysis. Martha Harris, with whom Bowlby had a warm rapport, was Bick's successor. The Bowlby/Harris duo represented different emphases but they worked together well, and their students understood that these disparate elements were a necessary part of their training. There was some space for individuals to go more in one or the other direction, and some of the early child psychotherapy trainees like Mary Boston and Dina Rosenbluth worked closely in Bowlby's research team with James Robertson (see Lindsay, Chapter 5).

As well as making this new training possible within the Tavistock Clinic, Bowlby contributed to the creation of the Association of Child Psychotherapists, which linked three trainings together: the one Anna Freud had started at a similar time in the Hampstead Clinic, the Tavistock Clinic training, and a third led by Dr Margaret Lowenfeld[1] (1890–1973), located in the Institute of Child Psychology. Bowlby's political experience and wisdom was needed to protect the new baby of child psychotherapy within a complex of institutional interest which could have throttled it; the Tavistock Clinic itself was dominated by adult psychoanalysis, and work with children was seen as second class at that time. The Institute of Psychoanalysis, on some of whose members' support the trainings had to be built to provide the personal analysis for students and the clinical supervision of cases, was ambivalent about training outside its own boundaries; the idea of non-medical practitioners taking on the intensive treatment of seriously disturbed children and adolescents and acquiring independent expertise and status was by no means universally accepted. Bowlby's loyalty to the project remained solid and meant an enormous amount to this tiny profession as it emerged.

Bowlby was part of a post-war generation who believed they could change things in quite profound ways for children and families, that they had a knowledge base to do this appropriately, and that research could and would expand our understanding of human relations further. It was a time of hopefulness about fundamental change. At the Tavistock Clinic the caveats about the negative forces in human beings which could unleash a world war and attack and destroy creativity were always part of the culture; the Kleinian tradition within British psychoanalysis had taken up some of the more pessimistic strands of Freud's thought, and ideas about the origins, nature, and forms of human destructiveness were much discussed. Bowlby's optimism and radicalism must have represented the positive pole in this small but intense hothouse. The people he disagreed with often shared vital elements in his perspective, and alliances could thus be sustained and work got done. Analytically minded clinicians and researchers were all outsiders in some ways; the dominant paradigm in psychiatry was certainly not either psychoanalysis or the beginnings of attachment theory, and the academic world remained hostile to all this with some small exceptions. Bowlby's efforts to make a link for the Tavistock Clinic with London University were rebuffed (see Kraemer, Afterword), making it clear that this was an organisation that had to stay on the margin, tolerated by the establishment in gadfly mode. How strange this now seems when we look at the international scope of attachment theory and research.

Bowlby's clinical thinking also deserves our attention. There are a number of significant contributions, but two retain a particular freshness. The first was a paper published in 1949: "The study and reduction of group tensions in the family". This is how it started:

> Child guidance workers all over the world have come to recognise more and more clearly that the overt problem which is brought to the Clinic in the person of the child is not the real problem; the problem which as a rule we need to solve is the tension between all the different members of the family. (p. 291)

What he goes on to demonstrate is his development of a model of experimental family therapy combined with individual work with family members, both child and parents. So here we have Bowlby the psychoanalytic family therapist, drawing on the theories of Wilfred Bion and Elliott Jaques about group functioning to adapt traditional models of parallel work with child and parents to one in which the dynamics of the family group can be addressed in joint interviews. In a fascinating final section of the paper, he also explores, in a very optimistic vein, the idea that benign processes in one social context (e.g., in a family helped by a clinical intervention) can influence much beyond the family's boundaries. Children go to school, adults work in the wider world, and so on, and their better states of mind will influence these contexts too, he argues. It is useful to keep this in mind when as clinicians we worry about how we can ever do enough to make a difference in the context of increasing expectations, evidence of higher levels of distress, and constraints in resources; one good piece of work can, Bowlby is pointing out, have a positive impact in complex ways. This paper is an instance of Bowlby's capacity to link ideas from different intellectual origins in creative ways. His approach to work with families became one vital strand in the Tavistock Clinic's development of family therapy.

He combined attention to unconscious dynamic factors in the minds of family members, with an exploration of the family system, and indeed much wider systemic influences. The later divergence between systemic and psychoanalytic thinkers was not consistent with Bowlby's convictions.

A second significant contribution is his paper "On knowing what you are not supposed to know and feeling what you are not supposed to feel" (1988b). The final version of this has a cognitive focus and feel to it, but its broader import was his version of the impact of real traumatic events on children's minds. He never tired of enquiring about what a child might have actually experienced as a crucial element in understanding anxieties and behavioural problems. Although he argued that psychoanalytic therapists were guilty of ignoring real events and overvaluing fantasy, the work of Selma Fraiberg (1980) and all that has developed in the field of infant mental health, to take one well-known example, allows us to open up the question of what is included in this category of "'real events". The unconscious identifications in a mother's mind are all too real when they have the character of the ghosts in the nursery she described. Similarly, Bion's theory of container and contained drew attention to the importance of the qualities of the container and the disastrous results of the absence of the containment of infantile anxiety on the development of a capacity for thought. I would like to suggest that, although Bowlby took a stance rather critical of analytic thinking and practice, he remained in many ways deeply in tune with its ideas while adopting other forms of description. Making therapeutic contact with a child damaged through massive neglect or projections which have undermined his or her sense of reality means the therapist getting to know at gut level about feeling driven mad, and the desperate psychological measures taken to protect the self in such circumstances. This is the work that cannot be avoided.

A recent clinical example which exemplifies Bowlby's impact on child psychotherapists comes to mind. The work is with a child with major physical and cognitive defects, and is taking place within his special school. Despite his enormous difficulties in verbal communication, his impulsiveness and aggressive behaviour, and his physical disorganisation and frailty, school staff felt there was an inner richness which could be reached by individual therapy. This proved to be the case, as his imaginative therapist found ways to perceive the rhythmic qualities he was reaching for, which could give some more shape and meaning to his life. As their conversational reciprocity began to grow, this little boy's awareness of his enormous and tragic limitations also came into focus. Alongside this was the evidence in the therapy of an internal maternal object which turned a blind eye to the reality of the child's damaged state, and work being done by a colleague with the mother in fact confirmed that denial, idealisation, and infantilisation characterised her relationship with her son. Here was a child using his therapist to help him to know what he was not being allowed to know within the family setting. The freedom to have his own experience which therapy provided seemed a vital step in his developing much greater verbal capacities.

My own experience of Bowlby's contributions to multidisciplinary case conferences underlines another characteristic of his clinical approach. The patient I was presenting was a highly disturbed six-year-old who had a grim early history, including major prematurity and a hospital admission without her mother's presence at twelve months of age aimed at forced weaning, in her mother's recollection, during which she cracked her skull by headbanging. The family history was also very distressing since her father grew up in Poland during the war years. In her sessions with me, the extremity of her mental state was expressed in unmistakably primitive terms. She was preoccupied with the dread of a destroyed inner world which could not be repaired and by the absence of protective good objects and their replacement by vengeful persecutors. I was astounded by the material which, week by week, seemed to demonstrate the accuracy of some of Melanie Klein's theories about early infantile life. At the same time, it put me in touch with how intergenerational trauma can impact on development: that is how powerful unconscious projections by parents can shape a child's mind. One example that stunned me was when my patient referred to the Auschwitz furnaces in her play; that was where bad babies were thrown, she said.

At the end of my clinical presentation, Dr Bowlby said that this was the kind of child for whom intensive psychotherapy was an absolute requirement. He suggested that there were undoubtedly elements of brain damage in my patient, and I think he was right about this, but that this was all the more reason for providing this treatment for her, to give her the best possible chance of developing her potential and making life for her and her family more bearable. As I was fully aware of the risk of a Klein vs Bowlby scrap over this case among the senior staff in the department, I was impressed by his dual kindness, to the patient and to me as a youthful child psychotherapy trainee. I think he would be pleased at the way in which child psychotherapists have proved themselves committed to work with groups of patients whose life chances are severely compromised. Work with deprived, neglected, and maltreated children, with refugees, and with children with learning disabilities, including autism (see Rhode, Chapter 17), are some of the everyday specialities of the profession he helped to bring into being. Bowlby noted that different therapeutic modalities sometimes converge and would probably have liked the more pluralistic clinical context we live in, but I think he would never have underestimated the difficulty of the work to be done and would probably have been politely sceptical about today's plethora of quick-fix remedies.

[Margaret Rustin's biography appears on p. 101]

Editorial note

1. Although she never worked there, the remarkable career of Dr Margaret Lowenfeld overlapped with the history of the pre-war Tavistock. Having qualified in medicine in 1914, Lowenfeld met the surgeon and social psychologist Wilfred Trotter (who was Wilfred Bion's mentor at medical school) from whom she learned about the work of Hugh Crichton-Miller, the Tavistock Clinic's founder, and became interested in psychotherapy. In 1928 she established the Children's Clinic for the Treatment and Study of Nervous and Difficult Children, one of the first child guidance clinics in Britain. https://psychology.wikia.org/wiki/Margaret_Lowenfeld

CHAPTER EIGHT

Balint groups

Andrew Elder

F or a generation of GPs who began their careers between 1960 and the 1980s the influence of Balint thinking on the role of the general practitioner was central. At that time most medical schools had not yet introduced undergraduate teaching about general practice, and it was still possible to become a GP principal without any training at all.[1] However, most young GPs secured a voluntary one-year training post with an approved trainer. I took up my post as a trainee to Harry Levitt, a colleague of Michael Balint's, in Lisson Grove, London in 1972. Within a few weeks of starting I was on my way to the Tavistock to be interviewed by Sandy Bourne about joining a "case discussion seminar". They were never called Balint groups at the Tavistock.

The College of GPs[2] was greatly influenced in its first thirty years by the thinking that arose from the first Balint groups. Many of its early luminaries had been members of groups led by Michael and Enid Balint. Their influence gave the newly emerging discipline two main things: an exploratory non-hierarchical group-based approach to training and a deeper appreciation of the GP's role as a generalist, and the significance of this within the structure of the Health Service. Half the members of the small working party who produced the College's publication *The Future General Practitioner* (Royal College of General Practitioners, 1972) had been in a Balint group. In the eyes of the College a GP was above all a generalist, easily accessible to patients, relationship-based, and giving long-term continuity of care across the whole spectrum of illness. Looking back, I feel very fortunate to have started my career at such a time. A Balint group was the best possible place for a young GP to begin to explore the personal meaning of such a role.

The Doctor, His Patient and the Illness by Michael Balint was published in 1957. It was based on the experience of the "first" research group which had begun its work at the Tavistock in

1951[3] (Soreanu, 2019). Written with great fluency in Michael Balint's third language,[4] it has proved to be a landmark in the history of medical education and professional training.

Prior to Balint there had been no systematic investigation of the therapeutic benefits, and pitfalls, of individual doctor–patient relationships. In *The Doctor, His Patient and the Illness* he expressed his challenge to doctors with characteristic directness. What do we know of the pharmacology of that most frequently prescribed drug: the drug "doctor"? What are its indications? What are its undesirable and unwanted side effects? Can we begin to describe diagnostic signs to enable the doctor to recognise these pathological processes in good time? A sustained and detailed examination of these questions continued for over forty years in a series of research groups led by the Balints and latterly their immediate colleagues. They all published accounts of their work: *Six Minutes for the Patient*, (E. Balint, & Norell, 1973); *The Doctor, the Patient and the Group* (E. Balint, Courtenay, Elder, Hull, & Julian, 1993); *While I'm Here, Doctor* (Elder & Samuel, 1987); and *What Are You Feeling, Doctor?* (Salinsky & Sackin, 2000). At the same time, there has been a widening of interest in Balint groups which are now held in many different countries and include groups for medical students, hospital doctors in postgraduate training, multidisciplinary teams, and other professionals, particularly psychiatrists.

Origins of Balint groups

Michael Balint was born into a middle-class Jewish family in Budapest in 1896, the son of a general practitioner. After qualifying in medicine in 1918 he became interested in psychoanalysis and studied in Berlin before returning to Budapest in 1924 to start analysis with Sándor Ferenczi. For a brief period, in the twenties and early thirties, before the repressive regime of Miklos Horthy took hold in Hungary, cultural life in Budapest was free and forward-looking. Among new ideas for the treatment of outpatients, an innovative "free" polyclinic—an early attempt to provide whole-patient medicine—was opened at the end of 1931. It was here that Michael Balint held his first educational ventures with doctors. After quickly abandoning formal teaching, he began to experiment with a seminar where the "discussion focussed on the everyday work of the general practitioners" (Soreanu, 2019). This was the earliest version of what later became known as a Balint group.

In 1939, with help from Ernest Jones and John Rickman, Michael Balint and his family left Hungary to escape the Nazis and came to the UK. Initially they settled in Manchester where he worked as a consultant psychiatrist before moving to London in 1945. In 1948, he joined the staff of the Tavistock Clinic where he worked until his retirement in 1961. It was during this time at the Tavistock that his most creative work was done and for which he is now widely remembered.

In 1948, at the Tavistock Institute of Human Relations, a group of social workers led by Enid Eicholz (later Balint) had begun to develop techniques for treating couples with marital problems in what they named the Family Discussion Bureau (see A. Balfour, Chapter 22;

Morgan, Chapter 23). Michael Balint joined her in this work and together they developed the "case discussion seminar" in which the focus of the group was on the interaction of the couple and between the couple and their social worker. Balint then instituted a similar training programme—"training-cum-research seminars" was his original term—for general practitioners to understand more fully the emotional problems they encounter every day in their practices. Michael's approach was influenced by his experience of the Hungarian tradition of psychoanalytic training with its emphasis on analysing the countertransference of candidates in supervision. The emphasis in Balint groups is on doctors developing their use of their countertransference and remains emphatically on the interaction between doctor and patient: not centring either on the doctor's personal difficulties or on the patient's illness. In his introduction to *The Doctor, His Patient and the Illness*, Balint defines the problem the seminar is to investigate: "Why does it happen so often that, in spite of earnest efforts on both sides, the relationship between patient and doctor is unsatisfactory and even unhappy?" (M. Balint, 1957). Doctors are encouraged to bring cases that are troubling them or in which they feel they have behaved uncharacteristically. They present their case without notes so that the ensuing group discussion becomes more akin to free association, in stark contrast to a conventional medical presentation. In this way Balint groups become laboratories for the skills of deeper listening: listening to feelings that lie behind the presenter's words; giving attention to thoughts that are only half expressed, pauses or changes of direction; to mood and the language of the body. This approach to listening—to self and other—is encouraged by the leader(s) in the way they listen and participate in the work of the group. The exploratory space in a Balint group is created by psychoanalysts and doctors working together in mutual respect.

The Doctor, His Patient and The Illness

In *The Doctor, His Patient and the Illness* (1957) Balint lays out his understanding of a new role for GPs who "will no longer be able to disappear behind the strong and impenetrable façade of a bored, overworked and not very responsible dispenser of drugs and writer of innumerable letters, certificates and requests for examinations; instead he will have to shoulder the privilege of *undivided* responsibility for people's health and well-being". Balint elaborates his key concepts through case histories and a detailed account of the working method of the seminar. Many of his aphorisms remain resonant: the collusion of anonymity, the drug-doctor, unorganised and organised illness, the mutual investment company, apostolic function. In an appendix for psychiatrists, he lays out his views about leading such groups:

> Perhaps the most important factor is the behaviour of the leader. We try to avoid, as far as possible, the ever-tempting "teacher-being-taught" atmosphere. Our aim is to help the doctors to become more sensitive to what is going on, consciously or unconsciously, in the patient's mind *when doctor and patient are together.*

Balint's principal premise was that any emotion felt by the physician in treating a patient should be considered a symptom of the illness.

The General Practitioner Training Scheme

After Michael Balint's retirement from the Tavistock in 1961, the General Practitioner Training Scheme continued to run a programme of weekly training groups for GPs for the next twenty years or so. At its height the Tavistock was training sixty to eighty doctors at any one time. Groups were led by Sandy Bourne, Mannie Lewis, Tom Main, Alexis Brook (see Elder, Chapter 9), and others. Every group had an "associate leader" sitting in as observer and seminars were regularly recorded for a verbatim transcript to be discussed at the "GP and Allied Professionals Workshop" which met at least once in every term. Every two years, the leader of a group would be changed so that the seminar members had a different experience and to lessen the formation of a dependency culture.

In 1972, while still a trainee, I joined a group with seven other GPs which was led by John Denford. I remained a member of that group for four years and it became one of the main components of my GP training. Group members came from far and wide. There was a doctor close to retirement who travelled down from Cheshire every week, a middle-aged GP from Surrey, a young woman doctor from Swansea, and three or four of us from a scatter of different London practices, some single-handed, others in group partnerships. For a start, I learned a huge amount from listening to the other GPs. Emerging from the medical school's insistence on "objectivity" it was a revelation to witness the extraordinary individuality and variation of the different members of the seminar—their personalities and individual styles of doctoring; sometimes very involved, going to great lengths to help patients, or more distanced and wary. I found it liberating and creative to be in a setting which valued feelings and ideas. Slowly it became clear to me that the "case" was always the inextricable mix of patient and doctor together.

I felt anxious bringing my own cases. What would the group think of my efforts? It can be a relief to bring a case that is worrying, but it is also an experience of vulnerability. Slowly I gained the confidence to bring cases to explore what I was doing with my patients, or they with me. Was it all right to drive a young schizophrenic who needed admission to a mental hospital in my own car late one night? Why was I often over-anxious and angry with alcoholic patients? How should I proceed with patients who I invited back for longer "talking" appointments at the end of surgery? This was the 1970s. After a year or so, I noticed that one of my colleagues always brought "the same" case—a different patient and a different situation, but somehow always "the same". I remember thinking: if that's true for him, it must also be true for me. Two members of that group remain good friends. Trust among members of a group grows; a Balint group becomes a safe place, a laboratory for deeper listening; listening to self and other during professional work, weaving listening into the daily practice of medicine.

Wider influence

Balint had an incisive intellect and soon collected around him a group of colleagues who found him both stimulating and exasperating. One of these, Bob Gosling, recalls, "With Balint around, the frontiers of understanding were forever being pushed further out … at times one might become alarmed at the amount of turmoil Balint's leadership encouraged … it was a genuine, shared exploration of unknown territory" (H. Stewart, 1996). Balint was certainly successful in transmitting his creative energy to others. In the 1960s and 1970s numerous publications appeared as a series of Mind and Medicine Monographs published by Tavistock Publications (see list of titles in bibliography below), among them *A Study of Doctors* (1966); *Night Calls* (1961); *Sexual Discord in Marriage* (1968); *Psychotherapeutic Techniques in Medicine* (1961); *Virgin Wives* (1962); and *Treatment or A Diagnosis: A Study of Repeat Prescriptions in General Practice* (1970). In all, there were twenty-three titles covering an impressively wide list of subjects, all associated with a detailed exploration of the interface between mind and medicine, nursing, or social work.

Gosling and his colleagues in the Tavistock Institute of Human Relations applied Wilfred Bion's theories of group functioning to understanding the GP groups and worked along similar lines with probation officers and social workers. As a result of their work they published *The Use of Small Groups in Training* (Gosling, Miller, Woodhouse, & Turquet, 1967). In the Introduction, Haskell Coplin, a visiting American professor of psychology, writes: "The GP who is insensitive to the complex interplay of his own personality with that of his patient, the social worker who 'shies away' from the implications of sexual conflict in a client family, the staff member of a penal institution who does not see that disapproved behaviour in one of his charges can be a covert attempt at communication—these are all alike in that an important dimension of human behaviour is being ignored with a resultant loss of effectiveness" (p. 7). Seminars were tried with several other professional groups including clergy and physiotherapists (Bourne, 1981). Another close colleague of the Balints, Tom Main, who was director of the Cassel Hospital, developed Balint groups as a method of training for family planning doctors treating sexual difficulties. The Institute of Psychosexual Medicine was founded in 1974 and remains the principal source of professional training in this work to this day (Skrine, 1987).

Interest in the general practitioner training scheme at the Tavistock gradually dwindled. Fewer GPs sought Balint training as other approaches to their postgraduate education expanded during the 1980s, and a new generation of psychoanalysts was appointed to the Adult Department who had little experience of the work. In the 1990s there were only one or two groups being held at the Tavistock and with the retirement of Sandy Bourne and Mannie Lewis the GP training scheme more or less came to an end. The locus of Balint work had moved from the Tavistock to the Balint Society which had been founded in 1969. By the 1980s many of the GPs who had been in groups now held positions as postgraduate educators and introduced Balint groups into their half-day release training schemes. By then, the Balint Society was running a regular Balint Group Leaders' Workshop held in the evening at the Tavistock—this became the successor to the original GP and Allied Professionals Workshop which had met for many years at the Tavistock, and earlier had started its life as a working meeting of colleagues in the Balints' residence at Park Square West, facing Regents Park in London. A small number of GP Balint leaders had always been invited to the earlier Tavistock workshop. I look back on the scrutiny given to verbatim transcripts at that workshop as one of the most searching and stimulating experiences of my professional life. Thus, a small group of GP leaders emerged who had worked with Enid Balint, Michael Courtenay, Tom Main, Antonia Shooter, Sandy Bourne, Mannie Lewis, and others. I became a Vocational Training Scheme course organiser at St Mary's between 1979 and 1992 and throughout that period ran a weekly Balint group for trainees who were attending the three-year programme. For a time, I led it with the psycho-analyst Joan Schachter who was then a consultant psychiatrist at the nearby Paddington Centre for Psychotherapy.

Between 1995 and 2000 I returned to the Tavistock (had I ever been away?) as a consultant in general practice and primary care based in the Adult Department.[5] Apart from continuing a programme of Balint groups (with Jane Milton), my role was to develop projects relevant to the interface between primary care and the Tavistock's training programmes. When appointed, my dream had been of laying the foundations for an eventual GP unit dedicated to the distinctive mental health role that GPs and primary care teams play in the Health Service. Throughout those years, the NHS was beginning to undergo rapid change; the Tavistock was struggling to negotiate its survival in that changing world; and primary care itself was in transition with the introduction of GP-led commissioning. The institution was in survival mode: it was no time for the realisation of dreams! Balint work has always represented a radical challenge to the culture of medicine. The institutionalised split between body and mind shows little sign of healing. Until it does, GP Balint work and psychotherapy in primary care are likely to remain extra-institutional: at home neither in the institutions of mental health nor in those of conventional medicine.

The Balint Research Project

Following *The Doctor, His Patient and the Illness,* four further research groups were convened. Michael and Enid Balint led a second research group between 1966 and 1971 which published its findings in *Six Minutes for the Patient* (E. Balint & Norell, 1973). Midway in its work the group shifted its attention to develop a technique that would suit typical brief GP consultations better. Up to this point group members had been encouraged to be selective and conduct long interviews with their more troubled patients. This approach had stimulated doctors to develop psychotherapeutic skill but did not sit comfortably within the timescale of GP consulting. It also had a side effect: that doctors might become dissatisfied with their ordinary medical work and want to train as psychotherapists. The "six minutes" group began to study how doctors can observe and make use of their feelings in *all* consultations. They came up with the concept of the flash—"The therapy lies in the peculiar intense flash of understanding between the doctor and patient in a setting where an ongoing contact is possible" (E. Balint & Norell, 1973). When the "flash" came to be recognised, its chief attraction for the group was that it was not time-dependent but intensity-dependent; that is, intensity of *observation*, of *identification*, and of *communication*. As the focus of observation changed, so also did the method of working in the group: less emphasis on history and background, more on observations in the present—with the patient and in the group.

The "six minutes" group (1966–1971) proved to be Michael Balint's last research project with GPs. He died in 1970. Following his death, Enid Balint remained actively involved in leading groups and encouraging and training leaders (mainly GPs). In London, she led two further research groups to extend the earlier work. *While I'm Here, Doctor: Study of Doctor–Patient Relationships* (Elder & Samuel, 1987) examined moments in which the doctor's feelings about a patient suddenly changed. And *The Doctor, the Patient and the Group: Balint Revisited* (E. Balint, Courtenay, Elder, Hull, & Julian, 1993) focused on the effects of a doctor suddenly feeling surprised by a patient, indicating a possible shift in the doctor's habitual assumptions about the patient. Only when doctors can be surprised by their own responses as well as those of their patients, can understanding be deepened. Surprises arise from the capacity to register *unexpected observations*.

In 2000, a group led by Michael Courtenay and Erica Jones, both of whom had worked with the Balints for many years, published their findings, *What Are You Feeling, Doctor? Identifying and Avoiding Defensive Patterns in the Consultation* (Salinsky & Sackin, 2000). This is the fifth consecutive volume in what must be one of the most sustained qualitative action research projects ever to be conducted in medicine (1951–2000). All the research studies used systems of recording that enabled long-term follow-up of the cases presented in the group, often for two years or more.

Enid Balint died in 1994 and had been actively involved in working with GPs and thinking about the therapeutic nature of their relationships with patients for over forty years. Throughout that time, she remained committed to exploring, in detail, the original research question asked by her husband during their early work together in the Family Discussion Bureau. It is clear from the Preface to the first edition of *The Doctor, His Patient and the Illness* that Enid Balint also played a significant part in the development of their ideas from the very beginning. Her personal contribution to Balint work was untiring. Until well into her eighties, she continued to conduct research groups, demonstration groups, and write chapters of books, as well as maintaining supervision by correspondence with colleagues all over the world.

It was one of the great good fortunes of my career to work with Enid from the late 1970s until shortly before her death. I worked in four different groups with her—as an associate at first, learning about leadership by observing, and then as a group member in her last two research groups, and fellow author. In all those years I don't think I ever heard her use technical language or jargon of any kind in a group. It was clear that she had come to a deep conviction about the value of the work that GPs do, but she was often surprised and interested by the fact that we found it so hard to recognise this ourselves.

Presenting a case in a group led by her was certainly a searching experience. Her presence created a secure but challenging atmosphere. She was tough-minded and deeply committed to the task but at the same time—with her soft and rather beautiful voice—always appeared calm and thoughtful whatever was going on in the group! Indeed, she had a remarkable capacity for stimulating a questioning, unknowing exploratory atmosphere around her. At a point of confusion in the discussion, she would often make a remark that seemed to come from a quite different direction, which then helped the group refresh its thinking by opening a previously unconsidered perspective. As her colleague Bob Gosling said, "as if the wind was blowing from a different quarter" (Gosling, 1996).

In the last of the research books to which she contributed, Enid wrote a chapter entitled "The Work of a Psychoanalyst in Balint Groups". In it she states her view that psychoanalysts need to allow themselves to be used by the group more "like a clinician in a professional setting, not to teach theories, but letting the group do the work, helping perhaps by telling it what it has said, rather than interpreting underlying meanings" (E. Balint, Courtenay, Elder, Hull, & Julian, 1993). Her emphasis was always on the need for understanding to be gained from within and not imposed from without. This emphasis came from the acuteness of her concern that the individual—the doctor or the patient—should have their autonomy strengthened as a result of the work and not as she put it "be neglected by being 'understood' in a way which is not understanding but misunderstanding" (E. Balint, Courtenay, Elder, Hull, & Julian, 1993).

Developments and change

As has already been described, after publication of *The Doctor, His Patient and the Illness*, the Balints' ideas percolated into the educational culture and have had a considerable influence on attitudes and approaches to medical education and professional practice. A Balint Society was founded in the UK in 1969 to further their ideas and the first international congress was held in London in 1972. An International Balint Federation (IBF) was formed in 1975 from the joint effort of national societies in France, Italy, Belgium, and the UK. IBF now has twenty-eight affiliated countries, the most recent being Brazil. For more than ten years an annual Balint conference has been held in a Beijing hospital to which around 100 (mainly hospital) doctors from different parts of China attend. IBF holds a congress every two years in which groups are held and research presented. In the last ten years IBF has also begun to hold alternating biennial international conferences for Balint group leaders from all over the world. At one of the recent international congresses (in Metz, France in 2015) a presentation was given entitled: "Bringing the world together through Balint: creating a virtual Balint group for doctors around the world" (Nease, et al., 2018). This paper described—and included a live demonstration of—the formation of a group of young doctors from different countries (indeed different continents) who meet regularly in an internet-based Balint group with leaders from the international federation. The world changes but the fundamentals of the Balint approach remain the same: no teaching, mutual exploration of the professional–client relationship within a clear framework to facilitate free association and observation of shifts in feeling: not "what *should* be happening" in the professional relationship but "what *is* happening".

At the outset, Balint groups were intended for established GPs and led by psychoanalysts. Meetings were held weekly and doctors would often attend for two or more years. The frequency of meetings is now more likely to be monthly. Weekend meetings are held in which there might be four or five group sessions. Leadership has changed, now more often being a partnership between a GP leader and a psychoanalytic psychotherapist. During the last twenty years a practice that originated in Germany has become widespread—inviting the presenter to sit out or "push back" and not take any active part in the group discussion while listening to the group explore their case. It is a mixed blessing. While furnishing a new generation of less experienced leaders with a technique to facilitate "reflection" it interrupts the unconscious parallel process between group and presenter. And the settings in which such groups are held has changed considerably—now sometimes being in GP practices, multidisciplinary settings, and on vocational training schemes for both trainee GPs and trainee psychiatrists; in hospitals, for junior hospital doctors, and increasingly in medical schools, for students (Yakeley, Schoenberg, Morris, Sturgeon, & Majid, 2011). The Royal College of Psychiatrists has made attendance at a Balint group a mandatory part of training to become a psychiatrist. Currently fifteen medical schools have established or are developing Student Balint Group schemes.

There has been a slow shift in the emphasis of Balint work from training to a more explicit concern with professional morale. Several factors have led to this change. Since the 1990s health services in most countries have been subjected to a series of organisational reforms and upheavals that have affected morale and the role of professionals in a fundamental way. Balint's original aim of "a limited but considerable change in the doctor's personality" (M. Balint, 1957) is more difficult to accomplish with the reduced frequency of Balint groups; leaders are less experienced than in the past; and there is a widespread concern about the state of professional morale with high rates of illness and burnout (Kjeldmand, 2006). In addition, health and education commissioners have needed evidence of effectiveness before supporting the introduction of Balint groups. Thus, in recent years the focus of research effort has mainly been on establishing the benefits of Balint groups using measurable outcomes often related to empathy, morale, and burnout. It remains the case that the implications of Balint's radical ideas for medical training have not yet been fully grasped. They involve nothing short of "a *transformation* that will affect everything the physician does" (McWhinney, 1998).

I will give a brief description of two current Balint groups.

An Israeli Balint group: loss and separation

This account of a Balint group in Israel is taken from a paper entitled "Family Physicians Leaving Their Clinic—The Balint Group as an Opportunity to say Good-bye" (Shorer et al., 2011). The group has existed for two years and meets every three to four weeks. A case is presented by a young woman doctor with three children who is shortly leaving her clinic and becomes unexpectedly aware of her anxiety about separation while presenting a case. The doctor describes her practice as "very close-knit, like a family". She begins, "… it's not urgent … I'm not sure if it's a problem at all, but if no one else has a case …" She speaks about a family whose eighteen-year-old son has been killed in a car accident. They are a family who don't consult often, and she is unsure whether to visit them or not … "If I invite them in, what will be the reason? If the loss is the issue, is this my task as a doctor to *open this issue up*?" During the discussion the connection between her own suppressed feelings of imminent separation and the tragic loss of the son in the family becomes apparent to her.

The authors summarise their report by saying:

> The cornerstone of family medicine is the belief in both the continuity and availability of care. These beliefs are challenged when a doctor leaves his or her clinic because of personal reasons. In the example cited, the involvement of colleagues in a Balint group led a doctor to an insight into her conflicting feelings related to leaving her clinic. The group process helped her to prepare and deal with her own feelings and needs, as well as those of her patients and staff. Balint groups are a secure place to explore and gain insight into the emotional aspects of attachment and separation of physicians from their patients.

And lastly, here is a brief account of a multidisciplinary Balint group I have been co-leading with a colleague, Anne Tyndale, a psychoanalytical psychotherapist and Balint leader.

A multidisciplinary organisational Balint group

Since October 2011, we have been co-leading a monthly multidisciplinary Balint group in the Practitioner Health Programme (PHP) in London. Founded in 2008 PHP provides a service for doctors (and dentists) with mental illness and problems with addiction. It is an NHS programme housed in an ordinary GP practice in south London. The invitation to establish the group came from the director who was concerned about the arduous nature of the clinical work and tensions that might arise within the team. The Balint group is attended regularly by the core staff, at present nine people: three GPs, two psychiatrists, a mental health nurse experienced in addiction, two nurses trained in CBT, and a psychotherapist. The practice ethos is a strongly primary care-based one with an emphasis on continuity of care, a non-hierarchical multidisciplinary team with regular meetings and a focus on the professional relationship.

The group functions as an organisational Balint group in which the discussion of troubling cases focuses mainly on the individual client–professional relationship but often also involves other team members who might know the patient being presented. Interdisciplinary tensions sometimes surface but not as often as might be expected. Sometimes a request is made to discuss an issue, but rarely: these have included anxiety about a nurse leaving who had occupied a full-time role within the service; a disturbing complaint against the service from an outside colleague, and a run of suicides. Nearly always the group discusses cases. Underlying the work of the group there is a palpable concern with personal and professional confusion and associated boundary difficulties.

Co-leadership has been vital. Many of the difficulties of the "doctor–patients" are connected to early emotional deprivation, omnipotent self-reliance, and denial of emotional need associated with high degrees of disturbance and addiction. The ethos of the team is deliberately designed to counter this with an emphasis on regular team discussion. The Balint group, and co-leadership, is part of that. The position of the leaders in an organisational Balint group is more of a visiting outsider than it would be in a traditional Balint group. The organisation has chosen to have a Balint group and we have been meeting for nine years. Clearly, a practice which is already mindful of the emotional dimension of its work is more likely to support setting up an in-house Balint group. But it is also true that once a group is established it will foster a feeling of secure attachment for the professionals within such a practice; a mutually enhancing relationship between group and organisation.

Conclusion

Unlike nearly all other approaches to improving doctor–patient communication, the Balints' approach involves a change *in* the doctor and therefore brings the potential for a genuinely "new kind of doctor" into being: one more able to be self-aware and to attend to the emotions involved in a clinical encounter. From his early years as a psychoanalyst, Michael Balint was a keen exponent of the value of applying psychoanalytic principles and insights to other fields of practice. In the encouraging and creative atmosphere at the Tavistock in the post-war period, presided over by J. D. Sutherland who was medical director at the time, Balint's energy and creativity was able to flourish and he produced a body of work and an approach to professional training which continues to spread and influence new generations worldwide.

Mind and Medicine Monographs, editor Michael Balint

London: Tavistock Publications—23 titles

1. *Psychotherapeutic Techniques in Medicine.* Michael and Enid Balint
2. *Night Calls: A Study in General Practice.* Max B. Clyne
3. *Psychological Illness: A Community Study.* E. J. R. Primrose
4. *Family Ill Health: An Investigation in General Practice.* Robert Kellner
5. *Virgin Wives: A Study of Unconsummated Marriages.* Leonard J. Friedman
7. *The Caseworker's Use of Relationships.* Margaret L. Ferard and Noel K. Hunnybun
8. *A Study of Brief Psychotherapy.* D. H. Malan
9. *Administrative Therapy: The Role of the Doctor in the Therapeutic Community.* David H. Clark
10. *Nurse and Patient: The Influence of Human Relationships.* Genevieve Burton
11. *Marriage and First Pregnancy: Cultural Influences on Attitudes in Israeli Women.* Esther R. Goshen-Gottstein

12. *One Man's Practice: Effects of Developing Insight on Doctor–Patient Transactions.* Ray S. Greco with Rex A. Pittenger

13. *A Study of Doctors: Mutual Selection and the Evaluation of Results in a Training Programme for Family Doctors.* Michael Balint, Enid Balint, Robert Gosling, and Peter Hildebrand

14. *Asthma: Attitude and Milieu.* Aaron Lask

15. *Neurosis in the Ordinary Family: A Psychiatric Survey.* Anthony Ryle

16. *Sexual Discord in Marriage: A Field for Brief Psychotherapy.* Michael Courtenay

17. *Psychopharmacology: Dimensions and Perspectives.* Edited by C. R. B. Joyce

18. *Motherhood and Personality.* Leon Chertok

19. *Contraception and Sexual Life: A Therapeutic Approach.* David Tunnadine

20. *Treatment and Diagnosis: A Study of Repeat Prescriptions in General Practice.* Michael Balint, John Hunt, Dick Joyce, Marshall Marinker, and Jasper Woodcock

21. *Focal Psychotherapy.* Michael Balint, Paul Ornstein, and Enid Balint

22. *Mental Illness in Childhood.* V. L. Kahal

23. *Six Minutes for the Patient: Interactions in General Practice Consultation.* Edited by Enid Balint and J. S. Norell

[Andrew Elder's biography appears on p. 93]

Notes

1. Mandatory postgraduate training for GPs was introduced in 1979.
2. Founded in 1952.
3. An earlier experimental group had met between April and June 1951 led by Michael Balint and Henry Dicks.
4. After Hungarian and German.
5. My GP and family therapist colleague, John Launer (2007), was based in the Department for Children and Families at the same time.

CHAPTER NINE

Alexis Brook: the contribution of a psychotherapist in primary care*

Andrew Elder

A lexis Brook was a pioneer in the field of psychosomatic medicine. Throughout his time at the Tavistock Clinic (1971–1985) and in his retirement, he worked with great tact and creativity with colleagues in other medical disciplines—with gastroenterologists and surgeons (at St Mark's Hospital), with occupational health physicians in industry, with ophthalmologists (initially at Queen Alexandra's Hospital, Portsmouth and later at Moorfield's Eye Hospital), and with GPs and their primary care teams. With his warmth, wisdom, and unassuming style he represented the very best of the Tavistock's approach to consultancy. Dr Brook was head[1] of the Tavistock Clinic between 1979 and 1985.

I was fortunate to have the opportunity of working with Alexis when we established a series of multidisciplinary case discussion seminars for eye professionals at the Tavistock Centre in 1996 (Brook, Elder, & Zalidis, 1998). It was a delight to work with him. In the seminars he was always encouraging and had an apparently effortless way of responding to very distressing cases with great sensitivity. The warmth and humanity of his approach enabled people quite unused to psychological ideas to feel safe enough to explore their work together. He never used technical psychoanalytic language and was often able to find a telling and evocative metaphor to illustrate his points. Alexis had a great gift for bringing colleagues together from different disciplines. He had a delightful sense of humour; it had always amused him that when the

---

* This chapter is an edited version of Elder, A. (2009). Building on the work of Alexis Brook: Further thoughts about brief psychotherapy in primary care. *Psychoanalytic Psychotherapy*, 23(4): 307–320. Copyright © The Association for Psychoanalytic Psychotherapy in the NHS, reprinted by permission of Taylor & Francis Ltd, http://www.tandfonline.com on behalf of The Association for Psychoanalytic Psychotherapy in the NHS.

Tavistock was built a basin was provided in every third consulting room. Clearly, the architect had been briefed about the three Tavistock disciplines—psychology, social work, and psychiatry—and doctors, of course, needed to wash their hands!

Alexis as innovator

In 1967 a paper appeared in the *Journal of the Royal College of General Practitioners* modestly entitled, "An Experiment in General Practitioner/Psychiatrist Co-operation" (Brook, 1967). This experiment entailed Alexis spending an afternoon every fortnight at two general practitioners' surgeries offering himself as a consultant to the doctors. During his visits he would see any patients referred to him for one or two assessment interviews and then discuss them with the GPs. Nothing similar had been carried out in the UK before. This was the first report of such an experiment in this country.

Alexis' approach had little to do with increasing the availability of psychological therapies, much more to do with the value of psychoanalytic listening being available to primary care teams and to patients who come in and out of a doctor's surgery. This stands in stark contrast to many of the more recent developments in mental health policy and to the implementation of the government's Improving Access to Psychological Therapies (IAPT) programme, in which there is little recognition of the role GP practices play in maintaining the mental health of individuals and communities; or indeed, even that GPs *are* key mental health professionals at all.

The 1967 report bears all the key elements of Alexis' approach to working with GPs. The paper describes the psychiatrist as being at the service of the GP, not going as a specialist with expertise but as a consultant to the doctor, who in Alexis' own words "should feel absolutely free to accept or reject any of the psychiatrist's formulations as he saw fit" (Brook, 1967). Such an attitude clearly conveys an unusual degree of respect for the professionalism and role of the generalist "whose particular expertise can so easily be overlooked" (E. Balint, Courtenay, Elder, Hull, & Julian, 1993). But most important, the conclusions Alexis reached after this first consultation with a practice in 1967 remain the foundation stones of the argument for (well-trained) psychotherapists working alongside GPs to the present day:

> Many patients said they valued the ease and informality of being seen on the doctor's premises … for some patients it would have been very difficult to overcome their fears if they had to go to a psychiatric clinic … several indicated their appreciation of the psychiatrist and GP talking over how best to help them … it became increasingly clear to the psychiatrist that what were referred to as minor psychological problems in general practice were far from that … and are sometimes major problems for the doctor in terms of how to help the patient … (Brook, 1967, p. 129)

This short passage makes a compelling case for the importance of "psychotherapeutic listening" being available in primary care: accessibility, lack of stigma, the particular value of its collaborative nature, the large number of patients who are not suitable for onward referral or are resistant to it, and of particular relevance at the present time, that GP patients frequently have *complex mental health problems*. In contrast to this, our present hyper-rational approach to mental health envisages an orderly progression of complexity from primary care (simple) through to secondary and tertiary care (more complex). However, in such a "stepped care" model many patients in primary care seem already to be off the scale!

It is also clear from Alexis' report that the experiment was of *mutual* benefit. The psychiatrist, says Alexis, had "now experienced at first hand what he had only understood intellectually before"—something of the frustration and limitations of being in the doctor's surgery (Brook, 1967). This emphasis on mutual change occurring between two professional disciplines was central to Alexis' approach. His strong encouragement to younger colleagues to take up GP work arose partly out of his belief in its value to *them* as well as to the primary care team to which they were attached. During the 1990s the Adult Department reinstated the opportunity for senior trainees (M1) to consult in primary care. The value of such an experience is well described in Jo O'Reilly's report, "The Practice as a Patient: Working as a Psychotherapist in General Practice" (2000).

Early influences

In the 1960s there was a great deal of interest in exploring new ways of using a psychiatrist's expertise (and also that of other professionals, particularly social workers) to support front-line professionals whose work had a bearing on mental health, and to whom people readily turned with their troubles. Much of this work originated from the Cassel Hospital. In 1961 Tom Main, the director of the Cassel, had read a paper to the Royal Society of Health entitled "New Developments in the Psychiatrist's Role" (Main, 1961). Tom Main was a close colleague of Michael and Enid Balint. And for Alexis, it seems to have been the experience of taking a case discussion seminar for GPs at the Cassel that led him to undertake his project. In its third year of work the seminar elected to study 100 so-called "ordinary" GP cases plucked at random from the participating doctors' morning surgeries (Brook, 1966). As a result of listening to these apparently "non-psychiatric" cases, Alexis decided to visit the doctors' surgeries and see the patients for himself. Thus, at first hand, he experienced the sheer scale of chronic unhappiness that afflicts a large proportion of patients seen in a doctor's surgery.

Of course, the presiding figure behind all these experiments in psychiatrist–GP collaboration at that time was Michael Balint who had begun his research-cum-training seminars with GPs in 1949, and had published his groundbreaking account of that work, *The Doctor, His Patient and the Illness*, in 1957. In this he had written, "I have mentioned that in Utopia the specialist will not be a superior mentor, but the general practitioner's expert assistant ... and he (the GP) will have to shoulder the privilege of undivided responsibility for people's health and well-being, and partly also for their future happiness" (M. Balint, 1957). Whereas Michael and Enid Balint were interested primarily in fostering a change in the individual doctors to help them respond more fully to their patients, Alexis' work can be understood as initiating a similar developmental change in relation to the role of the practice itself. "The aim of our project was to study how a worker with psychotherapeutic skills could help general practice to develop its resources as well as exploit its special advantages in the field of mental health" (Brook & Temperley, 1976). There is a similarity in the way the Balints described the role of a psychoanalyst while leading a group of GPs and the approach adopted by Alexis and his colleagues when visiting a practice: not teaching but listening, tuning in to the doctors' concerns, having an exploratory attitude, and only introducing ideas that were consonant with the doctors' own understanding of their role.

Tavistock Community Unit

Following his appointment to the Tavistock Clinic in 1971, Alexis continued to develop his interest in primary care. The Community Unit of the Adult Department at the Tavistock launched a project to study the impact of experienced mental health professionals (well advanced in their training as psychotherapists) visiting a general practice on a regular weekly basis. Four practices volunteered to participate in the scheme initially; others were recruited later. This project laid the foundations for therapists seeing patients in GP practices. It inspired a new generation of psychotherapists to take an interest in this work and had a lasting impact on the participating practices, which continues in some until the present day. The key ingredients of the project were *careful discussion* in setting things up; discussion between the collaborating workers about each patient *before* any management decision is taken; ultimate responsibility remaining with the general practitioner; and a weekly workshop focusing especially on interdisciplinary aspects of the work (held at the Tavistock) to which two members of the practice team were invited.

The Tavistock "clinic workers" were left free to decide how to respond to the various requests for help they received in the practices. Different patterns of collaboration emerged: sometimes the "clinic worker" saw the patient themselves for a period of brief therapy; at other times they conducted an assessment followed by discussion with the referring clinician (patients were seen for between thirty and sixty minutes); or they directed their attention to the practice "team meeting" by offering consultation to the doctors on their difficult cases or on roles and relationships within the team. It was felt to be important for those working in a surgery to be experienced enough *to tolerate what cannot be achieved* for patients and therefore to help the surgery staff tolerate this as well. Several publications appeared describing the different aspects of the project's work (Daws, 1985; Graham & Sher, 1976; Smith, Gross, Graham, & Reilly, 1983). The overall account of this important study was published in 1976 in the *Journal of the Royal College of General Practitioners* as "The Contribution of a Psychotherapist to General Practice" (Brook & Temperley, 1976).

From the 1980s onwards there was a steady increase in the number of counsellors in primary care; by 2007 as many as 88% of GP practices had access to practice-based counselling

(Barnes & Hall, 2008). Much of the thinking that influenced the attitudes and philosophy of the GP practices who were at the forefront of this expansion originated from the Tavistock project (Pietroni & Vespe, 2000; Wiener & Sher, 1998). With increasing experience of the primary care setting (episodic contact in the context of a continuing relationship with the practice) psychotherapists began to explore how their techniques and approach might be modified to take "therapeutic advantage" of the characteristics of the setting. For instance, it may be more useful in primary care for the approach to be one of "in quickly, out quickly" where *intensity of contact* is the key rather than length of time and working through. Such therapy might be better thought of as "*brief-in-long*" given the long-term timescale of general practice. This technique is reminiscent of the approach developed in the earlier Tavistock Brief Therapy Workshop (Malan, 1963; see Malan, Chapter 25). Similarly, an analyst working more recently in primary care writes, "The setting provides the containment necessary for therapy with very disturbed patients partly through availability of medication, ease of referral on to other services, and importantly, through case discussion" (Bravesmith, 2004). One of the practices originally visited by Brook and his team has just published a report describing the value of a "reflecting team in primary care". The authors are a group of systemic practitioners who have worked together (with some changes of personnel and one constant) in a GP surgery for over thirty years (Kraemer et al., 2018). In 2000, the Association for Psychoanalytic Psychotherapy in the NHS (APP) established a primary care section which continues to provide a network for psychotherapists working in primary care and holds regular seminars to focus on the unique characteristics of this work. The thinking initiated in the Tavistock Unit continues to be developed (J. D. Smith, 2013, 2019; Wilmott, 2019).

Essence of the Tavistock approach

In their description of the project, Brook and Temperley state clearly, "Our aim was to reduce the amount of splitting and dissociation that so often occurs in patient care when different professionals may be played off against one another. This splitting can be a reproduction of the patient's need to keep various aspects of themselves in separate compartments; it can also result from the staff's reluctance to bear looking at the patient's situation *in toto*" (Brook & Temperley, 1976). Alexis always emphasised how easily the tensions within the doctor–patient relationship can lead to premature referral and result in frustration for both patient and doctor. The range of problems and the pressures of clinical work in general practice cannot be overestimated. Jan Wiener, an experienced psychoanalyst who worked in primary care for many years, likened the GP surgery to a *souk*, a chaotic Arab bazaar, where everything is potentially available "… like a practice, where GPs have to maintain a gate-keeping function with often limited resources. GPs have to cope with whoever walks through the door and must decide what is treatable and what must be borne or managed" (Wiener & Sher, 1998). In such work, the complex tensions that surround decisions about "referral" or the need for "treatment" are critical. Such decisions can arise from a number of sources—only one of which is the patient's clinical need. Decisions to refer may also arise from pressures within the doctor–patient relationship as well as other sources. Alexis made this point with characteristic clarity in a letter to the *BMJ* entitled "Be honest about referrals". He gives four reasons for referral to a psychiatrist (or any other professional for that matter): to provide or arrange specialist treatment; to assess and clarify a situation and provide expert advice so that the GP can then continue treating the patient; the GP wanting to share the burden and responsibility of looking after a patient for whom little can be done but who insists on more and more investigations; and lastly, when the GP wants to be relieved of the patient for a while. He states that the "latter two are primarily in the interests of the doctor" (Brook, 1994). The essence of the Tavistock approach is to look as far as possible at the whole picture: the needs and presentation of the patient, the pressures on the doctor, and any tensions that there might be in the doctor–patient relationship. Without such an understanding, fragmentation soon follows, and cycles of unfounded hope, frequent frustration, and disappointment ensue. The extent of this phenomenon is not easily recognised, particularly where the research instruments employed to study outcomes are themselves too narrowly focused to reveal the individual narrative and contextual links behind the "treatments" studied.

In the present environment of financial restrictions and competitive commissioning, the Tavistock manages to maintain two schemes through which teams of mental health professionals support GP practices; one in Camden TAP (Team Around the Practice) and the other in Hackney through the City and Hackney Primary Care Psychotherapy Consultation Service. Both services continue to offer experienced psychotherapeutic listening and consultation to GP practices and exhibit the Tavistock's continuing commitment to the value of psychoanalytic thinking in primary care (Carrington, Rock, & Stern, 2012; Hard, Rock, & Stern, 2015; Rock & Carrington, 2011, 2012; Stern, Hard, & Rock, 2015). Both owe their origin and inspiration to the work of Alexis Brook.

Where are we now?

Today, primary care mental health services operate in a very different environment from the era in which the Tavistock Community Unit was founded. Therapists now often work in multiple surgeries which makes it more difficult to become a known and trusted member of the practice team; communication is often by computer rather than in person; GPs no longer have freedom of referral and have to make referrals to a "mental health team" which decides on an appropriate "treatment" for the patient—sometimes referring the patient on to a counsellor or psychological therapist working in a different practice. In such a system, little value is placed on the GP's experience and knowledge of the patient. Equally important, however, is the slow loss of understanding of the wider role of a therapist as an integral member of a practice team: availability for discussion, participation in team meetings, known personally as a member of the team, undertaking a collaborative role in relation to the mental health work of all members of the primary care team. Where such collaboration flourishes, the doctors and nurses grow in the use of their own psychological skills, and therapists take on a deeper understanding of the therapeutic opportunities gained by working in a medical setting and learn to adjust their technique accordingly.

At the same time as mental health services have become more bureaucratic and less flexible, GPs are increasingly being driven by a strongly disease-centred and measurable performance-related contract. Such a framework leaves little incentive for integrated thinking or genuine whole-patient care.

Thus the current contractual underpinning of GPs and psychotherapists in primary care, sadly, is tending to a further aggravation of the separation between body and mind; a split which is so often central to illness, and for which thoughtful collaborative work in GP practices can sometimes bring about healing. The essence of work in primary care lies in a flexible and creative response to the setting, which needs to be regarded as an opportunity rather than a restraint.

At Paddington Green, we were among the first practices to invite a counsellor to work with us. Between 1978 and 2018 (when funding was eventually withdrawn) a counsellor or psychotherapist was an integral member of our primary health care team, offering individual sessions, joint consultation, discussion of patients, and attending our weekly multidisciplinary meeting. We never set an arbitrary limit to the number of sessions and never had a waiting list (96% of referrals seen within three weeks), although the average number of sessions for which patients were seen was eight. A few patients were seen for a year or more and many for only three or four sessions. A valuable partnership grew up over time between GPs who had become more psychologically minded and therapists who became more primary care-minded (Elder, 2005, 2009b; Sharifi & Jayyusi, 2004). It is a sad loss to the human fabric of the National Health Service (and the development of thinking about primary care) that nearly all such provision has now gone.

The practice as a secure base

Michael Balint used the metaphor of a "*mutual investment company*" for the process by which trust is built between patient and doctor which can then be "drawn down" or used when needed. Alexis Brook's work enabled GP practices to think about their role as a mental health provider. A GP practice has been aptly described by John Launer as "a community of listeners" (Elder & Holmes, 2002). All members of a primary care team benefit from developing their understanding of the special nature of a GP practice as a setting for psychotherapeutic work. Michael and Enid Balint (1961) wrote that "The importance of the setting in which the doctor works is such that it largely determines the techniques used and the results obtained." Medicine has been slow to incorporate the implications and research possibilities of attachment theory and it is not difficult to see how such research might be used to underpin and extend the understanding of how trust (and mistrust) develops between patients and their doctors. GP practices can become familiar and trusted places. Attachments grow in the course of medical care. The doctors, nurses, and counsellors who work in GP practices often contain knowledge of the significant events and patterns of illness that have shaped the lives of their patients. In a sense this knowledge comes to reside in the practice itself, which then begins to take on some of the characteristics of a secure base to its patients. This notion of the practice as "a secure base—a place to which both patients and professionals become attached in characteristic ways" (Elder & Holmes, 2002, p. 2)—is noticeably missing in present-day thinking about mental health. Such a concept would help in understanding the role that practices play in maintaining the health and well-being of their patients and in understanding the need for professionals to be listened to themselves. "A sensitive recognition by the practice of a particular patient's pattern of insecurity, for instance, may well lead to a more secure attachment relationship to that doctor and the practice ..." (Elder, 2009a, p. 58).

Conclusion

Whatever advances there are in specialist services, much will always depend on the sensitivity and skill exhibited in the many thousands of daily contacts that patients make with their local doctors and nurses. The report *Psychological Therapies in Psychiatry and Primary Care* makes the point clearly: a "significant and lasting improvement in mental health in the population will depend on ... enhancing the psychological awareness and therapeutic skills of the existing healthcare workforce, in addition to providing dedicated psychological therapy services" (Royal College of Psychiatrists, 2008). Further, the quality and effectiveness of all clinical work in a practice is enhanced by teamwork and a culture of communication between professionals working together. Contact with patients in primary care frequently involves high levels of distress and disturbance. Often an experienced mental health professional is needed to facilitate the necessary teamwork and discussion from which support and professional development may follow. Alexis Brook always stressed that therapeutic help is not so much about treatment but about listening; listening to people (professionals as well as patients) and learning to notice how people use the setting of primary care. Listening is part and parcel of good medical care wherever medicine is practised. The recognition and lasting value of such an approach owes a lot to the pioneering work of Alexis Brook.

Note

1. Formally, chairman of the Tavistock Clinic Professional Committee.

* * *

Dr Andrew Elder FRCGP DEd (Hon)

Andrew Elder was a GP for thirty-six years in inner London and retired from his practice at Paddington Green in April 2008. In addition to full-time clinical work as a GP, he was involved in postgraduate and undergraduate teaching throughout his career. He joined his first Balint group in 1972 at the Tavistock Clinic in London. He worked with Enid Balint from 1977 until her death in 1994 and contributed to two books which arose out of research groups with Enid Balint—*While I'm Here, Doctor: Study of Doctor–Patient Relationships* (Elder & Samuel, 1987) and *The Doctor, the Patient and the Group* (Balint, Courtenay, Elder, Hull, & Julian, 1993). He has had a long-standing interest in all aspects of psychotherapy in primary care. He co-edited *Mental Health in Primary Care* with Jeremy Holmes (Elder & Holmes, 2002). He was a consultant in the Adult Department at the Tavistock Centre (1995–2000) and president of the UK Balint Society.

Dr Elder was the first co-chair of the primary care section of the Association for Psychoanalytic Psychotherapy in the NHS (APP) and a founding member of the committee for the Association for Infant Mental Health (AIMH). Until recently he was coordinator and chair of the International Balint Federation (IBF) leadership task force (2009–2016).

After retirement he led groups for medical students at University College Hospital (UCH), GP registrars at the Royal Free Hospital, and currently leads a Balint group for the multidisciplinary team at the Practitioner Health Programme (PHP), a service for doctors with mental illness and problems with addiction. He consults to the mental health team at TAP (Team Around the Practice) a Tavistock service for Camden practices. In 2017 he was awarded an honorary doctorate from the Tavistock/University of East London in recognition of his work in mental health and primary care.

This chapter is based on a talk given at the Alexis Brook Memorial Conference held at the Tavistock Centre in October 2008. A full version of the talk was published as: Elder, A. (2009b), Building on the Work of Alexis Brook: Further Thoughts about Brief Psychotherapy in Primary Care. *Psychoanalytic Psychotherapy*, 23(4)—a special issue: *Psychotherapy, Medicine and the Body: A Tribute to the work of Alexis Brook*.

CHAPTER TEN

Extending the reach of the "talking cure"

Margaret Rustin

This is the story, as known to me, of what happened over the second half of the twentieth century to the Tavistock's post-war ambition to reshape community mental health. I arrived at the Tavistock in 1967 to begin the child psychotherapy training and, after qualification, went on to become a staff member and later head of discipline, and also to take on central roles as dean and subsequently chair of the Professional Committee. I was amazed to find myself first watching and then joining this small group of clinicians who shared such large and ambitious ideas about influencing the shape of the new NHS's approach to mental health. How were these ideas about the health of the mind and the nature of what nourished human potential to travel?

One significant moment was the success of the plan to have a new building providing space to expand both treatment and training activity. The opening of the purpose-built Belsize Lane building was evidence that there was government interest in very different ways of thinking about forms of intervention for the mentally ill population and specifically in the idea that this had to be addressed across the whole life cycle. No wards and no beds, but spaces for outpatients of all ages to receive attention from multidisciplinary teams, whose expertise would be in understanding the experience of their patients' states of mind and whose approach would be first to listen and only then to talk.

The tight space available in the old building in Beaumont Street had been an obvious constraint on growth and visibility. The new building, renamed the Tavistock Centre to signal important changes in its scope, had lecture rooms, a proper library space, and facilities like one-way screen rooms available for teaching; and it housed, in addition to the Clinical Departments and the Tavistock Institute of Human Relations (the two interconnected arms of the Tavistock conception), the Child Guidance Training Centre (CGTC; see Hopkins, Chapter 14) and the Family Discussion Bureau. This last was the predecessor of what is now Tavistock Relationships (see A. Balfour, Chapter 22; Morgan, Chapter 23), and was then the seedbed for innovative thinking about couple relationships.

In 1967, when the new building opened its doors, the trainings within the Tavistock Clinic were quite limited. They included those for specialist medical senior registrars, working towards consultant roles as either consultant psychiatrists in adult mental health departments, or in child and adolescent psychiatry; a small cohort of a postgraduate training for social workers; trainees in educational psychology (often former teachers); and child psychotherapy trainees embarking on a four-year postgraduate training. This latter was the course initiated in 1948–1949 by Esther Bick, invited by John Bowlby to set up a training for non-medically quali- fied people with a background in work with children and adolescents, who could become the core of a new NHS profession of child psychotherapy. There were also some junior staff posts in the different disciplines represented in the clinic's establishment which gave opportunities for post-qualification experience and further psychotherapy training to small numbers of psy- chologists, social workers, and psychiatrists.

The trainees on all courses shared common lectures on human growth and development and on psychoanalytic theory, to which all the senior figures of the Clinic, TIHR, and the Family Discussion Bureau contributed. These included John Bowlby, Pierre Turquet, Martha Harris, Bob Gosling, Irene Caspari, Douglas Woodhouse, and Sandy Bourne. There were also other shared events, including "study groups", that is, groups whose aim was to study the processes unfolding in the group as a way of learning about group life, and in particular the anxieties and defences stirred by being in a group situation (see Armstrong & Rustin, Chapter 3). Another shared event was the opportunity to watch, through a one-way screen, group therapy in the Adult Department, and then to discuss what had been taking place with the group's consultant. Infant observation, which was a central part of the child psychotherapy training, was another training experience sought by many from among the other disciplines. There was a student common room on the ground floor, and a bar on the top floor, as well as the canteen. So there was quite generous space for social life among the trainees and staff. Many of the students came from outside the UK and the international atmosphere was unmistakable and enlivening. The mix across disciplines, departments, and cultures was the essence of the place.

During the 1970s there was substantial growth in training activity particularly by the child psychotherapists, led by Martha Harris, an inspirational head of discipline. She was a deter- mined person who aimed to make learning from experience available to hitherto untapped professional groups. She instituted an annual instead of biennial intake of child psychotherapy trainees, and her development of "work discussion" (Rustin & Bradley, 2008) opened opportu- nities for thinking psychoanalytically to a much widened range of interested professionals. One outcome of this was a new course for teachers from nursery staff through to tertiary education, a year-long one-evening-a-week course combining lectures and work discussion groups, which gave attention to the emotional experience of teachers as well as the understanding of their pupils (Wittenberg, Williams, & Osborne, 1993). This was a hugely successful and exciting initiative. Alongside this was an expanding group of applicants for a pre-clinical course based on infant and young child observation, work discussion, and theoretical teaching which came to be known as the Observation Course. For some, this was a precursor to clinical training, usually in child and adolescent psychotherapy, but it also served a much broader purpose in providing an introduction to psychoanalytic thinking for social workers, child care and nursery workers, teachers from primary to university level, and others from diverse backgrounds including law and journalism. This course represented a desire to build a wider community with an informed interest in psychoanalytical ideas, and their relevance to all interested in children's development. The new generation of child psychotherapists was quickly involved in this expanding teaching activity. This programme is one whose example and influence has spread widely in Britain and across the world.

By the end of the 1970s the extent of Tavistock training activities had grown considerably. When the challenges to continued NHS funding and to the relative independence of the Clinic became more acute, it was thus more than possible to respond to the demands of the various reports on our future which were being commissioned, with a robust assertion that we could function as a national resource for the training of health and other professionals relevant to improvements in the nation's mental health. The early years of systemic family therapy had by this time added an important dimension to the range of psychotherapeutic approaches within the Clinic (Papadopoulos & Byng-Hall, 1997). This non-psychoanalytic paradigm had unsurprisingly been a source of much debate and disagreement as it challenged the centrality of the Tavistock's post-war identity as a fundamentally psychoanalytic set-up, but its vitality and fresh insights attracted powerful voices, and its link to the wider Tavistock aim of understanding social systems and organisations was obvious.

We were thus able at this point to offer training for people tackling mental health problems across the lifespan in the following modalities:

- Group and individual psychotherapy with adults, both brief and long-term
- Psychotherapy for children, adolescents, and their families
- Family therapy, both systemic and psychodynamic
- Brief counselling approaches to adolescents, and to parents and babies and pre-school children
- Work with couples
- Consultancy to a wide range of organisations in the health and social sector
- Group relations training in understanding institutional life.

The Clinic's conception of itself was based on the integration of clinical work, teaching, and research, with the assumption that senior staff needed to be involved in all three of these. To be expert as trainers, staff needed to continue to work as clinicians and engage in new clinical and research projects. Protecting this balance was a fundamental responsibility of those running the Tavistock.

In earlier years, there had been organisational separation between the management of NHS-funded clinical work and the teaching and research work, which were housed in TIHR. This came to an end amid mixed views about what would best protect the broad aims of Tavistock training and research, when Clinic staff voted for further integration, and the Tavistock Clinic thereafter took on the administration of the full range of training activities. This was more welcome to some than to others, the Adult Department (see Garland, Chapter 29; Lousada, Chapter 28; Steiner, Chapter 27) still being predominantly interested in clinical work, treasuring its links with the British Psychoanalytical Society and having a top-down model of influence in the NHS. They believed that psychoanalytically trained consultants would spread good practice in NHS psychotherapy departments, as they indeed did, and this together with research, for example David Malan's (see Chapter 25) on brief therapy, had remained their main commitment.

There had been recurrent unsuccessful efforts to make links with London University in the 1950s and 1960s, including by John Bowlby, which, despite the Tavistock's highly respected research activity, were not responded to warmly (echoing similarly frustrated efforts by J. R. Rees in the 1930s; see Kraemer, Afterword). The attacks on psychoanalysis by such influential figures as Karl Popper and Hans Eysenck, and a narrow conception of what constituted scientific work, had influenced the universities in their rejection of the Tavistock, but this situation began to change with the establishment of new universities with their widening interest in interdisciplinary work, and their broadening of subjects deemed suitable for academic study (see Rustin & Armstrong, Chapter 4). The NHS review of the Tavistock's activity in the 1980s insisted, as one of its demands, that university links be established, so that the major professional courses, previously only recognised by relevant professional bodies, namely the medical Royal Colleges, the British Psychological Society, and the Association of Child Psychotherapists, should now also obtain academic recognition. The first courses to pilot this possibility were the post-qualifying social work course, which built a partnership with the University of East London (UEL, formerly a polytechnic) and the Family Therapy and Educational Psychology courses, with Brunel University (formerly a college of advanced technology). These pioneering efforts were helped along by the unusually talented people attracted to train at that time, as well as the self-confidence and determination of the course tutors and their colleagues in the two universities.

What could now be seen to work well, and to lead to the award of master's qualifications and PhDs, and to enhance the professional standing of the graduates, opened the minds of other Tavistock staff groups to the potential of such partnerships. This was a period of large university expansion, creating a pool of well-educated young people who might be attracted to postgraduate education in the mental health field. It also coincided with the professional upgrading of social work, a path to be followed later by nursing, and the idea that nursing too should become a graduate profession. In the 1990s a large raft of trainings were validated by UEL, our most receptive and supportive partner during this period of creative expansion, leading to a moment at which more than 1,000 students were registered for higher degrees.

Within the Tavistock, in recognition of the new centrality of our educational project, the oversight of training and its development became more distinct. The post of dean of postgraduate training to lead the process was introduced, and soon vice-deans in each clinical department were added. All these posts, like the chair of the Professional Committee, were elected by the senior staff, a practice only ended in response to disquiet from the Trust board some years after the Tavistock and Portman clinics had come together to form an NHS Trust. The requirement to be elected by peers meant that the office holders, who were all themselves clinicians/trainers, were entrusted by their colleagues with the responsibility to sustain this tradition of clinician-led teaching. The new training committee turned out to be a lively and enjoyable one, with each discipline having representation and the multidisciplinary nature of our work therefore strongly in view, as well as the recognition that it was fundamentally the distinctive disciplines, including the new one of systemic therapy, which were the engines of training growth.

One of the major aims in this period was to increase the geographical spread of Tavistock courses in a number of ways, the most effective of which were partnerships with senior local professionals. These were people who had been trained at the Tavistock and were now keen to use courses they were familiar with which they could deliver locally. The child psychotherapists and family therapists were particularly energetic in this regional activity, and the adult psychotherapists followed suit. We created a lovely map of the UK showing the range of links made, which included almost all the health regions. Senior staff did a lot of regular travelling to support the initial years of such courses, and the courses themselves then developed in individually distinct ways. Sometimes a local university was interested to validate a course, rather than making use of the indirect connection to UEL through the Tavistock. New course ideas could also emerge from among our partners, for example the course on Infant Mental Health (see Daws, Chapter 12) which was initially planned from Bristol.

By 1997 when we conducted a strategic review of our trainings, we were running three full-time four-year trainings, fourteen of a two-year duration, and nine lasting one year. We had a model of transition from a postgraduate certificate or diploma, to an MA or MSc, and we had three professional doctorates, with others in the pipeline. This internal review took place in the context of our awareness of another major and challenging external review of NHS psychotherapy services. When this external review appeared, it was quite supportive of our contribution while noting the "anomalous position" of the Tavistock as a national provider with a national training contract, while the NHS direction of travel was for locally commissioned education and training. However, our work in the regions was acknowledged and applauded and we were encouraged to develop greater access to supervision, CPD courses, research into the effectiveness of our training, and training for managers in the increasingly complex NHS systems. The overall theme was that we must be responsive to what was needed across the country.

One area in which we had been working was to find ways of providing post-qualification training for nurses (see Griffiths, Chapter 33) and GPs (see Elder, Chapter 9), disciplines not previously represented in the Tavistock workforce. New senior posts for GPs and nurses had to be created to make effective the NHS's greater emphasis on community mental health outside hospital systems. Another growth point was the expansion in our training of psychologists, the discipline (see Lyon & Dowling, Chapter 31) now growing most strongly within the NHS, by offering a qualifying training in clinical psychology in addition to the well-established post-qualifying courses and conference programme. All these efforts were intended to make real our breadth of commitment to the wider workforce and demonstrate our awareness that psycho-therapeutically informed mental health services had to embrace all the relevant professions. This was also how we could achieve our own long-term aim to influence the zeitgeist of NHS thinking about mental health and illness across the lifespan.

Over the years many specialist interests pursued by staff gave rise to short or longer courses, and our expanding conference programme also grew from the fertility of staff activity. The relevance of our theories and practices for patients with a learning disability, for the physically disabled, for those with eating disorders, for women with perinatal problems and problems of infertility, for adolescents, for older patients, for adopted and fostered children, and for those in state care were all instances of service developments which led to course development. The integration of our clinical work, new thinking, and training was the guiding principle.

The success of our training expansion was therefore considerable. There was an atmo-sphere of looking for opportunities and responsiveness when they emerged. The national dimension I have outlined was echoed in a modest way by international activity, inspired by the original effort of Gianna Williams (Chapter 18) in taking child psychotherapy to Italy, and promoted by numbers of ex-Tavistock students and staff starting projects in many differ-ent parts of the world, for example the USA, India, Australia, South Africa, Taiwan, France, Germany, Brazil, and Argentina. Staff members were invigorated by invitations to teach in all the continents, and conferences were enlivened by substantial and vigorous international par-ticipation. The intellectual work taking place within the Clinic at this time was wide-ranging, and included the launch of the Tavistock Clinic Series of books (see Waddell, Chapter 43), and at one stage no fewer than four different peer-reviewed professional journals being edited by Tavistock staff.

However, the imbalance of income from training, which for a period comprised about 70% of our total earnings, was of increasing concern. Clinical activity was shrinking and research and consultancy were also making only a small contribution. The model of the interdepen-dence of all these endeavours was at the heart of the Tavistock's identity, and keeping them all in good order was clearly important. As we entered the new millennium, these other areas of work became an important focus, most notably in respect of research. A number of profes-sorships and other posts held jointly at the Tavistock and one of our now increased range of university partners was an important marker of this. This academic acknowledgement of the value of the Tavistock's traditions of training and research (see Rustin & Armstrong, Chapter 4) was significant in making possible the major research projects which were so important in the early years of the new century.

By the year 2000, the range of training courses in place and the high quality of what they offered was indeed a major contribution to achieving the aim of the Clinic's founders to influence the mental health of future generations for the better.

* * *

Margaret Rustin

I came to the Tavistock (the new building) in 1967, to start the child psychotherapy training, having been interviewed by Martha Harris and John Bowlby a couple of years earlier at Beaumont Street, and was encouraged to start analysis and get more experience with children and young people. This latter aim led to a combination of teaching a small group of difficult to integrate children in an infant school in Paddington, babysitting a family of three, and lecturing on philosophy at North London Polytechnic.

Bowlby was chair of the Department of Children and Parents, and Mattie, as everyone called her, was head of child psychotherapy. I loved the training, and knew I had now found what I wanted to spend my life doing. I qualified in 1971, then had two children while working part-time as a Tavistock staff member and starting to supervise and teach infant observation.

I was given opportunities to develop clinically, to join various training activities, and to do consultations to a school and later a children's home. I became chair of the Psychotherapy Programme, which meant arranging weekly staff meetings to deal with referrals and for clinical discussion. Starting a brief consultation service for parents and under-fives (see Miller, Chapter 13) was one of the highlights of this period.

I had a year away in the USA in 1984 and when I returned was asked to apply for the post of head of child psychotherapy. That is the job I held from 1986–2009. This was a time of expanding training, both at the Tavi and nationally. I became dean of postgraduate education in 1993 and later chair of the Professional Committee. I retired in 2009, though remaining as a supervisor and as a trustee of the Tavistock Clinic Foundation.

I have taught in all the continents, as the Tavi has been a very international place. Since the 1980s I have written and edited many books intended to make Tavistock thinking widely available. The first of these, *Closely Observed Infants*, is still in print after more than 30 years!

Part II

Pregnancy and under-fives

The psychopathology of publications concerning reactions to stillbirths and neonatal deaths

Sandy Bourne

During my psychoanalytic training whilst a senior registrar at the Tavistock Clinic I encountered a patient who had had a stillbirth a few years previously and remained isolated, secretly depressed, preoccupied with it, instead of "pulling herself together and trying to forget about it", as most people supposedly did. I'd previously had a similar case when I was a registrar at the Maudsley Hospital.

Searching to get some therapy started with this case, I looked it up and was astonished to find absolutely nothing about the psychological sequelae of stillbirth in the medical or psychoanalytic literature; nor anywhere else. I slowly realised that this was perhaps the most interesting thing I had stumbled into, rather than just being an exasperating block in my own work. There was a considerable and respectable psychiatric literature on bereavement and mourning in general but nothing on mourning a stillbirth—almost as if there was nothing for the mother of a stillborn baby to mourn about and nothing special for doctors to think about—or to feel blocked about. This astonished me at the time. It was obviously an awkward subject, but doctors are not generally paralysed by awkward subjects nor struck dumb so easily. The silence was in itself striking, significant, and relevant.

Stillbirths were notifiable for the official register of births and deaths in each district, like live births and all deaths, and some notifiable diseases. I had thought (naïvely) that I could put this register to good use to discover other cases, and find out more about what reactions happened generally following a stillbirth. Eventually I did get very reluctant permission to explore notified cases by sending a questionnaire to 100 GPs in the county of Middlesex who had notified a stillbirth in the previous year; and to send a parallel questionnaire to another 100 GPs who had notified a live birth in the same period. This permission was given, after some anxious resistance, on condition that I undertook not to contact any of these women myself.

I later learned that the mothers of stillbirths in general were distressed and angry that their doctors seemed to avoid them, to be afraid to get involved; and friends seemed to cross the road if they were seen coming. Nobody seemed to want to know about them. About 90% of the 100 GPs in the live-birth series responded at varying length to the questions about how their patients had responded to the various pleasures, pains, and alarms of normal pregnancies and childbirth. It was gratifying that some GPs were explicitly glad that here was someone interested in their work and opinions as GPs; and several mentioned spontaneously that they were pleased to be asked.

In contrast, in the stillbirth series few doctors replied at all. Of those who did reply, the majority returned totally blank forms. Those who gave information showed a marked tendency not to know, not to notice, and not to remember anything at nearly every point. Answers tended to be confined to yes/no wherever possible; further spontaneous thought and comment were impoverished in contrast to the live-birth doctors, even regarding non-psychological aspects of their cases. The stillbirth doctors seemed driven to not-knowing, not-noticing, and not-remembering anything.

Publication

I sent a report of this work and these strikingly impoverished findings to *The Lancet* which rejected it immediately, explaining that my findings were nothing new (which was quite untrue), and then to the *British Medical Journal* which apparently forgot it for about a year, until I chased it up. The *BMJ* had turned it down but then mislaid it, forgetting to tell me. I woke up eventually, and then sent the paper to the *Journal of the Royal College of GPs* which more creditably did publish it almost immediately, in 1968 (Bourne, 1968). It turned out that this paper was actually a "world first" on this topic in the medical literature, so far as I ever managed to find out when searching later—which was very odd in itself. I should also emphasise, in contrast, I have also found that the *BMJ* does not generally ignore awkward subjects.

Reactions to this paper and developments following Dr Emanuel Lewis' advent

The reaction was silence in print and there was no easy solution, as the Tavistock Clinic had no obstetric department. This changed when Dr Mannie Lewis, who had formerly trained in the Department for Children and Parents at the Tavistock Clinic, became a consultant psychotherapist at the Charing Cross Hospital. There he could devote time to work in the obstetric department.

In particular, he was able to teach and encourage the midwives in a new policy to help the mothers of dead babies to hold them, and to feel free to examine them and cherish them as long as they needed. Previously, the midwives had been taught to whisk stillbirths away to unknown graves. He discussed his cases with us in our marital psychotherapy seminars.

There were parallel developments around the world in the medical and other literature from around 1960 onwards as interest in stillbirth increased. There was a massive change in Britain following an item in *The Guardian* in 1976 by journalist Bel Mooney, shattered by the experience of giving birth to a dead baby herself.

* * *

Sandy Bourne studied medicine at UCH and psychiatry at the Maudsley Hospital before coming to the Tavistock Clinic as a senior registrar and then as a consultant. He was a lively member of the Adult Department coming under the influence of Pierre Turquet and Bob Gosling. He was especially prominent in the organisation of therapy groups with patients and of Balint groups with GPs. For some time he chaired the GP and Allied Professions Workshop where a wide range of groups was discussed. He extended these to involve other professions including teachers and his seminar with physiotherapists formed the basis of his book, *Under the Doctor* (Bourne, 1981). He also organised seminars with solicitors and probation officers. It must be remembered that during his time group therapy was a major treatment service provided by the Adult Department when nearly everyone on the staff ran at least one and often two therapy groups, and for a long time these were coordinated by Sandy.

Another major contribution was the study he initiated into the effect of stillbirth on the family (Bourne, 1968). Together with Mannie Lewis (Bourne & Lewis, 1984) he went on to study the way stillbirths were dealt with in obstetric units and discovered a shocking neglect of this important source of distress to bereaved families. They wrote and spoke widely about their work, which changed the culture of many obstetric units and led them to take stillbirth seriously. In the course of this work they made many related observations, for example, that it was particularly difficult for a mother to mourn the death of a parent if she was herself pregnant or nursing a newborn at the time. It seemed that the pleasure in the new baby made mourning difficult and the loss of a parent made pleasure in the newborn difficult.

Sandy also took an active part in the ordinary running of the Adult Department. For a time he ran one of the clinical intake units and he also organised several of the teaching courses.

Biographical note by John Steiner

CHAPTER TWELVE

Parent–infant psychotherapy at a baby clinic and at the Tavistock Clinic

Dilys Daws

In 1975 I started to work, half a day weekly, as a child psychotherapist at the baby clinic of the James Wigg General Practice in Kentish Town, which I continue to do. I see families with babies where there are serious disturbances of feeding and sleeping, excessive crying, or difficulty in bonding between mother and baby, and post-natal depression in mothers. Many of these can be helped by routine primary care work from doctors and health visitors, but when these problems persist they may be referred to me, to see what the emotional and relationship issues may be.

When I had my own second baby there were feeding problems, and difficulties in my marriage. I had already trained as a child psychotherapist, and I went back to my psychoanalyst to talk about my anxieties. She was very helpful, and I wondered, "Who would I have gone to if I had not been in the therapeutic world?" I thought that there should be someone easily available in primary care, and I should start to be that person. After a few years working at the Child Guidance Training Centre (see Hopkins, Chapter 14) I talked to John Bolland, its medical director, who was very interested in the idea, and then to Alexis Brook at the Tavistock Clinic, later the chair, who introduced me to the James Wigg practice where he was a pioneering visiting psychiatrist (see Elder, Chapter 9). He trained others, including myself, to help GPs "increase their skills in identifying and tackling the psychological problems they meet in daily life" (Brook, 1978). As described elsewhere in this book (Elder, Chapter 8) Michael Balint—also at the Tavistock—is widely known for his groundbreaking work in thinking with GPs about the psychotherapeutic value of their communications with patients, and later the GPs Andrew Elder, John Launer, and Sue Blake continued this work.

At the time I started at the baby clinic, counsellors were working with adult patients in GP practices, but no one was working with children or infants, though John Bowlby had done so briefly (Bowlby, 1954). My first paper on the subject was called "Standing by the Weighing Scales" (Daws, 1985). It was about being visible and available to colleagues in the baby clinic (while trying not to get in their way!). I was gratified when this phrase caught on with colleagues to jokingly describe their own ventures into outreach work. I later discovered that the psychoanalyst Hyla Holden who had also worked at the Tavistock had published a paper on his work in general practice with the similar title "Propping up the Filing Cabinet"! My paper outlined the usefulness of consulting to doctors and health visitors in the baby clinic, but also, even though the practice I visit is friendly and welcoming, the vulnerability of working in an institution not one's own. I gave a paper at a Tavistock Clinic Scientific Meeting and Sebastian Kraemer asked what qualities were needed to do this work. I replied, "A very thick skin!" Of course a deep respect for these colleagues' work is also essential.

The consultations with GPs and health visitors help them to identify the problems in families with infants. It also helps them to manage their own stress in dealing with distressed patients. When they are confronting the symptoms described by parents in their babies it helps them not to rush to offer advice, and to reflect on the context of the problem. Instead of "Have you tried such and such?" they might say "Tell me more about it." I am encouraging them to be braver in letting patients talk about difficult matters even in the limited time surgeries allow.

To help with this I sometimes see cases jointly with a referring professional. I saw a depressed mother and her two hyperactive toddlers together with their health visitor. The mother cried while she told a story of many losses, and the HV put her arm round her. Afterwards the health visitor and I discussed the meeting. She was impressed with how much the mother had confided in us, but then confessed, "At first I couldn't stand the silences." I thought, "What silences?" Compared with a psychoanalytic session it had been all talk! I believe that professionals of all kinds can extend the scope of their work and be braver. The idea of how much to talk with patients is therefore important. Some of us psychotherapists have learned to talk more, but other workers need to do so less. The idea of free association, of allowing patients the space to follow the line of their own unconscious is difficult. For example, post-natally depressed mothers may, given the chance, relate shocking thoughts of anxiety, anger, self-hatred, hatred of the baby or partner, disturbing dreams, and damage that has or might happen. The urge to cheer people up, to keep things under control rather than hear the content of depressing or upsetting thoughts can be overwhelming. There is evidence that a series of meetings with a health visitor can greatly help these mothers. What does hearing this kind of material do to the worker? Anyone who takes on this work needs supervision and support, and work discussion groups (see, for example, Hale, Chapter 35) are an important way of providing this.

Sleep problems

At the baby clinic, I found that many of the referrals were for sleep problems and that many of these could be "cured" in the first one or two sessions, though the work might need to be consolidated over a few more weeks. This led me to look at the process within the family, and to write about it (Daws, 1989). Although this work is psychoanalytically inspired it is actually very simple and many other disciplines have found that they are able to follow it: the key to it is attuning to the emotions of families so that active offering of solutions is replaced by reflective listening. Parents are relieved at feeling understood and may find their own solutions.

Exploring the reasons for a baby's sleep disturbance often leads to a human drama in the family, sometimes going back to the parents' own experience in their childhood. Repeatedly this involves separations (Daws, 1989, p. 56). With sleep problems, as with any other presenting symptom, I take the nature of the problem seriously. The effects of sleepless nights are likely to leave the family exhausted, distressed, and angry. I start by letting parents talk to me in their own way, so that I get the flavour of what they consider to be the problem and its origin. I also experience their emotion in all its intensity, anger, anxiety, or responsible concern, and think of it as similar to the emotion the baby is finding directed towards him during his sleepless nights. I explain that I would like to ask about the baby and family in general, so we can discover what links there may be. Once I am asking questions in tune with the family's atmosphere I am perhaps felt to be looking after them, and the emotional intensity often subsides.

Asking for details of the baby's timetable, a vivid picture builds up in my mind of what happens in this family, and what they feel should happen. I am interested in the minutiae of detail of their lives—fascinated by the practicalities and symbolic importance of breasts, bottles, spoons, cots, and beds. It begins to clarify a confused situation, as the parents both inform me and think about the logical connections of what they are telling me.

"As dramatic and moving as any work of literature"

Second, I make a free-ranging enquiry into memories of the pregnancy, birth, and early weeks. I say I need to know the baby's life story to make sense of what is happening now. Finally I ask about how the parents met, their relationship—both with each other and with their families of origin—to see the bigger picture of which this baby is a part.

The parents I see have usually been offered much advice already, and often tell me they have "tried everything". However, because I do not at once offer solutions, they are less likely to react negatively. They are able to free associate, unconscious threads draw together, and connections emerge as their minds move freely from one related theme to another. It seems as though all ordinary parents have a story to tell about their baby, as dramatic and moving as any work of literature. The unfolding of this story is a major part of the work, and this first session is the key to it. Jumbled incoherent thoughts come together as I listen to this story. One of the functions of dreaming is said to assimilate the events of the day into settled long-term memory. The parents of sleepless babies have lost much of their time for dreaming. These consultations may allow parents to assimilate their jumbled thoughts and make sense of them.

As the family's story unfolds themes emerge about the nature of their relationships. The meaning of not sleeping may change with the age of the child, but underlying it always seems to be some aspect of separation and individuation between mother and baby. Feeding and weaning problems are closely related. Bereavements, marital conflict, difficult births, miscarriages and stillbirths, psychosomatic tendencies can all link with sleep problems. At its simplest, putting a baby down to sleep can feel unbearable for a parent who has experienced traumatic loss. Ambivalent feelings are a crucial factor in all this. Making these links enables parents to separate their experience from that of their infant's, and frees them to solve the problem themselves.

When a family is able to discuss such ideas, allowing the therapist as the outsider to have some new ideas, shows they are ready for a change. With older babies the thought of a "transitional object" (Winnicott, 1971) is raised by my asking if the baby has a teddy bear. I may be told she has several cuddly toys, but when I suggest that one significant toy could be important, parents may be able to create a shared idea with the baby that a particular toy has a job to do: "Kiss Teddy goodnight." Blankets, dummies, or the baby's own thumb may also become the source of satisfaction that allows separations from the mother at the same time as providing a link or memory. If the therapist's attunement to the stuckness in the original problem can encompass an idea of change, then the parents' belief in the possibility of change between them and their baby may be liberated. The therapist needs not to have a rigid idea of how the family should change, but share with the family a "transitional space" where thoughts of the satisfaction of sucked thumbs or cuddled teddies are mutually enjoyed by all in the room.

One big advantage of having the baby in the room is the chance to observe the baby.

This can be a shared activity and can quite naturally allow silences that give time for thoughts to grow. Babies are often in tune with the emotional atmosphere, and there may be a remarkable connection between what parents talk about and small babies' actions and vocalisations. The fact that some babies cry excessively may connect with some inconsolable experience in the parents' own history. When the parent is able to talk about this with the therapist they may then be able to console the baby (Hopkins, 1992). The parents' reaction to a baby crying in the session may in itself be useful material. They might want to take the baby out for a walk in the corridor as an attempt to get away from painful issues stirred up in the room. Persuading them to stay in the room with their crying baby may enable them to share difficult feelings with each other for the first time.

One mother attempted to soothe her baby silently. On having this pointed out to her she said, "If I did say anything to him, it would be too horrible." The opportunity to put her "horrible" thoughts about the baby into words to the therapist came as a release. Once such thoughts are spoken out loud they may become more bearable.

A therapist who is able to be non-judgemental, attuning to a wide range of emotions, can allow parents to own their hostile feelings towards their baby. In this case, the mother was able to have a different feeling towards her baby, to hold him close to her, and put into words what he might be experiencing. Having had her own feelings understood, she was no longer preoccupied with the force of them. The baby sensed this difference and could now be comforted by her. In this kind of parent–infant work the therapist can be thought of as carrying out a symbolic containing of the emotions in a family, which parents can then pass on in turn to their baby.

I was working in the Child Guidance Training Centre (CGTC; see Hopkins, Chapter 14) while developing this work at the James Wigg GP practice baby clinic. At the same time the Department for Children and Parents at the Tavistock Clinic had set up an Under Fives Counselling Service. Lisa Miller describes this in the following chapter.

Trainings and clinics for work with under fives

Juliet Hopkins and I joined this service when the two clinics merged in 1985. It was managed from an Under Fives Workshop, chaired by Lisa Miller, later renamed the Infant Mental Health Workshop. This led to a one-year course in under-fives work created by Juliet Hopkins, where many already experienced workers came together to enhance their work with a psychoanalytic experience of infant observation and theory seminars. Many of the students on this course went on to create other trainings and services for infants round the country. Later Paul Barrows in Bristol, Juliet Hopkins, and I created M9, the Tavistock postgraduate masters diploma (MA/PG Dip) in infant mental health, which was headed by Louise Emanuel. This course greatly helped the spread of infant mental health in the UK.

This work is also a very successful example of brief work that helps families to deal with current problems and often helps them manage emotions and relationships better in the future. I was pleased that the first referral I had for sleep problems at the Tavistock came from David Malan in the Adult Department, a pioneer of brief psychoanalytic work (see Malan, Chapter 25).

Spreading the work

As part of the Tavistock's "mission" and as a child psychotherapist, my own clinical work, teaching, and consultation has led me to want to spread it to other professions and other parts of the country. When I was chair of the Child Psychotherapy Trust in the mid-1980s and 1990s I supported child psychotherapists in setting up trainings outside London. My husband, the psychoanalyst Eric Rayner, was similarly working to help psychoanalysis outside London and we encouraged each other. I grew up in Yorkshire, his mother came from Liverpool. He claimed that few psychoanalysts knew that anywhere "North of Watford" existed. He and colleagues worked towards helping candidates outside London train in psychoanalysis without having to move to live in London, and this led to the setting up of the Northern Psychoanalytic Training based in Leeds, where a child psychotherapy training had already started. My task in often helping local child psychotherapists deal with sceptical colleagues and managers was in alliance with the Tavistock, especially Margaret Rustin. Its influence then spread to many regions.

Health visitors

One of the pleasures of working in the baby clinic was the contact with excellent health visitors. To name just two, Helen Utidjian and Linda Ashken taught me much about how parents manage the ordinary development and the crises of disturbance or disability in their babies. Passing on psychodynamic ideas to several generations of health visitors and helping them keep going with difficult patients led to me writing about these (Daws, 2005). One aspect of this was post-natal depression. Mothers with post-natal depression can be greatly helped by talking to health visitors. But those who need it most often turn it away. The most severely depressed can be so flat, elusive, and dismissing that it is easy for the health visitor to feel unwanted, and in turn not to be readily available for the mother.

This contact led to me campaigning for the profession of health visiting, which was seriously undervalued. I lobbied the government, and was part of the Regenerating Health Visiting project that led to the creation of the Institute of Health Visiting, which has transformed the professional image of health visiting.

Infant mental health

Belonging to the World Association for Infant Mental Health I attended and spoke at their world congresses. In 1995 Eric Rayner and I spoke at a regional conference of the Australian Association for Infant Mental Health (AAIMH). I was impressed with the way that the various professions involved with infants and their families got together. On the long plane journey home I thought, "We could do that." Inspiration born of boredom! Back home I wrote to various professionals, all of whom replied positively, and we had the start-up meeting of AIMH-UK in the Tavistock committee room, on March 1, 1996. The Tavistock supported this initiative and its chair, Nick Temple, got us a grant of £600 which paid the legal fees for setting up a limited company and writing the memorandum and articles consistent with those of the World Association (WAIMH). AIMH-UK has been successful in connecting many of the professions working with infants, and encouraging developments, especially in supporting front-line workers with the psychodynamic training they have previously missed out on.

Wanting to get the ideas out to parents I wrote a book with a younger Tavistock colleague, Alexandra de Rementeria, then on maternity leave. The book *Finding Your Way With Your Baby: The Emotional Life of Parents and Babies* (2015) won the BMA Medical Books Awards first prize for Popular Medicine in 2016.

The Tavistock Clinic has had a major part in spreading psychodynamic ideas about infant mental health throughout the NHS and the wider community.

Further reading

Emanuel, L., & Bradley, E. (Eds.) (2008). *What Can the Matter Be?: Therapeutic Interventions with Parents, Infants and Young Children (Tavistock Clinic Series)*. London: Karnac.

Horne, A., & Lanyado, M. (Eds.) (2015). *An Independent Mind: Collected Papers of Juliet Hopkins*. London: Routledge.

* * *

Dilys Daws

I trained as a child psychotherapist at the Tavistock Clinic in Beaumont Street, Marylebone, and qualified in 1963. After a year travelling and working at a clinic in Australia I had my two children, and joined the Child Guidance Training Centre and its Day Unit in 1971. Mary Boston and I edited the first ever British book on child psychotherapy, *The Child Psychotherapist and Problems of Young People* (1977). When the CGTC merged with the Tavistock Clinic in 1985 I became a consultant child psychotherapist in the Child and Family Department. At times I was head of a clinical team, and of the Under Fives Counselling Service, co-led the Infant Mental Health Workshop, and helped set up the PGDip/MA in infant mental health. I was chair of the Association of Child Psychotherapists, and later of the Child Psychotherapy Trust. I was the founding chair of the Association for Infant Mental Health, and in 2002 received the WAIMH Award for services to the World Association for Infant Mental Health. I was awarded a PhD for published works in 1999.

I started as a visiting psychotherapist at the baby clinic of the James Wigg practice in 1975 and still work there. I consult to therapists running infant mental health services around the country, and am adviser to AIMH-UK.

My father (Dr Jack Kahn) was a GP; after the war he trained as a psychiatrist and there was Freud on the dining room table!—one of the inspirations for me to train as a psychotherapist. My degree at Cambridge was in social anthropology which influenced me as a child psychotherapist to think about families and social settings. Born in Yorkshire (to a Russian-Jewish family), as an officer of the Association of Child Psychotherapists I realised one day that three of the four officers meeting in a room in London were from Yorkshire and I wondered why we were all there, and not still in the North! As chair of the Child Psychotherapy Trust I then encouraged colleagues who set up trainings outside London. My husband, psychoanalyst Eric Rayner, similarly helped spread psychoanalysis across the country. Much of my work has been in disseminating psychoanalytic ideas and in supporting front-line workers in other professions, both in writing and teaching around the country and abroad, and in political lobbying.

CHAPTER THIRTEEN

Service for under-fives in the child and family department at the Tavistock: short-term applications of psychoanalytic practice and infant observation

Lisa Miller

The original service for brief work with children under five and their parents was set up in the early 1980s. The germ of the idea came from Margaret Rustin and the close group of leading child psychotherapists, like Sheila Miller, who were aware of the importance of infant observation. This involved observing a baby growing up in the context of its family in great detail over a period of two years and was instituted in the Tavistock child psychotherapy training by Esther Bick. From this has emerged much deep knowledge of, and sensitivity to, the relationships and early development of the infant and small child which can be helpfully applied in psychoanalytically oriented work.

Offering up to five sessions, bearing also in mind that all five might not be wanted or needed, seemed a highly economical way of proceeding in a time of decreasing psychotherapeutic resources. Two things had been noticed: the lack of psychological attention given to babies and toddlers (partly through fear of pathologising anxieties which seemed within the norm, things which would be "grown out of") and the paradoxical surge of awareness of the importance of the earliest years in the whole process of growing up.

We saw fathers and mothers who were anxious about babies who would not eat, would not sleep, or would not be quiet for any length of time. There were parents anxious about bereavement or divorce, babies who refused to be weaned, toddlers suffering tantrums and jealousies, and those in the throes of nameless and apparently inexplicable anxieties. They came for counselling; they came to think with an experienced outsider about the difficulties and miseries they were undergoing in themselves or in their children. And the workers in the service thought of themselves in these terms, rather than as experts about to deliver advice.

Flexibility, promptness, and informality characterised the service. We used to see family members in various groupings; where there were two parents we liked to see both, but we were quite willing to take what came and work with it. The service prided itself in being able to give an appointment quickly, sometimes very quickly, believing that where anxiety involves an infant or a small child help is needed now, and can be used at once. A telephone call secured a session. People needed, of course, to have decided they had a problem, and it required courage to pick up the telephone. But beyond that we tried to put few obstacles in their way.

The professionals, sometimes two, who took on the case were members of a multidisciplinary workshop where psychiatrists, social workers, psychologists, and child psychotherapists met regularly to discuss cases they were holding, and other aspects of the emotional development in earliest childhood. I joined it in 1985, when the most influential people were the psychologists Elsie Osborne and Denise Taylor, and the social worker and child psychotherapist Alan Shuttleworth. The discussions were tremendously eager; everyone enthusiastic when they heard that a baby had slept through the night, or a toddler was observed in the session no longer to be climbing up the bookcases but playing thoughtfully while her mother was deep in talk with the worker. As time went on the workshop got bigger, enlarged by lively and welcome newcomers with fresh opinions and thoughts: there were Juliet Hopkins and Dilys Daws who brought their very well-established interest in this kind of work to the service when the Child Guidance Training Centre (see Hopkins, Chapter 14) was amalgamated into the newly formed Child and Family Department in 1985. There were younger psychologists like Judith Bell and Sally Hodges; Elizabeth Bradley came from her post as consultant child psychiatrist at Croydon Child Guidance Clinic and was fascinated by the potential of this different approach, and there was Gillian Markless, a social worker from King's College Hospital who brought vigorous and useful new ideas like the absolute necessity of trying to work with fathers.

Our thinking was to add a psychoanalytical approach to the attempt to intervene early enough in a child's life. The parents knew something was going wrong. We hoped to foster the parents' capacity to observe both their children and themselves. The work relied upon the knowledge that a good deal of change can be brought about in a family when a child is still tiny. It is a time of high-speed growth and development, when much emotional heat is generated in a family. Potential for psychological growth in the parents exists in relation to growth in the baby—and indeed in all family members, like siblings who need to change and adapt to a newcomer. Interventions can be effective, occasionally startlingly effective, in the intimacy of the nursery.

The psychoanalytic elements that the service incorporated were fundamental ones: the ingrained understanding that things will occur at an unconscious as well as a conscious level; the use of transference and countertransference especially the negative transference, and the corresponding confidence that change occurs in moments of contact with another mind. The members of the service tried to bring a mind that watches and receives, and to comment even lightly on feelings occurring in the room.

Observation of the patients and of oneself turned out to be an important tool. As one might expect, strong feeling was aroused in both worker and family which needed to be absorbed calmly. The receptive frame of mind turned out to be all-important. Forging a link which might be called parental with the parents—two entities who joined together in trying to look after the child—could at best reactivate what was parental in the pair or within the single parent.

So, what did we learn and how well did it work? Perhaps one thing we learned was not to be naïve, not to think that our efforts would be entirely well received out in the community. I remember giving a paper at a conference where I was asked, "What are you doing that a half-way good health visitor couldn't do?" What indeed? But there is an answer: we took on problematic families that had already been constant visitors to the health centre. They had already had excellent help, help that suffices for the great majority of worried parents. We could, albeit modestly, offer something in the way of emotional insight and containment, the capacity for which is nourished and deepened by the child psychotherapists' and others' experience of infant observation and close long-term supervised work. Training tells.

We learned a good deal about the usefulness of this kind of work. Probably in about a quarter of cases it worked very well indeed, sometimes surprisingly well. In maybe half it was a distinct source of help. In another quarter we had trawled in highly disturbed families and we then could perform a useful function in either transferring them or returning them to other agencies, but with the capacity to contribute some thinking based on a handful of sessions in some depth.

This form of work turned out to be gratifyingly exportable. An under-fives service could be started in all sorts of places at home and abroad. I was very touched when I went back to Milan ten years after my initial presentation there and found the service still strong and thriving in the same form. At its peak the then chair of department, Dr Caroline Lindsey, referred to it as "our flagship service". It is gratifying to discover a doctoral candidate undertaking a piece of research at present which involves a pilot project taking on five cases to treat in this way with the hope of setting up a service like this in the CAMHS clinic in which she is employed.

Bibliography

Emanuel, L. (2006). A slow unfolding—at double speed: Reflections on ways of working with parents and their young children within the Tavistock Clinic's Under Fives Service. *Journal of Child Psychotherapy*, 32(1): 66–84.

Miller, L. (2008). The relation of infant observation to clinical practice in an under-fives counselling service. In: E. Bradley & L. Emanuel (Eds.), *"What Can the Matter Be?" Therapeutic Interventions with Parents, Infants and Young Children (Tavistock Clinic Series)* (pp. 38–53). London: Karnac.

Rustin, M., & Emanuel, L. (2010). Observation, reflection and containment: A psychoanalytic approach to work with parents and children under five. In: A. Lemma & M. Patrick (Eds.), *Off the Couch: Contemporary Psychoanalytic Applications* (pp. 82–97). London: Routledge.

* * *

Lisa Miller was a consultant child psychotherapist in the Child and Family Department for many years, much involved both in clinical work and in training. She was a member of a clinical team and also for some time ran the Department's Under Fives Counselling Service and chaired the multidisciplinary workshop which underpinned it. Before she retired she was the department's last elected chair.

Though she always regarded herself as a generalist, she had a particular interest in work with babies and small children, and for fifteen years was the editor of the *Infant Observation Journal*. She has taught and lectured widely both in this country and abroad and published on various topics. She continues to work as a visiting lecturer at the Tavistock, teaching and supervising child psychotherapists, though her heart has remained with literature ever since she read English at Lady Margaret Hall, Oxford.

Part III

Children and adolescents

CHAPTER FOURTEEN

The Child Guidance Training Centre 1929–1984

Juliet Hopkins
with additional material from Marcus Johns, Judith Trowell, and Gillian Miles

It is not widely known that the Tavistock Child and Family Department was formed in 1985 by the merger of the Child Guidance Training Centre with the previous Tavistock Department for Children and Parents. The following account describes the history and achievements of the Child Guidance Training Centre (CGTC).

The Child Guidance Training Centre opened in 1929 in an elegant house—Tudor Lodge in Canonbury Place, Islington—under the name of the London Child Guidance Clinic (also known as the Canonbury Child Guidance Clinic). Its aim was to be a demonstration and training clinic for the new, scientific practice of child guidance: a psychological approach to children's problems, particularly delinquency, which had developed in America, especially under the leadership of William Healy who helped to introduce Freudian thought into the United States. Among his contributions to the field of criminology are his book *The Individual Delinquent* (Healy, 1915) and his "multifactor theory" of delinquency, which broadened the field and moved it away from European criminology's stress on genetic factors. Healy developed an elaborate methodology for "the complete study of the offender by a variety of specialists" (Snodgrass, 1984, p. 333). These included medical, psychological, and social work professionals working together. In 1922 the newly created Commonwealth Fund[1] supported the establishment of a network of court-affiliated child guidance clinics. Healy's Judge Baker Foundation[2] became the model for these new clinics to establish multidisciplinary working teams. The value of this scientific approach was recognised by psychologist Cyril Burt who chaired the newly formed Child Guidance Council in 1927. The Council arranged for eight representative professionals to study in America before returning to initiate the London Centre. Burt declined the offer of directorship of the Clinic and Dr William Moodie (1886–1960)[3] became its first director. Though the East London Clinic for Children had been set up two years earlier by the Jewish

Health Organisation of Great Britain, this was the first secular child guidance clinic in the UK. American money from the Commonwealth Fund fully supported the work of the London Centre for its first five years (J. Stewart, 2013).

Following Healy's design, the Centre was from the start multidisciplinary, involving cooperation between psychiatrists, psychologists, and psychiatric social workers. Engagement of patients began with a diagnostic procedure in which the psychiatrist ascertained the child's physical and mental health, the psychologist assessed his intelligence and attainments, and the social worker his home environment. A conference, chaired by the psychiatrist, then enabled agreement between these professionals about the nature of any further intervention. Still in charge, but much less hierarchical than any previous intervention in child mental health, the psychiatrist prescribed treatment. This form of teamwork was known as the medical model, and was regarded by many professionals as an encroachment upon their particular profession. Precisely because it was multidisciplinary it was also later difficult to fund under any particular system of governmental administration.

Despite early difficulties, and much public scepticism, the first medical director, Dr William Moodie, reported in 1936 that "… the Clinic's thorough, unobtrusive and scientific practice has helped so many that today it is generally regarded as sound, constructive and helpful, even as a necessity" (Gwen Thorstad, unpublished, 1984). One of the first social workers recalls Dr Moodie's ability to ensure

> enough harmony among the staff to get a lot accomplished. It could be aggravating to some that he didn't take a stand; he was an extremely good father-figure. He didn't antagonise the social work agencies who had never heard of this kind of thing before, and were very critical … You've got to take both ends of that and see what's good and what's not so good, but some people couldn't easily tolerate his not taking more of a stand about psychiatry. (Bowlby, 1987, p. 1)

John Bowlby's recollections of his experience as a trainee there in the 1930s give an idea of the change in hierarchy required for a multidisciplinary team to flourish:

> Robina Addis had no qualms about putting conceited medicals in their place. She used to tell how on one occasion a young man training to be a child psychiatrist called her to fetch some papers from across the room for him. "Go around the table and fetch them yourself," she retorted. "I expect social workers to bring things when I want them," he insisted. "And I expect a man to stand up when I come into the room!" replied Robina, one of the large family of a director of the Bank of England. (Bowlby, 1987, p. 2)

Treatment of the child was usually weekly and took the form of individual or group play, drawing, discussion, and games; it was mainly conducted by psychiatrists, while social workers made an essential contribution through their weekly work with parents. Liaison with schools and special teaching for children with learning difficulties was provided by psychologists. A different form of service was provided by contributions to the surrounding community. These ranged widely over the years but involved teaching, training, and consultation to a variety of organisations, hospital departments, schools, and children's care homes.

The training of professional child guidance staff was of equal importance to providing a clinical service. At first only psychiatrists and psychologists were trained, but psychiatric social workers were soon added to their number; their course was linked to a new degree in mental health at the London School of Economics[4] paid for by the Commonwealth Fund. They also had placements at the newly opened Maudsley Hospital. These became the only trainings for psychiatric social workers until the 1940s. After training at the London Child Guidance Clinic John Bowlby joined the staff (1936–1940). His classic papers "44 Juvenile Thieves" (Bowlby, 1944a, 1944b) were based on case notes from the clinic. He felt he learned most from the psychiatric social workers (Bowlby, 1987, p. 2). They had a psychoanalytic orientation and paid much attention to children's real-life experiences. He may also have been impressed by Dr Moodie's view that "It is emotional safety within the family that matters" (Van Dijken, 1998, p. 78). When in 1946 Bowlby became chair of the Tavistock Clinic's Unit for Children, he brought with him the multidisciplinary medical model that he had learned at the London Child Guidance Clinic and which was to remain an enduring cornerstone of future practice throughout CGTC's history.

In 1940, after the outbreak of war, the London Clinic closed and a skeleton staff followed the movement of the London School of Economics to Cambridge, then to Oxford and lastly to Muswell Hill. At the war's end Dr Moodie returned from military service and the clinic thrived again after finding accommodation at 6, Osnaburgh St, Regents Park, and changing its name to the Child Guidance Training Centre (CGTC). There is relatively little information available about the life of the CGTC in the post-war years. It appears to have run a smooth course in spite of various moves: first, briefly to Cosway Street, near Marylebone Station, in 1962, then to 33 Daleham Gardens in Hampstead in 1963, where it stayed until the move to the Tavistock Centre in 1967, a building it shared with the Tavistock Clinic.

During this post-war period CGTC continued to be organised on the medical model, each consultant psychiatrist being responsible for the running of his own team or unit. Early in the 1970s, the first child psychotherapist, Frances Tustin, was appointed to the staff and shortly afterwards a child psychotherapist was added to the staff of each unit. Units dealt with referrals in whatever way they judged most beneficial. Children and parents were generally seen separately but over time more families were seen for assessment together. Psychoanalytic theories were increasingly used and the majority of the consultants were psychoanalysts.

In each of CGTC's locations links with schools and hospitals were made by staff who offered consultation and teaching. For example, while in Daleham Gardens, links were developed by psychologists with the Hospital for Sick Children, Great Ormond Street, by psychiatrists with High Wick Hospital and with the Paediatric Department of the Whittington Hospital (see Kraemer, Chapter 16), and by a child psychotherapist with a GP practice (see Daws, Chapter 12).

Training continued to be largely through an apprenticeship system depending on ample supervision by staff. The interdisciplinary nature of the units which was such a strong feature of diagnosis and treatment was also a strength of the training for students who learned much from each other and staff as they met in the comfortable coffee room. Students learned also from case conferences and fortnightly staff meetings which discussed policy and considered new ideas. After the move to the Tavistock Centre a new rotation scheme was devised for the psychiatric registrars to have more hospital experience. The proximity—one floor up—of the Tavistock Clinic meant that many children whom CGTC could no longer treat were referred to the Tavistock child psychotherapists, an example of a few shared activities, such as placements of Tavistock child psychotherapy trainees in CGTC units and visits from outside speakers, which developed before the merger. Informal contacts in the canteen were also important as, of course, was the shared use of a splendid library.

The Day Unit 1968

The move to the Tavistock Centre enabled the fulfilment of a long-held wish for CGTC to open a Day Unit for seriously disturbed children (see Nicholson & Johns, Chapter 15). This was made possible in the now vacated Gloucester House in Daleham Gardens. After negotiation between health, education, and social services, the new unit opened in 1968 with places for up to twelve children. It provided prolonged diagnostic observation, psychotherapy, and education for children with serious developmental and behavioural difficulties, unable to profit from ordinary schools. Like the other team units at the CGTC, the Day Unit staff were led by a psychiatrist, supported by a senior psychologist, child psychotherapist, and social worker. The education authority appointed a teacher-in-charge, two class teachers, a remedial teacher; three assistants were independently employed. The unit flourished and in 1984 it joined the merger with the Tavistock Clinic to become the Tavistock Day Unit.

The threat to close CGTC
with contributions from Judith Trowell and Gillian Miles

The Child Guidance Training Centre had played a central role in the development of the child guidance movement for fifty-five years and was keen to continue, but the area health authority was aware of a disparity between the excellent child guidance provision in Camden and the relatively poor service provision in neighbouring Islington; it consequently proposed that CGTC should move back to Islington where it had begun. CGTC was willing to move but Islington Community Health Council refused to support an expensive national teaching and training centre at a time when many of its citizens' more basic medical needs were unmet.

At this point Hampstead Health Authority decided to close CGTC. They did not want two child mental health clinics in the same building. The then chair of the Tavistock's Department for Children and Parents (DC&P), Dr Judith Trowell, saw that there were unmet mental health needs in Camden: adolescent drug and alcohol abuse, homelessness (particularly young runaways arriving at mainline stations), physical and sexual abuse, learning difficulties, and neurological difficulties such as spina bifida and epilepsy. She joined forces with the vice chair of CGTC, Gillian Miles, to plan a merger. The organisation of the Tavistock department was no longer based on a child guidance model, where each team was led by a consultant psychiatrist. Instead there were clinical "programmes" based on the modality of treatment—brief therapy, psychoanalytical psychotherapy, family systems therapy—in which any senior member of staff could take full responsibility for his or her patients. This was, at the time, a revolutionary move away from medical dominance in health services (see also F. Balfour, Chapter 20). Methods of training were correspondingly less multidisciplinary in DC&P.

From outside the clash between conservative and progressive clinics might have appeared as the "narcissism of minor difference" (Freud, 1930a); to the participants the struggle was for some very real and painful, but for others also quite exciting. Some CGTC staff took retirement rather than merge, fearing, as they had done for years, that "the Tavistock will swallow us up" (reported in 2020 by Dr Mary Lindsay who had briefly been a CGTC consultant almost twenty years earlier). Gillian Miles was delegated by her colleagues not to permit change in their well-functioning practices. She and Judith Trowell recall unpleasant rows between them, which required consultative help from Eric Miller at TIHR. Yet, in support of joining forces were the already existing close clinical and training links between the two clinics: Frances Tustin, Salo Tischler, and George Stroh, all from CGTC, ran a training on psychotic and autistic children which many Tavistock colleagues found invaluable. Dr Arnon Bentovim, working mainly at Great Ormond Street Hospital, had three sessions in DC&P and together with the CGTC social worker, Carolyn Okell Jones, started a joint workshop for assessing children who may have been sexually abused (see Trowell, Chapter 34). Few, if any, such services existed at the time. An enormous amount of institutional—effectively group relations—work between the two clinics over eighteen months resulted in an agreement that all become part of a new Tavistock department, the Child and Family Department, with continuity as chair provided by Judith Trowell until the end of the decade. DC&P and CGTC were no more.

Personal experience

I enjoyed work as a child psychotherapist in CGTC for twelve years until the merger. I found myself in a remarkably supportive and apparently conflict-free environment. Responsibility for administrative decisions was taken off-stage by the consultants and the roles of each professional discipline were respected and undisputed. Referrals seemed to happen at a rate compatible with a manageable case load and no child waited long for therapy. A "coffee lady" provided fresh coffee and biscuits at mid-morning when staff could be sure of finding each other briefly available for discussion. Drinks were also provided in the waiting room where parents often lingered after appointments and children enjoyed a rocking horse. All this comfort and security can subsequently be seen as living in an ivory tower. Although an increasing amount of work was being done in the community, the staff had not yet realised how much more they could have contributed. Referrals from social services had scarcely begun, most child patients were seen individually once a week, and the immense possibilities of family therapy were only just beginning to be realised. It is hard to imagine a more different situation than that which prevails in child mental health today.

Resources

Brochure (1978). *Child Guidance Training Centre and Day Unit*. London: Camden and Islington AHA(T).

London Child Guidance Clinic Report 1929. https://wellcomelibrary.org/item/b18589558#?c=0&m=0&s=0&cv=1&z=-0.0451%2C0.1882%2C0.9309%2C0.4478. London: Wellcome Library.

Lost Hospitals of London. https://ezitis.myzen.co.uk/cgtc.html

Thorstad, G. (1985). A Brief History of the Child Guidance Training Centre. Presented at the Department Day, September 18, 1985.

Notes

1. An American charity founded by Anna Harkness in 1918 and dedicated to the "welfare of mankind" https://www.commonwealthfund.org/about-us/foundation-history

2. Harvey Humphrey Baker was appointed the first judge of the Boston Juvenile Court by Governor Curtis Guild in 1906. Judge Harvey Baker believed strongly that there was more to "juvenile delinquency" than just a "bad kid." He wanted to create a place where research and treatment could help these children and their families. https://jbcc.harvard.edu/history-serving-children-1917

3. A brief biography of Dr Moodie from the Royal College of Physicians. https://history.rcplondon.ac.uk/inspiring-physicians/william-moodie

4. The director of LSE at that time was William Beveridge. He had been appointed there by the Fabian Society. This indicates a subtle socialist influence at work in the child guidance movement.

* * *

Juliet Hopkins, PhD

My attachment to the Tavistock Clinic began in 1956 with a plan to join my uncle, John Bowlby, and his research team, but once I had experienced life at the Tavi my plan to research was quickly undone by the greater appeal of psychoanalysis and clinical work.

During the following years I had the privilege of completing three clinical trainings (clinical psychology, child psychotherapy, family therapy) and was further greatly privileged to become a staff child psychotherapist, first in 1974 in CGTC, and then (through institutional merger) in the new Child and Family Department of the Tavi, where I worked until my official retirement in 2000. During that time I took a training in family therapy at the Tavistock Clinic and in adult psychotherapy at the British Association of Psychotherapists. It is hard to overestimate the stimulus and satisfaction I gained from having great colleagues and students.

During various breaks early in my career I was fortunate to be able to spend three two-year periods working and learning abroad: at Yale University Child Study Centre, Hong Kong University, and Princeton Child Guidance Clinic. These experiences of difference made it easier later to embrace and accommodate the new developments in child guidance at home, such as attachment theory, the prevalence and injuriousness of child abuse, trauma, and the value of family work. In 1982 I became a founder member of the Independent Psychoanalytic Child and Adolescent Psychotherapy Association (IPCAPA) which I continued to support. I have consulted and taught widely.

Throughout my career I aimed to share new insights by writing clinical papers, now collected and published as *An Independent Mind*, edited by Anne Horne and Monica Lanyado (2015).

CHAPTER FIFTEEN

Gloucester House: a story of endurance, inspiration, and innovation

"Working together for learning and development"

Nell Nicholson
with added material from Gillian Miles and Marcus Johns, together with his addendum

Introduction

Gloucester House was established by the Child Guidance Training Centre as a Day Unit for "seriously disturbed children" in 1967 at 33 Daleham Gardens. This was possible when the CGTC vacated the house to move into the newly built Tavistock Centre at 120 Belsize Lane nearby. The Tavistock Clinic's Department for Children and Parents amalgamated with the Child Guidance Training Centre in 1985 and the Day Unit became the Tavistock Children's Day Unit.

This is an important acknowledgement of the significant proportion of clinical staff working in what might otherwise appear to be just another special school; and that it is uniquely placed within the Tavistock and Portman NHS Trust. The building is an Edwardian house nestled in the heart of Belsize Park. It could—on first glance—be mistaken for one of the local wealthy homes but the NHS signage proclaims its difference and specialness. The Day Unit provision is a unique blend of educational and clinical professionals working together to support the learning and development of a small group of children with complex social, emotional, and mental health difficulties. For more than fifty years Gloucester House has pioneered therapeutic educational work with children. During this time it has experienced many changes: of leadership and day-to-day practices. It has had periods of intense external financial pressure and internal rifts about approach; it has been impacted by wider social contexts and attached to different organisations, changing its title to fit the context. However the two things that have stayed remarkably constant have been its home in Daleham Gardens, and its adherence to the fundamental principles of multidisciplinary approaches in supporting the emotional and educational development of troubled children.

In recent years it has expanded its impact in the community by developing an outreach service. This provides support to other schools and services that have asked for help in understanding and managing their most complex and hard to reach children.

History

In 1899 the Elementary Education Act recognised the need for the provision of special education up to the age of sixteen. From then on such provision increased due to the understanding, drive, and compassion of dedicated individuals. One of these dedicated individuals was Dr Frederick Dodd. When the Tavistock Clinic was founded as the Institute for Medical Psychology in 1920 Dr Dodd was on the staff and was frustrated by the absence of provision for treating the neuroses of childhood. He was interested in the relationship between physical ill health and psychological disturbances and concluded that more help could be given to children in a natural home environment. Hence he set up a small residential school for disturbed boys in Blackheath. He was encouraged in this by Dr Hector Cameron, the physician in charge of the Children's Department at Guy's Hospital. Hector Cameron was the first to say, "Give a child a bad name and he will try to live up to it … give him a good name and he will do likewise." Frederick Dodd moved to a larger house when he married and where he continued to provide for about twenty emotionally troubled boys and girls between the ages of five and fifteen. Dodd continued to work at the Tavistock Clinic and in 1929 was able to establish a precedent with the Board of Education to pay for the placement of an eight-year-old girl away from home because of her psychological difficulties.

Another of these pioneers was Barbara Dockar Drysdale who set up the Mulberry Bush School in 1948. She had close links with the Tavistock Clinic and created her school as a therapeutic community to "provide an experience that will compensate and challenge all that has gone before, and help [children] develop a capacity to think and understand". Happily that link has been maintained, and the Day Unit was even known for a few years as the Tavistock Mulberry Bush Day Unit (see below).

As a part of the Child Guidance Training Centre, the Day Unit's ethos and approach had been developed from the multidisciplinary child guidance model. The child guidance movement began after the First World War at a time of significant social change. This saw an increasing interest in child development, not least through the emerging concept of childhood experience as a critical factor in adult lives. Child guidance sought to be a form of preventive health care promoting children's mental well-being. One of the central tenets of the approach was that a child might experience "maladjustment" due to internal as well external factors and that approaching the issues with multidisciplinary collaboration—clinical, educational, and social assessment with interventions working together—would be an effective way to address this.

The Child Guidance Training Centre (CGTC) was founded in Islington in 1928 as the London Child Guidance Clinic (see Hopkins, Chapter 14). In the 1930s John Bowlby (see Rustin, Chapter 7) worked there and after the war became chair of the Children's Unit at the Tavistock

Clinic, and deputy medical director of the whole clinic. After several moves, in 1963 the CGTC arrived at Gloucester House and in 1967, moved from there into the newly opened Tavistock Centre, its final home. The staff of the CGTC welcomed this opportunity to use the now vacant Gloucester House building to set up a therapeutic Day Unit as a full-time placement to help very troubled children who were struggling at home and at school. The length of stay was up to two years, and the aim was, if possible, to help them back into normal schooling. The unit was staffed by three full-time teachers with teaching assistants, and alongside a part-time multidisciplinary team from the Clinic; the unit was headed up by Dr Margaret Collins, one of the four analyst consultants in the Clinic, with child psychotherapist Eve Richards (soon to be replaced by Dilys Daws), and social worker Gillian Miles on the staff. The whole team met together on Friday afternoons to think about the children and to bring together the teaching and clinical contributions to our understanding, the better to think about each child's treatment needs.

During the 1970s—from 1975 under the leadership of Dr Marcus Johns—the Day Unit was made up of three groups of around six children each staffed by a teacher and an assistant. The groups were organised by age ranges: from four to seven, from seven to ten, and from ten to fourteen (remarkably similar to the current configuration). The idea of having two members of staff per class was to provide a model of a parental couple who could work together in the best interests of the child. The domestic feel of the unit was maintained in having a married couple as caretaker and housekeeper who cooked food in the kitchen for children and staff. All ate together in the dining room. During the 1970s and early 80s there was stability with consistent leadership and developmental thinking within the organisation.

Through the 1980s, child guidance clinics closed or became subsumed in other entities. This was due to the loss of the Inner London Education Authority, the overoptimistic opinion of the Fish Report (ILEA, 1985[1]) that all children could be managed in ordinary schools, and the growth of bureaucracy at the expense of care provision. In 1985, when CGTC and the Tavistock Department for Children and Parents merged, the Day Unit was incorporated into the newly formed Child and Family Department of the Tavistock Clinic.

The teachers became officially employed by the Mulberry Bush School in Oxford, and the service was named the Tavistock Mulberry Bush Day Unit. Both organisations were committed to therapeutic education but the links were more in name rather than a true partnership. Though the Tavistock Clinic amalgamated the organisations, the Day Unit had belonged to the Child Guidance Training Centre. Neither the Mulberry Bush nor the Tavistock had any sense of ownership. There followed a period for Gloucester House of feeling orphaned; unwanted and unvalued, caught in a battle for survival under intense financial pressure disrupted by the fractured visions of its parental institutions. This led to a crisis when in 2000 Gloucester House failed its fire report and closed temporarily. The service was severely at risk but, due to the commitment and passion of dedicated staff with their roots embedded in the earth of child development, endured. The apparent institutional ambivalence for the service, combined with its resilience to survive in the face of adversity, provides a notable parallel to the struggles of the children and families we serve.

In 2004 Dr Kajetan Kasinski took up leadership and reinvigorated an integrated service in which education and clinical staff would work again more collaboratively. This brought in a more diverse range of clinical interventions such as family therapy and nursing.

Personal reminiscence

When I was recruited, in a temporary capacity in 2005, the organisation's survival hung in the balance. Though there were positive green shoots of potential and commitment to the task, Dr Kasinski was going on paternity leave, there was one permanent teacher, and the service's viability was fragile; I was interested in the unique integration of education and clinical practice. The model at this time was predominantly co-located education and child psychotherapy but with significant divisions between practice and approaches. I was energised by this combination and the potential fusion. The emerging vision was to integrate the clinical and educational teams more fully and incorporate systemic and therapeutic community ideas.

There was discord in the senior management team which I saw as reflective of passion about ideas and approaches. However, the impact of these differences was troubling. The deputy headteacher Julie O'Dwyer and I built the education team and brought together systems and structures to support the development of an educational and behavioural framework. My commitment to the unit and my belief in the value of its work grew and I took up the permanent position of headteacher in 2006.

We approached Ofsted to get the school recognised in its own right and applied for a DFE number. Some were apprehensive that Ofsted would never understand us, but we were well prepared and confident. We had our first visit from Ofsted in September 2006 and were awarded our school status in February 2007. During this period pupil numbers rose and we appeared to be flourishing. Part of Dr Kasinski's vision was to incorporate psychosocial nursing approaches, and Gloucester House employed its first nurse in 2012. The nurse, Kirsty Brant, brought together education and clinical approaches effectively. She demonstrated being able to work in the moment, hand in glove with the education staff, bringing clinical experience and expertise to the day-to-day interactions in the classrooms and the playground. This successful innovation was bittersweet, however. The bleak wind of austerity was blowing through local authorities and in 2011 referrals had started to dwindle, despite their manifest appreciation of our achievements. With our finances becoming precarious we embarked on a tour of local authorities to argue our case.

In the summer of 2013 Dr Kasinski took a sabbatical to write up the audit we had conducted on twenty-nine children who had left the service over a period of seven years. The findings were remarkable: 82% maintaining stable placements a year on, numerous testimonials describing tangible progress in children's behaviour and maturity, and academic attainments in their subsequent placements. This was particularly striking to me, having previously been headteacher of a pupil referral unit where parallel achievements were less marked and sustained, with too many children reverting back into secondary services despite our best efforts.

In this context of flourishing innovation and proven outcomes it was devastating to think that we might be coming to the end of the road. The number of children referred remained low and financial pressure increased. In February 2014 the decision was made that the unit would indeed close. We had not yet communicated the decision publicly, and as fate would have it, two days after the decision was made, Ofsted visited. After a thorough immersion into our approach they gave us a glowing review. This gave us tangible evidence to take to the Tavistock and Portman Trust board where the Tavistock's new CEO, Paul Jenkins, was persuaded to agree to a reversal of the decision. It was a tense moment, but we were rewarded with a limited reprieve. We were to be extended a probationary period to trial our proposed new operational model. This kept the principles of multidisciplinary integration and therapeutic education at its heart. It still included psychiatry and psychotherapy, increased mental health nursing, and included family therapy and other therapeutic approaches, but would be led by education and be presented as a school. This was a major change for all concerned but maintained the psychoanalytic and multidisciplinary foundations of the Tavistock Clinic.

The current endeavour

During the transition to the "new model" we were careful to monitor the quality of our work and keen to develop innovations without reduction in quality. Numbers of referrals rose rapidly and we soon opened a third class. In the developing team the nursing/education partnership strengthened and the lead nurse became the clinical lead for the service. The senior leadership team combining nursing, teaching, and psychoanalytic psychotherapy created a unique fusion of approaches to address the needs of our children.

The influence of psychoanalytic thinking, with the importance of unconscious action and reaction, is deeply embedded within the service. Our psychotherapist Ruth Glover comments that it is exceptionally unusual to have so much psychoanalytic child psychotherapy throughout an institution's history. Children get therapy they would otherwise not be able to access but this is not only as a treatment, but also as an essential part of the ethos. Psychoanalytical thinking is present in the therapy room, in the classroom, and at lunch.

Applied therapeutic community approaches inform our concept of community and emphasise our commitment to "working together for learning and development". Clinical and educational approaches are integrated throughout the working of the unit with great attention paid to planning the details of each child's day. Reflective practice is central to all parts of the work: with the staff in multidisciplinary planning meetings, during time set aside for staff to focus on dynamics and with the children for the exploration of individual behaviour, examining simplified restorative justice approaches, community meetings, and committees led by the children. Many of our children have had difficult family experiences which makes sharing a challenge; strong feelings of deprivation and rivalry surface. Most of the children have a limited capacity to tolerate uncomfortable feelings which they therefore tend to attribute to others, away from themselves. This makes group work essential. The importance of self-awareness as the foundation of personal growth is a golden thread that weaves its way through the fabric of our approach, reinforcing the child's sense of his or her true self.

Work with parents and carers is core to our approach. Parent/carer days keep our practice embedded within the community. Through therapeutic work with families we ensure that our interventions are attuned to the specific needs of children and their families. Parents arriving here are often at the end of their tether when there is extreme behaviour at home, school has broken down, and children have not been able to access mental health services. At Gloucester House all clinical work takes place within the school day—within or outside the classroom setting—making it easy to access mental health support. Children at Gloucester House and their families have often struggled in the past to attend appointments, or even engage with traditional mental health services. By embedding this resource within the school, children and families often feel more comfortable and can receive support within the setting.

A case history: Peter, aged 11—a wiry, watchful child with a keen mind and short attention span

Peter and his younger sister were adopted when Peter was four and his sister was two. Peter's birth family was chaotic and characterised by severe neglect and emotional harm. Neither parent could prioritise the basic needs of their children. Their relationship was volatile and unstable with significant levels of domestic violence, further compounded by alcohol and substance abuse. Peter had four foster placements, some separate from his sibling, before being adopted.

After his adoption Peter initially attended a mainstream school. However, his behaviour escalated with increased opposition, unsafe behaviours, and aggression towards staff and peers requiring physical intervention. Despite efforts to contain his behaviours at school, by the time of his referral to Gloucester House his place there was breaking down. Having been put on an individualised reduced timetable, he was rarely mixing with his peers or accessing academic learning. His behavioural difficulties escalated both at home and school, and the family was in crisis.

When Peter came to us we used our whole team meeting forum to assess and review his needs and strengths. We noticed that he was hyper-attentive which affected his concentration and engagement, yet this anxiety appeared mixed with a curiosity about the other children. In response to noisy verbal aggression between other children, Peter needed reassurance from staff to show that he was safe, and that the adults were not hurting the children. He conveyed an anxious mistrust of the adults, their intentions, and their capacity to protect him. When he was more aroused and defiant, he behaved as if nothing mattered—that he simply "didn't care". The adults were made to feel useless—he was the boss, desperately trying to be in control. At such times he would split the staff team, creating a polarised position in which the adult would be pulled into battle where someone had to win or lose. At such times the adults' challenging task was to be able to take a more thoughtful and reasonable position, while maintaining firm boundaries.

Peter conveyed a strong need for containment through routine and certainty. He could be very concrete and literal, thus demanding that staff were extremely explicit and clear in their communication with him. He was unsettled by changes and by instances that he might see as mistakes. When adults forgot a boundary Peter was frightened and made them feel that they were incapable of holding things together. In class he competed for adult attention and would act out negatively if his teacher was working with another child. He struggled to believe that he could be held in mind if the adult was not actively engaging with him and would become extremely destructive and omnipotent. Over time he managed to accept consequences and boundaries, developing a capacity to repair and take responsibility for unruly behaviour.

Peter's treatment plan included three times a week intensive psychotherapy; being part of a "nurture group"; and, for his parents, regular therapeutic consultations with a clinical nurse specialist together with a child and adolescent psychotherapist. Through these interventions he formed some positive relationships and began to use his peers constructively for help, often looking to them for guidance if he was unsure of something. He became able to hold onto the hope that even if things are difficult they can get better and be worked out. Despite a poor initial prognosis and potential downward trajectory this experience supported his gaining confidence and ability so that he could now reintegrate into mainstream education; initially with support from our team but eventually independently.

Conclusion

We are proud that our outcomes remain consistently impressive. The success of Gloucester House and an increasing demand from schools and local authorities for specialist support to help children with SEMH (social, emotional, and mental health) and behavioural difficulties to stay in their existing schools, has led us to develop the Gloucester House Outreach and Consultancy Service. Led by a clinical nurse specialist (see Griffiths, Chapter 33), this service brings our model into mainstream and alternative provisions, which enables us to provide support, capacity, and training to schools. This also enables us to work with children who are out of school and with the networks around them.

The concept of "belonging and non-belonging" weaves its way through our history; mirroring the struggle within the institution for children and families to feel they can "belong" and for wider society to understand these children as vulnerable and in need. It is the essence of a civilised society not to reject and marginalise those who carry the aspects of humanity we as individuals would rather deny and place far outside ourselves.

* * *

Addendum: The CGTC Day Unit in the 1970s and early 80s

Marcus Johns

I came to the Child Guidance Training Centre, with special responsibility for the Day Unit, in 1975, after being at the Earls Court Child Guidance Clinic working with a multidisciplinary team of senior social workers, educational psychologists, educational therapists, and child psychotherapists. The other child psychiatrists there were Alan Wilson and Jim Templeton who were also working at the Cassel Hospital and brought with them the experience of a pioneering therapeutic community (Main, 1981). I had trained in child and family psychiatry at the Tavistock Clinic with John Bowlby as my clinical tutor, and also attended seminars at the Anna Freud Clinic. I had completed my training as a psychoanalyst in 1972. I was also a consultant to schools for autistic children, maladjusted children, and a girl's probation hostel. I was delighted to come to the Day Unit where the ethos aligned to my own, bringing together health, education, and social services.

The Day Unit that I arrived at, and remember most fondly, had retained its original form: a charming, non-threatening, elegant Edwardian family house with a containing garden, a welcoming porch, warm oak-panelled lobby with a stained-glass door leading to the main hall and wide stairway, large fireplaces lined with blue and white Dutch tiles, a butler's pantry, and providing an essentially domestic environment. In the classrooms there were cushions and pillows where a child could rest or sleep. We investigated the possibility of creating some bedrooms in the loft space where children, in temporary difficulties at home, might be able to sleep overnight but this proved to be impracticable. We had a dining room where the children and teachers ate together, and at least once a week were joined by all staff. The food was prepared in the kitchen by the housekeeper, Mary Newman, and her caretaker husband, Bill, sometimes helped by the children. This was such a good place to work, with mutual respect and friendliness alongside skilled experienced teachers, teaching assistants, social workers, psychologists, and child psychotherapists.[2]

It was from this domestic environment, along with all that I had learned from our experienced staff, that, when I was in South Africa in 2001, I was able to encourage some replication. I had been asked by Tony and Hillary Hamburger to advise on the setting up of a children's day unit on the edge of Alexandra township in Johannesburg. I visited the proposed building, then empty, listened to what was planned and made suggestions on the set-up of the classrooms, domestic arrangements, the containment of the playground, and the facilitating of staff relationships. I was delighted when I returned a year later and was greeted with "Marcus, come and see. We've done all you suggested and it works!" Tony and Hillary Hamburger had established the Ububele Educational and Psychotherapy Trust (ububele.org). In 2007 they received the Inyathelo Award for Community Philanthropy. I was able to thank all our Day Unit staff for the input that I had given on their behalf. Unfortunately I was unable to maintain the domesticity of our own unit due to financial pressures: we lost the services of our cook, Mary, to be replaced by institutional meals delivered from the Royal Free Hospital. Her husband, the caretaker Bill Newman, left with her. We lost the oak panelling in the lobby to dry rot! Though I could not replace the oak panelling we were able to obtain a new caretaker, Mr Stone, a wonderful man. Having retired from the travel industry he brought to the Day Unit something of the domestic presence of a firm and kindly grandfather. He was always "Mr Stone". He asked to establish a workshop with a lathe in the butler's pantry and from there he produced toys for the children: brilliantly coloured wooden macaws that balanced on the edge of a table, somersaulting acrobats strung between wooden handles; and also gifts for the staff: beautiful iridescent dragonfly and butterfly brooches, skilfully turned small and large wooden bowls.

We had placements of trainees from the Anna Freud Clinic, from the Jungian child therapy training, and from the Tavistock child psychotherapy training. I regretted that I could not be there full-time as I also had an outpatient unit in the main Centre. Giving enough time became more problematic when I became chairman of the Child Guidance Training Centre in 1981. During this time the Centre was generously given an amusingly illustrated brochure introducing its work, produced by the well-known cartoonist, Nicholas Garland. In 1985 the Centre joined the Tavistock Clinic to join the newly named Child and Family Department.

At the Day Unit I had a room on the first floor next to those of the psychologist and the teacher in charge, a tall imposing man with a sonorous voice and significant presence. Our rooms looked over the lawns and the large tree which was home to families of squirrels; kestrels flew by. During my time, we were able to install in 1988 an all-weather play surface and climbing frame thanks to the voluntary work of our receptionist, along with the receptionist from the Tavistock Clinic and her husband, who raised generous funds from a number of charitable organisations.[3] One of the first things that I needed to do was to preserve the stained glass in the inner door of the lobby with perspex panels because the children tended to use the glass as push panels; the next was to master the intricacies of the antique switchboard with its little knobs and levers so that we were not out-of-contact when our receptionist/secretary and guardian, Margaret McIlvenna, needed to be looking after her elderly mother.

I particularly enjoyed the Day Unit as I would also be called upon to fulfil various roles somewhat outside the usual for a psychiatrist: a doctor examining children with rashes, sprains, cuts and bruises, a bicycle mechanic to get a chain back on its cogwheels, a pest control officer to deal with the swarms of flies when a bird had died in one of the fireplaces during a holiday break, an animal trainer when a squirrel with very sharp claws fell down the chimney into a classroom!

We took a wide range of troubled children, all of whom were unable to sustain placement in ordinary schools because of severe behavioural difficulties: Ivan the Terrible who bombed cars below with paint pots from the top of his council block; Sam whose psychotic mother did his homework for him but denied her involvement and who was groomed by a paedophile for access to the boy which we only heard about from the police after Sam had left the unit; Simon whose mother suffered a paranoid schizophrenic breakdown and for whom we had to arrange admission when she was taking Simon around graveyards at night looking for the Devil who would kill him and we feared for his life; Elizabeth, an elective mute whom we didn't understand but after nine months told us that she was ready to go back to her ordinary school; Michael who told us he knew where his father kept his secret uniform to go to secret meetings; Anne who was a little autistic girl. We tried taking older children but the little boys of twelve quickly had their growth spurts and became an adolescent gang casing the local houses, so we stayed with the 5-12 age range. We had considerable support from mainstream education who would take children part-time, and local children's homes who would send one of their staff to accompany a child.

Notes

1. ILEA (1985). *Equal Opportunities for All? (the Fish Report)*. London: Inner London Education Authority
2. Staff members: David Hass, Doris Liebowitz, Sue Strasser, Dilys Daws, Virginia Bruno, Jane Walby, Freya Davy, Judith Edwards, Elizabeth Abrahams, Sheila Eimmerman, Theresa Healey, Jane Leverton, Maya Wallfisch, Lavinia Gomez, Lee Marsden, Beverley Loughlin, Nadia Poscotis, Lesley Holditch, Janine Sternberg, Valerie Sinason, Wendy Tromans, Joyce Piper, Rachel Nathan, Victor Stone, Paul Cahill, Jane Osborne, and Francesca Bartlett.
3. Charitable donors: Variety Club of Great Britain, Hampstead Wells & Camden Trust, ILEA, BBC Children in Need, Help a London Child, The Diners Club, Tesco Stores Ltd., Parents and Friends of the Day Unit.

* * *

Nell Nicholson has been the headteacher of Gloucester House, the Tavistock Children's Day Unit and Outreach Service since 2005. She has diverse experience of leading and managing in mainstream and special schools, pupil referral units (PRUs), and in complex multidisciplinary teams. At Gloucester House she has championed integrated approaches and wrote her systemic master's degree dissertation on multidisciplinary teamwork. She worked alongside Dr Kasinski to broaden the field of clinical approaches in Gloucester House and led Gloucester House through some dark times from near closure in 2014 to a thriving, growing innovative service in 2020. She has also developed Gloucester House Outreach Service which works with schools, networks, and families to facilitate thinking holistically to support children. Nell consults to school leaders to audit systems and implement new systems in their schools around behaviour and staff support.

Nell has an MA in applied systemic theory from the Tavistock and Portman/UEL which focused on working systemically with families and working in and with organisations. She has provided training and organised and spoken at many conferences about therapeutic education for children with social, emotional, and mental health difficulties.

Marcus Johns trained in medicine at Charing Cross Hospital, The Strand, London, and worked on one of the first artificial kidney units at St Philip's Hospital. He then trained in psychiatry at the Maudsley Hospital and went on to train in child and family psychiatry at the Tavistock Clinic. John Bowlby was his clinical tutor. During this time he was also training in psychoanalysis. Hanna Segal was his training analyst. In 1972, at the same time as completing the analytic training he became a consultant psychiatrist at Earls Court Child Guidance Clinic. During this time he was also a consultant to Northcroft School for Maladjusted Children, Harborough School for Autistic Children, and Katherine Price Hughes Probation Hostel. Three years later he became consultant at the Child Guidance Training Centre with special responsibility for the Day Unit. Between 1981 and 1984 he was also chairman of CGTC. He became a consultant at the Tavistock Clinic when CGTC was merged with the Tavistock Department for Children and Parents in 1985.

He maintained a part-time private practice in psychoanalysis. He was deputy director of the London Clinic of Psychoanalysis between 1994 and 2003 and editor of the *Bulletin of the British Psychoanalytical Society*. He was a contributor to the *Collected Works of D. W. Winnicott, Volume 5* edited by Lesley Caldwell and Helen Taylor Robinson, and also chair of the trustees of the International Pre-Autistic Network.

CHAPTER SIXTEEN

A foothold in paediatrics

Sebastian Kraemer

The Child Guidance Training Centre started life in Canonbury in 1929, but after the Second World War it migrated through three places until finding a home in 1967 on the first floor of the newly built Tavistock Centre (see Hopkins, Chapter 14, and Nicholson & Johns, Chapter 15). The Tavistock Clinic's larger Department for Children and Parents was on the second floor, entirely independent of CGTC, whose identity was thus rather submerged. It was not an ideal location for one of the very first child mental health clinics in the country.[1] From the mid-1970s onwards there were many discussions about moving back to Islington where there was a greater need for child mental health services. Although the Whittington Hospital had been seriously considered, in the end no place could be found.

In parallel with this story there was a very small-scale mental health innovation in that hospital. In 1960 a determined young child psychiatrist, Dr Dora Black, needed to get some experience in paediatrics and persuaded the eminent consultant paediatrician, Dr Sam Yudkin (1914–1968), to give her unpaid experience working alongside him in his outpatient clinic at the Whittington Hospital. He was so impressed with what she could do that he decided a few years later to appoint a consultant child psychiatrist, Dr Margaret Collins, to join him, giving up two of his sessions to pay for her. Dr Collins had been on the staff of CGTC since 1954 and arrived at the Whittington[2] a year or so before her clinic moved into the Tavistock Centre.

I was appointed to a consultant post at the Child Guidance Training Centre in 1980 which included Dr Collins' sessions—now increased to three—at the Whittington Hospital. The appointment committee took place while I was in the middle of the annual Tavistock Institute Leicester group relations conference (see Rustin & Armstrong, Chapter 4; Shapiro & Carr, 2012). These are extraordinary ordeals, from which lifelong learning about oneself in organisations can be gained. My performance at the interview was undoubtedly affected by a state of heightened consciousness. I had trained in paediatrics before starting psychiatry but had no experience of working as a psychiatrist in this specialty. While the child guidance sessions I took over were part of a well-established clinical organisation, the place of psychiatry in the Whittington paediatric department remained fragile, barely a foothold. I knew this was a single-handed post but arrived at the hospital to find that, besides having no mental health colleagues, I also had no secretary, and had been allocated a room with no windows. This tiny outpost of CGTC was all that was left of its yearning for a return home. Shortly after my appointment the search was abandoned. Five years later CGTC was no more, having been absorbed into the Tavistock Clinic to create the newly minted Child and Family Department. I knew none of the history at the time. I was very pleased to get this job and thought it a good opportunity to apply what I had learned as a trainee at the Tavistock Clinic in the preceding four years.

Passing the test

Though he had no vote on the appointment committee the head of the paediatric department Dr Max Friedman (1931–1987) was keen to have a colleague with a paediatric qualification, which probably got me the job. The first case he referred to me was a girl with abdominal pains who had stopped eating. I saw her with her parents on the ward, which seemed to resolve the symptoms quite quickly. I felt I had passed a test. In those days there were few emergencies so that it was possible to focus on patients with what are now known as medically unexplained symptoms (MUS). The most immediately useful clinical preparation for this was my training in systemic family therapy, under the ambitious leadership of psychiatrist Dr John Byng-Hall (1937–2020) and social worker Rosie Whiffen (Papadopoulos & Byng-Hall, 1997). Building on a relatively modest interest in therapy for families from the 1930s onwards, these pioneers carved out a significant space for it in the Tavistock Clinic during the 1970s. They set up an intensive training for internal and external clinicians, while forging inspiring links with then world leaders in the field such as Dr Salvador Minuchin (1921–2017), Marianne Walters (1930–2006) and Harry Aponte from in Philadelphia, with Lynn Hoffman (1924–2017) from New York, and Drs Gianfranco Cecchin (1932–2004) and Luigi Boscolo (1932–2015) from Milan. All made several visits to the Clinic to supervise and teach us. These were revolutionary times. The "family therapy programme" became within a few years the now thriving systemic psychotherapy training and service (see Helps, Barratt, & Daniel, Chapter 24) with its own distinct profession.[3]

It is significant that when he took over the leadership after the war John Bowlby renamed the Tavistock children's department "the Department for Children and Parents". With little antecedent literature or practice to go on he was already interested in families as clinical entities. Virtually inventing it from scratch he started doing family therapy (Bowlby, 1949). At the same time he set up the first training in child psychotherapy (see Rustin, Chapter 7) but as his energies became diverted towards attachment research, family therapy did not develop as much as child therapy.[4] By the time Bowlby retired from clinical work in the early 1970s the prevailing ethos in the department was psychoanalytic child psychotherapy, along with infant observation, work discussion, and group relations training. These were also core aspects of training in child and adolescent psychiatry at the time, which is how I began mine. Only a few of us were later drawn to the still new, and very different, approach to therapy with families. An immersion in both systemic and analytic thinking turned out to be a good preparation for the hospital challenge.

Where is the anxiety?

The system around a sick child includes not only her family, but also the doctors and nurses responsible for her care. When early on I asked a paediatrician who had referred a patient to me if she could join me in the family consultation, she said afterwards, "I see what you are doing," which surprised me, because I had not quite seen it myself. She realised that I was not going to take over the clinical care of her patient but instead, through shared consultations, wanted to enhance what she was already doing. There the families could witness our liaison relationship—*a therapeutic process in itself*. This is not what other specialists, such as neurologists or gastroenterologists do, because they are, rightly, more concerned with children's symptoms than with their experiences.

A doctor confronted with MUS is inclined to think that there must be a mental problem in the child. Actually the problem is in the mind of the doctor herself, who should therefore be included in any attempt to solve it. Children with inscrutable symptoms are distressed by these symptoms, rather than by any emotion behind it. Psychoanalysis began with this predicament but in children, troublesome anxieties may more easily be found somewhere else in the family (Kraemer, 1983; Minuchin & Fishman, 1979). Neither paediatric patients nor their parents are likely to see any sense in an appointment with a psychiatrist. They might even be offended at the suggestion. A better strategy for engaging one is for the paediatrician to say to the family that *she* is the one who needs help. "I am puzzled about these symptoms. We have done enough tests for now, so I am going to need a colleague to look at this in a different way. I want him to join me to help me work out what's needed here" (Kraemer, 2016, p. 75). A therapeutically useful system is thus created.[5]

Within a few years the hospital saw a need for more mental health sessions and found money for another part-time consultant, and Dr Peter Loader, from Great Ormond Street Hospital, was appointed. From his research on psychosomatic families he could see that with our limited resources we should focus on paediatric patients only, and stop accepting referrals from outside the hospital; thus a dedicated paediatric liaison team was born. By the 1990s the mental health presence in the department had been enhanced by several more gifted colleagues, all part-time; Dr Jane Roberts, replacing Peter Loader (both were also family therapists), a consultant psychotherapist, Maggie Cohen, who worked in the neonatal intensive care unit and was also a trainer at the Tavistock, a child protection expert, Carol Edwards, a senior psychiatric trainee from the Tavistock Clinic on placement each year, and a (full-time) local authority social worker, Annie Souter (1953–2014). Annie's leadership provided a third boundary, alongside medicine and mental health, for clinical staff. This containing triangle played a significant part in the success of the Whittington paediatric department as one of the most popular places in London for doctors and nurses to train. Throughout these years the head of paediatrics was the fearless Dr Heather Mackinnon who led the way in cross-disciplinary collaboration with social services and mental health. She regularly demonstrated the necessity of robust disagreement between colleagues in complex child protection cases (see Trowell, Chapter 34).

A bigger system

Problematic cases are shared not only in clinical consultations but in departmental discussions. Before I arrived Dr Friedman had already established a weekly multidisciplinary group of ward and clinic staff and trainees, of which I became a regular member, rarely missing a meeting over the following thirty-five years. This group originally crowded into a tiny room where people sat on a table or the floor, but after a few years, when the ward had moved to a new building, we met as the "multidisciplinary team" (MDT) in a larger space with seats for everyone. The meeting was always chaired by the consultant paediatrician on duty. Those attending were a number of other consultant paediatricians and juniors, senior ward and specialist nurses, social workers, safeguarding leads, mental health staff, hospital specialist teachers, play specialists, physiotherapists, speech and language therapists, nursing and medical students (and, in earlier decades, the hospital chaplain), plus any visiting colleague, such as a social worker or health visitor who was involved in the care of one of the patients being discussed.

Having a senior paediatrician in the chair—as there had been already before my time—made it clear to everyone that this was proper medical business, and not a marginalised "psychosocial meeting" which important people need not attend. In Tavistock terms, the MDT had to have a *primary task*. After many years, and much debate, our "terms of reference" were formulated thus:

> The aim of the MDT is to provide a weekly space for reflection on complex or troublesome cases and on themes arising out of these. The discussion is intended to be facilitative, supportive and educational to all those working in the wider team. There are no rigid criteria for the types of cases to be discussed but they will always include: non-accidental injury/safeguarding, serious/life-threatening illness, deliberate self-harm/acute mental health, complex cases involving many teams and agencies, *or any case in which the child or member of family is generating curiosity, anxiety or concern in any staff however unclear this may be.* (Italics added)

This is a disconcerting setting for medical and nursing staff. A typical ward round is a hierarchy of decision making, with a consultant at the top and students at the bottom. The principle that everyone in the MDT, including visitors, students and trainees had an equal voice in the discussion needed regular reinforcement: "Hang on a minute, I think our visitor has something to add."[6] The task is to make observations, not decisions. To encourage people to speak their minds no minutes were kept. Meetings would often start late, and the discussion be waylaid by exciting distractions, but over the decades the MDT served its function well enough.

Joining a paediatric department in this way was a form of participant anthropology. Through our daily visibility on wards and in clinics mental health staff became domesticated. We wanted to change the culture to one of inquiry, to slow down rapid-fire—often competitive—diagnostic talk and ask in conversations about puzzling cases, "What is happening here?", and how the way we were behaving with each other could be related to the case we are caught up in (Britton, 2005; Mattinson, 1975). This kind of thinking is routine in the Tavistock, where it had grown out of wartime experiments in leadership and group dynamics (Bion & Rickman, 1943), but is quite alien almost everywhere else in public services. Its fundamental premise is that any contribution, however inarticulate or even offensive, reflects a significant aspect of the case, and should be given equal value to any other, possibly more carefully formulated, contribution. In work discussion, "There is not one 'right' way to do whatever is being studied; instead there are some facts that can be viewed in many different ways, yielding new lines of enquiry" (M. E. Rustin, 2008, p. 12). Note that the mental health team's comments were not made from the privileged position of a group consultant but as regular members of the MDT, who had to present and discuss our own clinical material along with everyone else.

In contrast, we gradually set up facilitated staff groups. In the neonatal unit Maggie Cohen started a work discussion group and asked me to join her. Alongside her remarkable observations of premature infants, she wrote about these meetings in *Sent Before My Time* (M. Cohen, 2003). We also ran regular groups with junior paediatricians, and with the consultants in the department (Kraemer, 2016). Only many years later—now working with Maggie Cohen's successor Judy Shuttleworth—was it possible to maintain a group with ward nurses, set up by an enthusiastic nursing tutor. "We don't know any psychology," they said, to which I replied "That's fine. Tell us about your patients." The discussion that followed showed how natural—yet how unusual in a busy timetable—it is to talk honestly about one's clinical experiences (Kraemer, 2018).

Canaries in the mine

Since the turn of the century the number of consultant paediatricians grew rapidly and there were smaller developments in what was now called the Paediatric Mental Health Team, but the most dramatic change affecting the whole department was the number of emergency admissions, mostly of teenage girls following suicidal self-poisoning.[7] This epidemic has made the need for mental health in paediatrics more visible to policymakers, but has not helped them understand the basic principle of our working in partnership. Poisoned people need doctors to assess the damage before any mental health help can be provided, but it is real collaboration— by which I mean conversations of some kind—between physical and mental health care that has the most profound therapeutic effect. Infant observation, both in analytic training (see Rustin & Armstrong, Chapter 4) and in the laboratory (Fivaz-Depeursinge, Cairo, Scaiola, & Favez, 2012) shows how attuned babies are to the relationship *between* the adults who look after them and how disturbing it is when they undermine one another. It seems that this capacity has survival value; that it is, so to speak, "wired in". It should be no surprise, then, that people of any age who are in a vulnerable state will be affected when physical and mental clinicians show little respect for each other. Though often concealed in warm words this antipathy is still prevalent in health services. The therapeutic function of an emergency medical assessment is destroyed if patients are then deposited on a paediatric ward, waiting to be seen by a psychiatrist who is unknown to the hospital staff, and takes days to arrive (Kraemer, 2019).

To manage the anxiety stirred up by the most troubling admissions it was necessary for the ward to have access to out-of-hours emergency psychiatric consultations. In 1998 I watched in admiration as Jane Roberts summoned senior managers from UCLH, Royal Free Hospital, Whittington Hospital, and the Tavistock Clinic to advise them of their obligation to organise and fund a rota of specialist trainees in child and adolescent psychiatry, and the serious dangers of not doing so. One trainee would cover the three hospitals each night and each twenty-four hour day of the weekend, always with phone access to a consultant psychiatrist from whichever hospital their patient had been admitted. This service, largely invisible to managers and daytime staff, strengthened the bond of good faith between paediatric and mental health colleagues.

Paediatric wards everywhere are under unprecedented pressure from emergencies. This has been building up throughout this century as young people see their parents suffer, and their own prospects for secure homes and jobs—even for a habitable planet—dwindling. Such considerations are beyond the grasp of a technocratic health service. Without a deeper view of the developmental origins of mental and physical illness the NHS will be overwhelmed.

At the foundation of the NHS the Tavistock Clinic had bold new ideas for early intervention. Staff would engage the population from the beginning of life in "Infant Welfare Clinics, Obstetric Units, as well as … such organisations as a Nursery School and a Juvenile Employment Agency"(Dicks, 1970). This compulsion to reach out remains a proud part of the Tavistock ethos, as several chapters in this book show. The post-war pioneers discovered, as we did at the Whittington, that it is possible for teams to do good work on a certain scale. What we have now witnessed is the danger that small creative organisations can easily be washed away by tidal social forces which can only be contained by political change. Compared to the 1940s we are equipped with a much richer understanding of human needs and behaviour, waiting to be woven into social policy.

Mental health in paediatrics is a fragile thing. Like a good marriage, it depends on tolerable degrees of conflict, which are not usually encouraged in public services. The whole point of liaison is to hold together in one place otherwise incompatible accounts of disease. This is more than diplomacy; it is professional friendship, which when it works well is always evident to patients and families. Many innovations that have extended the scope of child health have their origin in fortuitous meetings, such as between Drs Black and Yudkin sixty years ago.

Acknowledgement

My thanks to Dr Dora Black for providing details of her work at the Whittington paediatric department in 1960. Dr Black went on to become a pioneer in British paediatric mental health, first at Edgware General Hospital from 1968 and then at the Royal Free Hospital from 1984 until her retirement. Her paper "Development of a Psychiatric Liaison Service" (Black, McFadyen, & Broster, 1990) was based on work done there.

Notes

1. The decision to put it there was probably due to financial pressure in the NHS from the looming devaluation crisis of that year.
2. When Dr Collins retired in 1975 a distinguished and also retired psychiatrist, Dr Jack Kahn (1904–1989), father of Dilys Daws (see Chapter 12), occupied these sessions as a locum until 1980.
3. The establishment of the systemic discipline in the Tavistock and Portman Trust in 2003 was supported by Margaret Rustin when she was chair of the professional committee around the turn of the century.
4. In an interview with Alice Smuts recorded in 1977 Bowlby recalled the arrival of his gifted trainee, the Canadian psychiatrist, Freda MacQueen (subsequently Martin). "She quickly adopted a joint interview technique [Martin & Knight, 1962] and as she progressed to senior registrar and staff status had a powerful influence on several members of staff. Although I gave her every encouragement and what help I could, as did Molly Mackenzie, I had too much else on my plate to make any further contribution myself" (John Bowlby, cited by Duschinsky & White, 2019, pp. 208–209). Dr Freda Martin (1932–2019) later became the chair of the Department for Children and Parents. She wrote elegantly about the interface between family and individual approaches (Martin, 1977) but left in 1975 to return to her native Canada.
5. What the early group and family therapist Dr Robin Skynner (1922–2000) called "the minimum sufficient network".
6. As John Rickman put it in a wartime paper—in two parts, the other written by Wilfred Bion—"Each individual member is valued for his contribution to the group … the group must have the capacity to face discontent within the group" (Bion & Rickman, 1943, p. 681). Rickman, a Quaker, had been analysed by Freud but was also influenced by the group psychology of Kurt Lewin (1939).
7. Badshah, N. (2018). Hospital admissions for teenage girls who self-harm nearly double. *The Guardian*, August 6.

* * *

Sebastian Kraemer

In 1976 I arrived at the Tavistock Clinic as a psychiatric registrar with a degree in philosophy and qualifications in paediatrics and psychiatry, but little training in thinking. Learning from experience began here; in clinical supervision—both through a one-way screen with families, and from written-up sessions with child and adult patients—in work discussion, infant observation, group relations, and in John Bowlby's reading seminar. In 1980 I was appointed consultant in the Child Guidance Training Centre with three sessions in the paediatric department at the Whittington Hospital.

The merger in 1985 of CGTC and the Tavistock Department for Children and Parents brought together their two training rotations for senior registrars in child and adolescent psychiatry. As a consultant in the newly created Tavistock Child and Family Department I took on the leadership of the now enlarged training scheme. This had several placements in the Clinic itself, at three local paediatric departments (including the Whittington), four CAMHS clinics, and four inpatient adolescent psychiatric units. It was at that time one of the largest programmes of its kind in the country and included quite a number of part-time trainees (all of them women with young children). Throughout these decades I was privileged to work in a very busy multidisciplinary clinical team with many inspiring colleagues, each joined by their trainees; a group relations event in itself. I retired from the Trust in 2003, and was awarded an honorary doctorate of education by the University of East London/Tavistock four years later. In 1999 I was a family therapist in the BBC TV series about the Tavistock Clinic, *Talking Cure* (see Holgate, Chapter 40).

During all this time I was building up an emergency and liaison mental health service in the Whittington Hospital paediatric department (described above), remaining there until 2015, thirty-five years in all.

My work now is largely facilitating NHS work discussion groups—in primary care, mental health, general medicine, and child health—and as a member of a "reflecting team" of family systems therapists in a GP practice (Kraemer et al., 2018). Since the 1980s I have been writing and lecturing on themes related to my professional and personal development: family systems therapy and its relationship with psychoanalysis; the role of fathers from anthropological and cultural perspectives; paediatric mental health liaison; learning from experience in professional development; the fragility of the developing male; the damaging effects of wealth inequality, and the perinatal promotion of secure attachments. Papers on these and other subjects can be found at www.sebastiankraemer.com.

CHAPTER SEVENTEEN

Early psychoanalytic approaches to autism at the Tavistock

Maria Rhode

The pioneering psychoanalytic work with children on the autistic spectrum that was carried out at the Tavistock between the late 1950s and early 1970s by Frances Tustin (1913–1994) and Donald Meltzer (1922–2004) has directly influenced clinicians around the world. It also continues to be fundamental to contemporary thinking in the UK through developments in the Tavistock Autism Workshop (Alvarez & Reid, 1999) and the publications of such clinicians as Anne Alvarez (1992), who has integrated their ideas within her own original approach.

Melanie Klein in 1930 published the first paper on a child who would now be seen as autistic, and Margaret Mahler and Anni Bergman, working in America within a classical theoretical framework, made seminal contributions beginning in the 1950s. The innovations associated with the Tavistock, however, could properly be called post-Kleinian in that they were influenced by the ideas of Wilfred Bion (1897–1979) and Esther Bick (1902–1983), both major presences at the Tavistock.

Donald Meltzer was one of the Kleinian child analysts who contributed importantly to the Tavistock child psychotherapy training when it was first established in 1948. He continued to supervise many generations of Tavistock child psychotherapy students, and the interest in treating autistic children that he developed in the United States before coming to England led to his forming, in the 1960s, a clinical research group on autism made up of supervisees. The resulting book, *Explorations in Autism* (Meltzer, Bremner, Hoxter, Weddell, & Wittenberg, 1975), included Meltzer's theoretical formulations based on four case histories of children who ranged from profound autism to "post-autistic obsessionality". Of these, three were contributed by Tavistock-trained child psychotherapists (John Bremner, Isca Wittenberg, and Shirley Hoxter).

Meltzer developed the concept of adhesive identification (Meltzer, 1975)—which, as mentioned below, was central to Tustin's work as well—together with Esther Bick. This was linked to his view that autism developed out of the interaction between a highly sensuous child and a mother who was depressed in his first year of life so that, when faced with the mother's depression, the baby easily fell back on attractive, isolated sense impressions that were not linked to information from other senses through the medium of attention. (It needs to be emphasised that this is no longer the received view: there are far more depressed mothers than children with autistic spectrum disorder). This absence of what Bion called "common sense" meant that the baby could form only an inaccurate and distorted picture of the world and other people. Meltzer called this isolation of information from different sensory channels "dismantling", and thought it was important in phenomena such as fetishism as well as in autism. He saw it as a gentle mechanism, unlike the sadistic splitting he encountered in schizophrenia. This linked with his view that children with autism were passionately possessive rather than envious and showed relatively little sadism, though he thought that dismantling could also be a way of avoiding oedipal anxieties. Another important theoretical contribution concerned mutism in relation to inner world constellations, for which Meltzer provided clinical illustrations from autism, manic depression, and schizophrenia, showing how the differing object relations in each condition led to differing impairments in the use of language. Later (Meltzer & Sabatini Scolmati, 1986) he proposed a variety of different pathways (failures of post-natal adjustment or of maternal containment as well as psychotic problems) that, like autism proper, could lead to inadequate mental development with autistic features.

Frances Tustin came to the Tavistock in 1950, as part of the second intake of trainees on the child psychotherapy training organised by Esther Bick. Her analyst was Wilfred Bion, and she was a member of Meltzer's research group, though she did not contribute to *Explorations in Autism*. Meltzer for some time supervised her work with her little patient John, from whom she learned about the existential anxieties associated with bodily separateness. It was John who showed her that he felt that he lost his mouth when he realised that the feeding mother was not part of it:[1] instead of a mouth, he then felt that he had a "black hole with a nasty prick". Other autistic children she saw had bodies that seemed not to fit together properly, so that the two halves looked noticeably different; or they talked about fears of liquefying, spilling out, and being "gone". Tustin had a particular gift for feeling her way into a child's bodily experience and for resonating to their existential anxieties. Like Bick and Meltzer, she emphasised the importance of adhesive mechanisms, in which the child seemed stuck to the surface of adults rather than being able to grow by internalising their qualities. In her own view, her most important contribution was the description of hard autistic objects (Tustin, 1980) which, like the misuse of the child's own body, could produce hard sensations that made the child feel strong; and of soft autistic sensation "shapes" (Tustin, 1984), deriving for example from breath and spit, that were used for self-soothing. These self-generated sensations allowed the child to "encapsulate" himself and to feel safe, but also cut him off from the potential of ordinary human contact. Tustin described ideas such as these in four books and many papers, written in vivid, ordinary language that resonated with parents as well as professionals. Her delineation of the bodily, asymbolic realm has obvious relevance to the current interest in unrepresented states.

Tustin valued the clinical descriptions of primitive experience that she found in Winnicott and Mahler, and her early theorisation followed their ideas concerning an early "autistic" stage of normal development in which mother and baby were undifferentiated. Later, and partly influenced by findings in child development, she revised her formulations, and held that "autism" was always an aberrant pathway (Tustin, 1991, 1994). Unlike Bettelheim (1967), she was emphatic in her belief that parents of children with autism were not to blame for their child's condition. After her death in 1994, Judith and Theodore Mitrani in Los Angeles established the Frances Tustin Memorial Trust,[2] which organises conferences and awards a prize for papers based on her ideas.

Both Meltzer's and Tustin's work has far-reaching implications beyond the clinical treatment of autistic children: their contributions are relevant to fundamental processes in the development of mind. These include asymbolic areas of experience; the evolution of the body image (extended later by Geneviève Haag in France and David Rosenfeld in Argentina); dimensionality; language development; the relation of autism and schizophrenia; and many others. Tustin drew attention to autistic anxieties underlying other conditions such as anorexia, school refusal, and psychosomatic symptoms, which, interestingly, converges with recent work by non-analytic child psychiatrists (Skuse et al., 2009). Sydney Klein (1980), a Kleinian child analyst who, like Meltzer, taught early generations of Tavistock child psychotherapists, has extended this to difficult-to-reach adults. Meltzer's and Tustin's many innovations continue to be developed by their supervisees throughout the world.

Notes

1. Tustin was subsequently made aware of an earlier, brief description by Winnicott (1963) of this phenomenon, and frequently referred to it.
2. Now headed by Alina Schellekes in Tel Aviv.

* * *

Maria Rhode is professor emerita of child psychotherapy at the Tavistock Clinic and University of East London, a member of the Association of Child Psychotherapists, and an honorary clinical associate of the British Psychoanalytical Society. She trained at the Tavistock Clinic between 1969 and 1973, and was supervised then, as well as later, by Frances Tustin and Donald Meltzer. She worked for many years at the Tavistock Clinic (where she was one of the co-conveners of the Autism Workshop), and later also at Camden MOSAIC (an integrated service for children and young people with disabilities, and their families) as well as in private practice with children and adults.

Her particular interests are in childhood autism and psychosis, language development, and infant observation: she has contributed many papers and book chapters on these subjects, and has taught and lectured in the UK and internationally. Her three co-edited books in this area have been widely translated (*Psychotic States in Children*, with Margaret Rustin and Alex and Hélène Dubinsky; *The Many Faces of Asperger's Syndrome*, with Trudy Klauber; and *Invisible Boundaries: Psychosis and Autism in Children and Adolescents*, with Didier Houzel). She has increasingly focused on the potential of early intervention for toddlers at risk of autism and their parents, and recently completed the audit of a case series. In 1998, she was awarded the Frances Tustin Memorial Prize (by the Frances Tustin Memorial Trust and the Psychoanalytic Center of California). Her most recent papers are "Object Relations Approaches to Autism" (*International Journal of Psychoanalysis*, 2018) and "Notes on 'Dick' in the Melanie Klein Archive" (in J. Milton (Ed.), *Essential Readings from the Melanie Klein Archives*, 2020).

CHAPTER EIGHTEEN

Eating Disorders Workshop—Tavistock Adolescent Department

Gianna Williams

When I joined the Tavistock Adolescent Department in 1975 there were many active workshops: Assessment Workshop, Group Workshop, Family Therapy Workshop, Brief Intervention Workshop, Young People's Counselling Service (see F. Balfour, Chapter 20). For a time there had been no Individual Psychotherapy Workshop (IPW). I was asked to join Arthur Hyatt Williams (Department chairman) in reviving the IPW.

The Workshop thrived in a cross-fertilisation between trainees and teaching staff of the Child Psychotherapy Training and members of the Adolescent Department, who almost all attended at different times over the first few years: Arthur Hyatt Williams, who was also co-chair of the workshop, Paul Upson, chair of the Group Workshop, Beta Copley, chair of Young People's Counselling Service, Dicky Bird, chair of the Assessment Workshop, Isca Wittenberg, head of Child Psychotherapy discipline, Anna Dartington, Sally Box, Eve Steel, Elisabeth Oliver Bellasis, Jorge Thomas, and many trainees from all the disciplines.

The work of the IPW was open initially to presentations on any type of individual psychotherapy. Over the years we found that we were gradually discussing, more and more often, presentations where the focus of discussion was on the patient's internal alliances, the ones fostering development and the unhelpful, destructive ones. "Matthew", an alarming "addicted to near death" adolescent presented by Maggie Cohen, was one of the cases we spent a great deal of time discussing. This new focus of the Workshop did not change its name but its character.

We often found that we were discussing cases where eating disorders were present and, in 1983, we decided to focus, at least for a time, on this specific interest. Arthur had been co-chairing the Workshop with me from the beginning and continued to do so after his retirement until the mid-1990s. He was especially interested in an exploration of this particular form of "the constellation of death". We founded the Eating Disorders (ED) Workshop in the early

1980s. I became curious to get to know more about the dynamics of eating disorders cases and began assessing a number of patients referred to the Adolescent Department. The referred patients were predominantly anorexic but some were bulimic, and predominantly, but not only, girls. In some cases the eating disorder was one of many symptoms.

Obviously I could not offer therapy to all the cases. But I gradually came to realise that, for some of these patients, the transition from the person assessing them to a new therapist could be very difficult, especially for the cases that I came to call "no entry" patients (Williams, 1997a, 1997b). If some contact had been made in the assessment, they were often not at all keen to open themselves again to a new person. I thought this might be less likely if the assessment was carried out in a group. I had come to realise that certain patterns involving the family of the patients were recurrent and I suggested that we offer initial family explorations for the eating disordered cases referred to the Department. I carried out a number of these family assessments with Arthur, by then my husband (Margot Waddell organised our engagement party with the Workshop members in 1984), and two papers "Psychic pain and psychic damage" (Henry [Williams], 1981) and "Una famiglia in fuga dalla pena depressiva" (Williams, 1998) were written on cases Arthur and I jointly assessed.

I also worked a great deal in family therapy assessments with Jorge Thomas, Beta Copley, and later with Richard Graham and Steve Briggs. We generally offered a "renewable contract" of four family sessions and in some cases the contract was extended to eight sessions, only on rare occasions to twelve. After one of these twelve-session assessments, the designated patient "Ophelia" who was initially very "hard to reach" accepted, and used, individual work very well, as did the other three members of the family. One of them was seen in the Adult Department— that was a time of plentiful resources.

The family work helped us to identify some recurrent patterns in the families we worked with: one or more members, not only the designated patient, may have a tendency to perfectionism. Obsessional traits were often present. Female anorexic patients often had a near symbiotic relationship with mother, and fathers tended to be excluded and denigrated.

One patient made this pattern very evident by literally "cutting" father out of all the family pictures. There could well be aspects of shared pathology between the designated adolescent patient and one of his or her parents. A glaring example of this came across in a family where mother and daughter were competing about loss of weight. Not only did they eat the same amount and type of food, but they checked, most carefully, on one another's amount of exercise. On one occasion mother hoovered the living room floor in the evening, when the daughter had already retired for the night to her room. The daughter heard the noise of the hoover and rushed to the kitchen to put a potato in the microwave. When mother completed the hoovering she was "ordered" by the daughter to eat the potato to compensate the amount of calories she had lost by hoovering. Mother obliged.

There were "many a typical case": a fourteen year old obese boy kept his hands in the pockets of his anorak all the time and "feigned" pregnancy. He had witnessed mother's traumatic miscarriage at home and was clearly suffering from post-traumatic stress disorder. In more than one case, patients who had become anorexic had perceived themselves as receptacles of parental projections. The attempt to keep out something toxic could stretch to a full "no entry" pattern of defences, which extended well beyond the rejection of food. By contrast bulimic patients were often more accessible to therapeutic work. They appeared to have been more "porous" to (imagined or real) toxic input. They often felt concretely full of persecutory "foreign bodies", very confused, and often relieved if helped to put some order in their states of mind.

In the late 1990s, I joined forces with a member of the Adult Department, Marilyn Lawrence with whom I later edited a whole issue of *Psychoanalytic Psychotherapy* on eating disorders (Lawrence, Mondadori, Simpson, & Williams, 2004). Marilyn had a keen interest in eating disorders and was to write a book about this topic (Lawrence, 2008). She helped me to transform the Eating Disorders Workshop into a PgDip/MA in conjunction with the University of East London (UEL). It took place on one full day and it included discussions in a large group and in small work discussion groups and theory seminars.

The course for "People Working with Eating Disorders" included participants from all professions involved in work with eating disorder patients. A parallel course was opened in the Faculty of Medicine of Bologna University and it was also accredited by the Tavistock and UEL.[1] Most of the students in this course were doctors specialising in adult psychiatry. All teachers in Bologna were also teaching on the London course. Some very interesting dissertations have been written both by the London and the Bologna students, some of which led to publication in the form of journal articles (Morra, 2015, 2018). Many students on both courses were working in different capacities in residential eating disorders units.

The severity of pathology of cases presented in both courses was greater than the one of cases previously discussed in the ED Workshop. There was a great deal of suicidal ideation and severe self-harm. Five patients in an eating disorder inpatient unit in Savona (Italy) had formed a group, or rather a gang devoted to "Thanatophilia": an anticipation of the current websites giving advice to eating disorders patients on "how to do better"—at losing more weight.

There is, even now, in the Tavistock, forty-five years later, an heir to the Adolescent Department Eating Disorders Workshop. It is part of the curriculum of the clinical doctorate in child and adolescent psychotherapy. I co-chair it with Roberta Mondadori, teacher for many years in both the London and the Bologna course. It is entitled "Workshop on Narcissistic Structures". Recently a case was presented very reminiscent of Maggie Cohen's alarming "Matthew" of the 1970s.

The time passes, but unholy internal alliances on the side of death still occur and the discussion continues to offer new and stimulating "food for thought".

Note

1. Italy is only one of the many countries regularly visited by Tavistock psychotherapists for teaching and supervision. The list, not complete, includes Turkey, India, Australia, China, Taiwan, Spain, France, Norway, South Africa, Mexico, Brazil, Argentina, Ecuador, Poland, Russia, Finland, USA, Canada, Germany, Sweden, and Zimbabwe.

* * *

Gianna Williams

I started teaching at the Tavistock half a century ago, in 1970, on the course on the Emotional Experience of Learning and Teaching. This is also the title of the book I co-wrote in 1983 with Isca Wittenberg and Elsie Osborne.

In 1975 I became a member of the senior staff of the Adolescent Department and began teaching on M7 (Working with Children, Young People & Families: A Psychoanalytic Observational Approach) and M8 (now M80, Child and Adolescent Psychoanalytic Psychotherapy Training). I have continued teaching on M80 to this day.

In 1976 I initiated, with the help of Martha Harris, a course in Psychoanalytic Observational Studies in Rome. The first colleagues to help me with the teaching were Isca Wittenberg and Anne Alvarez. In 1978, again with the help of Martha Harris, the Rome course was "Tavistock Accredited" by the Professional Committee of the Tavistock Clinic, when Robert Gosling was chair.

Students who had completed the course in Rome could apply for the clinical training in London. Later, clinical training started in a number of Italian towns. Again Martha Harris made it sound easy and it was. Martha Harris and Donald Meltzer taught on these Italian courses from 1979 to July 1984. In 1979 I inherited, together with Mary Boston, the role of organising tutor of M7. I carried on this role on my own from 1981 to 2001.

In 1992 I revived, with Simonetta Adamo and with the help of bursaries from the Istituto Italiano per gli Studi Filosofici, a bilingual course (the first of its kind at the Tavistock) on Working with Disruptive Adolescents (Adamo & Williams, 1991), started by Sally Box but then dormant for many years. In 1999 I started a Tavistock/UEL course in Eating Disorders at the Tavistock and at Bologna University Faculty of Medicine.

During my years in the Adolescent Department I revived, with Arthur Hyatt Williams, the Individual Psychotherapy Workshop, later to become the Eating Disorders Workshop. For seven years I also ran a workshop on Ethnic Minorities. I have published more than thirty papers and chapters in English and co-edited three books in Italian centred on Tavistock courses. In the area of eating disorders, I published (to start with in English) *Internal Landscapes and Foreign Bodies* (1997) and co-edited the two volumes of *The Generosity of Acceptance*: *Exploring Eating Disorders in Adolescents* (2003) and *Exploring Feeding Difficulties in Children* (2004).

CHAPTER NINETEEN

The creation of a service for children and adolescents facing gender identity issues*

Domenico Di Ceglie

An opportunity to pause and reflect on how one got to a particular point in the development of one's own interests should not be missed. In this case, it is the creation of a service for children and adolescents facing gender identity issues. This remains a mystery to me and it is still surprising how apparently unpredictable sets of events determine shifts in interests and professional activities.

In my case, it was an encounter with a sixteen-year-old in the early 1980s who had been referred by a colleague, Dr Jill Vites, to the Adolescent Department of the Tavistock Clinic. This young person had taken three overdoses and was claiming that she was a boy but in a female body. I knew little about this subject but I decided to take on this case out of curiosity and to expand my training experience. I thought I would also learn more about what it meant to be male or female and the differences between the two. After an initial assessment, I offered this girl, or should I say boy, psychotherapy, which was accepted. At the time she did not ask to be addressed with male pronouns. The impact of this relationship was an unexpected one. I learned very little about gender and sexuality as a good deal of the sessions were spent in silence. My patient would say a few sentences and I would make a few interpretations. The end result was that I could record very accurately what happened verbally in the session. What went on non-verbally—that is another story. I got the impression that there was something very profound about her sense of identity of being a boy which could not be easily explained and that was fundamental to her being.

* This chapter is an edited version of an article by Domenico Di Ceglie originally published as "Castaway's corner" in *Clinical Child Psychology and Psychiatry* 7(3): 487–491. Copyright © 2002 SAGE Publications. Reprinted by permission of SAGE Publications, Ltd.

Colleagues were saying that she was confused about her gender. I discovered instead that *I* would become at times confused during the sessions about her identity, whereas *she* seemed to be very clear that she was a boy and that there was nothing more to find out about this. I was at times made to feel extremely curious in the sessions, only to find out that my curiosity would be frustrated and that it was pointless to pursue my enquiries.

I started to read the work of Robert Stoller (1968, 1975) and other literature on trans-sexualism. These articles concerned mainly work with adults. I found, however, that this reading didn't help as much as I'd hoped in understanding the complexity of this young person's experience. This patient had to move to another town and so her exploratory therapy with me had to come to an end after two years. In one of her last sessions she said that perhaps this form of help had come too late, and that her parents should have been aware of how she was feeling by the way she behaved. She wondered why they had not sought help for her when she was a child. Her thoughts made me wonder why there was no service for children with these rare and unusual experiences. This planted in me the seed for the creation of such a service.

Soon after the end of this experience I became a consultant in child psychiatry in Croydon and started a workshop there with two or three members of staff who were interested in this area. We tried to see all the cases in the London Borough of Croydon—with a population of about 300,000—who presented with gender identity difficulties and we ended up with three or four cases. Some were seen in family therapy and I took one case into individual therapy. This child had some of the features that Stoller had described. However, in the clinical sessions I could find no evidence of a "blissful" relationship with the mother. Stoller (1992) writes: "When extremely feminine boys are studied in childhood, I find that their mothers try to maintain indefinitely a blissfully intimate symbiosis with their son . . ."

I used to see a seven-year-old boy after school as my last case. He made few demands on me as his therapist. This seemed to be the perfect patient to have at the end of a hard day. As soon as he walked in the room he would start to play with the dolls' house, placing all the dolls, which I had provided, in the little rooms, apparently totally ignoring me and tidying up everything near the end of the session. The problem started when I asked him what he was playing. He came up with very elaborate fantasies on how all the children in the house were going to be killed by various means, including the use of poisonous gas released by a cylinder. I was shocked to find out that so much was going on in his mind in spite of the mild appearances of his behaviour. Within a Kleinian perspective (Klein, 1932), if the dolls' house represented the body of the mother, or his unconscious relationship with the mother, there was very little of a benevolent nature going on there. So much for the "blissful" relationship!

By now, I had become convinced of a need for a service for children with gender identity disorders, as they were defined at the time. In 1987 at the international conference of the European Society of Child & Adolescent Psychiatry I had the opportunity to meet Robert Stoller in person. During a coffee break I mentioned to him my project to start a service for children and adolescents. He was very encouraging. He thought that there was a real need for such a service and predicted that there would be many referrals and a lot of interesting work. He suggested that I read and make contact with Richard Green who had been doing clinical work and original research on children (Green, 1968, 1971, 1974).

Some time after that I met for lunch with Peter Hill, at the time professor of child and adolescent psychiatry at St George's Hospital Medical School, to discuss my project. He enthusiastically agreed to support the establishment of a gender identity service for children and adolescents within the Department of Child Psychiatry at St George's. I decided to call it Gender Identity Development Clinic as the emphasis would be in promoting the development, particularly that of gender identity, in the children/adolescents coming to the service. So in September 1989 the service started. The staff included a social worker Mary Lightfoot, a psychotherapist Barbara Gaffney, and a senior registrar Martin McCall. The clinic was held one afternoon fortnightly and then weekly. Later an eminent paediatric endocrinologist from Great Ormond Street, David Grant, offered to run a paediatric liaison clinic once a term in the Paediatric Department at St George's, during which the child/adolescent key worker from our service would join him in seeing the child and the family.

I referred to these two settings as the "theatre of the mind" and the "theatre of the body" to use Joyce McDougall's fitting metaphors (McDougall, 1985, 1989). In our minds as professionals these two spaces need to be integrated and, hopefully, they will then become integrated in the minds of our clients. However, they needed to be seen as clearly definable and visible to meet the psychological needs of the children, in particular teenagers, coming to our service. I also conceptualised some aspects of the paediatric intervention as offering a transitional space, which allowed the engagement of some teenagers who wouldn't otherwise have considered working with us. This mind/body integration, visibly represented by the working together of a paediatrician with professionals involved in psychosocial interventions (see Kraemer, Chapter 16), became one of the primary aims of our therapeutic model.

In 1992 our service, in association with the conference unit at St George's, organised the first international conference on gender identity problems in children and adolescents. John Money presented a paper on the history of the concept of gender identity and gender identity disorder, which was published in 1994 (Money, 1994). The conference allowed a creative sharing of experiences with colleagues who had developed similar services in other parts of the world, particularly Peggy Cohen-Kettenis in Utrecht and Ken Zucker in Toronto. I presented a paper on our model of working in which altering the gender identity disorder per se was not a primary therapeutic objective. Our primary therapeutic objectives were instead the developmental processes, which, from clinical and research experience, seemed to have been negatively affected in the child. Particularly useful was the work of Susan Coates (Coates, Friedman, & Wolfe, 1991; Coates & Spector Person, 1985) on attachment patterns in children with gender identity problems. This therapeutic approach was obviously a paradox for a service for children with gender identity disorders in whom the primary aim was not the psychological treatment of the disorder, which meant the necessity of adapting the mind to the body, as many professionals and people expected at the time. Our stance was to maintain an open mind as to what solution an individual would find to the mind/body conflict. Our task was to assist the child/adolescent and the family in the gender identity development and in the search to find the best possible solution to the identity conflict. Addressing developmental processes, however, might secondarily affect the gender identity development. I remember vividly the controversy that this approach provoked during the discussion which followed my paper. Some professionals seemed shocked that our energy was not devoted to treating the disorder, whereas other members of the audience, particularly representatives of the self-help organisations, appeared relieved that we were not trying intrusively to change these children at all costs.

The method of achieving these aims relies on therapeutic interventions ranging from work with individuals, families, groups, and support and educational groups for parents, to professional network meetings involving teachers, health visitors, social workers, general practitioners, and other mental health professionals involved with the child. In some cases only one therapeutic intervention for a short period was deemed appropriate. In other cases a combination of these interventions was necessary over a longer period. A regular review of the needs of the child/adolescent and the family within a multidisciplinary team was necessary to determine which intervention would be the most appropriate and effective at a particular stage of development (Di Ceglie, 1998).

Over the years we did not have reason to radically change this model and the number of children and teenagers referred to the service gradually increased. However, the model was refined over the years, particularly with reference to physical interventions in adolescents with a transsexual outcome (Di Ceglie, 2014). A committee set up by the Child and Adolescent Faculty of the Royal College of Psychiatrists produced a Guidance for Management for Gender Identity Disorders in Children and Adolescents in January 1998. I refer to this model as the staged approach (Di Ceglie, 2000). Since the start of the service other areas of needs emerged, such as the gender identity and psychosocial difficulties of some children with intersex disorders (now Disorder of Sex Development—DSD) and the management issues raised by children of transsexual parents, particularly in relation to residence and contact disputes.

In 1996, the clinic transferred from St George's to the Tavistock and Portman Trust, based at the Portman Clinic. It organised two further international conferences in 1996 and in 2000. Some of the papers presented at the conference in 1996 were published in a book, *A Stranger in My Own Body* (Di Ceglie, 1998), which also contained a chapter on children of transsexual parents. In the 2000 conference therapeutic models of management of children and adolescents with gender identity problems were reviewed and debated, but a special feature of this conference was the psychosocial management of children with intersex conditions (now DSD). Milton Diamond presented a paper summarising his lifetime's work in this area and giving his views on the management of this condition (Diamond & Sigmundson, 1997). His presentation generated an interesting debate involving a number of self-help organisations. By then it had become clear that there was a need for a specialised service of this kind, covering three areas: (i) gender identity disorder (now gender dysphoria), (ii) some aspects of the psychosocial management of some intersex conditions (now DSD), and (iii) provision of specialised counselling to children and families with a transsexual parent.

During the life of the service, staff and users contributed creatively to its development. For instance, a mother of a child with gender identity problems who was involved in a dispute over contact with her ex-partner, asked me during a court break if she could meet other parents facing similar issues. This was the start of a new development—the running of a group for parents of children with gender problems (Di Ceglie & Coates, 2006). This group became an important feature of our service and then led to the formation of a self-help organisation called "Mermaids". Mermaids had been the focus of discussion in one of the parents' groups in an attempt to understand the fascination that some children have for these mythical creatures. "Mermaids" was a complementary organisation to our service, which offered the kind of help and support that we, as professionals, could not. Its social activities and networks provided a space within society in which children and teenagers with unusual gender development could feel accepted. Their social isolation was reduced and they could start to feel part of a community. Over the years Mermaids became more nationally based and an independent organisation.

With the help of some families within Mermaids, the service became involved in a television programme, *The Wrong Body*, in 1993. The programme featured some of the dilemmas a thirteen-year-old with a gender identity problem had to face within the family and social network. Should this teenager be addressed as he or she and in which gender be accepted in the school? Another dilemma was the timing for the start of physical interventions. This was a courageous teenager who, with the support of his family, wanted to share his experiences with society in an attempt to reduce the isolation and stigma which experiencing this condition attracted. The process involved in the making of this documentary was a very interesting experience for the whole service. At a crucial point during the filming a child protection conference was organised by social services involving a number of lawyers. Two main issues were at the centre of the debate: first, can a teenager of thirteen give informed consent to a programme describing his unusual experience? And second, are the parents really protecting their child by supporting his wish to make public his unusual experiences? In this case, after a lengthy debate a clear decision was made that the programme could go ahead if after seeing the documentary the adolescent and the family agreed to its being broadcast. The programme was shown in 1995. It highlighted clearly the intensity of feelings and convictions experienced by this teenager. A transcript of the relevant part of the interview was published in an article (Di Ceglie, 2009). This documentary had a strong emotional impact on those watching it and was thought-provoking. People were made aware of the seriousness and deep-rooted nature of the identity issues involved. Some teenagers wishing to be open about their atypical gender identity with peers and teachers in school used this video to promote some understanding of their condition.

In this chapter I have described the beginning, the foundation, and the early years of the Gender Identity Development Service. In 2009 the service became nationally funded and

I retired as director. The national funding facilitated the succession plan and created equity in the country regarding access to the service. A new base has been established in Leeds and outreach clinics have been created in other locations. Referral rates have increased considerably in comparison with the early years. In 2004 Parliament passed legislation recognising new gender identities (Gender Recognition Act 2004).

The area of atypical gender identity development remains controversial particularly with regards to physical intervention in young people (Di Ceglie, 2018). Models of care will change as clinical experience and empirical research increase and a new language may develop to describe the experience of diversity in gender identity.

Finally, I hope that GIDS will be able to retain a broad-based approach to issues of gender identity within the context of the multifaceted process of identity development, in line with the Tavistock tradition of thinking.

* * *

Domenico di Ceglie (born 1947) MD, DipPsychiat (It), FRCPysch, is a lifetime honorary consultant child and adolescent psychiatrist at the Tavistock Centre, London; founder and former director of the Gender Identity Development Service (GIDS) at the Tavistock and Portman NHS Foundation Trust, London; honorary senior lecturer, Department of Clinical, Educational and Health Psychology, University College London; Docente, Scuola di Specializzazione in Psicologia Clinica, La Sapienza University, Rome (2015–2018); honorary doctor of education (honoris causa), University of East London, and WPATH emeritus member.

Previously he has been a consultant child and adolescent psychiatrist in the Adolescent Department, Tavistock Clinic; honorary senior lecturer, The Royal Free and University College Medical School, London; visiting professor in adolescent psychiatry, University of Perugia, Italy (1992–1996); psychotherapist (retired), Lincoln Centre for Psychotherapy, London, and a member of the Tavistock Society of Psychotherapists.

He has a long-standing interest in adolescence and has worked in adolescent inpatient units. He has been widely involved in consultative work to organisations and to professional networks. He has been organising tutor of an MA course accredited by the University of East London in adolescent mental health for professionals.

In 1989 he founded a specialist service for children, adolescents, and their families facing gender identity issues at St. George's Hospital, London, now based at the Tavistock and Portman NHS Foundation Trust. He was the service's director until March 2009. GIDS provides a multidisciplinary service countrywide, consultation, training, and research, and has been nationally designated and funded. He has developed models of care for children and adolescents with gender variance and dysphoria and has been involved in research projects. He has widely published papers about his work and co-edited a book, *A Stranger in My Own Body—Atypical Gender Identity Development and Mental Health* (Karnac, London, 1998). He was highly commended in the Health & Social Care Awards, 2004. He gives frequent lectures worldwide.

CHAPTER TWENTY

The establishment of the Young People's Counselling Service*

Fred Balfour

The YPCS owes its existence to the creative vision of two distinguished psychoanalysts, Moses and Egle Laufer, who subsequently went on to develop the Brent Consultation Service. In the late 1960s, a charitable foundation financed the Laufers' proposal for a counselling service for young people on the condition that eventually it should be absorbed into the National Health Service. True to the condition set by the foundation, once the service was sufficiently established, the Laufers opened discussions with the then Tavistock Adolescent Department chairman, Dr Derek Miller, to test whether the Department could absorb a counselling facility. This took place shortly after the Tavistock Clinic, together with The Tavistock Institute of Human Relations moved into their new, purpose-built accommodation in Swiss Cottage in 1967.

There were the expected problems associated with establishing what was to be a non-medical service within what was widely recognised as a medically run psychiatric outpatients clinic. As this was such a significant departure from the Clinic's culture up to that point it may aid an understanding of the YPCS if what was involved in achieving the change is set out briefly. At the time, the psychotherapeutic treatment provided in virtually all the Tavistock's clinical units was conducted by consultant psychiatrists, their senior registrar colleagues in training, and, on occasion, supernumerary doctors on training courses who worked under the supervision of a consultant psychiatrist. Non-medical staff provided diagnostic and associated support work. (Child psychotherapists were an exception. In the then Department for Children and Parents and the Adolescent Department as well, they treated patients supervised by their

---

* Though its initials have remained the same, the YPCS is now the Young People's Consultation Service. https://tavistockandportman.nhs.uk/care-and-treatment/our-clinical-services/young-peoples-consultation-service-ypcs/

senior psychotherapist colleagues with a named consultant psychiatrist who was kept informed of progress and who took medical responsibility for the conduct of the work.)

Referrals came from GPs who were familiar with the prevailing culture. GPs expected that the patients whom they referred to the Clinic were either directly or indirectly under the care of a consultant psychiatrist who was responsible for their treatment. So a completely non-medical, non-treatment unit taking responsibility for its own work was an unusual addition. Until then, all the work that was classified as treatment was in the hands of doctors who carried a responsibility for the care of all patients. From the perspective of the present, the concern felt at the time about the change in culture may seem both odd and exaggerated. But the way in which the YPCS expected to function had to convince all concerned that professionally responsible work comparable to the securely established medically provided psychoanalytic psychotherapy treatment services would be offered to those using the service.

This meant that the YPCS had to have a clear definition that made it distinct from the general treatment culture of the Clinic. The Clinic's normal task was to train senior registrar level psychiatrists and child psychotherapists for work as psychotherapists in the NHS and in doing so provide a clinical service to referrers. The YPCS, by contrast, was to be a non-treatment, counselling service for young people who had been self-referred, and operated in a way that was independent of medical supervision and medical responsibility. (Care was taken not to encourage the notion that the YPCS could be used as a side door into the psychotherapy service of the Adolescent Department. Nevertheless, it was of great benefit to the nascent service that it had as a backdrop a sophisticated psychiatric clinic from which advice could be sought from medical staff and, when appropriate, have some young people referred on to one of the clinical treatment units.)

The reason for this detailed description of the culture into which the YPCS was born is to emphasise that, for the first time in the Tavistock Clinic's history, *a preventative service* was offered. While its counselling work was in ways similar to the practice of psychotherapy, the differences marked it out as distinct from the psychoanalytic psychotherapy provided in each of the three departments of the Clinic.

There was an additional and timely justification for the provision of the approach to the emotional and psychological problems of the mid-adolescent to young adult population. The policy of the Adolescent Department in those days was not to offer a consultation to anyone unless there was a treatment vacancy available following the initial consultation. Adolescents, it was judged, had enough to contend with as a result of their psycho-biological stage of development not to have to endure the uncertainties of a waiting list prior to being taken on for treatment. (The Adult Department on the other hand, always beset with more referrals than it could handle, had no choice but to operate a waiting list both for initial consultations and then again as it sought to find a therapeutic vacancy for its patients.) In contrast, because the young people seen in the YPCS were self-referred and not expected to be offered more than four sessions, the number and speed with which counselling appointments could be provided was so much greater than could be managed in the psychotherapy arm of any of the Departments.

There was another sense in which the incorporation of the YPCS into the Adolescent Department proved to be particularly timely. When adolescents took up a departmental psychotherapy vacancy, almost invariably the time scale for the treatment was expected to be for as long as was considered to be clinically necessary. Consequently, professional staff were soon fully booked and could not predict when their next vacancy would arise. However, an examination of the Department's appointments records over a period of time showed that, even when provided with an open-ended offer of individual psychotherapy, roughly one in three of those taken into treatment dropped out of the work within six sessions of the start. A further third dropped out within eighteen sessions. It seemed, therefore, that the culture of an open-ended offer of treatment was most suitable for the remaining third of those thought to be in need of long-term psychoanalytic psychotherapy. That raised the possibility that something about what may be termed the adolescent process might be inimical to long-term commitments and to the level of personal exposure involved in long-term depth analytical work.

That notion additionally backed the strategy adopted by the YPCS. It was believed that, ideally, not more than four psychoanalytically informed counselling sessions, aimed at confronting the current, major point of concern of the young person and an exploration of the underlying factors which may have caused or exacerbated their problem, might help them to take better charge of their lives and enable them to move forward. If such a benefit could result from limited help, the hope was that it might also support their efforts to manage other emotional challenges in the future. Finally, it was hoped that a positive experience of seeking help might allow them to approach counselling and psychotherapeutic services and make better use of them should they find that to be necessary in the years to come.

Of course, the professional staff of the unit realised that, because young people were to be self-referred, the service would attract not only those who were suitable for the limited work on offer but others who were not. (Clinical departments, in their offer of psychotherapy, saw cases referred to the Clinic screened on the whole by GPs who judged their expected suitability for treatment prior to their first consultation.) The YPCS, it was realised, without a similar screening barrier might find itself confronted with a Pandora's box full of psychiatric disturbance which might defeat the limitations of a brief counselling service. Happily, experience showed that not to be the case. Young people who were too disturbed to have their condition addressed adequately within the restrictions of the service provided by the YPCS were referred on for more extensive help either internally or externally to the Clinic. It seemed possible that many of those who were thought to be unsuitable for counselling may have been aware of just how disturbed they were but feared to have that confirmed by a psychiatrist. We assumed that for them it helped to have a gradual, hopefully a benign, first experience of asking for help—thus finding it easier subsequently to accept a referral to a proper treatment facility.

During its early years, it was not possible to assess adequately the efficacy of the YPCS. Having to face the emotional discomfort involved in the self-examination required in the work showed that the experience could be seriously exacting for those who undertook it.

As a result, it was regarded as important and, perhaps, even significant if young people were able to tolerate and work effectively within the constraints of the counselling. As a temporary measure of the value of the service, the evidence that young people completed all four of the consultations they had agreed to attend, was taken as some, hopefully not too slight, measure of the value of the service in appropriately addressing the young person's problem. Needless to say, the aim of the counselling was to provide an experience that was accurately diagnostic and therapeutic in its effect. But the work was conducted robustly and could in no way be seen as only supportive of the young person in distress. That made the capacity to live up to the verbal agreement entered into at the outset of the counselling all the more important in supporting the hope that subsequently the young person might be able to manage his or her life with less distress and without further professional intervention. Weekly staff case conference meetings (see "the seminar group", Young & Lowe, 2018) supported the staff which comprised child psychotherapists, clinical psychologists, and social workers, to assess the progress of each other's work and provide guidance with referrals when help beyond counselling was required.

* * *

Fred Balfour (1934–2019) was a psychoanalyst and a consultant clinical psychologist who worked at the Tavistock Clinic from 1962–1996, initially in the Adolescent Department, moving to the Adult Department in the late 1960s. He founded the Young People's Counselling Service and was one of the group of staff who originally set up the Tavistock Interdisciplinary Training in Adult Psychotherapy (M1). He was also involved in the establishment of both the United Kingdom Standing Conference for Psychotherapy and the British Confederation of Psychotherapists (BCP, now BPC, the British Psychoanalytic Council), representing the British Psychoanalytical Society in this endeavour and serving as the BCP's first registrar. He also worked as a consultant at the Institute of Marital Studies (now Tavistock Relationships).

CHAPTER TWENTY-ONE

Facing it out: the Adolescent Department

Margot Waddell

It gives me particular pleasure to be contributing to this book a brief overview of the Adolescent Department. The Department was, in bygone days, appropriately located on the middle floor of the main Clinic building—sandwiched between the Department for Children and Parents on the ground floor and the Adult Department on the third. This was my clinical home and I have Anton Obholzer to thank for realising that that was where I might find my own place.

Bearing in mind the inspiring work with children that had begun with Melanie Klein, Anna Freud, and Hermine von Hug-Hellmuth in the wake of the First World War, it is rather astonishing that it was not until the end of the Second World War that work began focusing on the nature and timing of the adolescent years. This was, perhaps, additionally surprising because Freud had long recognised the significance for development in those years between childhood and adulthood, and had been an admirer of G. Stanley Hall's prescient insights at the beginning of the century. Hall's classic two volumes, *Adolescence*, had been published in the United States in 1904 and were much admired by Freud (whom Hall hosted for Freud's first and only visit to America in 1909).

As its "biographer", Henry Dicks (1970) gave an interesting and comprehensive account of *Fifty Years of the Tavistock Clinic* from its establishment in 1920. He describes the origin of the Clinic as providing psychodynamic thought to the treatment of shell-shocked soldiers. Dicks also stresses the Clinic's commitment, from the first, to understanding the patient as a product both of his environment and of his own history. The multidisciplinary team, then comprising the psychiatrist, the psychologist, and the social worker, was regarded as central to the study of all aspects of the personality: "the child as father of the man and parents as conditioning the new generation of children". The Clinic was positioned "somewhere between official psychiatry and medicine on the one hand, and 'orthodox' psychoanalysis on the other" (Dicks, 1970, pp. 1–2).

When the Clinic first became part of the NHS on July 5, 1948, it was located in Beaumont Street, in central London, and was divided into the Adult Department and the Department for Children and Parents. It was not until the end of the 1950s that a nascent unit for the treating of adolescents, nearby in Hallam Street, was also established. This was staffed by Dugmore Hunter, Elizabeth Hunter, Derek Miller, and also Isca Wittenberg who went on to set up the Young People's Consultation Service (see below). In 1965 under the leadership of Jock Sutherland, the foundation stone for a new clinic was laid. The building, in Swiss Cottage, was opened in 1967, and a space was available to create a department especially for work with adolescents in this newly built Tavistock Clinic. Miller had been working with adolescents at the Menninger Clinic in the United States, and Dugmore Hunter was dedicated to realising a professional initiative that would offer a service to the mounting problem of "disturbed and anarchic youth" (Dicks, 1970, p. 262), but also to their families and to the social settings that were involved in their care.

Under John Bowlby, as head of the Department for Children and Parents, it was Esther Bick, a close colleague and collaborator of Melanie Klein, who was chosen to be the first organising tutor of the child and adolescent psychotherapy training, and she remained so for eleven years. The training brought together strong links with the community (the welfare state and the public sphere generally) and with a rootedness, through Mrs Bick's work, in observation. Observation was a discipline regarded by Freud, Klein, and certainly later by one of Klein's analysands, Wilfred Bion, as essential to a psychoanalytical frame of mind. Such links were central to a training in adolescent psychotherapy. The goals and functions of the child and adolescent psychotherapist, or psychoanalyst, became clearer: to understand and to render meaningful troubled aspects of the personality by bringing insight to bear on the nature of the internal world and its mixed population of figures, benign and persecutory.

Where adolescence was concerned, and as Hall had emphasised forty-five years earlier, the worlds of this population must always be seen as significantly entangled both with the changes in the youngsters' bodies and brains and also with the external familial, social, cultural, and educational realities in which the teenage years are lived out. Members of the Adolescent Department over the years, whether support staff, trainees, psychiatrists on placement, or staff from all disciplines, attest to the very special nature of a Department in which ways of teaching and learning attracted professionals who thrived on being part of a "work group" of psychoanalytically, systemically, community-minded professionals who worked in the Department, often for many years.

The staff group was always strong and adventurous with a wonderful line of chairmen and women—among them Anton Obholzer and Robin Anderson. Those were the days when staff elected their leaders—that is, the Adolescent Department was always a collective and was dedicated to the creative effort to remain attuned to the time that was, perhaps, first officially recognised by Philippe Ariès (1960). Ariès describes the cost to the younger generation of, as he put it, the "calamitous war of youth slaughter". It was with this slaughter, during the First World War, "in which troops at the front were solidly opposed to the older generations at the rear", that, Ariès suggests, "the awareness of youth really began" (1960, p. 28). (W. R. Bion's early experience of war as a tank commander at the front, aged nineteen, throws a fascinating and terrible light on the madness of the whole enterprise, as he described in *The Long Weekend*, 1982.)

It was also a Department that, true to its original founders, maintained the services that it set out with. Interestingly, of central significance, and rightly so, was the Young People's Consultation Service (see F. Balfour, Chapter 20)—a self-referral opportunity for youngsters of up to 30 years old to engage in four consultation sessions with psychoanalytically trained therapists. In the course of my many years' work in this service there were numerous occasions when I would listen to comments, made movingly or anxiously like the following: "Oh—I never thought of it like that," or "This is a revelation, I need to think about things in a different way now."

In its position at the heart of the new building, the Department became central, too, to the evolution of the Tavistock's identity and its impact both nationally and internationally. It was about learning what "being a grown-up" means, and the flexibility that the Department always embraced, as to the time frame of what could be regarded as "adolescence" was crucial. The little boy who said to me, many years ago, "When I grow up I want to be a dult," could have had little sense of how great was the difference between looking "grown-up" and *being* grown-up.

In his foreword to an exceptional book on adolescence, one published early on in the Tavistock Clinic Series, A. Hyatt Williams wrote eloquently about his sense of the work of the Clinic, and later of the Adolescent Department in particular. The book, *Facing It Out: Clinical Perspectives on Adolescent Disturbance* was edited by Robin Anderson and Anna Dartington (1998). It forms a remarkable collection of papers about a wide range of adolescent problems and their impact on the families concerned. I shall conclude with the foreword written by Hyatt, as we knew him, some years after his distinguished staff role in the Department itself.

> "Facing it Out" is a challenge and a history. It sounds determined and "Churchillean" in tone in that it inspires enthusiasm and effort which will be revealed as the book is read.
>
> Many times during my work in a forward area in the Burma Campaign in the early 1940s, doing what was called Forward Psychiatry, I met senior colleagues who told me about the Tavistock Clinic. I was interested in the psychodynamic approach and by then realised already the fact that an emotional breakdown was made more chronic for every 100 miles the psychiatric casualty needed to be evacuated away from the battle area and the comrades he knew and liked. I was impressed that the Tavistock medical staff seemed to know how to deal with the complicated therapeutic task with which we were confronted. They seemed to be interested in understanding and solving these problems both from a scientific and human perspective.

After the war was over it was many years before I managed to obtain a post at the Tavistock Clinic, and was then a "foiled circuitous wanderer". This was in 1962. In 1966 the large modern building was built and consequently projects and work with patients were greatly facilitated. Thus it was possible for the Adolescent Department to have a proper home of its own.

In 1969 my work at the Tavistock Clinic was increased and I was based in the Adolescent Department. From then until I retired in 1979 was the happiest professional time in my life. "How can we do it" was the question, not "How can we avoid doing it". In the three departments and the closely associated Tavistock Institute of Human Relations, there was a constant flux of creative enthusiasm dynamised by a devotion to both intrapsychic work and work on the complexities of interpersonal relationships. This attention both to the external struggles in the world of adolescents and the significance of their deepest inner feelings is what is special about the Tavistock Clinic and the work of the Adolescent Department. I have encountered nothing like it anywhere else in the world.

The battlefields may look different, but the environment of our 1990s inner cities does not provide an easy setting for development and the young people who succumb are no less in need of help. Often what is lost is the capacity to have hope. Without it whatever resources there may be available cannot be utilised. One of the primary therapeutic tasks in working with young people and their parents is to help them recover hope but this requires those working with them to have the inner and collective resources to sustain themselves against all-pervading despair which can so easily infect those that work with the mentally ill.

I am very glad that the current generation of clinicians in the Adolescent Department is continuing to provide this unique combination of science and humanity to the current generation of adolescent casualties (Hyatt Williams, 1998, pp. ix, x).

[Margot Waddell's biography appears on p. xiii]

Part IV

Couples and families

CHAPTER TWENTY-TWO

A brief history of Tavistock Relationships

Andrew Balfour

In the 100 years since the birth of the Tavistock Clinic, a number of organisations have been part of the wider "Tavistock family" of institutions. These have included: the Tavistock Institute of Human Relations, the Tavistock Institute of Medical Psychology, the Tavistock Career and Education Consultation Service, and Tavistock Relationships. The eminent psychiatrist Henry Dicks, writing at the time of the fiftieth anniversary of the Tavistock, saw it as having a corporate identity, within which these separate, constituent organisations "... are not only preserved but positively valued" (Dicks, 1970). Tavistock Relationships is the organisation formerly known as the Family Discussion Bureau (FDB) when it was launched in 1948. For an organisation that has specialised in developing the psychoanalytic understanding of the couple relationship, it is apposite that it began its life as the progeny, so to speak, of a couple—Enid and Michael Balint—both of whom knew something of the difficulty of couple relationships as, for each of them, theirs was a second marriage. Needless to say, although this offers us a neat "oedipal" dimension to our beginning, the reality is a little more complicated. Perhaps though, before we move on to discuss the historical detail it is worth observing that this "creation myth" of a founding couple which linked the Family Discussion Bureau with the Tavistock Clinic, contains a truth—of the history of the close relationship between the two institutions. Throughout its lifetime, Tavistock Relationships has been a "sister" organisation to the Clinic, with a history of personal and professional links and sharing a common approach of rigorous grounding in clinical work as a basis for research, training, and the application of analytic thinking to the broadest range of human problems; a mission to reach people and touch areas of human experience that have not before had the benefit of analytic understanding. It is this distinctive "Tavistock approach", with its focus on developmental challenges and developmental possibilities throughout the lifespan, which has been at the heart of the work of Tavistock Relationships since its inception.

This account could begin in a number of places, but, to set the scene, perhaps one foundational element is the social policy context, and the Denning Report of 1947. This paved the way for state sponsorship of psychotherapeutic work with couples, and for the positioning of the organisation as one dedicated to social welfare, but operating outside formal structures of the welfare state. As Denning conceived it: "There should be a Marriage Welfare Service … sponsored by the State but not a State Institution … (it should be) a function of the State (to support) marriage guidance as a form of social service" (Renton, 1990).

The organisation began its life as the "first non-medical channel in Britain for professional work with families" (Trist & Murray, 1990b, p. 7). Unlike the Tavistock Clinic, it did not join the new National Health Service when this was launched, but stayed as an independent organisation. Since 1979 it has been an operating arm of the Tavistock Institute of Medical Psychology, the charitable organisation that was the first, pre-NHS, institutional home of the Tavistock Clinic when the latter began in 1920. The Family Discussion Bureau had its roots in the aftermath of the Second World War, and the challenges of rebuilding social cohesion and stability. Families had been devastated by separation, loss, and displacement; returning fathers were often traumatised by their experiences and the civilian population had been directly affected by bombing, separation, and many other privations. There was tremendous social upheaval and disruption to social structures, particularly the place of women—who had taken on traditionally male occupations on the "Home Front". It is hard for us now to imagine the speed and the scale of social and emotional disruption to which families of the time had to adjust.

In 1946, Enid Eichholz, working for the Family Welfare Association in London, established the Family Discussion Bureau in which volunteers offered basic talking therapy to couples in distress (Kahr, 2017). She appreciated that, in order to develop this pioneering work, she would require assistance from senior mental health professionals and so she turned to Dr Tommy Wilson (A. T. M. Wilson), a psychiatrist at the Tavistock Clinic in London who, after the war, specialised in the resettlement of British soldiers (Wilson, 1947, 1949; Wilson, Trist, & Curle, 1952). Wilson championed Eichholz's project and introduced her to his colleagues at the Tavistock Clinic, who offered support, encouragement, and clinical supervision, notably, Dr John Bowlby and Miss Noël Hunnybun, as well as Dr Michael Balint.

In 1953, Enid Eichholz married Michael Balint (which at the time was regarded as a scandal, as both were divorcees) and at this point Lily Pincus, a Jewish émigré from Germany, became the director of the Family Discussion Bureau, which eventually became housed within the Tavistock Clinic itself. Pincus collaborated closely with Dr Jock Sutherland, who was the medical director of the Tavistock Clinic, and who championed the development of marital therapy. Enid Balint published very little about the early work on couple psychotherapy, but Lily Pincus, a much more passionate writer, harnessed her colleagues to share their experiences in print and in 1955, the Family Discussion Bureau published its first book, *Social Casework in Marital Problems: The Development of a Psychodynamic Approach* (Bannister, Lyons, Robb,

Shooter, & Stephens, 1955). With these foundations in place, the institution began to develop not only a clinical service but also a professional training, a research arm, and a series of publications. This early focus on writing and publication has been sustained and, since then, Tavistock Relationships has produced more than 700 publications, which have had national and international influence in the development of the field of couple and family mental health.

In the early years the clinical service was provided by non-medical "caseworker" staff, working in pairs as co-therapists, supported by regular case discussion groups chaired by a medical, psychoanalytically trained consultant—initially, in "Balint groups", where staff were helped to think about their countertransference arising in the work. This method later became associated with GP training (Pincus, 1960; see Elder, Chapter 8). These groups constituted a forum in which psychoanalytic theories of individual development were translated into an understanding of interactive processes in couples and also service delivery relationships (see, for example, Bannister & Pincus, 1965). As part of the Tavistock Institute of Human Relations, this learning was supplemented by group relations training. These developments ran alongside work in the Tavistock Clinic (Dicks, 1967), with which there was a cross-fertilisation of ideas.

Lily Pincus was succeeded by Douglas Woodhouse as chair of the staff group in 1963, a position he held until his retirement in 1980. The FDB changed its name to the Institute of Marital Studies in 1968 to reflect its status as a practice-informed training and research body. The 1960s saw a spurt in the growth of training, including the creation of intern fellowships for experienced practitioners working in other agencies and providing extra-mural training for, in particular, the Probation Service (which undertook marital and divorce-related work at the time) and the National Marriage Guidance Council (now Relate). It also saw the IMS housed in the same premises as the Tavistock Clinic in Belsize Lane.

In the 1970s the IMS extended its reach into understanding the functioning of couples suffering from learning disability (Mattinson, 1973), brief work with marital problems (Guthrie & Mattinson, 1971), specific illnesses in children (Mainprice, 1974), and the dynamics of supervisory relationships (Mattinson, 1975). The decade also saw the Institute's first major action research projects: investigating work with couple relationships in a group of social services clients (Mattinson & Sinclair, 1979) and developing a preventive intervention programme for couples expecting their first child (Clulow, 1982). The IMS also contributed to the development of public policy informing a national review of services to couples (Home Office, 1979). During this decade there was a significant amount of interaction between the IMS and the Clinic, lubricated by a bar situated on the fifth floor of the Tavistock Centre overseen by "Lofty" Simpson, head porter and self-appointed quartermaster, whose wife served as company secretary of the Tavistock Institute of Medical Psychology for a period in the late 1980s and early 1990s.

Janet Mattinson succeeded Douglas Woodhouse as chair of the IMS in 1980 until 1987, when she was succeeded by Chris Clulow until 2006. The 1980s was a decade of transition. Responding to the drive for non-adversarial proceedings in the management of divorce, the Institute undertook an action research project with a team of Family Court welfare officers to explore the feasibility of mediating between parents whose disputes had resulted in court-ordered welfare reports (Clulow & Vincent, 1987). The decade was one that saw rising rates of unemployment resulting in the Institute undertaking a study of the meaning of work and loss of employment on marriage (Mattinson, 1988). There was also research on telephone helplines (Colman, 1989) and inter-agency collaboration (Woodhouse & Pengelly, 1991). Alongside this "external" work the Institute produced another text on the practice of couple psychotherapy (Clulow, 1985) and a book for the layperson (Clulow & Mattinson, 1989). Papers from its fortieth celebration conference were published (Clulow, 1990), an occasion used to add the name "Tavistock" to its title to indicate the specific approach to "marital studies" it was taking. A significant development during the decade was establishing the first couple psychoanalytic psychotherapy training in the UK, and setting up a professional association for its graduates. Part of the background to this was a movement towards the registration of psychotherapists, discussions in which staff of the Institute played an active part—which led to the establishment of the British Confederation of Psychotherapists (now British Psychoanalytic Council). The decade saw the staff title change from the psychodynamic social work term "caseworker" to "marital therapist", a title that was to be succeeded by "couple psychoanalytic psychotherapist" in the 1990s.

The 1990s witnessed a step change of focus in thinking about the theoretical underpinning of psychoanalytically informed couple psychotherapy that has been summarised in conceptual histories of couple psychoanalysis in the UK (Clulow, Nyberg, & Hertzmann, 2018; Morgan, 2019a). Three major publications assembled this post-Kleinian perspective on the internal world of the couple (Fisher, 1999; Ruszczynski, 1993; Ruszczynski & Fisher, 1995), providing a strong conceptual and methodological basis for the training of couple psychoanalytic psychotherapists. In order to provide a feeder for this specialist training (a pyramid model of training with broad courses at its base and increasingly specialist training at its apex) the Institute organised a series of interdisciplinary events and lectures addressing the changing context of family life. These were assembled into publications (Clulow 1993, 1995, 1996). By the end of the decade the Institute had entered into an agreement with the University of East London enabling it to offer academic degrees for some of its courses at certificate, diploma, MA, and professional doctorate levels.

During the decade, and partly in response to growing pressure from funders for evidence of the effectiveness of psychotherapy, the Institute debated what kind of research might satisfy the scientific community without compromising the essence of its work that addressed unconscious processes operating in couple and in psychotherapeutic relationships. Two approaches from developmental psychology were pursued, with support from the Adult Department of the Tavistock Clinic and colleagues from the United States. One was based on attachment theory (Fisher & Crandell, 2001) and one on Kleinian theory (Lanman & Grier, 2001). Drawing on the resources of the Clinic to think about outcome research was not new; an attempt to apply an approach used in the Adult Department had been trialled in the 1980s (Balfour, Clulow, & Dearnley, 1986). This research emphasis was evident in the conference celebrating the Institute's fiftieth anniversary (Clulow, 2001). This was a welcome exchange across departmental boundaries in the Tavistock Centre, as was the production of the "Tavistock Pantomimes", a cross-departmental event, which one member of the Institute co-authored and co-produced (Pengelly & Sprince, 2011; see Sprince & Pengelly, Chapter 42). The decade also saw a growth in international contacts and multidisciplinary training around divorce and separation in the context of the 1995 Family Law Act, work on the impact fertility problems and the death of a child have on couples, sexuality in later life, and cross-cultural marriages. A significant invest-ment was made in developing "training the trainers" consultative programmes (Hughes & Pengelly, 1997), aimed at front-line mental health and social care settings, which continued to operate well into the early 2000s.

In 2004 the name of the organisation was changed to the Tavistock Centre for Couple Rela-tionships, acknowledging the diverse forms of partnership in contemporary society. Clinical work continued in conjunction with the Tavistock Clinic, entering into a partnership project with its Marital Unit and a publication coming out in the Tavistock Clinic book series (Grier, 2005). Perhaps the most significant development during this period was the decision to absorb into its operation the clinical and training services that had been offered by London Marriage Guidance before it went into administration in 2004. This increased the size of the organ-isation substantially, and resulted in services being offered from two sites in London rather than one, affording the organisation its long sought-after critical mass of staff on which sub-sequent developments could be based. In 2006, Susanna Abse became chief executive and in this period the organisation was able to build on this opportunity, with significant growth in the size and scale of its operations. In 2009 TCCR moved from the third floor of the Tavistock Clinic building to its own premises, in Warren Street. This was a significant development for the organisation, for the first time occupying its own separate space with room for expansion, which happened quickly over the following decade. As part of this, a strategic shift was made to devote more resources to influencing the public policy landscape. One of the aims was to raise awareness of the growing research base linking the quality of the parental couple relationship to children's development, making the case to funders for the importance of intervention with parental couples to improve child and family outcomes.

While clinical research had always been at the heart of the institution's ethos, and there had been some innovative research projects undertaken in the 1980s and 1990s as well as ear-lier, in the 2000s more formal outcome research was initiated. Regular research seminars were established, developing new projects and supporting the organisation's academic training pro-grammes. Two studies in particular inaugurated this new approach of quantitative outcome research—one, adapting a psychoanalytic measure developed in the Tavistock Clinic (Hobson, Patrick, & Valentine, 1998; Lanman, Grier, & Evans, 2003) to look at the effectiveness of psycho-analytic work with couples (Balfour & Lanman, 2012); the other, evaluating a couple-oriented parenting support programme in partnership with a mental health agency (Clulow & Donaghy, 2010). Tavistock Relationships also published an international evidence review (Abse, Casey, Hewison, & Meier, 2016).

The organisation also took the step of conducting a randomised control trial, evaluating an intervention for parents experiencing high post-separation conflict (Hertzmann et al., 2016).

At this time, a long-standing relationship with two academic and clinical psychologists, Professors Philip Cowan and Carolyn Pape Cowan, reaped significant rewards. They had developed couple-focused programmes showing good outcomes for children in the US (Cowan & Pape Cowan, 2009). Tavistock Relationships was funded by government to trial this approach in the UK, and over five years successfully delivered the intervention to more than 500 couples with significant outcomes in improved couple relationships, parental mental health, and children's well-being as well as reducing couple conflict (Casey et al., 2017). In 2016, an analysis of the outcome data gathered from more than 850 patients seen in Tavistock Relationships' psychoanalytic clinical service was published (Hewison, Casey, & Mwamba, 2016), in what was the largest naturalistic study of couple psychotherapy outcomes ever undertaken worldwide. Results showed significant effects on both mental health and relationship quality.

I became chief executive in 2016. Throughout these years, Tavistock Relationships continued to build on the social mission that the organisation had always sustained, seeking to develop new interventions directed at key social problems. These have been grounded in psychoanalytic thinking and formulated in ways which aim to attract support from commissioners and policy makers. This work has included interventions and services for couples in high-conflict divorce (Shmueli, 2018); separated parents in entrenched post-separation conflict over contact arrangements with their children (Ministry of Justice, 2018); couples living with dementia (Balfour, 2014, 2020; Balfour & Salter, 2018); couples in conflict around parenting (Hertzmann et al., 2016); couple therapy for depression, developed as part of the NHS Improving Access to Psychological Therapies programme (Hewison, Clulow, & Drake, 2014); couples facing retirement (Khan, 2018); adoptive couples (McCann & Polek, 2020); parental couples where there has been domestic violence (Benjamin, Chahal, Mulley, & Reay, 2018); and, most recently, taking a lead role in training staff and delivering clinical work as part of Reducing Parental Conflict Programmes being rolled out nationally by the Department for Work & Pensions (DWP); working in partnership with an inner London local authority to develop psychotherapeutic work in the area of learning disability and mental health; developing a new approach to working with inter-parental conflict in the context of alcohol dependence, funded by the Department of Health and Social Care (DHSC). All of these projects have been undertaken within a research design framework that enables rigorous evaluation and which supports their longer-term development.

Over the decades surveyed here, Tavistock Relationships' psychoanalytic clinical services have remained at the heart of its work and informed the development of its wide range of innovative programmes. These clinical services have expanded significantly and today the organisation delivers more than 20,000 sessions a year of psychotherapy, with three psychoanalytic/psychodynamic clinical trainings offered at master's degree level. At the same time its international influence has grown significantly, as Mary Morgan describes in Chapter 23 in this book. This is reflected in the trainings, lectures, and joint working that have taken place across the globe over the past decades, in Australia, China, the US, and Europe—and in our popular annual summer schools which attract a diverse international group of clinicians to Tavistock Relationships.

In 2018, Tavistock Relationships held its seventieth anniversary conference, when it launched its two most recent books, one celebrating the range of its innovative work (Balfour, Clulow, & Thompson, 2018) and the other, a landmark text on the theory and technique of psychoanalysis with couples (Morgan, 2019a). In 2019 the organisation moved to a new building in Hallam Street, a few doors away from the site that in the 1950s and early 1960s housed the Family Discussion Bureau, the Tavistock Institute of Human Relations, the Tavistock Clinic's Adolescent Department, and its library. Tavistock Relationships was moving back to its roots, so to speak, though what is evident from this brief survey is how it has never really left them—with the essence of its early approach, of working on the borderland of internal psychic life and external social problems and tackling these in distinctive ways, still very much in evidence today, as in 1948. Despite different degrees of relative emphasis on clinical work, research, and training at different points in its history, what is evident is the inextricable linkage between them throughout the life of the organisation. This key integration of elements is what Dicks (1970) termed the "internal integrate or matrix of the total Tavistock organization". It is this which, most of all, identifies Tavistock Relationships as part of the "Tavistock family"—holding throughout to this distinctive synergy of practice, training, research, and innovation that is traceable from our earliest beginnings, remains strongly evident in the work of subsequent generations, and which provides a creative foundation for the future.

Acknowledgements to Susanna Abse, Chris Clulow, and Brett Kahr for their help.

* * *

Andrew Balfour trained as a clinical psychologist at University College London and then as a psychoanalytic psychotherapist in the Adult Department at the Tavistock Clinic, where he subsequently worked for more than ten years, developing work in the area of later life. He also trained as a couple psychotherapist while working at Tavistock Relationships, where he was clinical director before becoming chief executive, a post he has held since 2016.

CHAPTER TWENTY-THREE

Tavistock Relationships and the growth of couple psychoanalysis 1988–2019: a personal memoir

Mary Morgan

When I arrived at Tavistock Relationships (TR) in 1988 as a student, it had just celebrated its fortieth anniversary. There were about ten members of clinical staff and a handful of students and together with long-serving administrative staff, we occupied part of the third floor of the Tavistock Centre. Though not part of my training or later job description I felt I had joined a kind of "special interest research group", with the expectation of building on the pioneering work of our predecessors such as Enid Balint, Lily Pincus, and Kathleen Bannister. This was underpinned by Douglas Woodhouse and Janet Mattinson having secured TR with government funding in the years immediately before I arrived. I saw TR as an organisation which could dedicate itself to understanding the couple relationship, in particular its unconscious components, provide an effective clinical service, and through training, research, and collaboration, support others in the wider field who were engaged in helping couples, families, and children.

In recognition of the close links to the Tavistock Clinic, that year it changed its name from the Institute of Marital Studies to the Tavistock Institute of Marital Studies (and several name changes later to Tavistock Relationships). In a publication celebrating the fortieth anniversary conference Chris Clulow wrote,

> Our roots have always been firmly in the Tavistock tradition. We have long years of association with the Tavistock Centre, we share a philosophy of life and a framework of beliefs with the Tavistock Clinic and with our parent body the Tavistock Institute of Medical Psychology. We have in common a mission to build bridges and understanding and practice between the wisdom of psychoanalysis and the ordinary experiences of everyday life. (Clulow, 1990, p. 21)

This Tavistock tradition feels palpable and enduring for those who have trained and worked within it. It came to my mind recently when teaching couple psychotherapy to a new group in Poland with Stan Ruszczynski. A student said to us, "You're different from other teachers in that you seem to be interested in what *we* think." It struck me that what he described—engaging with others, learning from that experience, and questioning and developing one's own thinking as part of that process, is so much a part of the Tavistock approach. Another is the close interrelationship between clinical work, training, research—central in TR and through much of the Tavistock. At TR it felt not just a description of the work we were engaged in but a state of mind. I experienced these three components existing, sometimes in great tension together, as each giving more life to the others. For example, although at TR one might be mainly focused on clinical work and training, this always felt imbued with a research mindedness. Perhaps because the theory and practice of analytic work with couples was still a relatively new discipline, there were questions, for example, about technique and the efficacy of treatment, the difference between co-therapy or one therapist, whether the gender of the therapist(s) mattered, how to think about the frame, along with concept building. Psychoanalytic concepts had needed elaborating in relation the dyad—for example, *shared* unconscious phantasy and *shared* defences (Bannister & Pincus, 1965), projective identification as it manifested in a *couple projective system* (Bannister & Pincus, 1965), and the reflection process (Searles, 1955) both in supervision and between the co-therapists (Mattinson, 1975). These kinds of modified concepts were developing out of clinical experience of analytic work with couples. New couple psychoanalytic concepts had developed and continued to do so—unconscious choice of partner and marital or couple fit (E. Balint, 1993; Cleavely, 1993), marriage as a psychological container (Colman, 1993), the idea of a marital triangle (Ruszczynski, 2005), a couple state of mind (Morgan, 2001, 2019a), and the creative couple (Morgan, 2005).

TR's training in couple psychoanalytic psychotherapy was only formalised the year before I arrived, previously knowledge and skills being transmitted through internships, including the special opportunity of being an apprentice by doing co-therapy alongside an experienced clinician. Once formalised, it became the foundational training for all core clinical staff and has contributed to the expansion of the small clinical staff group to a staff group of core and visiting clinicians of 150, in 2019. The training became MA validated by UEL and also as a professional training, the only one to be accredited by the British Psychoanalytic Council (BPC) in its psychoanalytical section. Since 2004 when London Marriage Guidance was incorporated into TR, there have been two other clinical trainings, one in couple and individual psychodynamic counselling and psychotherapy and another in psychosexual therapy, as well as an introductory course and many continuing professional development events.

By 1988 several collaborative projects had taken place or were underway, applying an understanding of relationships to other settings, something that has grown and continued to the present time (see A. Balfour, Chapter 22). During my time at TR, there was also an expansion of trainings offered to those who wanted to develop an understanding of analytic work with couples, particularly internationally. This followed the dissemination of a growing body of knowledge about psychoanalytic work with couples, now described in many parts of the world as couple psychoanalysis (see Clulow, 2009; Fisher, 1999; Grier, 2005; Morgan, 2019a; Ruszczynski, 1993). The international journal *Couple and Family Psychoanalysis* was established in 2011, superseding the former *Psychoanalytic Perspectives on Couple Work*, which had started in 2005. The work of TR has contributed to an important shift from analytic work with couples being seen as an adjunct to individual analysis or therapy to a treatment of choice—a valid therapeutic process in its own right.

Collaborative work with other institutions who shared an interest in analytic work with couples and families developed and continues today with either current or former staff of TR, for example with the Washington School of Psychiatry and the International Psychotherapy Institute, which is reflected in publications (Scharff & Savege Scharff, 2014). Between 1992 and 1995 we joined Swedish colleagues in delivering a three-year accredited couple psychotherapy training in Sweden and in 1999 we began the delivery of a three-year programme for colleagues in San Francisco, a fruitful partnership which led to them setting up their own training based on the TR model in 2010 (Nathans & Schaefer, 2017). There were also several visits to Finland to contribute teaching to a four-year programme on couple psychotherapy, and between 2013 and 2015 two years of providing seminars to colleagues in New York. Currently there are two collaborations in Poland, one in Warsaw that has been ongoing since 2013, and a three-year collaboration that has begun recently with a group who come together in Poznan. Next year will be the fifth conference in Poland on psychoanalytic work with couples and families, which attracts more than 350 participants. In recognition of this development a new couple analytic section will, in 2020, be created by the Polish Society for Psychoanalytic Psychotherapy. There have also been teaching events by TR staff in other parts of the world, for example Australia and China.

The theory and practice of TR's psychoanalytic approach to couples is also represented on the International Psychoanalytical Association's (IPA) Committee on Couple and Family Psychoanalysis (COFAP), which has put on conferences in Washington, Buenos Aires, Madrid, Naples, and San Francisco, with another planned for Beijing, and has produced many publications (Keogh & Palacios, 2019; Scharff & Palacios, 2017; Scharff & Vorchheimer, 2017). There are also links with the couple and family section of The European Federation for Psychoanalytic Psychotherapy (EFPP) and the International Association of Couple and Family Psychoanalysis, which, because of its roots in French and Spanish speaking analytic worlds, has enabled the interchange with different analytic perspectives on the couple, notably an understanding of "the link" (*el vínculo*) (Berenstein, 2012; Pichon-Rivière, 1980).

The founding caseworkers of TR (then known as the Family Discussion Bureau) turned to psychoanalysis to help understand the conflicted and distressed couple relationships they were encountering in their work. This relationship between psychoanalysis and the ordinary lives of people—adults, adolescents, families, children, and couples—that is so much part of the Tavistock tradition—has been creative and globally influential and sparked developments very alive today.

* * *

Mary Morgan is a psychoanalyst and couple psychoanalytic psychotherapist, fellow of the British Psychoanalytical Society and senior fellow of Tavistock Relationships. She is an honorary member of the Polish Society for Psychoanalytic Psychotherapy.

She joined Tavistock Relationships in 1988 as a student, coming from a background in psychiatric social work and later casework with the Family Welfare Association. She developed and led multidisciplinary teams in newly created family centres. She joined the staff of Tavistock Relationships in 1990, later becoming the head of clinical services and then until very recently, reader in couple psychoanalysis and head of the MA in couple psychoanalytic psychotherapy. Her career at Tavistock Relationships spanned thirty-one years.

She has been particularly interested in contributing to the theory and technique of couple psychoanalytic psychotherapy or couple psychoanalysis. She has published more than thirty articles in the field of psychoanalysis and developed concepts which are widely used such as "a couple state of mind", "the creative couple", "unconscious beliefs about being a couple" and "a projective gridlock". She edited with Andrew Balfour and Christopher Vincent *How Couple Relationships Shape Our World* (2012). In 2019, her book *A Couple State of Mind: Psychoanalysis of Couples and the Tavistock Relationships Model* was published by Routledge. It is considered a landmark text which describes both the theoretical and clinical approach of Tavistock Relationships developed over the last seventy years and her own conceptual thinking and technique.

She has taken a leading role in disseminating the Tavistock Relationships model internationally through writing, supervision, participating in conferences and teaching in many parts of the world. She has been part of setting up and teaching on courses and trainings in Sweden, San Francisco, New York, and Poland. She is on the boards of several scientific journals in psychoanalysis and couple and family psychoanalysis. She is also the European member of the IPA Committee on Couple and Family Psychoanalysis (COFAP), whose aim is to share and learn from different analytic approaches to couples and families and to support those working in this field within the wider community.

She currently works in private practice as a psychoanalyst, couple psychoanalyst, and supervisor and maintains links with Tavistock Relationships.

CHAPTER TWENTY-FOUR

Family therapy across the decades: evolution and discontinuous change

Sarah Helps, Sara Barratt, and Gwyn Daniel

Introduction

The story of the creation and evolution of family therapy and the systemic discipline at the Tavistock, like all stories, takes multiple forms. Each teller brings forth different and partial aspects of reality, reflecting different contexts both past and present. However, one shared narrative is that of immense pride in the way that the Tavistock Clinic has pioneered systemic psychotherapy in the UK and beyond over the past five decades.

In this chapter, we each comment on different aspects of the rich history of systemic psychotherapy at the Tavistock Clinic, our own particular experiences of training, therapy, research, and management, as well as highlight some of the most important recent developments.

The first fifty years

Systemic family therapy is a youngster compared to its psychoanalytically informed colleagues. But the principle of taking a holistic and contextual approach to people's difficulties is discernible from the inception of the Clinic in understandings of people within their relational context. In his account of the first fifty years of the Tavistock Clinic, Henry Dicks says that

> Emanuel Miller [1892–1970] was probably among the first in Great Britain to include something like the whole family in the treatment. The concept of family therapy, of regarding the family as a unity and the [child] patients' difficulties in no small measure related to the interpersonal nexus with the parents, runs with great continuity through the

theoretical base on which the Tavistock Clinic and the later Institute of Human Relations was developing. (Dicks, 1970, p. 58)

In the wake of the Second World War the first reference to treating groups and couples was the establishment of the Family Discussion Bureau in 1948 (see Morgan, Chapter 23), the first incarnation of Tavistock Relationships. This was formed by social workers and psychoanalysts with the purpose of exploring why families were struggling, focusing on issues such as post-war family disruption and trauma, the changing roles of women, and increasing understanding of the impact of early years development. In the 1950s and 1960s, after a decade or so of working with children and parents, a research strategy was established by John Bowlby and Jock Sutherland (deputy director and director of the Tavistock Clinic respectively), exploring both therapeutic and family processes, using transcribed recordings. This emergent relational research in part set out to test their notion that children's presenting difficulties were linked to tensions within the family, including the sequelae of loss by separation or death.

A similar interest and indeed similar research methods were shared by family and therapy researchers across the globe (McQuown, 1971). Gregory Bateson's pioneering work on family influences on schizophrenia (Bateson et al., 1956), led to his "double bind" theory. Ronald D. Laing, who was training at the Clinic at the time, learned of Bateson's work from John Bowlby.[1] "In 1962, the Tavistock paid [Laing] for a research visit to the USA, where amongst others he met Gregory Bateson … which profoundly influenced Laing's thinking on the functioning of families of schizophrenics" (Lucas, 1998, p. 1234). Laing later became a leader of the "anti-psychiatry" movement. While his accounts of family processes were brilliant and poetic, a tendency to blame parents and especially mothers did not always lead to productive therapeutic engagement with families.

As the clinical service developed as part of the recently formed NHS, Bowlby, chair at the time, outlined the tasks of the department: promoting the health of children and families within communities, understanding what makes for healthy development and enhancing the range of techniques to support healthier functioning. Bowlby gave priority to referrals where the identified patient was under five and "the hitherto neglected step of seeing fathers at the time of diagnosis was given particular attention" (Dicks, 1970, p. 190). Even so, while the basis for working with families, groups, and wider systems was emerging, the idea of "family therapy" itself was yet to assume significance.[2] Over the next decades there was an extraordinary blossoming of new theorising and innovative clinical practice, brought about by an expanding group of talented clinicians who drew upon radical ideas and influences from outside the Tavistock itself.

In 1969, John Byng-Hall (1937–2020), child psychiatrist, joined the Tavistock Clinic, eager to learn from Bowlby and to develop thinking about families (Byng-Hall, 2002). Key to his approach was the notion of attachment, and the importance of engaging with families in enhancing their own resources to overcome difficulties, rather than the more traditional "diagnostic" approach espoused by earlier clinicians. As a trainee at Hill End Adolescent Unit Byng-Hall was co-author of a landmark paper "The Reason for Admission as a Focus of Work for an Adolescent Unit" (Bruggen, Byng-Hall, & Pitt-Aitkens, 1973) written in parallel with, but without reference to, the structural therapy of Minuchin (1974) and his colleagues.

In the early 1970s Byng, Hall's reorientation included family stories or "myths", which evolved into notions of the family script, the "story" through which families organised and regulated themselves, thus providing a bridge between the individual and the family (Byng-Hall, 1973). In his early papers the language of psychoanalysis, of defences and the unconscious featured strongly, as it did for Sally Box (1979) who used a similar approach when working with families in the Adolescent Department. But over the years family therapy developed a different language, influenced by colleagues such as Rosemary Whiffen, a social worker who was instrumental in bringing in new ideas from across the Atlantic. While attachment frameworks were more consistent with prevailing theories at the Tavistock, the new systemic thinking presented a "discontinuous leap". Understanding individuals and families within the ecology of their relational and social worlds, finding frameworks for exploring relationship patterns, analysing the complexities of communication and the levels of context within which they are embedded required new conceptualisations. Explanatory frameworks now drew upon systems theory, cybernetics, and the natural rather than the human sciences. In particular the work of Gregory Bateson was pivotal.

While much theory thus emerged from outside the clinical context, these influences were accompanied by an unparalleled flowering of innovative therapeutic techniques, many presented by American therapists such as Salvador Minuchin and members of the Ackerman Institute in New York. It is important to emphasise that social worker/clinicians such as Rosemary Whiffen and Gill Gorell Barnes, who took leading roles in developing family therapy at the Tavistock Clinic, brought a perspective which included the impact of the social environment, class inequality, poverty, and family structural change. Work with poor or marginalised families, especially those who were recent migrants and with families where a member had a "psychosomatic" illness was hugely enriched by the work of Salvador Minuchin (Minuchin & Fishman, 1979), who came to the Tavistock in 1972 and 1978; in the latter working with staff and trainees in the Department for Children and Parents. (His earlier visit was confined to a sabbatical in the Adult Department where he had no impact on clinical practice there.) His intense, challenging, and proximate engagement with families and his use of experiential moves within the session aimed at creating structural change. Minuchin's confidence that families have the resources to do things differently seemed to upend many cherished assumptions about the nature of the therapeutic process.

The other key influence was from the Milan group of family therapists who developed an elegant and compelling application of Bateson's ideas to clinical practice (Selvini Palazzoli, Boscolo, Cecchin, & Prata, 1980). Their work was taken up at the Tavistock Clinic by David Campbell, Ros Draper, and Caroline Lindsey, producing many influential publications and—not without much contention within the systems team—a separate clinical training, based on the Milan approach. Although this never developed into a "split" it did reveal some profound differences, primarily in relation to theory. While Minuchin's therapeutic practice might appear highly unorthodox in the Tavistock context, its theoretical approach could nevertheless be seen to lie on a continuum which delineated "healthy" and "unhealthy" family functioning. The Milan approach, while it explored family interactions and their relationship to intergenerational patterns and beliefs, took a rigorously neutral therapeutic position which avoided making judgements regarding normal or abnormal functioning. The emphasis was instead on the opening up of new systemic connections through the use of circular and reflexive questions and a stance of openness to unexpected or idiosyncratic outcomes. The Milan approach lent itself particularly well to work with organisations, and Campbell, Draper and other colleagues' work in this area has had a particularly profound impact across the globe (Campbell, 1995; Campbell & Huffington, 2008).

The 1970s was thus an exciting period for family therapists within the Tavistock and outside; many were also involved in creating the Institute of Family Therapy, and there were creative links with the Maudsley and Great Ormond Street Hospitals and with the Marlborough Family Service.

In 1975, John Byng-Hall and Rosemary Whiffen had initiated the first Family Therapy training, centring upon the innovative practice of live supervision within small therapeutic teams. For those of us who did this training, what was inspirational, if initially discomforting, was the opportunity to have our own therapy observed and to receive direct feedback from supervisors on the process of therapy itself and, crucially, our own part in it. It also meant that the interplay between theory and practice was a live, open, and accessible process in which each could be seen to reciprocally act upon the other. For example, teamwork brought to life and grounded in our process the systemic concepts of multiplicity, of feedback loops, and of reflexivity. As systemic ideas and practices become more embedded, so critiques began to emerge, many directed at assumptions of therapeutic expertise and the need to consider issues of gender, culture, and power (Burck & Daniel, 1995).

Sara Barratt

I joined the Tavistock in 1996, with responsibility for some of the systemic trainings. Despite the national and international reputation of our family therapy group, and the extensive trainings we developed, we were employed within our first professions and it was not until 2003 that systemic psychotherapy became a recognised profession within the Tavistock and, as the first "Trust-wide" head of systemic psychotherapy I represented the group, for the first time, as the lead of a recognised profession within a largely psychoanalytic institution. My aim was to promote our ways of working, and to highlight the importance of teamwork in thinking about the needs of children and families. Alongside this, all Clinic teams within the Child and Family Department included systemic psychotherapy as we dispersed into different geographical and specialist teams. Although I worked hard to develop services with the Adolescent and Adult Departments, the discipline remained largely employed within the Child and Family Department.

Much of my experience reflects Gwyn Daniel's contribution below. The Clinic has always been an exciting place to work, with colleagues developing systemic practice with a wide range of client groups in the UK and overseas. Family therapists were centrally involved in pioneering work with refugees, in schools, with families with a serious illness, with fostering and adoption, family violence, divorce, and with parental mental illness. The expertise provided by those working with children and families in the Sexual Abuse Workshop, convened by Arnon Bentovim, Carolyn Okell Jones, and Tilman Furniss (see Trowell, Chapter 34), was crucial in ensuring that child sexual abuse was recognised and that professionals were provided with skills to listen to and protect children.

In our multidisciplinary teams we contributed new ideas about engaging often reluctant families and of affirming their relationships in ways which increased motivation for change. This was especially welcome in a clinical context where deficit and pathology were so often the dominant discourses. It could lead to tensions with other members of the Clinic teams if our approaches were occasionally seen as naïve or superficial, or verging on the collusive, and where there were disagreements about the frequency and duration of therapy. But we were also aware of how much systemic thinking and practice was valued by many of our colleagues especially in understanding and intervening in the complex nexus of inter-professional and inter-agency relationships surrounding children and families.

Gwyn Daniel

When I took up a clinical and training post in the Child and Family Department in 2000, having worked in both child and adult mental health, I was keen to make connections with the Adult Department where family therapy had yet to make much impact. I was invited to give a presentation there. On my way up the stairs I encountered a systemic colleague who asked where I was going and on being told, responded: "You are very brave!" I never felt that such divisions and polarities were helpful and indeed one of my most pleasurable experiences at the Tavistock Clinic was providing live clinical supervision to groups of psychiatrists undertaking psychoanalytic training. I had long experience of training systemic psychotherapists in this way but the interchanges and mutual challenges that emerged in our discussions—often heated in the cauldron of the therapeutic process—were especially stimulating and rewarding.

The desire to engage with "upstairs" and to provide clinical services to adult families continued and has been addressed in a small way though the provision of a service via the Lifespan team, an all-age service for people with autism spectrum conditions and their families (Helps, 2016a; Helps, 2016b). Indeed, as Sara has observed, it is often in the context of specialised work with a group of service users such as these who require a multi-model and multidisciplinary approach that the most interesting and valuable creative edges develop.

Having left the Tavistock Clinic in 2006 and now involved mainly as a visiting lecturer I look back with great nostalgia and affection at the ambience within the systemic team. No group of professionals is without its tensions and rivalries of course but there was a particular atmosphere of openness to new ideas, generosity, humour, and mutual support among the team that felt very special. Alongside the adoption of social constructionist and narrative approaches, systemic therapists included issues of power and wider social contexts in their thinking. Questions of diversity, marginalisation, racism, and gender constraints and inequities became increasingly central to our approach. The systems team not only did a great deal of innovative thinking on these subjects but challenged ourselves on our own cultural assumptions and how they affected our interactions with families and indeed with each other as colleagues. Our students both within the UK and from overseas trainings have played a pivotal role in provoking new thinking and new actions. Colleagues such as Inga-Britt Krause, Reenee Singh, Gillian Hughes, and Taiwo Afuape have pioneered cross-cultural work and influences from ethnography, from narrative therapies, and from liberation psychology have been especially effectual in recent years.

Sarah Helps

Recent developments

Clinically, systemic psychotherapists now sit firmly within all teams within the Child, Young People and Family Directorate and the Gender Identity Development service, numbering about fifty staff. We are the largest group of systemic psychotherapists in the UK. Inevitably, as the populations we serve change and as the commissioning landscape alters, services evolve. After many years of leading the field (Amias, Hughes, & Barratt, 2014), the Refugee team was reshaped and staff now utilise their expertise within the context of the borough-based CAMHS teams. Systemic input to services for children with gender dysphoria has expanded dramatically, as has all the work in this area. While faced with the evolving shape of services and teams, wherever possible we continue to work using a reflecting team model; even so, the challenges of finding the necessary physical and staff space, despite the evidence for the efficacy of this way of working, keep mounting.

Clinical trainings remain a core aspect of our work and, in partnership with the University of Essex, we support students from their first foray into systemic thinking through qualifying level courses and beyond. The systemic doctorate at the Tavistock is the longest standing in the UK. Multi-theoretical workshops and longer training courses have also evolved, which situate systemic theory and practice alongside psychoanalytic and cognitive-behavioural models.

Together with the staff at the Institute of Psychiatry, Psychology & Neuroscience, Tavistock staff have contributed to the development of the systemic arm of the Children and Young People's IAPT training. This training is designed to boost the knowledge and skills of mental health clinicians providing a working knowledge of systemic theory and practice to enable them to work in an evidence-based way with children, families, and broader systems.

There has been a long history of training social workers to work systemically and this has continued apace in recent years within the context of the reclaiming social work movement. Camden social workers have all been trained in systemic ideas and now use a reflective and reflexive model of systemic supervision as standard practice (Dugmore, Partridge, Sethi, & Krupa-Flasinska, 2018).

When I took up the post of Trust-wide head of discipline in 2016, there was an increasing shift towards rigidity of boundaries between clinical, research, and training tasks. This created fragmentation, inflexibility, and a partial undermining of job satisfaction by constraining the creativity that emerges from productive interactions between these domains. Despite this, the clinician-trainer model is still highly regarded.

While completing research remains a challenge within limited resources, the systemic discipline produces a steady stream of publications drawing on evidence-based practice and practice-based evidence (see for example, Barratt & Lobatto, 2016: Burck & Hughes, 2018; Helps, 2018; Krause, 2019; Partridge, Dugmore, Mahaffey, Chidgey, & Owen, 2019) We are proud to host the Family Therapy and Systemic Research Centre, pioneered by Charlotte Burck, which collates and celebrates research that informs and is informed by systemic theory and practice. Our master's and doctoral research students continue to produce high quality and influential papers (see for example, Watson, 2019).

Contemporary systemic clinical, teaching, and research practice at the Tavistock involves diverse and innovative clinicians who hold the professional tension of being dual-trained. A cornerstone of all practice is a reflexive consideration of the positioning of the therapist as both influencing and influenced by the work, a commitment to anti-discriminatory and socially just practices, and a commitment to working across difference. While there continue to be robust and spiky discussions across a variety of theoretical divides throughout the building, space to work across difference in the service of the families who we see and above all to stay in dialogue remains ever more important.

Notes

1. Alongside Laing, Bowlby cites Bateson, Jackson, Haley, & Weakland's double bind paper in a footnote in Volume 2 of his trilogy (Bowlby, 1973, p. 363).

2. In a 1977 interview with Alice Smuts, John Bowlby describes opposition to family therapy from his departmental colleagues. "One of them, I recall, accused me of cruelty to the children involved" (Duschinsky & White, 2019, p. 208), but he did have psychiatric colleagues, such as Freda Martin, who while still a trainee published a paper on initial meetings with both parents, without the child, challenging prevailing child guidance practice. "It seems to us that this pattern is one with which the traditional child guidance procedure appears actively to collude, and that, once established, such collusion may be difficult or impossible to break. Often its effect is to make the father retreat still further, and appear to be unaware of difficulties in the family or unconcerned about them" (Martin & Knight, 1962; see also Martin, 1977).

* * *

Sarah Helps initially trained as a clinical psychologist. Working at the child and family mental health and liaison service at King's College Hospital in the 1990s she became fascinated by structural family therapy and so completed her initial systemic training at the Institute of Psychiatry, after which she completed her qualifying training at the Institute of Family Therapy. She has worked in the NHS in and around London over the past twenty-five years. Combining her psychology, neuropsychology, and systemic interests, her clinical work involves working with children whose early development has gone awry and is concerned with the impact on the child, family, and wider system. Following in Sara Barratt's clinical footsteps, she currently works with children who are in foster or kinship care, children who are adopted, and their families and networks. She also works as an expert witness in the family courts and has written (Helps, 2015) about the challenges of doing this work from a systemic and social constructionist perspective.

Recent research publications include writings on the ethics of researching one's own practice (*Journal of Family Therapy*, 2017), systemic work with families where a person has an autism spectrum condition (*Journal of Neurorehabilitation*, 2016), and using autoethnography to explore use of self (*International Perspectives on Autoethnographic Research and Practice*, 2018). She completed a doctorate in systemic psychotherapy at the University of Bedfordshire in 2019 and used multiple qualitative research analytic methods to explore clinical material created with families who came to a CAMHS clinic.

Sarah is now Trust-wide head of systemic psychotherapy at the Tavistock and Portman NHS Foundation Trust where she holds clinical, supervisory, training, and leadership roles.

Sara Barratt is a systemic psychotherapist, supervisor, and trainer, working privately and in general practice. She is the training standards consultant to the Association for Family Therapy (AFT), and a member of the AFT course accreditation committee. She is also a visiting lecturer and mentor to supervisors on the qualifying training at the Tavistock Clinic, where she is part of a team providing systemic consultation for local authority social service teams.

Her first profession was in social work and she qualified as a family and systemic psychotherapist in 1989. She worked as a social worker in child protection and adult mental health from 1970 until moving to CAMHS in 1990.

After working as director of training at the Institute of Family Therapy, Sara joined the Tavistock Clinic in 1996 and, over the next twenty years was the chair of the introductory and intermediate courses on Systemic Approaches to Working with Individuals, Families and Organisations. She was joint chair with David Campbell of the master's degree course in systemic psychotherapy until 2003 when systemic psychotherapy became a recognised discipline within the Clinic and she became the head of systemic psychotherapy. She joined David Campbell, Charlotte Burck, and subsequently Laura Glendinning to teach on the systemic supervision course and co-chaired a training programme in Malta.

Her clinical base was as team manager of the Fostering, Adoption and Kinship Care team. The multidisciplinary team specialised in working with adoptive and kinship families and looked after children with their social workers and carers. Alongside a range of different therapeutic approaches, the team provided groups for adoptive parents and children, and worked closely with other specialist services to develop our thinking and practice in this specialism.

Alongside professional articles and chapters, she co-edited (with Charlotte Burck and Ellie Kavner) *Positions and Polarities in Contemporary Systemic Practice: The Legacy of David Campbell* (Karnac, 2013) and (with Wendy Lobatto) *Surviving and Thriving in Care and Beyond: Personal and Professional Perspectives* (Karnac, 2016)

Gwyn Daniel is a systemic psychotherapist, supervisor, and trainer in private practice in Oxford and a visiting lecturer at the Tavistock Clinic. She has worked in the NHS since 1971 in child psychiatry, CAMHS, and adult mental health settings. Her first profession was in social work and she trained as a systemic psychotherapist at the Tavistock in 1984. In 2000 she took up a post in the Child and Family Department at the Tavistock Clinic and was joint chair, with David Campbell, of the master's degree course in systemic psychotherapy. In her clinical work in the department, Gwyn specialised in working with families where there is high conflict between parents, and with children and families where a parent has a diagnosis of psychiatric illness. She ran training workshops and short courses on this topic and (with Reenee Singh) developed an open access course, Families and Beyond, which introduces systemic thinking to a wide range of professionals and non-professionals. An online version of the course has been accessed by people from all over the world. As well as numerous professional articles and chapters, her publications include, with Charlotte Burck, *Gender and Family Therapy* (Karnac, 1995), with Gill Gorell Barnes, Paul Thompson, and Natasha Burckhardt, *Growing Up in Stepfamilies* (Oxford University Press, 1998), and, co-edited with Charlotte Burck, *Mirrors and Reflections; Processes of Systemic Supervision* (Karnac, 2010). Her latest book is *Family Dramas: Intimacy, Power and Systems in Shakespeare's Tragedies* (Routledge, 2019).

Part V

Working with adults

CHAPTER TWENTY-FIVE

Brief psychotherapy: practice and research

David Malan

I trained as a psychoanalyst, used analysis in therapy and recognise that the insights from analytical thinking remain as valid as ever, but I have always been concerned that the process takes a long time. As a way of resolving emotional problems only a relatively small number of patients can be treated. Therefore I have tried to find the most effective treatment that can help a greater number of patients in the shortest possible time, and my research and writing has focused on this.

As a senior registrar and psychotherapist at the Tavistock Clinic in 1956, I joined a group of experienced colleagues working with Michael Balint, researching whether brief focal therapy was effective. We treated patients using a radical interpretive approach and evaluated the results according to specified criteria and, in general, the results were highly encouraging. In 1967, as a consultant in the Tavistock Adult Department, I developed a Brief Psychotherapy Workshop. All trainees were required to attend and present cases using the principles of brief psychotherapy under my supervision. The aim was to achieve effective therapeutic results in the fewest number of sessions and to research the factors that made this possible.

A cornerstone of the method of treatment was the integration of the "two triangles"—the "triangle of conflict" (defence, anxiety, and hidden feeling) and the "triangle of persons" (current, transference/present, and past) and this has become central to much of experiential dynamic therapy. The triangle of conflict illustrates the relation between anxiety, defences, and the underlying impulses or feelings. The triangle of persons shows the links between the relationship with the therapist, with current people in the patient's life, and with people from their past. In therapy, the relation between them for the patient at any given moment can form a reliable basis for many of the interventions that the therapist makes.

In the workshop the technique used was actively interpretive, using the integration of the triangles as the key. Research from the workshop exploded the "myth of superficiality" by which critics maintain that brief psychotherapy is a superficial treatment that can only be effective with superficially ill patients, bringing about superficial results. In my view the aim of every session is to put the patient in touch with as much of their true feelings as they can bear and the long-term outcome should demonstrate deep and lasting changes. The work does not have to be focal and limited to specific problems but can lead to therapeutic changes that are wide-ranging, deep-seated, and permanent.

An account of twenty-four therapies completed by trainees from the Adult Department using this active interpretive technique is summarised in *Psychodynamics, Training and Outcome in Brief Psychotherapy* (Malan & Osimo, 1992). It is based on the follow-up of a series of patients treated as part of the Brief Psychotherapy Workshop and demonstrates that good therapeutic results can be achieved even by trainees if they are well supervised.

In 1974, Dr Habib Davanloo visited the Tavistock Clinic and showed his work using videotapes. When a surgeon in Iraq, Dr Davanloo observed that a patient's recovery could be helped by the use of psychotherapeutic interventions and so he did an analytic training. He became a therapist and, after moving to Montreal, for twenty years videotaped his sessions with patients—with their consent—reviewing them to see which interventions were the most productive and effective. Dr Davanloo's active, interventionist, and often challenging approach was antipathetic to colleagues at the Clinic but as a scientist I could not dispute the results which were conclusive and convincing. The tapes showed undeniable evidence that patients could be treated in relatively few sessions (forty or fewer) and fully recover from a range of long-standing emotional and psychosomatic illnesses. The essence of Dr Davanloo's approach—called intensive short-term dynamic psychotherapy (ISTDP)—is to enable the patient to reach and experience hitherto unconscious feelings which have been governing their emotional responses leading to deep-seated neurotic patterns of behaviour that in many cases have crippled their lives.

The essential intervention is to ask the patients what they feel. Then to block the tactical defences, including those in the transference, persistently and systematically until their buried feelings can be truly experienced. The therapist does this by challenging the defences that the patient has been using to avoid painful feelings of loss, grief, anger, hate, and guilt about people whom they loved and/or needed when children. Dr Davanloo's technique was often abrasive which was an anathema to me but then I realised that the challenge was to the defences, not to the patient directly, and the relief and gratitude of the patients at their recovery was self-evident. Although it could be a painful process, the therapeutic results were compelling.

Initially my therapy had been actively interpretive but after seeing the work of Dr Davanloo it shifted in emphasis to a more affective, experiential approach. Dr Davanloo and I worked together for twelve years from 1974, leading to many conferences and workshops worldwide, with Dr Davanloo showing his tapes while I outlined the rationale and objectives of his technique and explained the elements of the therapy itself. At the same time Dr Davanloo was doing core trainings teaching his method.

After my retirement in 1982, I collaborated with Dr Davanloo on many books and articles as I am convinced that he has developed a very effective and powerful form of treatment which is applicable to a wide range of patients, often resulting in their complete recovery in relatively few sessions. Later it became clear that the therapist does not have to be so abrasive when challenging the defences but the same results can be achieved by persistently and repeatedly blocking them much more gently until they dissolve. This then enables the patient to experience the buried painful feelings, the avoidance of which underlies many of their neurotic and psychosomatic symptoms.

A number of ex-trainees from Dr Davanloo's core trainings formed a group using intensive experiential dynamic psychotherapy (IEDP). I became honorary president of the IEDP Association which adheres to the basic tenets of ISTDP—namely, to help patients experience their buried, previously unconscious painful feelings and thereby become freed from their reactive power, while giving the therapists greater flexibility in how they reach that point. All sessions are videotaped if patients give permission, and most do, so that the work can be reviewed by the therapist, and supervision is more focused.

In 1991, the first International Experiential Dynamic Therapy Conference was organised in Milan by Ferruccio Osimo, who had trained and worked in the Adult Department at the Tavistock Clinic. It was immensely successful and many subsequent conferences and training courses followed internationally. Having repeatedly seen videotapes overseas showing impressive outcomes with long-term follow-ups that demonstrated that the therapy was often truly life transforming, I decided that the tapes should be shown in the UK, and hopefully ISTDP would come to be used in the NHS.

To this end two conferences were held in Oxford in 2006 and 2008, with a range of therapists lecturing and showing videotapes of their work. After these conferences a significant number of people completed core training courses. Also an interest group was formed, attended by therapists and students who could not afford the time and/or financial commitment needed to do the three-year part-time core training. Subsequently a number of conferences have been held in the UK, and currently several experienced therapists who have completed the training successfully are running core training courses in London and in the North of England. Many other therapists who have come into contact with the theory and practice of ISTDP use elements of it to make their work more effective, both in private practice but also in the NHS.

For many years I continued to lecture and write extensively about intensive short-term dynamic psychotherapy. As part of this, collaborating with Patricia Coughlin, we co-authored *Lives Transformed—a Revolutionary Method of Dynamic Psychotherapy* (Malan & Coughlin Della Selva, 2006). This outlines the concepts of intensive short-term dynamic psychotherapy and illustrates the therapy of seven patients and the follow-up outcome data.

Some therapists trained in traditional methods are resistant to hearing about this technique. Perhaps they can be forgiven, because often the results do seem to be exceptional. Yet surely it is not unfair to use the following analogy; suppose a team of reputable physicians were to report that they had discovered a uniquely effective, widely applicable, and permanent cure for cancer, would traditional oncologists decide that they simply "did not want to know"?

In this form of therapy, when properly conducted, the transference neurosis does not develop, termination presents no problem, at follow-up there is no evidence of unresolved transference, and the results typically amount to total resolution of even severe neurosis. Unquestionably, ISTDP is an extremely effective and efficient technique for resolving deep-seated emotional problems. There are centres of excellence in Canada, the USA, and in many European countries where training is available. However, therapists who use this technique need not only to be deeply empathic but also to be able to bear the pain experienced by patients and, where necessary, the intense anger and rage associated with their most heavily defended, previously unconscious, feelings and impulses. They must also be capable of leading patients carefully but persistently towards these feelings and to carry them through the process of experiencing them.

Moreover, therapists trained in psychoanalysis and traditional psychotherapy have to undergo a considerable reorientation in thinking and in "therapeutic reflexes". For instance, in the early stages of therapy they need to curb entirely one of the fundamental aspects of their training—namely, the tendency to give interpretations. Although the technique is challenging to learn and the therapy demanding to do, the rewards when the skills have been mastered are truly immense for both therapists and, most importantly, patients.

* * *

David H. Malan DM FRCPsych was born in India in 1922 and aged seven, after his father died, came to England with his mother. During the Second World War he worked for the Special Operations Executive (SOE) doing secret research developing devices for resistance fighters and then as part of a team that devised an effective incendiary bomb for use in the Far East. In 1947 he began medical and psychoanalytical trainings, having analysis first with Michael Balint then with Donald Winnicott. Following psychiatric and psychotherapy trainings at the Maudsley Hospital and at the Tavistock Clinic, he became a consultant in the Tavistock Adult Department in 1966. There he developed the Brief Psychotherapy Workshop which attracted students from around the UK and overseas. He later collaborated with Dr Habib Davanloo (*Intensive Short-Term Dynamic Psychotherapy: Selected Papers of Habib Davanloo*, 2001). His outcome research has demonstrated many times that brief psychotherapy and intensive short-term dynamic psychotherapy can transform in a profound and lasting way the lives of patients who have deep-seated and long-standing emotional problems.

His 1979 book *Individual Psychotherapy and the Science of Psychodynamics* has been translated into eight languages and, following a second edition in 1995, is still in print as a classic textbook for psychotherapists. It was based on actual sessions with patients that demonstrated significant psychodynamic incidents. Dr Malan believes that psychodynamic processes should be scientifically studied and that one of the most important tools for the "objective study of subjective matter" is long-term follow-up interviews to obtain reliable psychodynamic outcome data.

Besides his important and widely read 1979 textbook and many peer-reviewed journal papers, Dr Malan has also published *A Study of Brief Psychotherapy* (1963; reprinted several times and translated into seven languages), *The Frontier of Brief Psychotherapy* (1976a), *Towards the Validation of Brief Dynamic Psychotherapy* (1976b), *Psychodynamics, Training and Outcome in Brief Psychotherapy* (with Ferrucio Osimo, 1992), *Anorexia, Murder and Suicide* (1997), and *Lives Transformed—A Revolutionary Method of Dynamic Psychotherapy* (with Patricia Coughlin Della Selva, 2006). In 2005, at the International Conference of Experiential and Dynamic Therapy, Dr Malan was presented with a Lifetime Career Achievement Award for his contribution to the research and practice of psychotherapy.

CHAPTER TWENTY-SIX

The Tavistock Adult Depression Study (TADS)

David Taylor

The Tavistock Adult Depression Study, known in brief as TADS (Fonagy, P., Rost, F. Carlyle, J. McPherson, S., Thomas, R., Fearon, P., Goldberg, D, Taylor, D, 2015) took more than fifteen years to complete, and cost something in the order of £1.75 million. It had been intentionally designed to provide a severe test of a psychoanalytic approach to a significant mental disorder suffered by many NHS patients. It was the first randomised controlled trial (RCT) of longer-term psychoanalytic psychotherapy, and was designed to test its ability to offer help to those suffering from the kind of chronic depression that was resistant to the usual treatments. Such treatments would take the form of antidepressants, and/or courses of counselling or cognitive behavioural therapy (CBT).

The decision to test a mainstream psychoanalytic therapy with this chronic, hard-to-treat patient group was strategic: depressive disorders are in many ways the central, most prevalent health condition. There was very little evidence in favour of the efficacy of other kinds of treatments for their more chronic "treatment-resistant" forms. Moreover, patients with this kind of depression are generally regarded as unsuitable for psychoanalytic treatments. To add to this, the condition itself is responsible for a large portion of the diseases associated with depression; thus it was unlikely that inveterate sceptics could argue that any gains from such treatment might have arisen through spontaneous remission. Also exceptional was the study's two-year follow-up period.

In brief, the main outcome findings were these:

- 44% of the patients who had received eighteen months of weekly psychoanalytic psychotherapy no longer met the criteria for major depressive disorder when they were followed up two years after therapy ended. This contrasted vividly with the 10% figure found in those receiving the usual NHS treatments.

- Complete recovery in those receiving the psychoanalytic psychotherapy was 14%, as opposed to 4% of those receiving the usual treatments.
- The TADS trial had provided three-and-a-half years of observation. For every six-month interval observed, the chance of the TADS patients having gone into partial "remission" of their depressive symptoms was 40% higher than for those receiving the usual treatments.
- At the two-year follow-up, depressive symptoms had partially remitted in 30% of those receiving the psychoanalytic therapy; in the control condition it was 4%.
- The quality of the participants' lives, general wellbeing, and their social and personal functioning was also observed; and a pattern of significantly more benefits were noted in those receiving psychoanalytic psychotherapy.
- Although those who responded to the psychoanalytic psychotherapy often continued to experience symptoms of depression, it was at a reduced level. Moreover, they had significantly less likelihood of a "relapse" over the two years following the end of therapy. The gains of control-group patients were generally smaller; they tended to be less stable and to disappear over time. It was as if the psychoanalytic treatment was conferring a limited degree of immunity to a relapse, or to the return of depression.
- However, some patients did not appear to benefit.

Yet the security of these findings also needs to be examined. For example, the "treatment-as-usual" group serving as comparison and control reflected what these patients would generally have received, rather than what might have been thought of as optimal forms of treatment. This was true for this group of patients both in terms of medication, or of possible cognitive behavioural treatments. Although this was corrected for statistically, the randomised groups, however properly constructed, nevertheless had important differences. These issues aside, the quality of the study was good.

This way of presenting findings is customary in trials of antidepressants in the United States, and in comparable studies. But many uncertainties remain. For example, we used the Hamilton Depression Rating Scale's definitions of recovery, remission, and response, and these are simply based upon convention. Depression is a disorder whose expressions may penetrate into every corner of the patient's life, and lie beyond the sensitivity of any current measure. It is in no way clear what these scales might indicate in terms of the patient's actual lived experience.

We feel it is clear that the methods of the psychoanalytic case study remain the best way of reporting the effect of psychological treatment at the level of the individual. The clinicians in TADS found that even in individuals who have had the disorder for many years, who seemed mentally dulled, and who had not responded to other treatments, it was often possible to make a kind of contact with them that became increasingly meaningful. There was a shift from a predominantly meaningless suffering to meaningful, if painful, experience, and this became associated with an increased sense of mental aliveness and connectedness.

Semi-structured interviews collecting narrative material from patients in an impartial semi-objective way can offer a middle ground between group-level statistics and individual experience. The TADS project coordinator, Felicitas Rost, has collected a unique series of "before" and "after" interviews with a sample of TADS patients and therapists; when this material is finally analysed, it will provide much useful information.

In conclusion:

- For those suffering with this kind of depression, there are few other equally well-evidenced and positive results available. We hope the encouraging findings reported from TADS about the effectiveness of longer term psychoanalytic psychotherapy will be taken into account in the ongoing revision of the NICE guideline for the treatment of depression in adults.
- It is important to maintain longer-term treatments in the mental health field. In the same way, well-designed random allocation controlled trials need to be designed with follow-up periods that are long enough to monitor the stability of short-term gains; also they need to be able to detect those that, although slower to develop, may ultimately be more lasting.

Should further such studies of the outcome of psychoanalytical treatments be undertaken? In what kind of format? To which mental health conditions should they be applied: to less complex forms of depression, psychotic disorders, eating disorders, and so on? What benefits—most importantly in terms of improved service provisions—might develop as a result of TADS; or indeed from future trials of a similar kind? And how are the immense practical, logistical, and funding challenges to be approached?

Questions such as these lurk in most of us. Yet even if my own position upon them contains contingency and uncertainty, as Clinical Director of the study, I have no doubt that if we wish to improve the range of what is available for patients in the NHS, we need to arrive at well-considered answers to these questions. The interesting and broadly positive nature of the TADS findings as to the beneficial effects of a longer-term psychoanalytical psychotherapy have increased the significance and urgency of the task.

* * *

David Taylor was born in Manchester in 1946. He studied medicine at UCLH, intending from the outset to specialise in psychiatry and psychoanalysis. During psychiatric training at the Maudsley Hospital, his exposure to psychoanalysis included such exceptional Kleinian analysts as Henri Rey, John Steiner, Michael Feldman, and Leslie Sohn. He was appointed a consultant at the Tavistock Clinic in 1981 and has held prominent positions there, including chair of the Tavistock's Adult Services and Medical Director of the Tavistock and Portman NHS Foundation Trust.

When most senior analysts were disdainful of research into the outcomes of psychoanalytic treatments, Taylor was aware of the trend towards evidence-based medicine and of the threat that it posed to the provision of psychoanalytic therapies in mental health services. Although recognising that demonstrating the therapeutic effects of psychoanalytic therapies might be challenging, Taylor thought that there was nothing to make it impossible in principle. From the year 2000 onwards, he became the Clinical Director of TADS. He was then responsible—with Phil Richardson and Peter Fonagy—for the study from inception to completion in 2015.

Taylor wrote the manual for the psychoanalytic psychotherapy that was tested and used in TADS. It required him to combine the technical procedures of outcome research with Kleinian clinical insights. His treatment manual therefore sets out a psychoanalytic approach to patients with chronic, treatment-resistant kinds of depression. It was adopted by a German trial, the LAC (*Langzeittherapien bei chronischer Depression*) and will also be used in a planned replication of TADS in Switzerland.

He is now an honorary consultant psychiatrist and psychotherapist at the Tavistock and Portman NHS Trust. He is a training and supervising analyst of the British Psychoanalytical Society, as well as being a visiting professor at the Psychoanalysis Unit at University College London.

TADS, he says, was a team effort. Its first principal investigator was Phil Richardson, who sadly died after a short illness. His place was taken by Peter Fonagy, who gave generously of his time and expertise.

Senior researchers were Felicitas Rost, Adam Campbell, Susan McPherson, and Jo-anne Carlyle; the junior researchers included Hannah Ridsdale, Lucy Gibson, Donna Oxley, Rachel Tucker, Lucy Chan, Peter Cairns, and Thomas Booker.

Research administration: Sharon Novara.

Research clinician: Rachel Thomas.

Affiliates: Maxine Dennis, Niloufar Noktehdan, and Hiroshi Amino.

Clinicians/therapists: senior members of the Adult Department, including Mary Bradbury, Cyril Couve, Stephen Dreyer, Marcus Evans, Gideon Hadary, Orna Hadary, Caroline Garland, Liz Gibb, Francesca Hume, Birgit Kleeberg, Julian Lousada, Michael Mercer, Monica Lanman, David Millar, Matthew Patrick, Philip Stokoe, and Nollaig Whyte.

Taylor is very grateful to the steering committee led by Sir David Goldberg (chair). Its members were A. Faulkner, S. Blake, M. Buszewicz, J. Cape, P. McCrone, M. Knapp, and I. Nazareth.

Funding: Tavistock and Portman NHS Foundation Trust; Tavistock Clinic Foundation; International Psychoanalytical Association.

CHAPTER TWENTY-SEVEN

Working at the Tavistock Clinic Adult Department 1972–1997

John Steiner

I first came to the Tavistock Clinic in 1972, holding a joint appointment with sessions also at the Maudsley Hospital in both general psychiatry and psychotherapy. Of course the Tavi was very different and it was a pleasure to find that psychoanalysis was respected and used. A liberal, tolerant, and generally relaxed atmosphere fostered by the chairman of the Professional Committee, Bob Gosling, contrasts with the current climate of pressure and tension which makes me feel I was exceedingly lucky to have been there at that time.

Partly following the Balint group tradition of work with general practitioners (see Elder, Chapter 8) a number of groups were held in the Adult Department and I was fortunate to be able to join a GP group run by Pierre Turquet. Once a month all the group leaders met to present their work and I remember animated discussions between Tom Main, Bob Gosling, and Pierre. Therapy groups were a major activity and all the members of staff conducted at least one weekly therapy group so that the department was very group oriented at that time and especially of course influenced by the work of Wilfred Bion. What impressed me was that a sophisticated understanding of group processes could be applied in a simple straightforward way to help patients with their life problems and GPs with ordinary work.

Another influential activity was led by David Malan (see Malan, Chapter 25) whose outcome studies on treatment by brief psychotherapy became internationally well known. Perhaps more interesting to me personally was the work of Sandy Bourne and Mannie Lewis who showed that commonly the medical management of stillbirth and neonatal death was inhumane and traumatic (see Bourne, Chapter 11). It seemed a real advance that parents should be allowed to hold their dead child and to grieve at a proper funeral.

After a couple of years I found that holding two posts at opposite ends of London was too stressful and I left the Tavistock for a couple of years in 1974 but was pleased to be able to return in 1976 when I left the Maudsley. Having worked as a general psychiatrist I was often consulted about difficult patients sometimes considered to have psychotic features. In respect to these, I was greatly influenced by the work of Henri Rey who thought of borderline patients as existing not only on the border of neurosis and psychosis but on many other borders, for example not being clear if they were adult or child, male or female, weak or strong, and so on. I developed the idea of a borderline position in equilibrium with the depressive and paranoid-schizoid positions described by Melanie Klein.

My interest in working with this type of patient led me to begin a weekly seminar where Tavistock staff and trainees could come to discuss the patients they were treating. It came to be known as the Borderline Workshop and the title stuck even though the range of patients we took on broadened and the diagnosis became less important and included all kinds of difficult patients and subsequently any patient that the therapist wanted to discuss.

Each member of the workshop presented his case two weeks running and then had to wait quite a time until his turn came up once more. We then proceeded to a theory seminar for which I had prepared a reading list. Mostly we tried to deal with basic concepts and of course because of my approach these were chiefly but not exclusively Kleinian. Many of the students had a different orientation but my impression was that all kinds of views were accepted and openly discussed.

The juxtaposition of a reading seminar with a clinical seminar turned out to be a useful teaching model which I have continued to use in postgraduate seminars. Invariably links could be made to theory in the clinical part of the seminar and the theory part could be directed to the clinical problems presented by patients. At the end of a student's stay in the seminar they were invited to present a paper based on the case that had been discussed. This introduced the members to the task of writing up clinical material and many of the papers were interesting and productive. Some formed the bases of papers that were subsequently published. The workshop began with about six members in 1976 and gradually expanded, remaining mostly at about twelve to fifteen, until in later years members of the Adolescent and Child and Family Departments joined and we moved into a larger room which could hold the thirty or so members.

I invited a number of visitors to conduct the clinical discussions. I remember Henri Rey, Betty Joseph, Hanna Segal, Eric Brenman, Elisabeth Spillius, Joe Sandler, Roy Schafer, and Otto Kernberg as well as two leading Lacanians from Paris. We had a memorable workshop with Herbert Rosenfeld which was popular and necessitated a move to the lecture theatre on the ground floor. Sally Weintrobe presented some vivid clinical material which enabled Rosenfeld to conduct what was later described as a master class.

Most of the patients were treated once a week for one to two years but exceptions were common and we were sometimes able to treat patients more intensively and for longer. Even though our resources set limits to what we could offer we were able to try to tailor the treatment to the patient's needs. It was common at the time to assess patients to see if they were "suitable for psychotherapy" and I tried instead to determine what treatment was suitable for a particular patient. The work was deeply grounded in psychoanalysis but especially in what we considered to be a psychoanalytic attitude in which priority was given to understanding. We argued that such an attitude could be sustained in once-a-week therapy allowing meaningful work to be done in an NHS setting.

Sometimes of course the analytic setting was disrupted by the patient's disturbance, for example when violence, suicide, litigation, and other disruptions threatened to intrude. This meant that the therapist had to see to managerial problems in order to attend to the patient's or the therapist' safety. At these times I suggested it was necessary to put on a managerial hat but we did not pretend that this was therapeutic and when the position stabilised we tried to revert to an analytic attitude.

At one point six members of the workshop became pregnant at about the same time and we decided to run a separate seminar to study the effect of a pregnancy on both the patient and the therapist. This work was published in a special number of *Psychoanalytic Psychotherapy* (Cullington-Roberts, 2004; Dufton, 2004; Gibb, 2004; Hernandez Halton, 2004; Hopkins, 2004; Steiner, 2004; Whyte, 2004), which showed that patients varied in their perceptions of the analyst's state. Some denied the evidence of the pregnancy while others were so sensitive that they seemed to know even before the therapist did. The therapists also varied and some became very anxious and protective of their pregnancy which they often felt provoked enormous hatred and envy from the patients. Again we tried to foster a psychoanalytic attitude in which the patients' need to negotiate conflicts related to pregnancy seemed to revive conflicts from their infancy.

In addition to the workshop I was involved in the ordinary teaching and clinical work of the department. For a number of years I ran one of the three clinical units, I supervised a good deal, and I became especially interested in consultations, for a time also running a consultations workshop. I took over the management of a rather poorly attended Introduction to Psychotherapy course and initiated both clinical and theory seminars as well as proposing that all the students should be in once-weekly therapy. Against many predictions this feature turned out to be very popular and the course, known as D58, "Foundations of Psychodynamic Psychotherapy", became sought-after and is still running now.

In the mid-1980s, following Bob Gosling and then Alexis Brooks, Anton Obholzer was elected chair of the Professional Committee, which led to a period of more active management in which the psychoanalytic approach continued to be supported. My poor attendance at committees at that time led to some complaints and I was again lucky to have Anton's support; it was a liberal attitude in which people were encouraged to do what they were good at. I was involved in a number of other initiatives; perhaps a significant one was to help to establish the Association for Psychoanalytic Psychotherapy in the NHS (APP), with a colleague from South London, Dr Michael Michalacopoulos. I served as its first chairman from 1982–1988 and helped to establish the journal *Psychoanalytic Psychotherapy*. Initially full membership was restricted to medically trained therapists and this produced vehement protests among the psychologists in the department. Thankfully the matter was quickly rectified.

I was very pleased to have been able to make links with staff and students from the Adolescent Department and the Department for Children and Parents, and at the Borderline Workshop the attendance of colleagues such as Margot Waddell, Margaret Rustin, Isca Wittenberg, Gianna Williams, and Elizabeth Bradley raised the level of discussion and of course created anxieties for the core membership, not least for me. Nevertheless it was an enriching experience and working at the Tavistock and the workshop in particular taught me a lot and was an enormous help in my own development as well as in sustaining a psychoanalytic attitude in a public sector environment.

* * *

John Steiner worked as a consultant in the Adult Department of the Tavistock Clinic between 1972 and 1997. He continues to work as a training analyst of the British Psychoanalytical Society, and although he has retired from clinical practice, he continues to supervise and write. He is the author of *Psychic Retreats* (1993) *Seeing and Being Seen* (2011), and *Illusion, Disillusion and Irony in Psychoanalysis*, (2020). He has also edited and written introductions to several books including *The Oedipus Complex Today* (1989), papers by Hanna Segal entitled *Psychoanalysis, Literature and War* (1997), and essays on Herbert Rosenfeld's clinical influence, entitled *Rosenfeld in Retrospect* (2008). Recently (2016) he has edited Melanie Klein's *Lectures on Technique* which she gave in 1936.

Steiner was born in Prague in 1934, and in 1939 after the Nazi invasion he was fortunate to be able to move to New Zealand with his family. There he studied medicine and worked for a period in neuroscience, completing his PhD in Cambridge in 1964. He then moved to London to train in psychiatry at the Maudsley Hospital where he was influenced by Henri Rey. He later held a joint post as a general psychiatrist and psychotherapist at the Maudsley before moving to the Tavistock Clinic. His work in the Adult Department is described above but included the establishment of an introductory course in psychotherapy, D58, which is still running, helping to found the Association for Psychoanalytical Psychotherapy in the NHS (APP), and running the Borderline Workshop.

He continues to lead an active life, supervising candidates and running two postgraduate seminars. He is also active writing and developing his ideas in psychoanalysis.

CHAPTER TWENTY-EIGHT

The Adult Department

Julian Lousada

Rereading H. V. Dicks' *50 years of the Tavistock Clinic* (1970) for these personal reflections on the Adult Department, I am struck by the suspicion and scepticism that greeted the emergence of psychoanalysis in the 1920s and their repetition in the latter part of the century. This sceptical state of mind was not sufficient to constrain a quite brilliant generation of psychoanalysts who secured and developed the department's intellectual reach, clinical practice, and its trainings in the post-war period. The mission of the Adult Department and the Tavistock Clinic more generally was to promote clinical services informed by psychoanalysis for the public sector. The emergence of psychotherapy services up and down the country was in no small way due to the reputation of the Tavistock Clinic as a whole. The competition between providers and the challenge to the effectiveness of psychoanalytic interventions grew once more in the 1980s and there is some truth to Harvey Taylor's view, in his unpublished 2013 discussion paper for the British Psychoanalytic Council (BPC), *U.K. Psychoanalysis: Mistaking the Part for the Whole*, that "The Psychoanalytic community was not as adept in its response as perhaps would have been helpful."[1]

I was appointed to the Adult Department in the early 1990s. It was a time of challenge to and change in what has been described as the "Welfare Settlement". The 1990 National Health Service and Community Care Act promoted the concept of "collaborative care", a process that encouraged not just interdisciplinary work in community mental health teams, but also the delivery of mental health services out of the hospitals and psychiatric units. The result was that over time many more "providers" entered and competed for mental health resources.[2] It was therefore the beginning of a period of transition in the delivery of mental health services, which would over the next period have a considerable impact on the future funding of psychoanalytic psychotherapy in the NHS. In this changing context, together with colleagues,

I consulted to—and ran—reflective groups for a wide range of mental health day and residential services. In the Community Mental Health Teams the task was to attend to the gap between the aspiration of collaboration and the difficulties of achieving it. Working with mental health and care staff in multiple organisational settings was predicated on the understanding that working "well" with the psychic projections and the distress of patients can be, and frequently is, distressing for the clinical and administrative staff who care for them. In the absence of attending to this experience there is an ever-present danger of enactments that put the patient, the staff, and the organisation at risk.

The multidisciplinary underpinning of the 1990 Act was not new for the Adult Department, which had a long tradition of multidisciplinary staff and trainees. Psychiatrists, psychologists, social workers, and latterly nurses held in common a commitment to psychoanalysis as well as to learning from, and contributing to, the differing professional settings and roles.

The Adult Department's reputation, as with the Tavistock Clinic's as a whole, was not least a result of its ability to attract an exuberant and talented staff, who not only provided clinical leadership and training but also published clinical and scientific papers and books offering new understandings of psychic distress, as well as exploring their application to the public domain. Many also contributed to the Tavistock Clinic Series of books edited so ably by Margot Waddell (see Chapter 43).

In spite of occasional family squabbles there was a palpable sense of community within the Clinic exemplified by the organisational democracy in which senior staff positions were elected, the shared monthly scientific meetings, and the notorious Christmas pantomimes during the 1980s (see Sprince & Pengelly, Chapter 42). No description of the Adult Department would be complete without reference to the collective fun associated with the play readings we undertook. The Adult Department, as part of a "community-as-a-whole", is perhaps best illustrated by the courageous and controversial decision by Caroline Garland and David Taylor to play a central part in the BBC's 1999 *Talking Cure* (Taylor, 1999; see Holgate, Chapter 40) to which Robin Anderson, Jenny Altschuler, Caroline Garland, and Margaret Rustin made moving contributions. Making the essentially private nature of psychotherapy public was not without its critics but it represented the belief that keeping mental distress and its treatments out of sight did more harm than good. Even a rather sceptical Andrew Billen wrote in the *New Statesman*:

> Ines Cavill and Polly Bide's programme take us to the NHS's Tavistock Clinic in London, a blank building with an Abandon-Hope-All-Ye-Who-Enter statue of Sigmund Freud at its gates. Fortunately the old boy's theories seem to have been discarded and the therapies performed inside look subtle and undogmatic. The talking cure is based on very careful thought about what makes human beings tick.[3]

Billen was right to be moved by the quality of the clinical work shown, but of course wrong that "the old boy had been discarded".

The Interdisciplinary Training in Adult Psychotherapy (M1) remains the department's flagship training, containing an important relatedness between the teaching of psychoanalytic theory and clinical work. What made, and makes, the training unique was the expectation that trainees would do assessments, see once-weekly patients, and have the experience of more intensive work as well as running a group, all under supervision. There was also the expectation that trainees would have the opportunity to work clinically in the more dedicated services, for example: group psychotherapy (Caroline Garland and Maxine Dennis), couple psychotherapy (Joanna Rosenthall), trauma therapy (Jo Stubley; see Garland, Chapter 29), the treatment of borderline patients (see Steiner, Chapter 27; Bell, Chapter 30), Balint groups for GPs (see Elder, Chapter 8), group relations conferences (Julian Lousada and Maxine Dennis), and latterly the opportunity to participate in the now well-known research project into treatment-resistant depression led by David Taylor (Fonagy et al., 2015; see Taylor, Chapter 26). It is hard to think of another training that prepared clinicians more fully to enter and lead other psychotherapy and mental health services.

Like many, I imagine, I knew about the Adult Department long before I had any reason to think I would be on its staff. My own journey towards psychoanalysis had been a slow one, but central to it were two graduates of the Tavistock Adult training. First, Martha Friedlander in New York where I was working with street gangs and then in a therapeutic community for children. Martha was an enthusiastic and deeply challenging supervisor and helped me understand the presence of the unconscious in group life. Second, Sue Holland with whom in the mid-1970s I started the Battersea Aid and Action Centre, who showed me that a psychoanalytic approach did not depend solely on the setting of a consulting room, but could be applied in community settings.

As a social work lecturer one of the most influential texts for me was Isca Salzberger-Wittenberg's *Psycho-Analytic Insights and Relationships: A Kleinian Approach* (Salzberger-Wittenberg, 1970). This book beautifully described the dynamics of working with the sort of clients whom the students encountered on their placements. It was Isca's willingness to accept my invitation to come and offer a master class each year that led me to my ambition to work at the Tavistock Clinic.

Having completed my training at the British Association for Psychotherapy (BAP), I was lucky enough in the early 1990s to be appointed as a senior member of staff in the Adult Department. It was as daunting an experience as it was exhilarating. The two tasks of training and clinical work were, and continue to be, undertaken with such commitment, enthusiasm, and rigour. In my experience, the Adult Department was far from austere, and far from being inward looking. Eric Miller[4] was one of my early neighbours on the fourth floor. I am eternally grateful for the conversations we had which led me towards an interest in groups and organisations. Anton Obholzer suggested that I attend the Leicester group relations conference, with the intriguing warning that on leaving I should remember that a red light was not an invitation to have a conversation! This was the start of many years of staffing and directing group relations conferences at the Tavistock and internationally.

The social work discipline of which I was a member was rather scattered on my arrival but with the appointment of Andrew Cooper (see Chapter 32) as professor of social work in 1996, the discipline developed a stronger sense of direction and purpose and the Centre for Social Work Research in collaboration with the University of East London added research to the reputation of the trainings it had already established.

Above all it was my clinical work that developed as a result of the constant exposure to the thinking that took place in the main three units, in dedicated workshops, and in the teaching and supervising of trainees. The department was a place of shared learning, a place of thoughtfulness, of questioning, and above all, a place where the reality and modesty of clinical work was faced. The truth is that there are multiple factors that contribute to psychic distress and it is as delusional as it is omnipotent to suggest that there are easily available solutions. Psychic change is never easy and the modest ambition principally concerned with the strengthening of a capacity for relationships is a worthwhile and profound objective.

Whilst it is invidious to single out individual members of staff, John Steiner's Borderline Workshop (see Steiner, Chapter 27) illustrated the "reaching out spirit" of the department. The workshop started as seminars for the discussion of difficult patients, and quickly evolved into a clinical presentation and discussion followed by the reading and discussion of a theoretical paper, a model that continues. The weekly workshops were attended by between twenty-five and thirty trainees and colleagues from all the departments at the Tavistock, as well as by some people from other clinics in the NHS. From time to time senior psychoanalysts were invited as guests. The outcome of this workshop was the now established, well-respected, and long-running course, "An Introduction to Psychoanalytic Psychotherapy", known as the Qualifying Course in Psychodynamic Psychotherapy (D58). Steiner was influential in establishing the Association for Psychoanalytical Psychotherapy (APP), which supports professionals in the public sector trying to use psychoanalytic thinking. Other initiatives followed: for example, developing an adult psychotherapy training in Newcastle, and D58 setting up in Leeds. The award-winning City and Hackney primary care psychotherapy consultation service initiated by Philip Stokoe and Brian Rock (Rock & Carrington, 2012), which continues to this day, was a collaboration with local GPs to manage the complex needs of people who often fall between gaps in mental health provision. The model developed by this project has been widely repeated in other mental health trusts.

There were three CEOs during my time at the Tavistock; Anton Obholzer, Nick Temple, and Matthew Patrick. Three very different men sharing the project of how to secure and develop the unique Tavistock brand. The Tavistock's democratic tradition strengthened a sense of ownership of the strategic direction departmentally and in the Clinic as a whole. Perhaps on reflection the celebration of our own self-government did not adequately prepare us to navigate the increasingly choppy waters stirred up by the managerial changes associated with becoming first an NHS Trust in 1994, and then a Foundation Trust in 2006. The collective confidence in the work of the department and the wish to develop increasingly had to encounter the unfamiliar question how best to survive. Scarcity of resources and the NHS internal market meant that local commissioning of services created an atmosphere of competition between providers at the expense of the collaboration necessary to provide a comprehensive mental health service. These factors and the advent of "evidence-based" commissioning within an ever more crowded psychotherapy marketplace posed real difficulties for the department and more broadly for psychoanalytic psychotherapy in the NHS. We have witnessed a tragic decline in psychoanalytic psychotherapy posts in the NHS together with the downgrading and outsourcing of non-consultant posts. The experience of being squeezed by the demand to change and our continuing commitment to psychoanalytic treatments was perhaps a situation that could never in truth have a completely happy ending, but the struggle continues.

I worked for more than twenty-five years in the Adult Department. It offered me so much as a clinician and for me and many others it was a tremendously stimulating and happy experience. I remain proud and grateful for the opportunity of being its clinical director for a number of years and above all I am indebted to all those from whom I have learned and with whom I have worked and sometimes played. My confidence in the project of the Adult Department remains undiminished. It seems to me essential for a responsive and sensitive mental health service to find and use the value that psychoanalytic thinking has to offer. This is as it always has been the task of the Adult Department.

Notes

1. In this paper the psychoanalyst Harvey Taylor proposed that key historical and institutional decisions have led inexorably to the current crisis in which psychoanalysis in the UK finds itself. This crisis takes the form of the almost complete disappearance of psychoanalytic work in the National Health Service (NHS) and the lack of a significant voice in public policy and debate.

2. This legislation created the "internal market" of purchasers and providers in health care and at the same time an obligation on health and local authorities to work together for people with mental health problems. https://scie.org.uk/publications/introductionto/adultmentalhealthservices/legalandpolicycontexts.asp It was led by the then health minister Kenneth Clarke, who had to fight Margaret Thatcher to prevent her from bringing in a US-style health insurance system. https://inews.co.uk/news/health/ken-clarke-health-secretary-nhs70-282504 (Ed.)

3. "Sick benefits", *New Statesman*, November 15, 1999 by Andrew Billen. https://newstatesman.com/node/150231

4. Eric Miller (1924–2002) a leading figure in the Tavistock Institute from 1958 until his death, Obituary. *The Guardian*, April 17, 2002 by Anton Obholzer. https://theguardian.com/news/2002/apr/17/guardianobituaries.obituaries

* * *

Julian Lousada is a psychoanalyst (BPA), originally a social worker. Following ten years as a senior social worker, he lectured at West London Institute, the North London Polytechnic, and New York University Silver School of Social Work. In 2005 he became clinical director of the Tavistock Clinic Adult Department and in 2015 chair of the British Psychoanalytic Council. He has co-authored two books, *The Politics of Mental Health* (Banton, Clifford, Frosh, Lousada, & Rosenthall, 1985) and, with Andrew Cooper, *Borderline Welfare: Feeling and Fear of Feeling in Modern Welfare* (Cooper & Lousada, 2005.)

CHAPTER TWENTY-NINE

The Adult Department: a group at work

Caroline Garland

In spite of the enormous burden of mental distress and mental illness carried by our patient population, the Adult Department contained a lively and energetic bunch of staff, making the department a highly enjoyable place in which to work. When I arrived to join the psychologists in the 1980s, the department was known, not altogether affectionately, as "The Gentleman's Club". It was male-dominated, moreover by experienced psychoanalysts, whose authority and clout both in and out of the Clinic was tremendous.

Although a few members of the "club" felt that their most important work was conducted in their analytic consulting rooms, the greater proportion of the staff were not mentally cloistered with five-times-a-week patients, but believed in the value of applied psychoanalysis. They—we—felt that analytic understanding was deeply important, indeed essential, in illuminating the problems that beset so many in the community. This was in a direct line with the foundation of the Clinic in 1920, as the outcome of work with "shell-shocked"—or traumatised—victims of World War One (see Armstrong & Rustin, Chapter 3).

The task of bringing this hard-won knowledge from what was learned on the battlefields, and in the community, to the population in general continued to inspire and enliven the work carried out in the Adult Department. Over the twenty-five years that I spent there, a great deal of work was begun and sustained over the decades with long-lasting problems: depression, stillbirth, trauma, chronic pain, refugees and immigration, eating disorders, borderline personality disorders, as well as many other areas of research and treatment.

I am going to concentrate on just three areas of work in the department, those in which I was most active and therefore found most productive personally: group treatment; the understanding and treatment of trauma (the direct link back to the Clinic's origins); and finally some things less directly related to the Clinic's primary task of addressing the mental health

219

of the population: the art collection and the Adult Department's play readings. Both had a part to play in maintaining staff morale. (See also Lousada, Chapter 28, for more on the Adult Department.)

The structure

There were four different groupings in the department: the patients, our *raison d'être*; the permanent senior staff; the trainees, all of whom were in personal analyses, and many of whom were concurrently engaged in the training at the Institute of Psychoanalysis (as were various members of the senior staff); and the administrative staff, who kept the whole enterprise documented, serviced, and running with, on the whole, great good humour. The clinical work of the department was carried out by three units, consisting of members of all four groupings. When I arrived, all three units were headed exclusively by white male analysts who were also psychiatrists. Over the years this began to change for the better, mirroring important, indeed vital, changes in society in general. Women and psychologists began to run the units, and all four staff groupings increasingly included people of all colours and nationalities.

Group as a primary form of treatment

There had been an important period earlier in the history of the Adult Department, which had originated in the work of Wilfred Bion in the War Office Selection Boards, and at Northfield Military Hospital (see Armstrong & Rustin, Chapter 3). Staff such as Pierre Turquet and Henry Ezriel (1952) had fostered the use of analytically orientated therapeutic groups as an important mode of treatment. This way of thinking had diminished by the time I arrived in the department in 1984, and by then patients, once assessed, were usually put on a waiting list for once-a-week individual treatment. (A few were allocated to three-times-weekly treatment, which was carried out by trainees under supervision.) Not surprisingly, the waiting lists were long, and the wait for treatment even longer, sometimes more than a year. This was a hopeless situation, perhaps reflecting how cut-off the department and the Clinic as a whole could be at times from the society whose needs it was created to address. Critics sometimes referred to the Clinic as "an ivory tower", though those of us who worked hard there found it anything but that.

I had been responsible for the supervision of group therapy (run by young psychiatrists in training) at the Maudsley Hospital, also no ivory tower, for some years before joining the Adult Department. I think the expectation and the hope was that I would do something of the same in north London. Deriving from a training at the Institute of Group Analysis, I came with a conviction that therapy groups had a value and significance of their own. Biologists, sociologists, psychoanalysts, and psychoanalytic therapists all see the drive for relatedness to other members of our own species as primary, an intrinsic part of our make-up. It is as fundamental to our being, to our well-being, our mental functioning, and to our very survival as human beings, as are the drives for food, shelter, warmth, and sex. This drive for relatedness, often damaged by adverse experience in early life, can be seen vividly to evolve and grow within the setting of group therapy: eight or nine individuals meeting weekly on a regular basis for two or three years.

However, within the National Health Service, there had been an implicit assumption that group therapy was a crude though economical form of treatment, suitable only for target-driven and publicly funded organisations: eight patients seen in the same time that it takes an individual therapist to see a single patient and make notes on the session. This was a very short-sighted view. From the moment of conception we exist within a social group, consisting of, at the very least, three members. Whether or not the father is an active presence in the mother's life, he (or some version of him) has an existence in her mind, as *the father* of this baby. "Three" is the basis of the internal grouping in the mother's mind, in the baby's mind; and this "three" is the basic social unit, the primary group, whether in individual analysis or in group treatment.

Every baby, every human infant, then has two major tasks to be faced. He or she has to develop as an *individual*, in touch with the internal world—impulses, phantasies, wishes, ideas, and feelings, whether pleasurable or unpleasurable: whether derived from and dominated by hate, or derived from and expressive of love. And as the baby contains inevitably at different times the capacity for both love and hate, he or she has to learn how to manage that fluctuating balance.

Psychoanalysts deal with the consequences of these early processes in our daily analytic work. And as psychoanalytic *group* therapists we could see the same processes being worked out in the to and fro of the interactions, often intense and sometimes explosive, between group members, and in the relation of the individual to the group itself. This is the second major task facing the developing child and it continues into adolescence and throughout adulthood: the child has to learn how to become *a member of a group*, while retaining his particularity, his individuality, his capacity to think for himself.

It is more easily said than done. To be a member of a group is to have to put into practice some of the earlier developmental steps to do with the balance between love and hate; to be able to hold back on personal aims and ambitions when the needs of the group require something other from each of its members. Bion (1961) described this process as a move from *narcissism* to *social-ism*; and the larger the group, the harder it is to achieve. Nevertheless, I believe the tremendous appeal of a leader such as Barack Obama may be because, in himself, he demonstrated something of the liveliness and energy of a man who knows that working on behalf of the larger group brings satisfaction, and a sense of value and meaning to individual lives.

We developed the Groups Waiting List. In the original consultations, we discussed with suitable patients the point and value of their joining a group, rather than waiting an indefinite period for individual treatment. We wanted trainees carrying out most of the assessments of patients to consider "group" as the primary form of treatment, with individual work reserved for those who could not be accommodated in a group setting: the paranoid, the sociopathic, those who had powerful alternative belief systems (for example, Jehovah's Witnesses), and the acutely narcissistic. In order to do this with conviction, the staff had themselves to believe in the significance of group treatment as valuable in its own right, not merely cut-price over-crowded travel instead of a seat in first class with a single dedicated therapist.

The Groups Workshop for trainees ran weekly, with a mixture of clinical presentation and theory, modelled along the lines of John Steiner's concurrent and highly valued Borderline Workshop (see Chapter 27). The requirements for training were altered: every trainee was to run a therapy group as well as taking on his or her quota of individual patients. Being a group therapist did not suit every trainee: some were clearly happier in the privacy of the individual setting, but for many it allowed them to gain both insight and confidence—they were not going to be overwhelmed by an angry mob, or forced to engage in a group orgy—and to see in action the capacity of the patients themselves to respond to each other at a deep level, and with feeling and understanding. Young therapists learned they did not have to be the only expert, making privileged interventions: they saw that patients discovered ways not only of learning about each other, but also in a reflexive and mirrored way about themselves. And this new-found understanding, and capacity to function well in a group setting, could be—and was—exported to life outside the clinical setting, with benefit for patients, their families, and their working lives.

In fact, I saw the department itself as a group, a working group with a structure, a setting, and a primary task, which in turn was broken down into subtasks to be carried out by the various units and workshops. Eventually a book emerged from this work (Garland, 2010), which contained theory and clinical practice, and even more importantly, a manual for future group therapists.

The Trauma Workshop

The Trauma Unit within the Adult Department began, with a generous helping of "seed corn" money allocated by Anton Obholzer, eighteen months after the terrible sinking in the English Channel of the *Herald of Free Enterprise*, in 1986. The news of this disaster, with the loss of hundreds of lives, had broken as half a dozen of us were celebrating our just-announced qualifications from the Institute of Psychoanalysis. Each of us felt, within the tradition of the department, that our brand new qualifications in the field of mental health should have a direct application in the area of external relations, as well as in the intrapsychic world of the individual. The next day, two of us travelled to Dover to offer whatever we could in the way of back-up, support, learning, and expertise. What we saw and learned that day (including the blunt fact that "helpers" arriving unasked at the scene of a catastrophe is not the best way to be helpful) was the first stage in the formation of the Unit for the Study of Trauma and its Aftermath.

What was distinctive about the approach taken by our unit was that it focused upon a psychoanalytic approach to the treatment of traumatised states of mind. We knew that to be caught up in a severely traumatic event would stir up many of the unresolved pains and conflicts of childhood. Thus we attended to the meaning of the events as well as to what had actually taken place, linking the present with the past. We did not believe in the advice, frequently heard, to "put it out of your mind".[1] When events were remembered and worked through, rather than being encapsulated in a no-go area, there was a chance that they could be incorporated into the whole of the individual's existence, instead of becoming its central focus—whether consciously or unconsciously.

We offered each patient referred four consultations, in which the practical and the emotional elements of the situation could be put together with the patient's history. Some patients felt sufficiently helped by this approach to leave it there; and some were then referred on either for group or for individual treatment. However, what seemed to us crucial was that any referral onwards should then be made for the person, not for the traumatic event itself.

Since my retirement in 2008, Dr Jo Stubley has taken over the leadership of the Trauma Unit. Its scope has enlarged primarily to address complex and developmental trauma. This includes work with asylum seekers and refugees, veterans and survivors of childhood abuse—physical and sexual, as well as survivors of interpersonal violence. The Tavistock Trauma Service—as it is now called—still holds a psychoanalytic understanding at the heart of its work, but also makes use of other ways of working. These include the use of trauma-focused cognitive behavioural therapy (TF-CBT), eye-movement desensitisation and reprocessing (EMDR), trauma art therapy, trauma psycho-education groups, and trauma yoga groups. The Trauma Service also engages with the issue of historical child sexual abuse: here it offers specialist groups for men and women, as well as individual work. It maintains a partnership with the British Red Cross, which helps asylum seekers to access the Trauma Service through direct referral by Red Cross caseworkers. The service also offers consultations to organisations working with traumatised individuals, including a number of front-line services after the Grenfell Fire. It continues to teach widely, and runs a one-year course on a psychoanalytic approach to trauma.

And as well: art and literature

There were two enterprises begun in the Adult Department which, while not contributing directly to the Clinic's primary task, yet in the way that yeast adds lightness to the daily bread, made some aspects of the hard work more manageable and more enjoyable. The first was the art collection, of which I was the first curator.

I contacted serious local artists, and local art galleries, to see if they had works they might consider having shown in the public spaces of the Clinic, purely on a loan basis. Without exception there were generous and enthusiastic responses, particularly from those painters who had works that were too large to be hung in the average home. Jamie Boyd contributed a painting that became enormously popular with the children attending the Clinic: *The Lion in the Bath*. A large lion stood in a bathtub under a shower, water splashing all over the floor: its magical realism and general exuberance graced the Clinic's entry corridor for many years. Anthony Whishaw contributed many superb works to enliven the grey utilitarian corridors and meeting rooms of the Clinic. The Clinic has continued this work with its subsequent curators. The paintings have maintained an attractive addition to the building's basic structure, which also, in my view, contributes to the emotional well-being of the staff. Our motto was "Good Art Is Good For You."

The second activity that was not "work"—that is, not directly related to our primary task—were the annual dramatised play readings done by the Adult Department staff purely for its own pleasure. I describe just one of these, Shakespeare's *A Midsummer Night's Dream*, because its dramatic structure fitted so well the structure of the department itself. The Court was played by the most august members of the senior staff; the Rude Mechanicals were the psychologists, who read with brilliant comic effect; the Lovers were played by the trainees; and the Fairy World were, of course, the analysts. All the costumes were devised by the players themselves, and the evening was a sensational success. Many other dramatised readings followed, as well as cabaret evenings (The Borderline Café) in which Adult Department members displayed their own individual talents in music, comedy, and poetry.

I hope that overall I have given some idea of why at the outset I described the Adult Department as a highly enjoyable place in which to work. A worthwhile task, good colleagues, a hard-working day that still had room for friendships and social activities made me pleased and privileged to have been part of this Clinic and its endeavours.

To give a final taste of the atmosphere there that enlivened the work and the task, I include the song that was sung at Anton Obholzer's eventual retirement party. Our best soloists sang each verse and the entire department belted out the chorus (in bold type) to the tune of the Captain's song in Gilbert and Sullivan's HMS Pinafore.

Anton's Progress

When Anton began in C and F
he was busy all day and never drew breath
for this was the start of a lifetime's trek:
he was aiming for the office of a Chief Exec!
He was aiming for the office of a Chief Exec!
He tackled every task and then some more
on his way to the goal of the very next floor.
He tackled every task and then some more
on his way to the goal of the very next floor!

His Dad was a swimmer with Olympic claims,
his sons won medals at the very same Games,
so Anton couldn't pause for a moment's rest
if he was going to dazzle as the very best.
If he was going to dazzle as the very best.
He was busy every hour on the second floor
and then he came a-knocking at the Adolescent door.

He was busy every hour on the second floor
and then he came a-knocking at the Adolescent door.

It didn't take him long to attain the Chair.
The department's elders tore their hair
for Anton used his offices as Nurserees,
turning all his acorns into very fine trees.
Turning all his acorns into very fine trees.
And yet that still didn't fill his cup:
the Professional Committee was the next step up.
And yet that still didn't fill his cup—
The Professional Committee was the next step up.

In Finance Simon hoped to shine
till Anton told him, "The whole lot's *mine*:
mine to dispose of, mine to dispense,
whether it's people or pounds or pence.
Whether it's people or pounds or pence.
Creative accountancy will help me do my job,
Now there's a street-wise cabby—just bring me Uncle Bob!"
Creative accountancy will help him do his job:
Now there's a street-wise cabby—just bring him Uncle Bob!

With Lotte on board he made his name
As a Chief Exec of national fame,
She ran the office and she knew the score—
With a Lotte for your totty could you ask for more?
With a Lotte for your totty could you ask for more?
So how did he thank her for everything she bore?
"I've found the very present, it's a bag of horse manure!"
So how did he thank her for everything she bore?
He found the very present: "Here's a bag of horse manure!"

Now Maggie Wakelin-Saint on her morning jog
Said, "How do I tackle this great bull-frog?
I'll say to the Trust Board right away
I'm your new Chief Executive, and here to stay."
I'm your new Chief Executive and here to stay!

He stamped and he roared and reduced her to a wreck:
"I'm the Boss here, lady, I'm the Chief Exec!"
He stamped and he roared and reduced her to a wreck:
He's the boss here, lady, he's the Chief Exec!

At the DoH he embarked on a war
to make the Tavi's future oh so very sure.
All the underground parkers paid their dues
and the NHS Executive shivered in its shoes
And the NHS Executive shivered in its shoes.
The Tavistock flourished with no soft soap:
He's Consultant to the Vatican, the People's Pope!!!
The Tavistock flourished with no soft soap,
He's Consultant to the Vatican, the People's Pope!!!

Yet one floor remained as a final goal.
It's the acme of ambition for a man with soul.
If elegant and witty and you're not a dinosaur
you can satisfy ambition on the very top floor.
You can satisfy ambition on the very top floor!
He's gone to join the Adults at the Tavistock's hub
as a celebrated member of the Fourth Floor Club!
He's gone to join the Adults at the Tavistock's hub,
he's a celebrated member of the Fourth Floor Club!

Now professionals all, whoever you may be,
if you want to rise to the top of the tree
just climb the stairs as you ply your trade
and always keep in mind there's a final accolade
And always keep in mind there's a final accolade.
Just come to join the Adults at the Tavistock's hub,
you'll be welcome as a member of the Fourth Floor Club!
Just come to join the Adults at the Tavistock's hub,
you'll be welcome as a member of the Fourth Floor Club!

Note

1. An insight made plain, with clinical examples from First World War traumas, by W. H. R. Rivers (1918).

* * *

Caroline Garland

I have spent many years as a clinician, teacher, and researcher both in the Maudsley Hospital, and then for more than twenty-five years in the Tavistock Clinic. Before beginning work in the NHS, I was an ethologist, studying the social behaviour of chimpanzees (I speak fluent chimpanzee), which was followed with a study of the behaviour of newborn babies in St. Mary's Hospital, Paddington. Subsequent clinical and academic work includes many publications, including three books: *Children and Day Nurseries* (1980), *Understanding Trauma* (1999, 2002), and *The Groups Book: Psychoanalytic Group Therapy, Principles and Practice* (2010). I teach and lecture widely, at home and internationally.

In 1987, following the tragic loss of a cross-Channel ferry, I founded the Trauma Unit, specialising in the understanding and treatment of trauma.

I have since made a point of presenting the work of the Tavistock Clinic, and its relevance for modern mental health provision, to the general public—for instance in the BBC2 series, *Talking Cure*, directed by Beth Holgate (see Chapter 40). These were the first programmes to have gone inside the consulting room to show genuine clinical encounters with actual patients. I have also had much experience in working with groups, including consultation to organisations in trouble, plus working in conflict situations at home and abroad—for example in Kosovo. As well, I was one of the senior clinicians treating patients in the Tavistock Study of Long-term Treatment-resistant Depression, under the direction of Dr David Taylor (see Chapter 26)—demanding but highly interesting work.

Apart from clinical work, I write, under the name of Beatrice Garland. I won the National Poetry Competition in 2001, the Strokestown International competition in 2002, and have published two collections of poetry (*The Invention of Fireworks; The Drum*). I am at work on a third collection. One of my poems, "Kamikaze", has been on the GCSE syllabus for the last three years.

I have two adult sons, and three grandchildren, plus four stepchildren and six stepgrandchildren, all of whom both individually and in a group give me much pleasure, work, and satisfaction.

CHAPTER THIRTY

The Fitzjohn's Unit

David Bell

The Fitzjohn's Unit, which was set up within the Adult services in 2002, has established itself as a unique treatment provision for those suffering from severe and enduring psychological disorders whose needs have been so marginalised within our current health service.[1] The difficulties these patients encounter cover a very wide spectrum but include those suffering from chronic severe depression, manic depressive disorder, and those usually described as suffering from personality disorder (though the service, in common with many patients, prefers not to use this term). Others have made suicide attempts, some have had psychotic breakdowns. Most have had lifetimes of chronic incapacity and social dysfunction. Usually patients have had multiple unsuccessful treatments in other services almost always of a short-term nature.

The unit's work embodies a strong Tavistock tradition centring upon a psychoanalytic developmental model. Uniquely within the NHS, the Fitzjohn's offer is of an unusually long period of continuity of treatment: twice-weekly individual psychotherapy with experienced psychotherapists for two years, followed by a group for a number of years. This way of working aims to help the patients secure, over time, a transition towards a meaningful understanding of their difficulties, the ways they have been affected by them, and to situate them within their own histories—a significant step towards developing a greater capacity to manage their lives. The unit also provides consultation to other services who seek help in managing an "impossible patient".

A major achievement of the service has been the establishment and maintenance of a very high morale among the staff, essential for the work with such difficult patients. This highly functioning hub of mutual learning and cooperation thus provides a developmental experience not only for the patients but for the staff too.

Engagement with such complexity and severity of disorder requires an equivalently strong and shared commitment on the part of the staff to both offering and working within the firm model of management and containment which, despite the immense stresses, the Fitzjohn's Unit maintains. This is sustained by the creative partnership between Dr Bell and Dr Birgit Kleeberg who work closely together to co-manage the service. The unit has always provided an external workshop/seminar for all the staff, a meeting which is kept entirely separate from managerial issues. This was chaired for many years by Mrs Edna O'Shaughnessy and is currently under the leadership of Mr Francis Grier.

Note

1. David Bell, *Mental Illness and Its Treatment Today* (British Psychoanalytic Council, 2015, https://bpc. org.uk/mental-illness-and-its-treatment-today-0?page=5

* * *

Dr David Bell has been a consultant psychiatrist in the Adult Department for twenty-four years and retires this year. He has led the Fitzjohn's Unit for eighteen years. He is a past president of the British Psychoanalytical Society.

He lectures and publishes on a wide range of subjects including the historical development of psychoanalytic concepts (Freud, Klein, and Bion), and the psychoanalytic understanding of severe disorder. For his entire professional career he has deeply involved himself in interdisciplinary studies—the relation between psychoanalysis and literature, philosophy and sociopolitical theory. His interest in Shakespeare is reflected in the making of a DVD 'Iago on the Couch' where he is in discussion with Simon Russell Beale and Terry Hands (past Director of the Royal Shakespeare Company) and psychoanalysts Don Campbell and Ignês Sodré.

For about eighteen years he has provided a very successful year-long course at the Tavistock (PC4), which traces the development of psychoanalysis from its earliest origins up to the present day, situating it within a cultural and philosophical context (see https://tavistockandportman.nhs.uk/training/cpd-courses/development-psychoanalytic-theory-lecture-series/).

Books include: *Reason and Passion, Psychoanalysis and Culture: A Kleinian Perspective, Living on the Border,* and *Turning the Tide,* on the work of the Fitzjohn's Unit (all in the Tavistock Series) and one small book, *Paranoia.* During his professorial fellowship at Birkbeck College (2012–2013) he focused on different forms of degradation of knowledge and thinking. He is one of the UK's leading psychiatric experts in asylum and immigration and a passionate advocate of the public sector particularly the NHS (see for example his *Guardian* article, http://theguardian.com/society/joepublic/2010/nov/03/welfare-state-ideal-good-society).

Over the last three years David has been deeply involved in thinking about the current debate over gender dysphoria in children and adolescents, trying to maintain a thoughtful and psychoanalytic perspective in a highly toxic and politicised climate. As a result he is invited to lecture at conferences both nationally and internationally.

Part VI

Psychology, social work, and nursing

CHAPTER THIRTY-ONE

The psychology discipline

Louise Lyon and Emilia Dowling

Introduction

Psychology has long been significant in the culture of the Tavistock and Portman. The first psychologists recorded as staff members were three educational psychologists who joined the staff in the 1930s. When clinical psychology emerged as a separate discipline the Tavistock Clinic was one of the two institutions providing the first training courses, the other being the Maudsley Hospital. In the context of the Tavistock tradition of multidisciplinary work, psychologists have been distinctive in their willingness to work flexibly, to adapt and devise approaches to changing needs, and to take our work out into schools, primary care, and other diverse organisations. Psychologists' broad basic training enabled them to work across the whole Trust. This training included working with children, adolescents, adults, and older adults as well as with people with learning difficulties or neurodevelopmental disorders.

Our core training as scientist practitioners led us to embrace research and evidence-based practice while retaining our concern for the individual patient, family, or indeed trainee. We have an eye to both the uniqueness of the clinical encounter and the broader picture of the context in which we work. Psychology is not inherently wedded to any one approach and seeks out different ways of seeing, understanding, and addressing people's predicaments. This has meant that psychologists were able to support the Trust's development through bringing in alternative perspectives to those already established. Until the 2000s, the majority of psychologists were employed at consultant level and were dual trained, in either psychology and psychoanalytical psychotherapy or psychoanalysis, or psychology and systemic psychotherapy. With the establishment of systemic psychotherapy as a separate discipline, a number of psychologists became members of both disciplines. These included some of our most creative colleagues such as David Campbell (1943–2009).

More junior psychologists with training in a range of models began to be employed in the 2000s with the expansion of services in the community such as Camden Child and Adolescent Mental Health Services (CAMHS), the innovative development of the City and Hackney Primary Care Psychotherapy Consultation Service in 2009, and the expansion of the Gender Identity Development Service (GIDS) as it gained national service status in 2009. Psychologists have been key to each of these developments; Rita Harris as Trust CAMHS director, Brian Rock as lead in implementing the City and Hackney Service, and Polly Carmichael as director of GIDS along with senior psychologist colleagues, Bernadette Wren and Sarah Davidson.

While both educational and clinical psychologists are trained to administer a variety of tests of cognitive and emotional functioning, the profession from the 1970s onwards sought to establish itself as having much to offer alongside such tests. At the Tavistock, psychologists had pioneered new forms of assessment such as the object relations technique, developed in 1955 by Herbert Phillipson (1911–1992), and used in assessment and research until recently. The Rorschach method was re-established as a tool through the interest of a group of psychologists including Sadegh Nashat, Judith Bell, and Justine McCarthy Woods who went on to become the president of the Rorschach Society and led on revising norms for UK use of the test.

In adult and forensic services, the senior psychologists were almost all psychoanalytically trained and applied their skills to providing individual and group psychotherapy and to delivering our unique NHS based training in psychoanalytical psychotherapy and its applications. Many psychologists were graduates of this very substantial four-year training and through this contributed to the wider NHS and public sector.

The psychology discipline has made a significant contribution to the work of the Trust through clinical work, training, research, and consultancy and through leadership roles in the organisation. We will now look in more detail at each of these pillars of the Trust's work.

Innovations in clinical work

Working clinically in education and directly with schools has been a key area of innovation for psychologists, beginning with Irene Caspari (1915–1976). She founded and developed the clinical method of Educational Therapy[1], paying attention to the emotional aspects of learning. Emilia Dowling, for many years head of psychology in the Child and Family Department, developed the work further, along with colleagues. In the 1980s, she and psychologists Valery Golding, Denise Taylor, and educational therapist Muriel Barrett pioneered the application of systemic ideas to working with families and schools, which culminated in a book that became a classic text in the training of educational psychologists (Dowling & Osborne, 1985).

This work continued through the "Shared-Talk" project developed by Judith Bell and through the innovative work of Mike Solomon (1967–2019) in Camden. Mike contributed a reflective compassionate approach to the education of some of the most challenging young people in the Camden Centre for Learning (Camden's pupil referral unit). He played a key role in redesigning all aspects of the provision—from the architectural design of the new schools to the psychological support to staff and young people.

Psychologists have been innovative in taking our work with children and families out into the community. Jenny Altschuler, Valery Golding, and Emilia Dowling developed collaborative work based in GP practices in Camden. More recently, Rachel James developed services for children and families in the community, leading on work with under-fives. Renos Papadopoulos and Maureen Fox developed innovative work and training in working with refugees. This was further amplified by Gillian Hughes and Taiwo Afuape who promoted the powerful "Community Psychology" approach and ethos in working with asylum-seeking and refugee children.

Some of the Trust's specialised services have drawn significantly on psychologists' expertise. Sally Hodges contributed to the development of the Learning Disability Service and published on the subject (Hodges, 2002). Nancy Sheppard built on Sally Hodges' work and progressed services for people with disabilities in both the Clinic and in the community. Psychologists have been key staff in the evolution of exploratory and treatment approaches at the Gender Identity Development Service (GIDS), as well as in research and the development of a clinical ethics forum for the service.

The psychology and the systemic psychotherapy disciplines have benefitted creatively from dual trained staff and their close collaboration. Emilia Dowling with Gill Gorell Barnes pioneered systemic work with children and families going through separation and divorce. They trained many students and supervised numerous research projects in this area (Dowling & Gorell Barnes, 2000).

Psychologists have led in a number of areas of innovation in adult services. Peter Hildebrand worked on brief therapy (see Malan, Chapter 25), using video recordings to develop his approach and train others. He worked early on with people with AIDS and also applied his approach to working with older adults. Rachael Davenhill and Andrew Balfour (see also Chapter 22) took this work with older adults further, applying what they had learned from psychoanalytic psychotherapy with individuals and couples to the study of the psychic process of ageing as part of the developmental process across the lifespan.

Caroline Garland (see Chapter 29) set up the Unit for the Study of Trauma and Its Aftermath following the *Herald of Free Enterprise* ferry disaster in 1987. She used a psychoanalytical approach to understanding trauma, later supplemented, as proposed by Linda Young, by cognitive behavioural therapy for post-traumatic stress disorder and eye movement desensitisation reprocessing. Responding to the need to offer shorter-term psychoanalytically informed therapies for adults, Alessandra Lemma developed the Dynamic Interpersonal Therapy (DIT) model, training in which was widely taken up (Lemma, Target, & Fonagy, 2011).

Early work on group psychotherapy at the Tavistock Clinic was led by Wilfred Bion. Caroline Garland (a group analyst as well as psychologist and psychoanalyst) substantially developed group work in the Adult Department and, along with Francesca Hume, started the weekly

Groups Workshop in 2003. This creative workshop led to *The Groups Book* edited by Caroline Garland with chapters by other psychologists (Francesca Hume and Jo-Anne Carlyle). It provides a comprehensive account of how group work in the Adult Department is conducted and the relative influences of both Bion and Foulkes (Garland, 2010).

The Groups Workshop was subsequently taken on by Maxine Dennis, now lead for group work. She has developed this further by setting up a qualifying course in Group Psychodynamic Training. Her work draws on Bion, Foulkes, and Garland and recognises the role of cultural issues, thus providing an integrated model.

Around 2000, psychologist and psychoanalyst Shirley Borghetti-Hiscock started the Pain Service. This is a Tavistock and Portman led service based at the Royal Free Hospital. Her interest in this area began with children and adults undergoing heart transplantation and evolved into a service for patients with medically unexplained symptoms in hospital. This service has grown and is now run by psychologist François Louw.

Training

Our Educational Psychology training is the only clinically based multidisciplinary training in the country. The Educational Psychology training was the second course academically accredited by Brunel University. Amongst its organising tutors were Elsie Osborne, Maureen Fox, Liz Kennedy, and Sue Rendall. Mark Fox developed the Educational Psychology doctorate in conjunction with the University of Essex.

David Campbell played a crucial role in the development of Systemic Family Therapy training, which became the first Tavistock course academically accredited by Brunel University, leading to a master's degree. Dual-trained psychologists and family therapists brought valuable research know-how to the systemic trainings when they became university-accredited at master's, and later doctoral, level.

In 1993 Emilia Dowling founded the first clinical PhD in the UK. In association with Birkbeck College, the Tavistock–Birkbeck Clinical PhD in child and family psychology offered clinicians the unique opportunity to develop research to the highest academic level in the context of a clinical training. The course led to significant research, publications, and a creative collaboration between Birkbeck and the Tavistock (e.g., Rendall & Stuart, 2005). Renos Papadopoulos and Stephen Frosh made substantial contributions to the course (Papadopoulos & Byng Hall, 1997; Frosh, Phoenix & Pattman, 2002).

Denise Taylor developed the consultation course, 'Consulting to Individuals, Groups and Organisations'. Deirdre Moylan was course director until 2009 and several psychologists such as Valery Golding, Emilia Dowling, Stephen Frosh, and Judith Bell contributed to the teaching over the years. In 2005 Deirdre and Judith initiated the doctorate programme in Consultation and the Organisation.

Clare Huffington and Rita Harris developed the Systemic Consultation course for clinical and educational psychologists. David Campbell and Clare Huffington published on the subject (2008).

Key to our understanding of life in organisations is group relations. Group relations experiences are offered to many students and trainees on our courses, to external participants, and to staff at any stage of their development. Psychologists such as Deirdre Moylan, Judith Bell, and Maxine Dennis have all played significant roles in group relations both in the UK and abroad.

Psychology is unique as a discipline within the Trust in organising an annual week-long workshop, in which participants attend a programme of lectures, small study groups, and a large group experience, which together offer a combination of theoretical, clinical, and experiential learning. This multifaceted approach provides graduate psychologists with both an introduction to psychoanalytical approaches and an experience of reflective practice. The workshop has been running since the 1980s and since 1998 has been led by Linda Young. During the 2000s a second workshop was organised jointly by Linda Young and Veronica Gore, clinical psychologist, which was based in Newcastle, and took the event to an out-of-London audience.

Phil Richardson and Louise Lyon supported the University of Essex to set up the Essex–Tavistock Training Course in Clinical Psychology, inaugurated in 2005. One of our key aims was to ensure that the course was pluralistic in its clinical approaches, giving equal weighting to cognitive behavioural therapy, psychoanalytic and systemic approaches to ensure that future psychologists had a rich conceptual and clinical basis on which to build innovative approaches to future needs. Maxine Dennis has for many years organised the psychoanalytic and diversity modules for trainees on this course.

Francesca Hume has led the Advanced Adult Psychoanalytic training (M1) for more than twelve years. As part of the training, she set up the Transference Workshop that ran for many years and was open to colleagues outside the Trust as well as staff and trainees within the service. With a keen interest in developing theoretical and technical concepts, she has played a significant role in stimulating interest in the Trust's psychoanalytical work through her writing and through running supervisions and seminars in many parts of the world.

Research

With our background as scientist-practitioners, psychologists have been active in supporting, and sometimes leading, research across the Trust. Bernadette Wren set up an annual doctoral conference bringing together contributions from all the doctoral programmes in the organisation. She has been specifically employed for many years to provide research modules on our psychotherapy trainings.

Psychologists contributed to the International Study of Childhood Depression under the leadership of Judith Trowell. Renos Papadopoulos, David Campbell, and Emilia Dowling had supervisory roles in this project. Jenny Altschuler developed innovative clinical and research work on illness in the family leading to publications (Altschuler, 1997, 2016). She also participated in the television programme *Talking Cure* (see Holgate, Chapter 40), interviewing a family with Barbara Dale.

Phil Richardson joined the Trust in 1999 as Trust-wide head of psychology and lead on outcome research. He was research lead for the Tavistock Adult Depression Study (TADS, Fonagy et al., 2015) until his untimely death in 2007. The early scoping exercise for the adult depression study was undertaken by Phil Richardson and Maxine Dennis. Maxine went on to conduct many of the psychodynamic interviews, along with Joanne Carlyle and Rachel Thomas.

A number of psychoanalyst psychologists were the treating psychotherapists for the patients in the study including Caroline Garland, Cyril Couve, Steve Dreyer, Francesca Hume, and, after the TAD study, individually and in groups, Maxine Dennis. Two research psychologists, Susan McPherson and Felicitas Rost, were vital to the rigour and successful completion of the project.

Consultancy and the wider organisation

The Tavistock Consultancy Service (now Tavistock Consulting) was set up twenty-five years ago by Jon Stokes former head of the Adult Department (see Chapter 39) and Clare Huffington. Clare Huffington, Deirdre Moylan, and Judith Bell were subsequent directors. Tavistock Consulting aimed to take organisational consulting beyond publicly funded services and now works with clients across most other sectors. Its staff has included those from psychoanalytic and systemic backgrounds and the development of a Tavistock model of systems psychodynamic consultancy relied on the interplay of both theoretical approaches. Specifically systemic work in organisations was developed by David Campbell (Campbell, 2000) and Clare Huffington (Huffington, Armstrong, Halton, Hoyle, & Pooley, 2004).

Both Judith Bell and Deirdre Moylan also held significant roles in the Clinic, Judith as head of child psychology following on from Emilia Dowling and Deirdre as director of the Adolescent Department. Perhaps this illustrates one of the pleasures of working in the Trust; many staff have been involved simultaneously across different areas such as training and clinical work or research and consultancy, or all four tasks over time. This has led to a complex interweaving with mutual benefit to each area, though inevitably stressful when demands compete.

At the Portman Clinic disciplines were deliberately less differentiated to support Clinic cohesion in working with the demands of their patient population but many of the staff come from psychology backgrounds and, as elsewhere in the Trust, they have supported research and exploration of innovative approaches.

Louise Lyon first joined the Tavistock Clinic psychology discipline in 1984 as a basic grade clinical psychologist in a training post in the Adolescent Department, when Paul Upson was the head psychologist in the department. Ten years later, she returned to a consultant clinical psychology post in the Adolescent Department with a remit to develop time-limited psychotherapy for adolescents, now further developed and described in, for example, Briggs and Lyon (2012). She went on to become the Trust-wide head of psychology in 2004, Trust director in 2008, and director of quality and patient experience in 2014. In this last role she championed equality, diversity and inclusion for staff, students, and patients, led on implementing quality improvement, and, following Sally Hodges' pioneering work, strengthened the role of the patient's voice in shaping all our services.

The current picture

Vicky Lidchi is the current Trust-wide head of psychology, the largest discipline in the Trust. She notes the changing profile of psychologists with the expansion of services, the Trust's shift in emphasis as a centre of excellence in psychological therapies, and the increasing influence of the National Institute for Health and Care Excellence (NICE) guidelines and "evidence-based" approaches. Psychologists have been recruited across the bands, from counselling, clinical and educational psychology, and trained in approaches other than psychoanalytic and systemic. They have contributed to introducing or developing therapeutic approaches such as dynamic interpersonal therapy and extending the use of cognitive behavioural therapy. Psychologists have played significant roles in developing new initiatives such as resilience building programmes (Laverne Antrobus) and video-feedback intervention to promote positive parenting (VIPP) (Rachel James). The Tavistock and Portman is now attracting a new generation of dynamic young psychologists who are anxious to develop the identity of the discipline and what it means to be a psychologist in the organisation.

The discipline strategy is to value its rich history but to develop capacity in different therapeutic approaches. The psychology discipline aims to develop and write about innovative ways of working and applying new psychological models/frameworks such as the 'Power Threat Meaning Framework' (BPS Division of Clinical Psychology, 2018). The latter is a source of inspiration to many members of the discipline who are interested in developing services and therapeutic innovations that meet the needs of service users and do justice to the important contribution of structural inequalities, violence, and poverty to psychological difficulties. Psychology is acutely aware of the need for a diverse workforce that reflects the ethnic, cultural, and class background of service users.

Publications by psychologists

The references in this chapter represent a selection of books written or edited by Tavistock psychologists which reflect the discipline's significant contribution to the professional literature.

Note

1. The Caspari Foundation (http://caspari.org.uk/) continues to promote educational therapy.

* * *

Louise Lyon is a clinical psychologist and psychoanalyst. She joined the Adolescent Department of the Tavistock Clinic in 1984 for a two-year training post. She returned to the department in 1996 with a brief to develop time-limited approaches for adolescents and young adults. She founded and chaired the brief therapy workshop and led the Young People's Consultation Service for a period. Interested in how to maintain and develop thoughtful and compassionate services in an increasingly regulated context, she took on a number of challenges in clinical governance and quality improvement, most recently leading the Trust through two Care Quality Commission (CQC) inspections. She also worked to bring in different perspectives through, for example, supporting training in diverse clinical approaches, using data, bringing in the patient's voice, and tackling inequalities. She was for many years a national assessor for senior psychology posts and lead national assessor for psychotherapy posts in psychology. Senior roles in the Trust include Trust-wide head of psychology, clinical director of the Adolescent Department, and Trust director from 2008 to 2014. As Trust director she held overall operational responsibility for clinical, training, and consultancy services and leadership of the Clinics Committee which included the Trust-wide heads of discipline. She has published on relationships in early infancy and time-limited psychoanalytic approaches.

Emilia Dowling is a chartered clinical psychologist and systemic family psychotherapist who worked for many years at the Tavistock Clinic where she was head of Child Psychology and was involved in postgraduate training, clinical practice, and research. She is a retired member of the Institute of Family Therapy and the Association of Family Therapy. Emilia has worked with families and schools for more than forty years including pioneering work "taking the clinic to school" and developing school-based projects with parents, children, and teachers.

Her interests include systemic consultation with families, schools, and general practice and she has many years of experience of working with families during and after separation and divorce. In all areas of her work she is particularly interested in the children's perspective.

She has published widely and co-edited with the late Elsie Osborne *The Family and the School— A Joint Systems Approach to Problems with Children* (1985, with later editions in 1994, 2003).

She is co-author, with Gill Gorell Barnes, of *Working with Children and Parents through Separation and Divorce* (2000), and co-editor, with Arlene Vetere, of *Narrative Therapies with Children and Their Families* (2005, second edition 2017).

In 2012 she published, with Di Elliott, a book for teachers, *Understanding Children's Needs when Parents Separate*.

CHAPTER THIRTY-TWO

Holding tensions: social work and the Tavistock

Andrew Cooper

S ocial workers have been a part of the multidisciplinary set-up at the Tavistock almost since its beginning, and are a recognised core NHS profession. Over the decades this has been a source of strength but also a site of tension. Shortly after its seventy-fifth anniversary in 1995 I arrived at the Tavistock as professor of social work and the first appointed, rather than elected, head of discipline. I quickly realised that some of these tensions would require my attention. Many social workers in the Trust at that time seemed at best ambivalently identified with their core profession; also qualified as psychoanalysts, psychoanalytic or systemic therapists, these parallel identities appeared to be more attractive, absorbing, and prestigious. Few members of the discipline conveyed much interest in or awareness of the wider world of mainstream social work practice or training.

For many years "clinical social work" had been in decline in this wider context, a victim of social work's own wars with itself about its social purposes and methodologies, but also of the baleful impact of government-sponsored attacks on the professions generally and efforts to modernise them in favour of an emphasis on skills, competencies, performance, and value for money. By the 1990s the Tavistock seemed like a last line of defence for therapeutically informed social work. Psychoanalytic "casework" had come under attack from "radical" social work; the high water mark of psychiatric social work and the child guidance clinics was in the past. The Child Guidance Training Centre (CGTC; see Hopkins, Chapter 14) had been one centre of excellence and influence for social work. At my own appointments panel, an external professor of social work referred to this culture of therapeutic social work practice and theory as "bizarre"; coincidentally I had encountered her a few months earlier on a validation panel at my previous workplace (where relationship-based practice was also valued) when she deemed it "quaint".

When I arrived there was, despite this context, some excellent work in train at the Tavistock; a thriving post-qualifying multidisciplinary child protection master's programme, a newer Advanced Social Work course, and continuing work on an infant and young child observation training for social work teachers and educators, probably one of the most effective social work interventions mounted by the Trust, aimed at sustaining and reviving a broader professional culture of attention to psychological processes in the everyday work of social workers (Trowell & Miles, 1991). Its influence across the UK and beyond is widely apparent to this day. Clinically, social workers were fully engaged in and valued as members of the many multi-professional services offered by the clinics, but always with this tension in play—how does the "outer world" of social life and its contribution to the adversity suffered by patients relate to the internal worlds of individuals and families? Attention to external world forces (which social workers were often assumed to be over-preoccupied with) could readily be interpreted as a defensive turning away from the rigours of attending to the internal world and the unconscious processes assumed to primarily underlie and explain mental pain, family dysfunction, or adolescent crisis. It seemed to me that this dynamic also played a role in a perpetual Tavistock game of disciplinary snakes and ladders—who is rising, falling, at the top, in the middle, and at the bottom of the unspoken hierarchy of the professions? Poor professional self-esteem is a chronic condition in social work, but at the Tavistock one could study aspects of how this was generated and sustained as disciplines projected forcefully into one another within the pecking order of the rather closed ecology of the organisation.

At this time it was the systemic social work practitioners in the Trust who probably most comfortably and effectively "held" the various tensions in their thinking and discourse. But as a group they were straining and striving to establish their own separate identity within the Trust as a recognised discipline. Ultimately, it fell to the Professional Committee of the Trust (at that time the central forum for clinical, training, and research cultures engaged with organisational policy, strategy, and decision making) to decide on this bid for secession. As head of discipline for social work, I felt divided. Here was a strong and articulate group of clinically trained staff who passionately believed in the distinctiveness of their modality, leaders in their field in scholarship and research, but constrained in their development by an enforced "housing" within other disciplines—psychology, medicine, social work. If they departed I had little faith that most of them would continue to contribute very actively to the core project of social work in the Trust; if they stayed it would be as a discontented and at worst corrosive subsystem within the wider social work grouping. In the end the right decision seemed to be to endorse their desire for secession, and subsequently the systemic discipline has thrived, grown, and developed (see Helps, Barratt, & Daniel, Chapter 24). Later, adult psychoanalytic psychotherapists began to bid for a similar charter of freedom but were unsuccessful, largely perhaps because of a less favourable context in the wider NHS environment.

If I conceived my project as bringing the best of Tavistock clinical and training culture into a more productive and effective relationship with the mainstream then I believe my bosses at the time backed me implicitly or explicitly. "Management is always management at the boundary" was one of Anton Obholzer's nostrums, echoed by some of the world-class consultants who were around at the time and of whom I availed myself. David Armstrong showed me how to think about leadership, how to use my many dreams about the organisation as a source of intelligence in role. Sustaining a dual identity as a social worker and psychotherapist was important for credibility, and to *show* that some of the fault lines could be bridged. I found a clinical home in the vibrant and creative Adolescent Department Family Therapy service where social workers like Jeannie Milligan and Anna Dartington were part of the leadership, as were psychoanalysts such as Robin Anderson and Louise Lyon, who seemed to "get" the need for clinical practice that responded to real world conditions beyond the therapeutic dyad (Anderson & Dartington, 1998). Here I felt I could function as a genuine clinical social worker, working in the thick of the turbulent and sometimes explosive dynamics that troubled adolescents and their families brought into the room, as internal and external world forces collided and clashed. Things were starting to fall into place, and I have never given up this adolescent family clinical work.

The academic partnership with the University of East London was a crucial platform for further development. The professional doctorate in social work programme was established in the later 1990s and subsequently the postgraduate qualifying MA programme. The first cohorts of doctoral students took time to complete but then the trickle became, if not a flood, a steady stream of often inspiring, innovative, creative applied practitioner research, frequently resulting in publications and policy impact (e.g., Foster, 2016; Jordan, 2019; Swann, 2015). Some of these practitioners now contribute to teaching in the Trust, and nearly all occupy influential specialist or leadership roles in the sector. Tavistock staff had now consolidated a clear vision of how therapeutically informed social work could be realistically and meaningfully taught and developed, and the MA programme has become one of the best and most sought-after opportunities for social workers in the country. This student body is a substantial presence within the wider environment of the Trust and they bring something different, and seemingly not always easily assimilated by the organisation. Derived significantly from East London minority ethnic communities, they are an expressive presence, not always finely tuned in to the nuances of the rather middle-class and (often) defensive and precious etiquette of the Tavistock clinical and training culture. At times this makes them a ready vehicle for subtle, and sometimes not so subtle, discriminatory responses from other parts of the student population, and staff too. As social workers immersed over many decades in anti-discriminatory practice, we are fairly capable of handling these dynamics, but they do persist.

In these respects the work of Frank Lowe, who established the long series of "Thinking Space" events in the Trust has been crucial (Lowe, 2014). Thinking Spaces are safe forums wherein the difficult, complex, and anxiety-provoking sources and dynamics of everyday micro and macro discrimination, marginalisation, othering, identity, and scapegoating can be aired, and the subtle interplay of subjective and social processes at work can be understood. Straddling intellectual and paradigm boundaries, this work may be the strongest embodiment of what modern social work has brought to the Trust—a capacity to work across boundaries, categories, and the constraining hold of binary thinking and practice, in pursuit of forms of engagement that challenge social injustice while respecting the particularity of people's lived experience. In the early 2000s I acquired substantial funding to appoint two part-time race training consultants, to further the project of tackling the organisation's systemic difficulties in diversifying its staff and student populations. Agnes Bryan, a social worker, and Inga-Britt Krause, a systemic therapist and anthropologist, worked tirelessly and painfully on this project, and I believe made a huge contribution to tipping the dynamics of the Trust towards acceptance of a more open and inclusive culture.

Clinically social workers have increasingly contributed to innovative service developments that reach beyond the Trust into local and national communities of practice. The Trust's Gender Identity Development Service (Di Ceglie, Chapter 19, describes its origins), local "complexity forums" in child protection work (Karen Tanner), and the Family Drug and Alcohol Court (Steve Bambrough) are cases in point (Bambrough, Crichton, & Webb, 2019). All are multidisciplinary endeavours, the latter initially as a local experiment in "relational justice" which subsequently developed into a national programme, informed I believe by social workers' innate professional ease with, and desire for, translating the headier aspects of Tavistock thinking and practice into realistic interventions in the messier and less boundaried world of the "front line". Of course, other disciplines are quite capable of this, and it became an increasing necessity as the Trust's "reach" and "footprint" has been required by commissioners to extend far beyond NW3 and London and the South-East.

More and more, social workers began to assume positions of leadership and authority within the Trust. Within four years of arriving I became dean of postgraduate studies, and for five exhausting years tried to blend this position with continued academic and professional social work leadership. Later I took on the role of Director of Research and Development. Social work colleagues have been clinical directors, associate deans of training, service leads, "freedom to speak out guardians", patient and public involvement leads, and so on. Sometimes we wonder whether this is a mug's game, as we sacrifice operational role expertise for the demands of leadership, perhaps in the service of bolstering our always precarious position in the organisational hierarchy, or assuring our somewhat uncertain clinical identities. More positively I believe social workers are good at multidisciplinary leadership because they have always swum strongly in the waters of collaboration, often against the tide. In the wider world social workers carry huge statutory responsibility for life-changing decisions, usually in collaboration with others, but somehow the buck often seems to stop with us, especially when "things go wrong". Ultimately we are not called "social" workers for nothing; the realm of the social is not a uniform place, but a complex network of relationships, often conflicting. Working with conflict, or the threat of it, is a central skill in social work, and of leadership.

Formal research has always had an uncertain position in the Tavistock scheme of things. Strong on clinical and practice-based scholarship, as evidenced by the remarkable Tavistock Clinic Book Series (see Waddell, Chapter 43), empirical research has held a less secure place in the organisation's ambitions. Stephen Briggs has done much to develop social work research at the Tavistock, founding and leading the UEL Centre of Social Work Research, and promoting the importance of new models of "practice near" research that are now widely referenced. My own career as a "proper" researcher foundered on the rocks of all the other responsibilities I came to hold; it is sustained vicariously through the task of wide-ranging doctoral research supervision and the creativity of the growing network of social work doctoral graduates. Many social work colleagues would love to undertake more research, but in the context of an NHS mini-university that is not adequately resourced for the job of fulfilling this identity, it falls by the wayside. Not so publication in the wider sense. Recent years have seen a flow of exciting applied scholarship with Marion Bower (2004), Clare Parkinson (Hingley-Jones, Parkinson, & Allain, 2017), Robin Solomon (Bower & Solomon, 2017), Stephen Briggs (2008), Julian Lousada (Cooper & Lousada, 2005) and myself (Cooper, 2005, 2018) among the leading contributors.

Alongside those of other disciplines, there is ultimately nothing exceptional about the story of social work at the Tavistock. Each has its distinctive tale to tell. However, the slow, quiet revival of "relationship based" social work in the national sector does owe something to our endeavours over the years. We have collaborated strongly with colleagues in other universities, Sussex, Bedfordshire, the West of England, East London, Essex, Southampton, and East Anglia prominent among them. They look to us, and we to them. Recent success in winning partnership bids to mount national programmes of practice development reflects our current strength as a networked organisation of national significance. In particular the social work Practice Development Supervisors Programme, led by Jo Williams, has extended the reach and impact of Tavistock approaches to reflective practice from both a psychodynamic and systemic stance.

This chapter is a story told through a rather personal lens. Others, such as Gill Rusbridger who has led the discipline strongly in recent years might tell it differently. There are exceptional staff not mentioned by name here. I hope they take no offence. I have tried to write something that encapsulates a quarter of a century of achievement at the expense of complete inclusivity. Of course that does run counter to the democratic sensibility that is a core part of social work's informal sense of identity, a sensibility that is as always a source of great strength, and sometimes of vulnerability, in the intensely rivalrous but also astonishingly creative institution that is the Tavistock.

* * *

Andrew Cooper has been professor of social work at the Tavistock Centre and University of East London since 1996. He is an adult psychoanalytic therapist who works in the Adolescent Family Therapy Service of the Trust. He set up and still leads the professional doctorate programmes for social workers and social care staff, now validated by Essex University.

Earlier in his career Andrew was a member of a cross-national research team looking at child protection and welfare systems and practices in European countries, an experience which taught him to never ignore experiential or intellectual context. He is interested in how psychoanalytic and systems psychodynamic thinking and practice can inform social, political, and policy analysis and behaviour. This is reflected in his many publications and in his co-ordination of the long-running Tavistock Policy Seminar series (see Cooper, Chapter 44). He now works part-time at the Tavistock, and devotes his remaining energies to later life parenthood, painting, and attempting to write fiction.

CHAPTER THIRTY-THREE

Nursing at the Tavistock Clinic

Peter Griffiths

Nursing presence

It is difficult to say quite when nursing first began to take up its presence as a discipline within the Tavistock Clinic. Isabel Menzies' study of nursing ("A case study in the functioning of social systems as a defence against anxiety") was published in 1960 and drew attention to the emotional experience and work of nurses in a general hospital setting. It importantly identified a paradigm for thinking about the evolution and presence of social defences against the primitive anxieties stirred up by the emotional experience of intimate care work. In their study, *Anxiety and the Dynamics of Collaboration*, Woodhouse and Pengelly (1991) used this framework to explore anxieties in the care work of a variety of disciplines, including health visitors and other workers. Menzies' paper became one of the most cited pieces of social science research, and a framework that has been used in other settings, by other disciplines, over many years (Armstrong & Rustin, 2015).

Isabel Menzies' study influenced perceptions about nursing work at the Tavistock Clinic and Institute for many years. It was often a staple requirement for reading on many different courses, in developing thinking about the effects of care work and the cultural and social structures created unconsciously as defences against the emotional experience of care work. Later it was used in thinking about institutional observations (Hinshelwood & Skogstad, 2000).

Valery Golding, who worked on the original study at King's College Hospital with Menzies in the late 1950s, later developed, with Anna Dartington, a short course in psychodynamic thinking for nurses at the Tavistock Clinic. It was a short course which ran until the late 1980s or early 1990s. Anna Dartington (1945–2007[1]) originally trained as a general nurse, just after Menzies' study was published. She then went on to undertake a post-qualification training in psychosocial nursing at the psychoanalytic therapeutic community, the Cassel Hospital (E. Barnes, 1968; Barnes, Griffiths, Ord, & Wells, 1998) before leaving to retrain as a social worker and then as a psychotherapist specialising in work with adolescents at the Tavistock Clinic.

Anna was influential in paving the way for the emergence of nursing as a discipline at the Clinic. This was brought about through her continued interest in nursing, through lobbying senior management about training for nurses and of their "absent presence" within the Clinic. Anna retained an interest in nurses and nursing throughout the remainder of her career, being a founder member of the Cassel nurses association in 1992, and through her work with Julia Fabricius (a nurse and psychoanalyst) with nurses in other settings. In a powerful and evocative analysis of the experience of nursing and of its effects upon others Dartington wrote:

> The intense emotions aroused [in nursing] are thought to threaten not only efficiency, but also the fabric of the institution itself … it seems to be the fate of those who work on the staff/client boundary, to carry and attempt to contain this anxiety so the rest of the organization can experience an emotion-free zone in which to operate. In order to maintain this, these frontline workers must be silenced, anaesthetized, infantilized or otherwise rendered powerless. (Dartington, 2019, p. 107)

While the Tavistock was not, nor is in any way an emotion-free zone, one can perhaps hypothesise from Menzies' comments made about nurses and nursing, and from comments made by Tavistock colleagues in other disciplines, that for a considerable time nursing was kept at an arm's length distance for this reason. Nurses and nursing were objects of study and interest but not until much later brought over the boundary in any meaningful way for a co-creative exploration as a discipline alongside others. In the early 1990s, it was recognised by the professional committee at the Tavistock Clinic that, while nursing was and remains the largest professional discipline within the National Health Service, it was not represented as a clinical discipline at the Clinic. Nurses had attended programmes of study at the Tavistock Clinic for many years. Some had undertaken psychotherapy trainings, but many had largely attended applied programmes. In fact, at one point, nurses were ranked third in the disciplines attending applied courses. Something more specific was required.

The appointment of nurses within the Clinic and development of training for nurses

As a professional discipline, nursing was only accepted into the Tavistock Clinic as a co-discipline some seventy-five years after the Clinic was established. This development was driven by political and economic motivations but equally by the sincerely held views of some senior Tavistock staff. Many of these had worked with nurses in other settings, such as at the Cassel and the

Maudsley and Bethlem Hospitals, and knew that nurses could both gain from and enrich the multidisciplinary milieu at the Clinic.

In 1995 the first nurse was appointed as a senior lecturer in nursing within the Adult Department. As a nurse and qualified psychotherapist, he was employed to develop the training of nurses in adult psychotherapy, within the Adult Department, but equally to develop training for nurses within and outside the Clinic. Two nurses began the adult psychotherapy training in the late 1990s, one a senior lecturer in nursing at Middlesex University. In collaboration with the Cassel Hospital and the Nursing School at Middlesex University, an MSc programme in applied psychodynamic practice was developed. The MSc in institutional and community care[2] was a successful course that ran for many years, training nurses who were later to become nurse clinicians at the Tavistock Clinic. The course was specifically created for nurses, social workers, and other allied healthcare professionals (AHPs), to provide a postgraduate education and training in the application of psychodynamic and social systemic ideas to practice in the settings from which the students came.

In 1999, the first nurse was appointed within the Child and Family Department, a joint clinical nurse/senior lecturer role between the Child and Family Department and Middlesex University. The remit of this role was to develop courses for nurses at pre-and post-registration levels at the university, as well as further courses and roles for nurses in clinical services at the Clinic. Alongside the development of the aforementioned MSc (M19), the role-holder enabled other Tavistock applied training courses to be professionally validated by the English National Board for Nursing (ENB) as accredited post-registration nursing courses: the Pg cert (D3) in applied systemic theory; the Pg cert (D33) in communicating with young people: adolescent mental health; the Pg cert (D30) in therapeutic communication with children, and the Pg cert (D11) in working with groups in the public and independent sectors.

These courses offered models of psychodynamic and systemic practice for nurses from varying fields of practice and working in acute and community settings, who were already involved in significant mental health work, but for which they had little preparation in their pre- or post-registration training. These included health visitors, school nurses, practice nurses, district nurses, paediatric nurses, and accident and emergency nurses. The aim was that the training would enable nurse practitioners to develop the appropriate psychotherapeutic skills and capabilities they needed to do this work. This modelled moving beyond medication and remedial action, to the importance of relational work with patients and their families. They were working towards significant change and development in clients, aimed more at promoting mental health and preventing mental illness, as well as caring for and treating existing mental ill health.

By the mid-2000s there was the development in the Adult Department of a programme of short bespoke courses for mental health nurses in the dynamics of mental health (D65). These were short courses developed at the South London and Maudsley Hospitals (SLaM), at CNWL, Oxleas, Camden and Islington, and Barnet, Enfield and Haringey mental health trusts and at

Broadmoor special hospital. As nursing became a graduate profession, for a period of time attendance at these courses could be used as a top-up academic training credit, for nurses seeking BSc degree awards.

The development of nursing practice within the Clinic

Gradually over time within the Child and Family Department (latterly the Children, Young Adult and Families Department, CYAF) and within adult and forensic services more and more nurses were appointed into clinical nursing posts and training posts. Within the Child and Family Department, this began with outreach nurses attached to the North and South Camden child and adolescent mental health teams, working out of the clinic into homes, cafés, or wherever they could reach difficult to engage adolescents, or working into Tier 4 (inpatient psychiatric) adolescent units to enable patients to have earlier planned discharge and receive care in their community. This has in more recent years become a nurse-led service—Camden Adolescent Intensive Support Service (CAISS)—providing an independent commissioned service that employs many nurses and serves other Tavistock clinical teams. A senior nurse lecturer, trained in systemic family psychotherapy, was appointed to develop further courses for nurses, as well as to specialise in working with the emotional sequelae of physical illness for individuals and families. Over time, nurses were appointed into the Family Drug and Alcohol Court Service (FDAC), the MOSAIC learning disability team, the North and South Camden CAMHS teams, the Arrest and Deferral service in Camden and Islington, the Camden drug service for young people, within the multi-agency liaison team (MALT), to work with the local authority, and into the Portman Forensic CAMHS team. More recently a nurse has been appointed into the Autism and Learning Disabilities team.

After an initial nursing consultation, a new nursing service was developed at Gloucester House (the Clinic's school; see Nicholson & Johns, Chapter 15), to work alongside teachers and child psychotherapists, creating a third integrating therapeutic space in work with severely troubled young people. This nurse-led service has grown in strength and developed an outreach service to families and schools.

Nurses work within both the Gender Identity Development Service (GIDS) and Adult Gender Identity Service. In addition to this there have been other more strategic developments of nursing, both in the establishment of the national headquarters of the Family Nurse Partnership (FNP) within the Tavistock Clinic but equally within the development of perinatal services. Student nurses now regularly undertake training placements at the Tavistock Clinic, working alongside Clinic nurses, as part of their nurse training at Middlesex and City Universities.

Historically, within the adult and forensic services, the staff posts to train as psychoanalytic psychotherapists were not available to nurses. This changed in 2010; nursing is now a recognised discipline and a nurse has undertaken an outreach role from within the Fitzjohn's Specialist Service. Nurses are working across primary care, in external psychotherapy services, and have taken up significant roles in working with patients with medically unexplained symptoms, working in GP practices within the Primary Care Psychotherapy Consultation Service in Hackney and latterly the Team around the Practice (TAP) in Camden.

The recognition of nursing skills and capabilities

In their own right, each nurse has developed a nursing specialism within their team. They draw upon a rich philosophy of nursing work that might be informed by a variety of psychological approaches, including psychoanalytical and systemic, but which also brings into play the core nursing skills of engagement: working alongside, sitting with distress, containing anxiety and sometimes huge risk, with a wide range of individuals; child, adolescent, parent, staff, and with other agencies. This pragmatism draws on nursing knowledge and authority gained in multidisciplinary teams and wards. The added value of nursing experience and ward-based authority can come as a surprise to non-nursing colleagues! Seemingly ordinary skills exploit the therapeutic potential of everyday activities. Such work can be at odds with a more professional distance held by colleagues delivering specific therapy within boundaried sessions, which can lead to tensions about the therapeutic frame. It is by way of a "working through" of these tensions—each learning from experience—that the nursing role has come to be seen as an important additional clinical practice within the Clinic.

In the field of training, this ability to work alongside others—other disciplines and other theoretical paradigms—led to the development of new tri-modal training courses, weaving human development and neuroscience, and psychodynamic and systemic ideas into applied courses for nurses and others working with children, adolescents, families, and young adults (D24 and D24A), and a new training in psychodynamic psychotherapy in working with children, young people, and families (M34).

In all, there are now some thirty-three nurses working in a variety of different services across the Clinic, in clinical services within it and in many outlying services based in and outside London. These nurses occupy leadership roles as consultant nurses, clinical nurse specialists, leaders of nurse-led services and other clinical services and practice initiatives within the Trust related to PPI (Patient and Public Involvement), the assessment of clinical risk, clinical service improvements, and leadership of work within the National Workforce Skills Development Unit (NWSDU). Nurses have undertaken research as part of their studies and within their clinical roles, but to further the aspiration of growing a nursing research community, an honorary clinical nursing professor has been appointed.

Increasing strategic influence within and beyond the Tavistock Clinic

When the Clinic became a Foundation Trust in the mid 2000s, a nurse was appointed to sit on the board of directors, as director of nursing, and this role has grown from half a day to be a full-time post. This appointment has led to an engagement with the profession of nursing at local, regional, and national levels, through for example the London Capital Nurse programme, with the Royal College of Nursing and other national and charitable nursing bodies.

There has been nurse-led research around nursing preceptorship schemes across London and the development of reflective learning training, for designated preceptorship nurse leads and other nurses in supervisory roles. There has been nursing research undertaken into the provision of work discussion groups for student mental health nurses, which alongside other nurse-led professional development schemes has led to a North London partnership, professional development programme for trainee advanced clinical practitioners (ACPs), many of whom are nurses.

There have been training events and national conferences, for instance to support nurses working with chronically ill patients who have inflammatory bowel disease, recognising both the impact of the illness on the patient, and of their clinical care upon the nurses. A nurse-led symposium, drawing a national membership, reviewed the work of Isabel Menzies-Lyth, evaluating the influence of her 1960 seminal paper sixty years on. It explored Menzies' own evolution of her ideas about nurses and nursing and their appropriation and use by nurses in the development of nursing practice, notably in the development of primary nursing and nursing development units (NDUs) in the 1980s and early 1990s and their loss through increasing managerialism in the late 1990s. It considered their contemporary relevance to the training of nurses today, and what happens to nurses as they qualify and what enables nurses to stay in nursing.

The symposium identified many rich themes and many tensions:

- A tension between meeting an increasing plethora of nursing training competences and nurses being able to really focus on engaging with "in the moment experiences", that give real importance to the therapeutic potential of human relationships within the work.
- The need for clinical supervision and a reflective culture, not just managerial supervision, both to register and to be curious and learn from these moments in order to better support patients and other nurses.
- That good mental health is not the same as developing resilience, which all too often can be a discourse that has come to mean survival and surviving.
- Moreover, that these and other tensions can interfere with the professional identity of what it means to be a nurse, all too often apologised for—"I'm just a nurse"—which denies and undervalues the real complexities of practice and the capabilities nurses possess.
- And that the seemingly perpetual language of a "crisis in nursing" does nothing to ameliorate this and needs to be thought about in terms of whom and what purpose this serves? (Griffiths, forthcoming).

Besides training specifically for them, many nurses are on applied courses including those at senior nursing leadership and managerial levels, for example on the MA course in consulting and leading in organisations: psychodynamic and systemic approaches (D10) or the Tavistock consultancy coaching course. Some nurses undertake training in systemic and psychoanalytic therapies while at the same time retaining their nursing discipline. Others go on to train as family therapists (M6), child psychotherapists (M80), and/or as adult psychotherapists (D58 & M1) but use their enhanced skills to further train nurses.

In conclusion—a positive beginning for a late starter!

Nursing may be a late entrant as a discipline to the Clinic but over the last twenty-five years of its existence it has made its presence felt within the Clinic. This has been through the development of nursing services, within existing services, and through new innovative nurse-led services. Equally its influence has been felt, through the development of a multiplicity of different courses, some specifically for nurses, and through nurses now teaching on training courses for other disciplines within the Clinic. There have been attempts to capture something of this experience over this quarter of a century, in a number of publications, some listed below. There are plans for a book capturing nurses' contribution to the Tavistock and Portman's clinical services.

Bibliography of selected Tavistock nurse publications

Evans, M. (2009). Tackling the theory practice gap in mental health nurse training. *Mental Health Practice*, *13*(2): 21–24.

Evans, M. (2014). "I'm beyond caring", a response to the Francis Report: The failure of social systems in health care to adequately support nurses and nursing in the clinical care of their patients. *Psychoanalytic Psychotherapy*, *28*(2): 193–210.

Evans, M. (2016). *Making Room for Madness in Mental Health: The Psychoanalytic Understanding of Psychotic Communication (Tavistock Clinic Series)*. London. Karnac.

Evans, M., & Franks, V. (1997). Psychodynamics as an aid to clear thinking about patients. *Nursing Times*, *93*(10): 50–52.

Franks, V. and Griffiths, P. (2001). Teaching emotional nursing. *Practice Nursing*, *12*(9): 351–353.

Franks, V. & Griffiths, P. (2002). Caring for patients who provoke strong feelings. *Practice Nursing,13*(5): 214–216.

Franks, V., & Griffiths, P. (2006) The caring professions—the role in the mind—Nursing as a case. Study paper given at Jock Sutherland Lecture, February 2005, Edinburgh, *Tavistock Occasional Paper Series*.

Glendinning, L. (2008). Making relationships through genograms. *Context, 100*: 27–28.

Griffiths, P. (2001). Child and adolescent mental health: A cause for concern in primary care nursing. *Mental Health Practice, 5*(1): 38–39.

Griffiths, P. (2012). Plotting a new course. *Young Minds Magazine, 117*: 36.

Griffiths, P., & Franks, V. (2004). Nursing mental health at the Tavistock. In: S. Tilley (Ed), *Psychiatric and Mental Health Nursing: The Field of Knowledge* (pp. 57–84). Oxford: Blackwell Scientific.

Lindsey, C., & Griffiths, P. (2004). Developing a comprehensive CAMHS. *Young Minds, 73*: 31–33.

Notes

1. In a powerful and learned exposition of the systematic social neglect of vulnerable people, Anna's husband Tim Dartington (2010) includes a section on his experience as her carer as she declined into Alzheimer's disease, still only in her fifties. This is followed by Anna's own account of this process: "My unfaithful brain" (A. Dartington, 2010). (Ed.)
2. M19, later to become the MSc in psychodynamic practice for nurses, social workers, and other care professionals.

* * *

Peter Griffiths, consultant nurse and couple psychoanalytic psychotherapist.

Peter trained originally as a general nurse (SRN), developing modes of primary nursing on what became a Nursing Development Unit at Charing Cross Hospital. This experience led him to train as a mental health nurse (RMN) at the Bethlem and Maudsley Hospitals and at Brunel University. Having developed an interest in psychodynamic relational nursing, he went on to train and then work at the Cassel Hospital for eleven years, where with others, he developed the Psychosocial Nursing course, training for workers in other settings, and researched and developed literature on psychosocial practice.

He was recruited to the Tavistock staff in 1999, as the first nurse in the Child and Family Department, to develop both the nursing service and applied courses, drawing on psychodynamic social systems and systemic thinking, for nurses in many varied settings. He undertook this role as a joint position with Middlesex University, where as a principal lecturer he developed family mental health nurse training for student and post-registration nurses. At the Tavistock Clinic he went on to develop tri-modal training courses at applied, pre-clinical, and BPC accredited clinical training levels, winning with others awards that recognised the innovative nature of these courses.

He has been involved regionally and nationally in developing therapeutic training for the NHS and for public and voluntary sectors' workforces, using training that makes use of group relations methodology to explore the complexities of multidisciplinary and inter-agency work. He has been a staff member and director of group relations conferences both within the UK and abroad. For eight years he was the CAMHS training cluster lead and then portfolio manager for psychological therapies at the Clinic, before retiring in 2017.

He now works part-time within the Child, Young Adult and Families Directorate (CYAF) and as a visiting lecturer in the Department of Education and Training (DET) at the Tavistock and Portman NHS Foundation Trust. He works clinically with families, parents, couples, and individuals, using a variety of therapies within the Trust, and as a couple psychoanalytic psychotherapist in public and private practice.

I would like to thank Chris Caldwell, Claire Shaw, Kirsty Brant, and Lynne Reed for their contributions to this chapter.

Part VII

Consultation, court, and organisations

CHAPTER THIRTY-FOUR

Child protection and the courts

Judith Trowell

Introduction

The development of child protection work at the Tavistock arose from small numbers of cases that caused concern and needed skilled help. In 1984 Dr Arnon Bentovim and social worker Carolyn Okell Jones started a monthly assessment workshop for possible sexual abuse cases. I had been working one day a week for the NSPCC and on a training placement there in 1979, amongst a range of abuse cases, saw my first case of child sexual abuse. Physical abuse was rarely referred to the Tavistock, only emerging at times in cases referred for other reasons. Dame Elizabeth Butler-Sloss, who chaired the Cleveland inquiry into child abuse (Butler-Sloss, 1988) confirmed from the physical, psychological, and narrative evidence that sexual abuse of children had occurred. There was widespread anxiety about child sexual abuse and profession-als needed expert assessments for their patients and clients. Emotional abuse and neglect were also often difficult to clarify and needed assessment. Where any of these cases showed probable abuse, court hearings would follow.

The law impacts on children, young people, and their families in many ways. The Family Division becomes involved when the state is concerned about children's development or when the parental care they receive indicates some form of abuse or neglect. The court is also involved in divorce when the couple have children. This is private law but the impact of family breakdown on children means that this aspect is now taken seriously. When the court decides children must no longer remain with their parents they then enter the care system and are fostered, or go forward for adoption. There are currently about 75,000 children in care and of these there are usually about 4,000 to 5,000 adoptions a year. The court plays a significant role in these children's lives. For example, the 2000 Leaving Care Act requires local authorities to support care leavers in this major transition into independence. Adoption can only be confirmed by the court. Recently the courts have recognised that many families break down, and their children come into care, because of parental drug and alcohol addiction. There have been attempts to modify the court process to assist these very troubled families.

An expanding area of legal work is with refugees and asylum seeking young people, particularly unaccompanied minors. Inter-country adoption has escalated, involving courts across cultures, for example where a parent from another jurisdiction takes the child out of the UK without the consent of the UK-based parent.

Why would one do this work, which takes hours of time and can be very challenging? Dr Sue Isaacs Elmhirst[1] thought, given that staff at the Tavistock were highly trained in communication with children, in child development, and child observation, and that they understood the complex family dynamics as well as the organisational conflicts that are enacted in the professional network, that we should—indeed we must—be active in the court domain. With our skills and experience we have an obligation to ensure the best possible outcomes for children.

The child abuse assessment team

This led to the development of the child abuse assessment team and later of the expert witness service preparing court reports and, if need be, giving evidence. It seemed reasonable to try to build on this in the Tavistock Clinic as a specialist service. External events played a part; social services departments became overwhelmed by referrals of protection cases, arising from physical abuse and neglect and, after Cleveland, sexual abuse referrals increased. As our expertise grew, the first step was recognition of the needs of the children, families, and professionals. We could provide help and support, child psychotherapy, family therapy, clinical work with parents and carers, and consultations with professionals alongside careful assessments.

Emerging from this experience came the view that the skills and knowledge acquired should be used to develop teaching arising from the clinical work. Trainings at different levels were set up at the Tavistock and beyond. There was an introductory training, a master's degree course, and a PhD programme. Many cases involved complex legal issues, and the legal workshop we set up provided a forum where a range of cases could be discussed with senior clinicians, lawyers, and a barrister.

Our influence spread, with participation in local and national policy working parties, and working conferences with the judiciary. The president of the Family Division of the Royal Courts of Justice (Elizabeth Butler-Sloss) decided to inaugurate a biennial conference, at Dartington in Devon, to keep the special family court justices up to date. I was on the planning group and gave presentations there, from which came other requests to lecture around the country. The emphasis on the voice of the child and the UK signing of the UN Convention on the Rights of the Child in 1992 were central.

Multidisciplinary working

Understanding the situations where children and young people are traumatised requires multiple perspectives on the children and their lives. As child abuse became better recognised, children's services within social service departments were overwhelmed and their staff often lacked the appropriate training. The Tavistock Clinic could now provide multidisciplinary teams to think about these cases and sometimes undertake the clinical assessment and treatment. We gathered together clinical psychologists, educational psychologists, mental health social workers, adult and child trained psychiatrists, sometimes forensic staff, and lawyers to clarify the legal issues.

This made it possible to understand the abuse in the round: family dynamics and parental mental health, the social and educational life of the child, and his or her development, intellectual capacity, and mental health. We looked for a range of problems, including emotional and behavioural disorders, post-traumatic states as well as psychopathology. All these findings would be put together in a report which would usually lead to the need for attendance at court.

In the tradition of the Tavistock, we had a staff group used to reflecting on the impact of these cases on ourselves. When major decisions had to be made that were going to be life changing, our discussions during the assessment helped whoever was to attend court—usually the psychiatrist—to avoid feeling a little godlike or a member of a "court club". The impact on a professional of a parent or parents sitting in court fighting for their child, weeping and having to describe why they could not continue to care for the child, could be gut wrenching. As local authorities became better trained, many cases were dealt with in their locality but we were still needed in complex, more challenging cases.

Containment

A cornerstone of the psychoanalytic stance and of the training at the Tavistock Clinic is containment. Our capacity to bear not knowing, to be able to avoid rushing into action or decision making, was crucial. Anxiety around referred cases was generally very high. We were asked for our expert opinion but often what was wanted was action or confirmation of action already taken. Of course in life-threatening situations keeping individuals safe has to be paramount, but in most cases what was required was careful assessment and time for reflection and discussion.

Unconscious processes could become part of the total picture, where the transference and countertransference of the clinicians, their gut feelings, and the dynamics within the staff group provided rich and significant information about the case. For this to be possible there needs to be a secure professional environment for clinicians to feel able to share their non-verbal experiences while working on a case. For example, the parents' relationship had broken down and each alleged that the other had sexually abused the child. Clinicians saw the child, the mother, and the father individually, and contacted the school. Staff meetings were tense and holding the case together became very difficult. The case consultant and then the wider staff team had to insist on case discussion to manage, digest, and reflect upon the meaning of all this. From experience of the "non-programme workshop" run in the 1970s by Dr Ron Britton (Britton, 2005) in the Department for Children and Parents we were aware of the capacity of professional groups to re-enact the dynamics of the troubled families we were working with.

The Orkney child abuse scandal

Arising from allegations of sexual abuse in February 1991 several children were removed from their homes in dawn raids on Orkney. In the subsequent inquiry, chaired by Lord Clyde (HMSO, 1992) later that year, I was asked to look at the social work practice. I interviewed social workers and read all the transcripts of the interviews and numerous other documents around the case. I had to read 320 hours of court transcripts of people giving evidence. What emerged was a complex system of organisational rivalry: social services at loggerheads with police, while the GP and paediatrician (his wife) hid the children from social workers who wanted to interview them. During the lengthy court hearing I managed to convey my concern that the children were somewhat lost in the interdisciplinary issues, a very vivid enactment of uncontained professional anxiety.

Psychoanalytic understanding of violence and sexuality

Human sexuality usually involves another who may be male, female, or gender fluid, and the sexual relationship provides mutual pleasure. Sometimes the sexual need turns in on itself and the person becomes self-absorbed, narcissistic. Other emotions are also present such as guilt and shame which may or may not be conscious. At times sexuality can become attached to love or hate in a perverse way that leads to sadism or masochism. Physical and sexual abuse can be sadistic, the perpetrator gaining a sense of excitement, power, and sexual satisfaction. Given that sexual release is addictive the repeated behaviour can be understood even when the individual may rationally want to stop.

In some abusers sexual satisfaction from a number of different activities including online pornography, group sex, and oral and anal sex have proliferated over the years. Our understanding is that children have sexual feelings and bodies capable of sexual pleasure but not mature adult sexuality. Normal childhood sexual awareness can be cut across if they experience full adult sexuality while deprived of a gradual flowering of their own sexuality, as these examples illustrate.

A girl of about eight years old whose mother had died quite suddenly became her father's full sexual partner. Asked about this, she insisted they were in love and would marry in due course. There were no concerns about the girl at school but neighbours were worried about the father and his inappropriate behaviour in the local community.

A man from another country lived with a British woman for many years. She had three children the younger two of which were his. The first problem that emerged was the sexual relationship between this man and the eldest child, a girl. Mother blamed her daughter whom she saw as her rival for the man, and the girl was taken into care. She had been vaginally abused for some time. Later the younger two, a boy and a girl, had serious problems in school. Mother became very concerned. The man disappeared, leaving behind two very damaged children. They were used to sexual activity with the man, with each other, and also with the family dog. The little girl was terrified she might be pregnant by the dog.

What did the Tavistock Clinic contribute in these cases? It was a slow process of unravelling what was going on. Anxiety was high, and managing the assessment process required considerable containment. It also required the capacity to think about what was happening in these families which at that time was much less recognised than now. There was deep scepticism about child sexual abuse—"Do people really do that?"—and suspicions about our motives, implying with unpleasant innuendo that we had our own problems.

The Tavistock's most important contribution was our determination to focus on the children and to secure the best possible outcomes for them in placements and therapeutic treatment.

Research

The research that followed from all of this was initially small projects:

a) To look at the effectiveness of the trainings (Yelloly, Loughlin, Rolph, Stanford, & Trowell, 1994)
b) To ask the children about their response to the child protection process (Stanford, 1992)
c) To look at different systems of child protection in other countries (Hetherington, Baistow, Katz, Mesie, & Trowell, 2002).

A bigger project funded by the Department of Health looked at treatment outcomes, based at the Tavistock and including the Royal Free Hospital, Great Ormond Street Hospital, the Maudsley Children's Department, and Camberwell Child Guidance Clinic (Trowell et al., 2002). Nine months of individual child psychotherapy together with parent work were compared with group therapy. All the children improved but the psychotherapy arm continued to improve after therapy ended. It seems that these children and their parent(s) had internalised some of the help received and also could talk more to each other.

One of the surprising findings from the initial assessment of the cases was the extent of depression in these children. At that time there were doubts about whether these children of six to fourteen years old could be depressed. This led on to the Childhood Depression Study

(Trowell et al., 2007). To obtain EU funding three EU countries had to be involved, so the study based at the Tavistock worked with colleagues in Athens (Greece) and Helsinki (Finland). In this study individual child psychotherapy together with parent work was compared with family therapy. As in the depression study there was random allocation. All the children improved and were no longer depressed. The children receiving family therapy improved more quickly, but the individual therapy cases continued to improve after therapy ceased.

These clinical outcome studies were important because by now social services and schools had gained expertise in assessment and were asking for therapeutic intervention, no longer demanding assessment and court work. The Tavistock was in a good position to provide effective interventions.

Note

1. Susanna Isaacs Elmhirst was a psychoanalyst and a consultant psychiatrist at CGTC, the last to be appointed before the merger with the Tavistock Clinic in 1985. Obituary, *The Guardian* 29 April, 2010. https://theguardian.com/society/2010/apr/29/susanna-isaacs-elmhirst-obituary

* * *

Dr Judith Trowell MB BS, DCH, DPM, FRCPsych, F Inst Psychoanalysis

After qualification at the Royal Free Hospital I did paediatrics which I loved. One admission stands out: a pretty child of five years with a serious head injury. Mother had hit her with her stiletto heel; the child thankfully died. Five years in general practice followed—the doctors five men and myself—with lots of children and women patients. I had to attend all child protection case conferences. By then I wanted to follow my preferred career in medicine. I came to see Bob Gosling at the Tavistock saying I wanted to be a child psychiatrist. He told me to go and get the MRCPsych (British psychiatric diploma). A part-time married woman's training post was created at Shenley Hospital and I loved it. I worked for some time on the Coombe Wood mother and baby unit. A memorable case was a mother who drowned her baby in a nappy bucket. I later worked at the Tavistock with mothers who had killed their babies. I noticed there that many of the mothers admitted had been delivered by Caesarian section, which led to my first research project (Trowell, 1982, 1983) for which I had to train with Mary Ainsworth in the Strange Situation Test.

I started as a registrar at the Tavistock Clinic in January 1975 and became a consultant child and adolescent psychiatrist at Watford Child Guidance Clinic in 1977. There I had a team member in every secondary school in my patch, a monthly physical and learning disability team meeting, and a time for GPs to phone in, amongst other services. In 1980 I moved back to the Tavistock as a consultant and became chair of the Department for Children and Parents in 1982. After the merger with CGTC (see Hopkins, Chapter 14), the Child and Family

Department took off as a national centre for child and family mental health. I remained the chair until 1990. I became vice chair of Camden ACPC (safeguarding board) and started the Monroe Young Family Centre (Trowell, 1996). I was on the Child and Adolescent Faculty at the Royal College of Psychiatrists (RCPsych) and various Department of Health child protection working parties. I supervised higher psychiatric trainees weekly at the Maudsley Children's Department and gave lectures on child abuse to judges and other professionals.

In my spare time I did the psychoanalytic adult and child trainings at the Institute of Psychoanalysis, and was chair of the child analytic training there. I helped develop trainings at the Tavistock for social workers with CCETSW and child protection trainings. I taught around the UK and in Europe, Israel, Australia, Argentina, and USA. I helped set up the chair in child and adolescent psychiatry for Professor Issy Kolvin and we began a programme of clinical research, some of which is cited below. I was in John Bowlby's research group and did the Adult Attachment training with Mary Main twice. I had hoped to develop the Bowlby research unit.

Besides formal research papers on psychotherapy for depression (e.g., Trowell et al., 2007; Trowell & Miles, 2011; Kolaitis et al., 2014) and child abuse (Trowell et al., 1999; Trowell et al., 2002), I have edited and contributed to books on child observation in training and court work (Trowell, Paton, Davids, & Miles, 1998; Yelloly, Loughlin, Rolph, Stanford, & Trowell, 2004), the emotional needs of young children (Trowell, 1996), on fathers (Trowell & Etchegoyen, 2002), children of mentally ill parents (Hetherington, Baistow, Katz, Mesie, & Trowell, 2002), assessing change in psychotherapy (Tsiantis & Trowell, 2018), supporting and learning from trainees (e.g., Trowell, Davids, Miles, Shmueli, & Paton, 2008), research methods (Long & Trowell, 2001), ethics, and multidisciplinary work in the family justice system (Thorpe & Trowell, 2007).

CHAPTER THIRTY-FIVE

Autonomic countertransference: the psychopathic mind and the institution

Rob Hale

Defences against madness and badness

Psychiatry is generally presented as an objective activity. Personal reactions are seen as an impediment to the scientific study of psychological phenomena—"countertransference" should be avoided or discounted. This chapter takes a very different view, namely that the study of countertransference in all its forms is essential to the understanding of patients and particularly of those with a psychopathic psychic structure.

For the past twenty-five years I have acted as external consultant to twelve forensic institutions, usually on a weekly basis, some less frequently, but always regularly. This is my attempt to chronicle these experiences and to extract some ideas on the nature and function of psychopathy. The consultation takes the form of a work discussion group with professionals from psychiatry, psychology, nursing, social work, occupational therapy, and occasionally administration. The topic is not decided in advance but is a current felt need—usually a clinical problem or an administrative crisis. Attendance at the group is voluntary—people are allowed to "vote with their feet", but once committed, people are expected to attend and they usually do; or they send their apologies. The groups are made up either of different professions or of a single profession; each has its advantages and disadvantages.

My "home base" has been the Portman Clinic for over thirty-five years with a spell of six years at the Tavistock Clinic. The Portman is an NHS outpatient clinic providing psychoanalytic psychotherapy for people with a history of violence or sexual perversion who may or may not have broken the law and received the appropriate punishment. My own training was as a general psychiatrist and as a psychoanalyst and my main clinical interest was the treatment of perpetrators of paedophilic acts. From quite early on I had run Balint groups for GPs and a lot of my own learning was in groups.

The first foray into the forensic world outside the Portman was in 1992 when I was approached by the then director of the Prison Medical Service to run a Balint group for prison medical officers at their training centre near Rugby. Attendance was sporadic, no doubt influenced by the threat of impending disbandment of the service. As is normal for a Balint group the participants would present a patient/inmate on a "felt need" basis. One week a PMO said, "I want to present a patient today; it's called Aylesbury Prison." A door had opened for me and for the group. From that time onwards my wish has been to focus not only on the relationship between the clinician and the patient but also on the relationship between the practitioner and the institution as well as the institutional "superstructure"—the agents of financial provision and probity and agents of authority. Outside this is the current legal and social context. And underpinning this understanding lies the question, "What function/s does society want our organisation to perform?"

Much of this is far from new, indeed as long ago as 1932 the psychiatrist and psychoanalyst Grace Pailthorpe carried out a psychological study of the inmates of Birmingham Prison and the report, which was published by the Home Office, was entitled "What we put in prison" (Pailthorpe, 1932) (not "Who we put in prison"), that is, "What is it in society that we want to be rid of and protected from?"

As I see it the toxic elements of society that we fear are madness and badness which we observe in our patients/prisoners; added to this is our own badness and madness which we project into them. We thus feel better when it is contained by an external force—be it the police, the courts, the prison, or the special hospital. What is in effect contained by the institution is anxiety, perceived at both a conscious and largely unconscious level. The response of the organisation is to set up systems such as rotas, data recording structures, or postgraduate education which serve a practical, necessary, and useful function but which preoccupy the staff and in so doing dilute their contact with the patients; the increasing anxiety in society, fuelled by the media and the blame culture, has led to ever increasing bureaucratic accountability which further dilutes direct contact with our patients.

Secure inpatient units tend to be closed boxes with little outside influence or independent view; the staff can become institutionalised with set ways of behaving and reacting to the patients; they long for external recognition of the work they are doing, yet paradoxically resent intrusion. This impact of the anxieties created by the work on the structure and function of a unit was first described in 1960 by Isabel Menzies' "A case-study in the functioning of social systems as a defence against anxiety: a report on a study of the nursing service of a general hospital". In his chapter "Managing social anxieties in public sector organisations" Anton Obholzer describes it thus:

> A way of protecting oneself against what is unbearable is to organise the work in ways that
> ward off primitive anxieties, rather than serving to carry out the primary task. A great deal

of what goes on is not about dramatic rescue but having to accept one's relative powerless-ness in the presence of pain, decrepitude, insanity and death.

Staff are ill-prepared for this in their training and in their work practice there is often no socially sanctioned outlet for their distress. This then expresses itself as illness, absen-teeism, high staff turnover, low morale, poor time keeping and so on. In a study on nurs-ing turnover (Menzies, 1960) it was found that it was usually the most sensitive nurses, those with the capacity to make the strongest contribution to nursing, who were the most likely to leave—perhaps those least willing to join in the institutional systems of denial. (Obholzer, 2019, pp. 179–180)

In a prison there are multiple tasks—removing someone from society, punishment, rehabili-tation, skills training, and so on, and what is regarded as primary will depend on the profes-sional's appointed position. For the inmate/patient the primary task is to get out. Should these defensive structures become excessive and become more important than the primary function of the institution, or should they fail altogether for whatever reason, the risk is that we will have a sick and dysfunctional organisation. This will be analogous to illness in an individual and will have its presenting signs and symptoms, of which more anon. Underneath, driving this pathological process will be the largely unconscious destructive purposes and actions of the patients. In my view, unconsciously, it is the function of the psychopathic patient to attempt to destroy the institution and its therapeutic purpose; equally and paradoxically it is the function of the institution to prevent him, for his sake, from succeeding. Thus the unconscious desires, purposes, and anxieties of the patients determine the shape and function of the institution. We think we design the institution; not so, it is the patients' unconscious processes to which we are responding.

Medicine is practised in three/four settings. In each case we respond to the specific anxieties which the patient brings to the consultation.

- In general medicine and surgery the anxieties are to do with death, dying, disfigurement, pain, and loss of control. ("Is it cancer? Is it terminal? How much will it hurt?")
- In the psychiatric setting the anxieties are of unbearable sadness or of madness—psychic disintegration.
- In a forensic institution, be it a prison or a secure unit, the anxieties are on one hand of cor-ruption and the power to corrupt—badness; on the other, violence, the wish to kill or inflict pain, again badness. Behind them lurks the descent into madness—far more frightening than badness.

In general practice all three are encountered, often with one overlaying another.

How do we, as individual professionals, protect ourselves from these anxieties? I described these protective mechanisms in my chapter with Liam Hudson on why our patients make us ill ("Doctors in trouble", Hale & Hudson, 1999). They include displacement, denial, intellectualisation, black humour, eroticisation, and acting out. For the most part they serve us well but when excessive they begin to fail us and we find the disturbance created within us unmanageable—we become sick, psychologically or physically.

So too an institution needs to protect itself with the same defensive manoeuvres, albeit the "symptoms" may take a different form. Displacement, for example may manifest as "The problem is the Department of Health or the Trust"; intellectualisation as "We only need to get the diagnosis/medication right and the problem will be solved". Eroticisation may take the form of sexualised relationships between staff members or dressing provocatively. Acting out may be at a personal level, such as excessive drinking or drugs; far more serious however is acting out with the patients (acting out in the countertransference). This may be through excessive use of medication, restriction of liberties, treating the patient in a disrespectful way, or treating him in a cruel or corrupt way. In its most extreme form it may involve breaking professional boundaries by entering into a sexual relationship with a patient. In all these boundary violations we, as staff, have identified with the psychopathic part of the patient and mimicked their actions; the guilt the institution then feels is, in part, the guilt the patient is seeking to avoid.

The autonomic countertransference

How is it then that these patients manage to affect us to the extent that we feel "infected" by something toxic without us realising it? The concepts of projection and projective identification may help us to understand this. Projection is the process whereby we resist acknowledging uncomfortable emotions within ourselves and attribute them to another person. In projective identification the recipient is unconsciously stimulated into experiencing these emotions or to enact the projected impulse. Ogden extends the concept thus:

> … it allows the infant (more accurately the mother–infant) to process experience in a way that differs qualitatively from anything that had been possible for the infant on his own. In projective identification the projector induces a feeling state in another that corresponds to a state that the projector had been unable to experience for himself. The recipient is enlisted in playing a role in an externalised version of the projector's unconscious state. (Ogden, 1984, p. 519)

What staff (that's all of us, by the way) do with that powerful and disturbing emotion will vary; they may rid themselves of it by actions which take the forms described above—essentially psychopathic and in the long term counterproductive and destructive of the institution. There is, however, an alternative as Ogden explains:

> When a recipient of a projective identification allows the induced state to reside within him without immediately attempting to rid himself of these feelings, a potential is created for the projector–recipient pair to experience that which had been projected in a manner that the projector alone had not been capable of. (Ogden, 1984, p. 519)

Within the therapeutic process this potential requires the therapist (or therapists) to recognise the emotion projected into him, or them, to name it to the patient in a timely and sensitive manner, and to seek to explore the many painful experiences and memories generating that emotion—to give it meaning and to attach it to people in the present and particularly in the past. It may sound simple but this is no easy task! It will only stand a chance of success if there is a forum for clinical discussion and for reflection and supervision, both individual and for the group.

The method by which the patient creates this reaction is important and in my view specific to situations dominated by psychopathic processes. I would suggest that this transfer of emotional disturbance fundamentally uses the autonomic nervous system which is predominantly outside conscious control. The autonomic system is divided into the sympathetic system and the parasympathetic system. The sympathetic system when stimulated by rage or fear prepares the body for fight or flight; the heart rate is increased, the pupils dilate, the skin sweats. Blood is diverted from the skin and the alimentary tract to the skeletal muscles, and the sphincters of the alimentary and urinary tract are closed. The parasympathetic system has the effect of counterbalancing the sympathetic system. It adapts the eyes to near vision, slows the heart, promotes secretion of salivary and intestinal juices and accelerates intestinal peristalsis.

Within the relationship between a violent individual and his/her victim there is contrasting sympathetic disturbance; the victim has sympathetic over-arousal, the flight response; but the perpetrator is likely to exhibit suppression of sympathetic activity as evidenced by an abnormally slow resting heart rate—a pattern demonstrated in four studies (Murray et al., 2016). The same autonomic sympathetic disturbance occurs, I believe, in the relationship between a violent patient and a therapist; by various means such as subtle intimidation or threats the violent patient may evoke a "fight or flight" reaction in the therapist, while remaining calm or even enjoying a feeling of being emptied of anxiety. Consider then the interaction between someone with a sexual perversion such as paedophilia and another; here the disturbance is in the parasympathetic system, the victim/therapist experiences nausea, the perpetrator sexual excitement: the same autonomic asymmetry. Because this projective process goes on in the autonomic system it bypasses conscious perception in both parties and as such is all the more powerful; hence my assertion that psychopathy is a diagnosis made in the countertransference.

The perpetrator, by his actions, leaves us to experience the highly disturbing emotion. Our subsequent reaction is likely to be avoidant or retributive, and uncharacteristic. We are likely to act in the negative ways described above and we feel guilty and ashamed of our retributive actions; it is the lot of the psychopath to bring out the worst in us.

Such was the situation facing Ashworth Hospital and identified by the Fallon Inquiry (1999) which concentrated on the Personality Disorder Unit and found the widespread availability of pornography, patients running their own businesses, and a child being groomed for paedophile purposes. The problem, as I saw it, was basically of blindness to corruption on the wards and at times complicity with corrupt and perverse actions. Some staff were removed from their jobs, some were moved. A new medical director was appointed who had no previous connections and thus no allegiances with existing staff. She approached me as director of the Portman Clinic to provide consultation to the whole hospital. It was agreed that I and my colleague Stan Ruszc-zynski would spend a day a week at the hospital. We were not employed by the hospital but by our own Trust. Of crucial importance was the fact that the initiative came from the "head" of the organisation. I remember Harold Bridger, who was on the second Northfield Experiment in the Second World War (see Armstrong & Rustin, Chapter 3), saying that any such project which was not based on an initiative and a commitment from the top of the organisation was bound to failure. The project lasted over five years during which we provided a weekly reflective space for each of the professions, for some of the wards previously affected by the dysfunctional practices, and, most importantly, for the management group of the hospital which included the heads of the disciplines and the chief executive. When we left, the subsequent medical director said, in his farewell speech, "You know you saved Ashworth Hospital." Not so; but I believe it was the willingness by the hospital to engage in an ongoing process of consultation which was a significant factor in the process of healing the damage which previous staff had unwittingly allowed to happen. What constitutes a well-functioning forensic organisation, including its position within wider society, could well be the focus of another paper.

I have said that badness and madness are the dominant forces in the psychopathic mind. Does he/she not experience normal sadness and anxiety? Of course he/she does, but to quote King Lear, "Where the greater malady is fixed, the lesser is scarce felt," (Act 3, scene 4). For the psychopath, acting out is the defence against consciously experiencing fear, loss, guilt, shame, hopelessness, sadness, and confusion. These emotions are projected into those around them and their institutions. The label we place on them is "dual diagnosis", psychosis and personality disorder, which may make us feel better, but doesn't do much for the patient. (For personality disorder read "psychopathy".) That is not to deny the reality of the badness and the madness and the need for containment and (dare I say it?) punishment of the badness, and pharmacological treatment of the madness.

"Creating his most feared scenario"

In a previous paper "Flying a Kite" (Hale & Dhar, 2008) I and Raj Dhar explored the relationship between psychopathic personality and psychosis. The clinical example I used was a man, Frank (not his real name), who killed an off-duty policeman. Here I am using the clinical material to explore the specific countertransference experiences in myself and those charged with his care.

Abandoned by his mother at birth, Frank had a lifelong history of institutional care in children's homes, prisons, and hospitals. Subsequent to the legal processes there was a Department of Health Inquiry on which I was the medical member and a detailed report of his life and care was published so the clinical details are already in the public domain. (However, were he still alive I would have sought his permission.)

Following sexual abuse by a staff member in an institution he became a teenage rent boy and embarked on major drug abuse. His criminal behaviour led to numerous non-custodial and custodial sentences for acquisitive and violent offences. When he was eighteen he had his first psychotic breakdown and was admitted to hospital. There the psychosis resolved rapidly with medication and he was very soon discharged because of his threatening and, at times, violent behaviour. When he was in prison, where the psychosis became manifest, he was seen as mad and in need of psychiatric care; when he was in hospital he was seen as primarily bad ("personality disordered") and the responsibility of the criminal justice system. In each place he disturbed the staff to the point where they rejected him. In essence he ensured that nobody wanted him—the story of his life from birth onwards.

For the psychopath there is no fundamental object constancy. From very early on he survives by learning to accommodate, never able to trust. For him the world is fickle and unpredictable. The consequence in adult life is the protean, constantly changing nature of the manifestations of the disorder. For the most part in descriptive psychiatry we see diagnosis as static—a still photograph; but, as Nigel Eastman so clearly pointed out in his evidence to the Inquiry, for a psychopath we need a cine camera to see the changing presentation of symptoms, signs, and actions which are integral to and, in my view, a defining characteristic of the disorder. Whether this constitutes a diagnosis is another matter. I see psychopathy as a defence mechanism in which the person holds on to some degree of psychic equilibrium by projecting their feelings of their own badness into others, distorting reality to protect their sense of sanity. Current events are described with a disconnected insouciance, without affect, causal relationship, or personal responsibility; again a series of snapshots to protect themselves from facing the reality of who they are, or more importantly, who they are not—an integrated person. It is a psychic survival mechanism, albeit a pathological one because ultimately it is they who suffer and who are the losers. The use of drugs is highly significant. Smoking large amounts of, say, cannabis can ward off anxiety (and perhaps guilt), buffering the person from external and internal anxiety. With continued and excessive use, and a progression to more powerful forms of the drug, ego boundaries start to dissolve and the outside world, which could previously be regarded with disdain, antagonism, and contempt now takes on an increasingly different complexion. It is now perceived as powerful, malign, and vengeful. An active paranoid state is starting to establish itself—a prodromal psychotic state. The response may be self medication with yet more drugs.

What we are observing is the failure of the psychopathic defence to ward off underlying psychotic persecutory anxieties which gradually break through as paranoid delusions. In this psychotic state the individual eventually encounters a situation which, to him, mirrors his unconscious feared fantasy or complex of fantasies. These will be primitive fantasies based on very early traumatic experiences such as rejection and alienation, intentional harm, the wish that the person should not exist in the first place, humiliation and self loathing, thoughts of being known and controlled by others, and so on. The current situation mirrors the past for the individual but is only recognised as having current relevance and the threat is responded to by an attack on the current persecutor. Thus the present-day psychotic state allows and even requires a symbolic attack, apparently to rectify the current injustice, but really to reverse the traumatic experience of infancy. A wished for revenge is now made possible by psychotic functioning. The victim who is perceived to be an "attacker" and so is attacked in an act of revenge, is not of course the true "attacker" but the person who happens to fit the bill in the current situation.

Frank

Such a process is revealed in the account given by the psychiatrists who saw Frank after the event. He told Dr L that he had seen a man, Mr G, parking his car and asked him for a cigarette. Frank said Mr G replied, "You shouldn't ask men like me for a cigarette," which he felt had some inference about the difference between their respective social classes. He also described Mr G hissing through his teeth and showing some annoyance which Frank took as an insult.

Another psychiatrist, Dr P, reported that Frank told him that he was "kicked out of Shenley Hospital" and claimed that he hadn't any medicines or an appointment to see a doctor. Eventually he was "kicked out of his hostel" and said he was walking the streets and sleeping rough. He told Dr P that he felt very down and out—"I don't know where my mum is and my dad doesn't want to know." He said he attacked a pensioner in order to rob him of his money to buy drugs. He said that on the night of the killing he watched television with a friend and the television said to him, "The only way you survive is if you kill." He explained, "It was trying to help me like God when he got inside Jesus and sent him down to die for our sins."

From these accounts we can surmise that Frank unconsciously created his most feared scenario with all its complexities. He rejected and was rejected by a caring maternal presence in the form of the hospital and the hostel. He regresses to a completely paranoid state: "The only way you survive is if you kill." Searching for the means to get drugs which might alleviate his psychic pain he encounters a man who treats him with what he perceives to be disdain and humiliation. Mr G then hisses at him through his teeth, penetrating his final defences. Previously he could intimidate, dominate, and control his objects, but now the position is reversed; it is his objects which control him. His psychopathic defence has failed and he is the victim of paranoid psychotic forces. With his affective control loosened by the drugs and his perceptions distorted by psychosis, this man (Mr G) now can and must be eliminated—"The only way you survive is if you kill." At the time of the killing the conscience is ablated by triumphant excitement. Afterwards, both reality and remorse return.

All of this history was from documents and professionals' accounts accumulated over a few months of the Inquiry. Painful as it was, it was largely an intellectual and fact finding process. It was only when the chair of the Inquiry and I went to see him in a high security prison that we experienced the full impact of this man's psychological capacities with all their contradictions. We went to see him on a Saturday in May—Cup Final day; his team were playing; not a sensible move on our part. We waited till half time and he reluctantly came to see us. The first impression was of his size—he was enormous and muscular—and then his glowering resentful demeanour. He answered our questions briefly and throughout made it clear that he was only talking to us on sufferance. Then something strange happened. One of the professionals we had talked to was the headmaster of his school, Mr S, who had clearly seen another Frank who was a rewarding and responsive child. Mr S and his school had brought out a good Frank who had clearly stayed in their minds—hence their contacting our Inquiry. We told him that his headmaster had asked us to remember him to Frank. He went silent; after about a minute we realised that he was crying. "Does he remember me? Does he really remember me?" After a couple of minutes he stood up and said in his previous assertive manner, "I'm going back to the football; you can push off." (Not quite his words.) Our experience was of feeling initially intimidated by him; we were pushed into fight or flight mode—an autonomic sympathetic response. Then through his tears we were exposed to his sadness for what he had lost and what might have been. But in this state of mind he was exposing to us, and to himself, his vulnerability and his longing for a good dependable object. This state of being is far too dangerous—he has lost control and he needs to regain the ascendancy, hence his aggressive dismissal of us.

This brief vignette demonstrates, I hope, the violent psychopath's capacity to stimulate in others a specific autonomic defensive response with the characteristic physiological features—changes in heart rate, blood pressure, respiratory rate, and so on. The result is that we as professionals feel like a small child, intimidated, fearful, out of control. We are driven to take back control and diminish him in some way. We are reluctant to help him and concerned only for ourselves. He has managed to bring out the worst in us, for which we then feel guilty and we hate him all the more.

Had our patient been a sexual psychopath, say a paedophile, a different set of psychological and neural pathways, the parasympathetic, would have been engaged in us; the final result is the same however. We treat the patient badly and feel guilty for it. Those of us who treat sexual deviants over a period of time consistently report two physiological responses in our selves—gut churning nausea and drowsiness, both of which are parasympathetic autonomic phenomena. The drowsiness removes us from the immediate response. Revulsion is the body's response to toxic and poisonous stimuli, whether they are physical or moral, which have been forced into us against our will and largely without our conscious knowledge. We know they are deceptive and destructive and we need to expel them as soon as possible. Vomiting is the self-preservative response. But the "poison" may be disguised as something acceptable or nice. (Deception is frequently an integral and sought-after part of perversion.) Again we as professionals are enlisted to experience the feelings the patient finds intolerable. In his glib triumph he makes it "our" problem if we find it distasteful or morally abhorrent.

Small wonder then that we find the patient in whom there is a significant measure of psychopathy so disturbing to us, both as individuals and collectively as an institution. It is because they affect us primarily at a visceral level and bypass our normal conscious defensive systems. The impact is primarily on our sympathetic and parasympathetic nervous systems over which we have little or no control. We recognise them by the way they make us feel. Subsequently we make conscious sense of the visceral experience. Psychopathy is therefore a "diagnosis" made in the countertransference, but it is experienced as a negative countertransference. They bring out the worst in us and we struggle to treat them decently.

In their interaction with the clinical team they are seen as unreliable, unpredictable, devious, deceitful, arrogant, and given to acting out often in a violent or self-injurious way. They split teams, some members hating them, some regarding them with sympathy and affection. The result is two factions locked in mutual antagonism. One has only to look at the traits identified in the Hare Psychopathy Checklist:[1] (glib and superficial charm, grandiose estimation of self, lying, conning, manipulativeness, callousness, parasitic lifestyle, etc.) (Hare & Neumann, 2009) to realise how unpopular they are. They are the patients nobody wants, not least because they attack the treatment and are therapeutically so unrewarding. How similar this is to the childhood they describe where their memory is of being abandoned, deceived, and used as a lever between adults. They crave love but fear it. By being hated at least they know they are in a live relationship.

A trap we can fall into is of reprisal for the pain they have caused, or indulgence towards their demands. In each case we have failed to maintain boundaries—too much of ourselves has become involved. In a most extreme form we too become corrupt or violent. A third state of mind we may employ is cynicism—we may mock our patients and communicate to them that we consider them a lost cause. We predict a poor prognosis and by failing to maintain any hope we ensure that prediction comes true.

How a supervision group works

Let's look now at the way a supervision group works. As with any group it takes time to get established. These are people who are working together on a daily basis and may have a hierarchical relationship with one another. There may also be rivalries between professions; the most frequent one I have encountered is between medics and psychologists but the split between nurses and "non-nurses" can be as powerful with barely disguised competition, criticism, and contempt. Again this represents how these tensions can become repositories for the conflicts between different parts of the internal world of the forensic patient. Gradually they may be able to establish a safe enough distance from their colleagues.

I ask for a present problem—a difficult patient, or a difficult organisational event which they have recently encountered. The presenter is not chosen—they volunteer spontaneously, telling the story in their own words without any notes. This may take ten to fifteen minutes; I ask very few questions. When the presenter has finished I ask the other members what has been left out of the account. In the subsequent discussion we focus on the affective response of the presenter as well as the affective response of the other members of the group as they listen to the story. As they listen, what do they experience in their minds and in their bodies? What does it make them feel like doing? From these experiences, and from the history, we build a dynamic pattern of the index offence or the critical incident. My emphasis is not on what I can teach them in a didactic manner but what they can learn from their own direct or second-hand experience of the patient. I encourage them to follow and value their own intuition and to examine the patient's symptoms and actions for their defensive function—for example, why has the patient become flippant or dismissive? What are they trying to hide? Or why have they turned to intimidation or violence which we know about from our own recognised anxiety? And what is the patient really frightened of but does not or cannot recognise?

Conclusion

Overall in psychiatry we are encouraged to be objective and logical. Our own feelings for and reactions to the patient are rarely discussed or seen as having any value. Yet it is precisely these feelings which, along with the symbolic meaning of their actions, give the greatest and most accurate access to the psychopath's mind. We are examining the interaction (or perhaps theatre) between our own mind and that of the patient.

I recently asked a group that has been running for about six years to tell me about their experience of being in the group. The first comment from each one of them was "It helps me to stay sane," the next word they used was "comforting". They went on to say that they found it comforting to hear about other people struggling, not in a gloating manner, but that it was a relief that they were not the only ones. They went on, "It gives a sense of relief from the feeling that you must have the answer—sometimes you haven't a clue." They talked about the sense of isolation as consultants and of the loneliness of leadership. They described the group as a forum that holds the anxiety, "a reflective space for things psychological". They commented that the regularity was very important (this is a group that meets for an hour every week). They said that such a group was only possible if facilitated externally and they valued my commitment which encouraged their own commitment to the process. A final comment was, "Every Tuesday you know there's a safe place to go."

Acknowledgements

In writing this I have been aware of how much I have learned from colleagues. Carine Minne, Stan Ruszczynski, Heather Wood, and Theresa Tattan have been particularly helpful and encouraging.

Note

1. *Hare Psychopathy Checklist—Revised: (PCL-R) Second Edition*. London: Pearson Clinical. http://minddisorders.com/Flu-Inv/Hare-Psychopathy-Checklist.html

* * *

Rob Hale FRCPsych, M. Inst Psychoanal.

After training at UCH and St Mary's Hospitals, he was appointed consultant psychiatrist at the Portman Clinic in 1980. His original interest was in suicidal acts based on a six-year study at

St Mary's of people who had attempted suicide. This resulted some time later in a book with Donald Campbell. *Working in the Dark* (2017) a psychoanalytic study of suicidal acts. At the Portman Clinic his interest was in perpetrators of sexual abuse and their treatment. From 1987 till 1994 he worked at the Tavistock Clinic where he was the postgraduate dean and while there he set up the MedNet service for doctors in need of psychological help. Returning to the Portman in 1994 he took up the position as director and established a number of connections with medium and high security hospitals throughout the country. He also started the first group treatment service for paedophiles.

In his retirement he continues a "grandparent" role providing weekly supervision to consultant staff in high and medium secure units.

CHAPTER THIRTY-SIX

The Tavistock legacy in America: making sense of society

Edward R. Shapiro and James Krantz

Apart from several cross-Atlantic interactions, most notably with Kurt Lewin, the most important Tavistock influence in the US began in the mid 1960s. The legacy of Eric Miller and Kenneth Rice was taken up through the establishment of the A. K. Rice Institute. The socio-technical perspective was brought to Los Angeles by Eric Trist in 1965 (Trist & Murray, 1993).

The socio-technical perspective

Socio-technical thinking was a foundational advance at the Tavistock. Beginning with discoveries in the coal mines, Trist and his colleagues developed an approach to thinking about organisations that relied on a dual perspective—recognising the importance simultaneously of both formal task systems and the social system, understood psychoanalytically—rather than privileging one or the other, as had guided theory previously. This theoretical advance laid the foundation for many signature contributions of the Tavistock Institute, including semi-autonomous work groups, contributions to thinking about industrial democracy, Miller and Rice's thinking about task and sentient systems, the quality of work–life movement, and a creative approach to labour-management relations. Trist's wide-ranging contribution was recognised in the UK when he was granted the OBE title.

Eric Trist (1909–1993) joined the faculty of the University of California at Los Angeles (UCLA) business school where he worked with colleagues on bringing socio-technical thinking to American industry. The socio-technical perspective adopted in the States was technocratic in nature, having split off the rich psychodynamic underpinnings of social system analysis.

Due to changing social and economic realities in the latter part of the twentieth century, the relevance of socio-technical theory faded, although many of its insights have informed and continue to play a role in approaches to today's organisations.

In 1977 Trist moved to the Wharton School in Philadelphia where he focused primarily on the impact of wider social and ecological forces on communities, people, and their organisations. He was deeply engaged in projects that brought the resourcefulness of local community groups to bear on challenges facing communities in the post-industrial era. His primary focus at that time was on "domain development", how local groups and associations could join in ways that improved the living and working conditions for everyone.

Eric actively encouraged cross-Atlantic collaborations. Especially during the 1960s and 70s there was considerable exchange, with many Americans visiting Tavistock, both the Clinic and the Institute, something which has faded over the years as the more pioneering aspects of the post-war years gradually diminished. He often tried to connect people who he thought might enrich each other's thinking.

Eric was an extraordinary teacher and mentor. He had the remarkable gift of bringing his exceptional intelligence into conversation with others in such a way that left the others feeling clearer and more intelligent rather than being in awe of him. Several of Eric's students from Wharton have continued as organisational consultants and group relations practitioners, some of whom have made important contributions to the ongoing development of practice and understanding from within the Tavistock tradition.

Group relations

Arthur Kenneth Rice (1908–1969) joined the Tavistock Institute of Human Relations in 1948. It was at the Tavistock that he developed his method of critically analysing society, in particular addressing problems facing managers in industrial settings. Rice worked with Eric Miller on a number of projects, including consultancy to an airline, a public (i.e., relatively privileged fee-paying) school, the clergy, and for the then Prison Commission. Out of this work he developed his ideas about group relations. Along with Trist and others, Rice instituted the first group relations conferences as a research programme into group and organisational dynamics. Rice directed the Tavistock Institute's group relations programme and training events, including the Leicester conference, until 1969, writing a book about his experiences (Rice, 1965).

News of Rice's work in group relations and the original ideas in his book *The Enterprise and its Environment* spread to the United States (Rice, 1963; Rice & Miller, 1967). He was briefly employed by Yale University and the Washington School of Psychiatry, where he met Margaret Rioch. Together, they put on the first US group relations conference in 1965 in Holyoke; Rice was the director. Following his death in 1969, Margaret Rioch, Eric Miller, and other colleagues established the A. K. Rice Institute (AKRI) in his memory, with a mission to explore the events and processes that produce non-rational behaviour in social groups.

Beginning in Washington and expanding to centres across the country, AKRI has had a rich, diverse, and at times tumultuous, history through which many people in the US have been exposed to systems psychodynamics. The work has had an impact on many organisations, communities, and families. Margaret Rioch (1975) was a passionate mentor, stimulating a number of young psychiatrists and psychologists to expand the reach of group relations training in AKRI centres across the United States.

The preoccupations of group relations conferences evolved along with emerging social and cultural issues. In the 1960s turmoil centring on Vietnam and race relations signalled a shift away from assumptive hierarchical authority to a recognition of the negotiated nature of authority. Group relations conferences were popular and AKRI began publishing its work in Group Relations Readers (e.g., Colman & Bexton, 1975). The increased numbers of books and papers about systems psychodynamics published in the US demonstrated the influence of conference learning (e.g., Gould, Stapley, & Stein, 2001; Krantz, 2019; Shapiro & Carr, 1991).

Several constituent centres of AKRI developed distinctive approaches to group relations, often reflecting regional differences. More recently, the pendulum of centralisation/decentralisation has swung back towards decentralisation, with the regional centres taking a more integral role within AKRI. In addition to AKRI's ongoing development, several academic centres have developed robust and generative programmes focusing on group relations approaches, most notably San Diego University, Teachers College, Columbia, Northwestern and George Washington Universities. Weekend and residential conferences began elaborating an increased diversity, with some focusing on social chaos and irrationality rather than maintaining a strict focus on leadership and authority. All of this shaped lively dialogue about the nature of conference learning.

In connection with its commitment to self-examination, a newly developed understanding of AKRI's mission has been articulated which recognises how group relations has a more direct application to society (Shapiro, 2020). AKRI's current thinking about its mission and role are best illustrated by the words of its current president:

> We want to tell a story linking Group Relations experiential learning about systems and roles to the experience at the heart of being a citizen. We recognize that many of us—in our work, family, and community life—are feeling targeted, polarized, angry, and disengaged. We know that we have something extraordinary to offer: AKRI offers experiential learning designed to make sense of the social chaos and irrationality that surrounds us. People who participate in this experiential learning can emerge with a greater capacity to join and fully engage in work, family and community life. Many find themselves newly energized, feeling more alive and significant. Ultimately, participants in Group Relations might discover how to claim their voices and feel more significant as part of something larger than themselves. These capacities are the foundations of the role of citizen, which our world desperately needs.[1]

Note

1. Marmostein, J. (2020). President's letter to AKRI members.

* * *

Ed Shapiro is clinical professor at the Yale Child Study Center and was medical director/CEO of the Austen Riggs Center from 1991–2011. An organisational and family consultant, he has published more than fifty articles on human development, organisational and family functioning, and personality disorders, presenting papers in the US and abroad. He has written two books, *Lost in Familiar Places: Creating New Connections between the Individual and Society* (with Wesley Carr, Yale, 1991), and *Finding a Place to Stand: Developing Self-Reflective Institutions, Leaders and Citizens* (Phoenix, 2020), and edited a third, *The Inner World in the Outer World: Psychoanalytic Perspectives* (Yale, 1997). He is on the boards of the A. K. Rice Institute and the International Dialogue Initiative, and on the advisory board of Partners Confronting Collective Atrocities. He is a principal in the Boswell Group of New York.

Dr Shapiro has received the Felix and Helene Deutsch Scientific Award from the Boston Psychoanalytic Society, the Research Prize from the Society for Family Therapy and Research, and the Isenberg Teaching Award from McLean Hospital. In 2007, he was named Outstanding Psychiatrist for Advancement of the Profession by the Massachusetts Psychiatric Association and since 2011 has been listed on the US News & World Report's list of "Top Doctors".

James Krantz is an organisational consultant and researcher from New York City, whose principal interests are in the unconscious background to work and organisational life; the impact of emergent trends on the exercise of leadership and authority; and the socio-technical dimensions of new forms of work organisation. He is the managing principal of WorkLab, a consulting firm that focuses on strategy implementation, leadership development, and helping organisations confront the need for change.

Jim holds a BA in philosophy and economics from Wesleyan University and a PhD in systems sciences from the Wharton School. He has taught on the standing faculties of Yale and Wharton, and at numerous universities including Columbia, Harvard, INSEAD, the Universidad de Chile, and currently at the School of Higher Economics in Moscow.

Jim is a member and past president of the International Society for the Psychoanalytic Study of Organizations (ISPSO); a fellow of the A. K. Rice Institute; member of OPUS; and former director of the Center for Socio-Analytic Studies at the Institute for Psychoanalytic Teaching and Research (IPTAR). He chairs the editorial management committee of the *Journal of Social and Organisational Dynamics* (OPUS) and serves on the editorial boards of the *Journal of Applied Behavioral Science* and *Socio-Analysis*.

CHAPTER THIRTY-SEVEN

Psychoanalytic thinking in organisational settings and the therapeutic community tradition

Jenny Sprince

In the mid 1980s, when I first arrived at the Tavistock Clinic, the building housed many different applications of psychoanalytic thinking. As well as individual psychotherapy for adults and for children, we were encouraged to explore psychoanalytic family therapy, group therapy, organisational dynamics, and group relations. Therapeutic communities were widely accepted as part of the psychoanalytic family, and many of my colleagues had—like me—started their progress towards a psychoanalytic training by working at the Cassel Hospital therapeutic community as nursing assistants, nurses, or psychiatric registrars.

I was fortunate to find a training post as a child psychotherapist in a boarding school for adolescent boys with emotional and behavioural difficulties. But I didn't think myself fortunate at the time. For a young woman, of less than average height, weight, and strength, being sequestered in an isolated consulting room and expected to provide individual psychotherapy to a series of violent teenage boys who came equipped with fists, scissors, and table legs was anything but a reassuring start to a professional career.

But there was time and sympathy available at the Tavistock from an international community of colleagues and senior staff. They offered suggestions: Did I have a teacher within call? A bell I could ring? A blanket I could throw? One of them—fresh from compulsory military service in his home country—gave me a short course in self-defence which we practised among the cake crumbs and dirty coffee cups of the first floor common room to the bewilderment of casual onlookers.

Then my tutor, Juliet Hopkins, suggested I should talk to Anton Obholzer. He was a large and daunting presence, but he convinced me that it wasn't my lack of physical strength that was the problem but the narrowness of my perspective. Under his supervision my vision expanded.

I began to see that it wasn't the individual boys who were my patients: it was the school as a whole. And armed with that recognition I no longer felt powerless and terrified.

How do you take on a whole organisation as your patient? I spent much of the next few years down the road at Hampstead police station, studying the impact of violence and trauma on a service that has to cope with it on a daily basis. With Anton's support I applied my learning to the boarding school and everyone who worked there, helping them to stay more emotionally responsive in the face of the children's powerful projections of anger, perversity, and dissociation. And I discovered that as my thinking helped the adults, the school became a more benevolent environment, and the children became less violent. From there it was a short step to the realisation that staff who were properly supported to know what they were doing, and were with the children twenty-four/seven, could do a lot more good than one child psychotherapist who could provide at best one hour a week to a handful of patients. I was determined to take this learning elsewhere.

The Peper Harow Community was well-known at that time. It had evolved from a Borstal, to offer therapeutic residential treatment to traumatised adolescents. When I left the Tavistock, I took on the job of consulting to its newly opened sister community, Thornby Hall, stipulating from the start that I would work with the staff and not with the residents. And I asked Anton to supervise me. The training that evolved at Thornby Hall, in collaboration with its directors, Alan Worthington, Rene Kennedy, and Phil Faulkner, continued to be firmly rooted in Tavistock thinking, and to be supported by Tavistock luminaries. Psychiatric overview was provided first by John Byng-Hall and then by Judith Trowell. The Adult Department of the Tavistock joined with Middlesex University to offer theoretical seminars in psychosocial thinking.

And in parallel, I provided consultancy and supervision to other, younger child psychotherapists working as consultants to residential units.

After several years we found that between us we had trained a large number of staff whose clinical expertise went unrecognised beyond the bounds of their own residential communities. Where were they to go when they wanted to give up the punishing shift work involved in residential care, without any formal clinical accreditation? This was a pressing concern, more especially as austerity was cutting the therapeutic services available to vulnerable children, and the number of therapeutic residential organisations became fewer.

So in 2011 Anton Obholzer, Judith Trowell, and I collaborated to found a new member institution of the British Psychoanalytic Council, the Association for Psychodynamic Practice and Counselling in Organisational Settings (APPCIOS). APPCIOS offers a clinical accreditation as an organisational therapist for psychosocial workers and other professionals—anyone working with vulnerable clients, and particularly those clients with needs too complex to be met by once-weekly psychotherapy. Our members apply psychoanalytic thinking to their interventions with individual clients, groups, and families, and also to the teams and environments in which they work and the professional networks with which they interact. We use the internet to make training accessible. You can find out more about us from our website, appcios.info. As well as offering training components to individuals, APPCIOS accredits existing courses designed to develop psychodynamic thinking in front-line workers. Some of these are courses that have been developed by the second generation: clinicians who learned their trade through the model of consultation that Anton had helped me to evolve at Thornby Hall.

One such course is provided by Placement Support (https://placementsupport.co.uk/)—a company that offers psychodynamic interventions to looked-after children and adopted families—and to the professional networks around them. Alongside child psychotherapists, it employs APPCIOS organisational therapists, working in teams together. This combination of organisational and individual psychoanalytic understanding has proved highly successful and is greatly appreciated by parents, children, carers, and social workers. The company is owned and managed by Mark Waddington, with the help of Phil Faulkner. They both worked at Thornby Hall for more than twenty years, and rose to be deputy director and director respectively; and they are both organisational therapists on the BPC's register.

Other courses have been set up by other Tavistock-trained clinicians. Here is what Ariel Nathanson, a Tavistock-trained child psychotherapist, says about a course he developed and that APPCIOS has accredited.

> I established this course after more than three years of consultation to a residential therapeutic care home for young people.
>
> Designing and delivering a formal course like this constitutes an acknowledgment that the learning and change experienced through psychoanalytic consultation amounts to the development of a professional therapeutic role and merits a distinct professional title. The course doesn't only enhance the development of the staff and the organisation: it also endorses the value of psychodynamic thinking amongst the professional networks who refer the children and monitor their progress.
>
> I really enjoy being able to offer this accreditation and recognition of the residential care workers who are so committedly invested in the lives of extremely disturbed young people. This feels in keeping with the spirit of my current work with carers at the Portman Clinic; and with everything I learned from my training.

APPCIOS recently launched an interactive community site to promote psychodynamic thinking in areas of the UK where it might otherwise be inaccessible: https://psychodynamicthinking.info/. Through this site we hope to extend the reach of the learning environment that typified the Tavistock Clinic when I first knew it: a place where creativity and comradeship could flourish, beyond the constraints of geography.

[Jenny Sprince's biography appears on p. 311]

CHAPTER THIRTY-EIGHT

Group relations and religion

Wesley Carr

It was a surprise to some in the early days of the Group Relations Programme to find consultants occasionally offering socio-political interpretations. But the programme was very much a thing of its age. And the Church (specifically the Church of England) inherited that context. The effect was to bring together society and the Church in a shared interpretative frame. The social context within which at least parts of the Church worked explored the implications of the small group for the Church. In the period roughly between 1969 and 1980 such groups abounded. One of the most prominent places for such work was the Diocese of Chelmsford in Essex where Richard Herrick was director of education and, later, provost of the cathedral.

"Dick" Herrick had been a member of one of the earliest conferences held at Leicester. With him, in one of the groups, was Dr Eric Miller from the Tavistock Institute. As often happens with good work, they struck up a friendship that outlasted the conference. Dick established the "Chelmsford Cathedral Centre for Research and Training" and invited Dr Pierre Turquet from the Tavistock to join this enterprise. Together with a powerful committee they built up an institution. It was, however, as Turquet pointed out, lacking something that was, in principle, essential for a religious related body, namely, a technically qualified theologian. The post was advertised and I was appointed, having been teaching in Cambridge. Not surprisingly, I was immediately signed up for the forthcoming Leicester conference. Soon after this I was invited to be the associate director of the Leicester conference and then the director. From that point, I worked at the ideas of the Cathedral Centre. Dick Herrick and I developed an intensive learning programme that focused on systems learning for the clergy at the Diocese of Chelmsford, one of the largest in England. Meanwhile, I developed some thinking on the Church and group relations, seeing these as ideas about the working church. Clergy came from a number of sources and some also were sent to Leicester, the central conference of the Tavistock Institute.

This work had a significant effect on teaching in the Church at large, although it unfortunately suffered from the death of some associated with it—Pierre Turquet (1913–1975) and Dick Herrick (1913–1981) being the two most prominent. Turquet had been the first consultant to Dick Herrick and the Institution. In his place Eric Miller (1924–2002) was appointed. This had, among other effects, a stronger link between the cathedral clergy and the Institute. In spite of the large number of people, both clergy and laity, and the original thinking by people involved, the Centre did not survive a change of staff in the cathedral. However, the work continued on a private basis and new thought was generated on the Church and its role in society.

There were a number of people who made particular contributions: for example, Bruce Reed (1920–2003) of the Grubb Institute, who elaborated a detailed theory of dependency. At Chelmsford, and later at Bristol, I wrote a great deal on the Church's ministry, taking as a model the dependent life of groups and institutions. But perhaps the most memorable definition of the Church's task was that provided by Gordon Lawrence and Eric Miller:

> Ministers have to be dependable. There is, inevitably, an element of child-like dependency
> in the relationship to the church, and thus to its representatives, in that, to some extent,
> they are asked to solve the insoluble, cure the incurable and to make reality go away.
> (Miller & Lawrence, 1993)

Herrick had some connections with group relations practitioners in the USA and arranged for me to be invited onto the consultant staff of a conference there. As noted above, such conferences often lead to friendships. This was the case with my conference work with a number of American members. Chief among these was Edward R. Shapiro (see Chapter 36) with whom I developed a close relationship. He acted as consultant to Austen Riggs, Stockbridge, MA as well as being a staff member in group relations conferences. We also wrote a book which was widely read and used—*Lost in Familiar Places; Creating New Connections between the Individual and Society* (Shapiro & Carr, 1991). This title is of particular interest since it endorses the point made above about the original Tavistock conferences and their emphasis on social and political interests.

Whether in the USA or the UK this type of work on group relations and the Church no longer has such a formative presence. This does not mean that nothing is done but the Church and society have both changed. Of course, this itself is partly a result of group relations study! In both countries there are still major conferences for a religious clientele which bring about change in their conference and consultancy work.

December 31, 2016

* * *

Rev Wesley Carr (1941–2017) PhD DLitt KCVO, dean of Westminster 1997–2006.

Wesley Carr was born in 1941. His parents were Salvation Army officers. He won a scholarship to Dulwich College, and from there read classics at Jesus College, Oxford, and theology at Jesus College, Cambridge, and prepared for ordination at Ridley Hall, also in Cambridge. In 1974, he moved to Chelmsford, where his work with the provost, Dick Herrick, brought him into contact with the Tavistock Institute and its work on group relations. With the emphasis on clarifying tasks and roles and the boundaries between them, it was found by many to illuminate and explain the functioning of teams and the dynamics of cathedrals and bishops' staffs.

Wesley was not only a much respected senior figure in the Church of England hierarchy—he was well connected in a variety of thoughtful group clusters in society, one of the key ones being his connection with the Tavistock Institute of Human Relations and in particular the Leicester group relations conferences. He had come into contact with these ideas when he was a junior cleric and immediately saw the relevance of seeing and addressing the underlying dynamics which occur in groups of various sizes.

Wesley was one of the few members of staff of the conference group who never had any psychoanalytic coaching or training, but he was a complete "natural" in the field and a source of support for, and insight into, many a colleague or outsider who felt puzzled by the sort of group processes that they were caught up in. His inner strength and resilience was also drawn upon in a powerful way when he had to come to terms with being diagnosed initially with early Parkinson's disease. At first he thought that it meant the end of his career, but he soon overcame this and lived with this burden for a long time before resigning from his work at Westminster Abbey.

Much of this was reflected in Carr's later books *The Priest-like Task* (1985) and *Brief Encounters* (1994), which became influential. One diocesan bishop said later that they were "so refreshing because of the sharpness of the observations and the sense that pastoral theology was an intellectual discipline of high importance, rather than simply all about getting on with everybody, smoothing ruffled feathers, and avoiding conflict". He added: "The more able found him liberating, whereas others could find him forbidding."

By Anton Obholzer with help from Ed Shapiro and excerpts from Church Times *obituary: https://churchtimes.co.uk/articles/2017/4-august/gazette/obituaries/the-very-revd-dr-arthur-wesley-carr*

CHAPTER THIRTY-NINE

The new landscape of leadership: living in radical uncertainty

Jon Stokes

I first came across the Tavistock Clinic as an undergraduate studying experimental psychology at Oxford University. I had hoped that somehow studying psychology would help me to understand myself better; in fact it turned out to be a rather dry scientific affair. In a bored moment preparing for an essay on the psychology of groups I came across Wilfred Bion's *Experiences in Groups* (1961) on the library shelf. At last an illuminating and often humorous account of the strange behaviour of human beings in groups. Hoping that Bion was still at the Tavistock I wrote asking how I might train there, and received a kind letter explaining he wasn't and that I might consider training as a clinical psychologist, and so I did. Bion's book spoke to me very directly and now I think I understand the reasons, of which I was entirely unconscious at the time. I had like many boys of my generation been sent to a boarding school where I was unhappy and was puzzled by why my parents thought it a good idea and why the other boys seemed to regard it as a privilege. It was the start of my interest in group and organisational psychology.

As I later discovered, Bion had been sent to a boarding school at the age of eight where he was also very unhappy and meant that he grew up in groups far away from his parents. He did not see his mother for three years "and then momentarily, did not recognise her"[1] (F. Bion, 1994, pp. 91–92). Hence very possibly his later interest in groups and the puzzle of how to be oneself and to be a member of a group with its swirl of irrational emotion and groupthink. John Bowlby, another central figure in the Tavistock story, was sent to boarding school at the age of eleven. He later told his wife he "would not send a dog to boarding school at that age" (Tizard, 2009). It is likely that his preoccupation with attachment and loss had similar early roots. It seems we may have more reasons than we might think to thank the English boarding school system for the origins of some of the central ideas of the Tavistock's two most influential thinkers!

Bion's concept of container–contained (Bion, 1962) is one such example. The attempt to make sense of painful experiences is one way of containing and attempting to repair the damage caused. Another is to choose work that provides an opportunity to repair others. For many of us drawn there, working at the Tavi provided just such opportunities, to repair others and at the same time ourselves.

The concept of container–contained was developed first within the frame of the pair relationship in psychoanalysis, but has come to be a central plank in the Tavistock tradition of understanding and working with families, groups, and organisations; understanding the individual within the group, within the broader organisation nested in a series of wider social systems (Stokes, 2019a). By joining the Tavistock and working there for more than 20 years I had found not just a job but a home to help me work at my puzzles. Having trained as a clinical psychologist and as an adult psychotherapist in the Adult Department, I went on to take up leadership roles firstly as the chair of the department for five years, and then as the founder of Tavistock Consulting which continues to provide consultancy services to leaders and organisations.

Understanding leadership

The traditional emphasis in understanding leadership has been a focus on the individual leader—the so-called Great Person theory of leadership. In the early years of the Second World War it became clear that the existing method of officer selection in the army which focused on exam results and an individual interview was not producing good results. Social and technological changes meant that effective leadership required different skills (see also Armstrong & Rustin, Chapter 3). The Tavistock group in the army, which included Bion, made the radical suggestion that selection should be based on observing the individual's performance in a group activity. Jock Sutherland, one of the members of this group who subsequently became the medical director of the Tavistock Clinic, reports that when he and Eric Trist were working together on this project, Bion often remarked "on the need to judge the 'quality of contact' the candidate had with others" (Bion, as quoted by Sutherland, 1985, p. 49). They felt that many different personalities could make good officers, but Bion sought that crucial quality, which is "a man's capacity for maintaining personal relationships in a situation of strain that tempted him to disregard the interest of his fellows for the sake of his own" (Bion, 1946, p. 77). Bion is here emphasising one crucial aspect of leadership that current methods of selection were not evaluating—the relationship between the leader and those who follow. And in fact this is where "leadership" resides, not in the individual but in the relationship. Much research on leadership still fails to take account of this fact.

Subsequent work at the Tavistock Clinic and Institute has enlarged our understanding of leadership by exploring the ways in which, in order to be effective, leaders need to understand not just the group as Bion did but the wider system in which they operate—the systems psychodynamic approach to organisations developed by Eric Trist, Ken Rice, Eric Miller, and Harold Bridger, among many others (Trist & Murray, 1990a). But what is the system in which today's and tomorrow's leaders will operate? Since leaving the Tavistock twenty years ago I have continued to consult with a wide variety of organisations and their leaders, and currently as a senior fellow in management practice at the Saïd Business School at Oxford University I have been researching leadership and the question of what leaders need to get better at in today's world.

The Fourth Industrial Revolution

We are now in the throes of the Fourth Industrial Revolution. We live in a hyper-connected era in which digital technology and related developments have blurred the boundaries between the physical and digital worlds, between mind and machine.

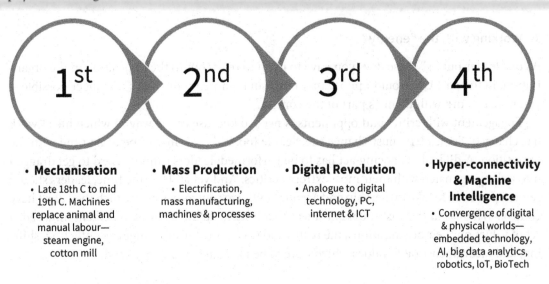

- **Mechanisation**
  - Late 18th C to mid 19th C. Machines replace animal and manual labour— steam engine, cotton mill

- **Mass Production**
  - Electrification, mass manufacturing, machines & processes

- **Digital Revolution**
  - Analogue to digital technology, PC, internet & ICT

- **Hyper-connectivity & Machine Intelligence**
  - Convergence of digital & physical worlds— embedded technology, AI, big data analytics, robotics, IoT, BioTech

The Four Industrial Revolutions

Like the industrial revolutions before it, this fourth revolution has produced a shift in the nature of power, in this case away from the preceding essentially vertical forms of power that use traditional command and control sources of superior information and knowledge, and the opaque use of financial data, information, and rewards: a style of exercising power now largely ineffective. Power and information are much more widely dispersed and transparent, based on horizontal forms of power across the organisation and beyond it. Members of organisations are no longer prepared to just "follow", they want to have influence and to have access to resources to enable this. What are leaders to do?

What do leaders need to get better at?

Leaders are under scrutiny as never before. Perceptions of character and competence are regularly and publicly examined. We are sceptical of their motives, why they want to be leaders, and their abilities, asking are they up to the job? Trust in leaders is at an all-time low.

Given this scrutiny of leaders I, together with my colleague Professor Sue Dopson (Stokes & Dopson, 2020), recently carried out a study of twenty-five current leaders heading up a representative sample of different organisations, as to what they thought leaders need to get better at. Two central themes lay at the heart of their responses:

I. Accountable but not in control

The game has changed. Leaders told us that traditional hierarchical power has melted away. No longer can they rely on rank or position to command action. Three aspects of this new world they described are worth considering in particular:

1. Working with the "enemy"

As one leader put it: "These days you have to learn to reach out to the opposition in the organisation; in the past you would oppose them or could ignore them. That's no longer possible—you have to work with them as part of the context."

Engagement with critics and opponents is needed because of the way in which life at work has changed. So, leaders must change their game too. This will mean spending time with the opposition. A difficult balancing act has to be performed: leaders cannot afford to get dragged into a slanging match with their most extreme critics. And yet at the same time, leaders should remain prepared to take ownership and accountability for outcomes over which they don't have control. Whereas in the past the mantra was that leaders defined, and to an extent imposed, a set of values on their organisations, the reality today is more one of a range of conflicting, shifting, and incommensurable values which have to be navigated and conciliated.

2. Leading in a glass box

"Everyone has access, you have to expect people will sooner or later know most things and particularly the things you don't want them to know about."

There are few if any secrets at the top anymore. The old maxim of "knowledge is power" no longer applies just for elites. Leaders will not be able to keep information confidential for very long. The leader's office, it seems, has glass walls and an almost permanently open door. Brave and competent leaders will deal with this. Restricting access to resources, knowledge, and information as a form of management power is no longer effective, and may indeed prove counterproductive. Leaders need to get used to being under 24/7 scrutiny. They have to accept they have vulnerabilities, and get comfortable making mistakes and learning in public.

3. Working with plurality—connecting is as important as directing

"These days it's all about subtler forms of influence, with your social media, your blog, not about command and control."

An organisation is not a culture—it is a multi-culture. The workplace is now diverse beyond the capacity of any one individual to comprehend all of its variations. Leaders need to accept that their point of view is one among many, and may even be part of the problem rather than the solution. Diversity is strength. Organisations can make better use of this plurality.

II. Shaping the context

Leaders will only have followers if they are making sense of the world people are operating in. Only leaders who can describe and explain the context will be worth following. They must learn how to shape the context of the work that they and their colleagues are undertaking, rather than primarily directing from the front.

There are three aspects of this shaping of context which the leaders we interviewed told us about that merit particular attention:

1. Developing the narrative

"Leaders need to get out and shape the story rather than work within the one you've inherited."

Leaders have to develop their "narrative competence", the capacity to tell a compelling story about their organisation and its purpose, using conversation to orchestrate the flow of ideas and harness employee curiosity.

2. Enabling a sense of purpose

"Work these days has to be much more than about just getting tasks done."

Today employees are demanding work that is socially meaningful if it is to engage their capacities and energy. Increasingly they want to feel that their organisation is contributing positively to society above and beyond shareholder value or government policy.

3. Leaning into uncertainty—leading in a swamp

"Sometimes my job is to resist the rush to action."

Regular disruption of existing practices is now an ordinary part of working life. Living with and in uncertainty is a permanent state of affairs. Leaders need to act decisively whilst at the same time holding uncertainty.

Living in radical uncertainty—the new landscape of leadership

Much research and writing about leadership suffers from the "Leadership Attribution Error"—the erroneous attribution of leadership effects without regard to the nature of followers, the situation for which leadership is required, and the wider social and economic context. Leadership is best viewed not as a quality of a person but as an emergent and shared property of the system in which the leader operates, consisting of four interdependent elements—leader, followers, situation, and context.

Five capabilities: from "ego" to "eco" leadership

The technological and economic changes central to the Fourth Industrial Revolution have significantly changed the context for leadership. Not all of leadership has changed, more traditional methods of leadership are not entirely outmoded. But older skill sets and capabilities are insufficient for effective leadership for the social ecology (Emery & Trist, 1973) of today and tomorrow.

A move away from "heroic", individualistic leadership ("ego") towards a leadership that recognises the organisation as a system nested in other systems ("eco") is needed. To achieve this shift five key capabilities which might be called Leadership 4.0, are required.

1. Shape the conversation

Leadership operates through language; an organisation is a set of conversations. When a leader speaks, the effect is not only to describe a given reality, but also to change that social reality. Leadership is a conversation, a way of talking about things with people, at all levels, within and beyond the organisation.

2. Cultivate collective intelligence

Knowledge exists in networks and collective capabilities as much as in individuals. Leadership is less about providing the answer, more about releasing collective intelligence, building internal connection and collaboration.

3. Nudge the context

Leaders are like farmers. Farmers don't grow crops, they create the conditions for crops to grow. Organisations are a response to context: leaders need to pay attention and nurture the ecosystem in which their organisation sits.

4. Co-create the structure

Organisations are structures of power. Organisational structures tend to accumulate power and attempt to maintain the status quo, becoming a constraint on further development. Reputation and status rather than competence to solve a problem come to determine organisational influence. Leaders need to challenge power bases within their organisation, focus on minimising structure and rules.

5. Pluralise participation

Organisations are tools to problem-solving. Leadership can be exercised by anyone at any level in the organisation. In order for solve complex problems leaders need to increase diverse participation. By excluding many people from problem analysis and solution, organisations are deprived of different perspectives and sources of creativity.

Conclusion—Leadership 4.0

Not everything about leadership has to change. The desire for leadership is fundamentally rooted in our nature as social animals. We seek leaders for a sense of security and reassurance. We need a source of coordinated direction and focused collective energy in order to survive and we have deep needs to belong. Nevertheless, styles of leadership change through history and between cultures, and across types of organisations. The leader-centric conception of leadership is misleading and outmoded. Norms of dominance and deference have radically altered. Technological and economic change are driving the need to invent new more collaborative forms of relationship between leaders and those who follow.

Indeed, the idea of "followers" is in many ways anachronistic; "members", "partners", or "colleagues" might be more accurate. As early as 1951 Eric Trist and Ken Bamforth (Trist & Bamforth, 1951) identified a new paradigm that they termed self-regulating workgroups without the need for directive management. The subsequent Tavistock socio-technical approach developed by Trist and Fred Emery in the 1960s and 70s (Trist & Murray, 1993) challenged the conventional hierarchical relationship between managers and workers and, while having some successes, it also ran into many resistances and vested interests. The Fourth Industrial Revolution is creating conditions where these ideas are more likely to have perceived relevance and resonance. Just as the early Tavistock pioneers and Operation Phoenix forged their ideas in the context of a world war, so we need to develop new thinking for the work of leadership for today's challenges.

Note

1. An experience matched some decades later by Laura, the subject of James Robertson's film *A Two-Year-Old Goes to Hospital* (see Lindsay, Chapter 5). (Ed.)

* * *

Jon Stokes is a clinical psychologist and associate fellow of the British Psychological Society. He is an SCR member of St. Antony's College, Oxford University and part-time senior fellow in management practice at Saïd Business School, where he teaches and researches leadership. Jon trained and worked at the Tavistock Clinic for twenty-five years and was chair of the Adult

Psychotherapy Department from 1994 to 1999. He was the founding director of Tavistock Consulting which provides organisational consulting and coaching services. Since 2000 he has been a director of Stokes & Jolly Ltd, a leadership advisory firm.

Jon's consulting work focuses on advising chief executives and boards on interpersonal, group, and organisational dynamics. He has worked with leaders from a wide range of companies in the energy, information, and finance industries, as well as with professional service firms in the fields of law, accountancy, private equity, investment banking, advertising, and management consulting. He also has extensive public sector experience. Jon has contributed to executive education programmes at the business schools of Oxford, Cambridge, and Cranfield Universities. He is a former associate fellow of the Institute for Government in London and a past president of the International Society for the Psychoanalytic Study of Organisations.

His publications include "The unconscious at work in groups and teams" and "Institutional chaos and personal stress" in *The Unconscious at Work* (Obholzer & Roberts, 2019), "Why do we work" in *Talking Cure* (Taylor, 1999), "Executive and leadership coaching" in *The Complete Handbook of Coaching* (Cox et al., 2018), "Using emotion as intelligence" in *Organizational Therapy* (Schein & Ogawa, 2017), and "Defences against anxiety in the law" in *Social Defences against Anxiety* (Armstrong & Rustin, 2015).

Part VIII

Performance, publications, and policy

CHAPTER FORTY

"Give them time"
Pigeon holes and pasta—the making of a
Tavistock TV programme

Beth Holgate

In the early days, we had a routine—pigeon holes then pasta. We were far from popular when we arrived at the Tavistock in January 1998 to research the series that became *Talking Cure*. A provisional agreement had been brokered by executive producer Polly Bide for the BBC and Anton Obholzer and Nick Temple for the Tavi, but the detail of quite what would be in the series had been left deliberately vague.

In the late mornings, my colleague Ines Cavill and I would check the pigeon hole that had been thoughtfully allocated to the BBC. Disappointed but not yet discouraged we'd post more requests for meetings before heading up to the top floor canteen and the best home-made pasta either of us had ever tasted. Over lunch we'd debate the wisdom of approaching clinicians in the corridors, or in the lift, or why not over the cannelloni? "It's a process, give them time"—was Nick Temple's advice—but that was the problem. Television time and processes were not the same as the Tavi's and anyway what was wrong with using phones and email (it existed) and getting back to people the same day, the same week even?

"If you fuck with us, I'll make sure you never work in TV again"—this was progress, I guess: a senior clinician in the Adult Department had agreed to talk to us, or rather to put us straight about what was at stake. A sobering encounter. The Tavi was not going to agree to the BBC filming its patients. The BBC was not going to agree to reconstructions using actors. We withdrew to the Child and Family Department where the wonderful Margaret Rustin had agreed to discuss how we might make a film about infant observation (BBC, 1999). This was less controversial—we found families who were happy to be observed and filmed, then clinicians Sarah Wynick and Maxine Dennis stepped up to do the year-long weekly observations. We also agreed that the filming and its impact on the observation process would be flagged up in the final programme. In early April, Bonnie Boskovic joined the BBC team as production manager along with editor Anna Liebschner, and we started filming.

The infant observation film got the ball rolling. We'd understood the impossibility of approaching patients in treatment, but what if the BBC were to advertise for people to take part in documentaries involving psychotherapy and what if that process was then made explicit in the finished programmes? I think it took us a while to grasp quite how terrifying the prospect of being filmed was for clinicians, and to this day I am grateful to the courageous few who gave us the benefit of the doubt—Caroline Garland for the Adult Department, Anton Obholzer for group therapy in the workplace, Sebastian Kraemer, Sarah Wynick, Barbara Dale, and Jenny Altschuler for the Child and Family Department. It is still a matter of regret that we weren't able to make films representing the work of the Adolescent Department and with clinicians in Child and Family working with autism—although we got tantalisingly close.

There was plenty to be terrified about. Advertisements relating to trauma and autism attracted a lot of callers and it was clear that the BBC and the Tavi had an obligation to all of these people regardless of whether they appeared in the final films. With the help of participating clinicians we were able to advise callers how to access mental health care in their areas but it was a sharp reminder of how much pain was out there and how stretched resources were. I don't imagine this has changed in twenty years.

We had some technical issues to solve. No camera operators in the room, no filming of patients in-between therapy sessions—no shots of the building inside or out to show any humans. As a consequence, there are rather too many shots of the Freud statue and tree branches in the final programmes. Crucially, cameraman Steve Standen was able to design and rig a remote filming system that came close enough to capturing what went on between therapists and patients without intruding upon it. By the autumn of 1998 we were in full production on six films. At some point the canteen changed hands and they stopped serving pasta.

Talking Cure was shown in October 1999 on BBC2 to modest viewing figures and reviews. My BBC bosses seemed pleased enough and there was even talk of a second series about group therapy but ironically after the Tavi, I didn't work in TV again—although not as a consequence of those early threats from a certain clinician in the Adult Department. I had given birth to my third child as the series aired, and by the time I was ready to return to the fray, the landscape had changed. Reality TV was the new thing and what I did was old hat.

BBC (1999) *Observation Observed: Closely Observed Infants on Film.*
https://vimeo.com/ondemand/observationobserved This film was made using much BBC footage, with additional material, as a resource for teaching infant observation.

* * *

Beth Holgate was the series producer of *Talking Cure*—the six part BBC series about the work of the Tavistock Clinic shown in autumn 1999. She joined the BBC in 1983 to train as a producer in the News and Current Affairs department and then moved on to work in Arts and Documentaries, coming to specialise in observational filmmaking. Her first contact with the Tavistock had nothing to do with TV—but was the result of a GP referral to the Under-5 clinic at Kentish Town Health Centre. Two thought-provoking sessions on how toddlers think appeared to make a difference to her own family dynamic, so when the BBC Tavistock project came along, she was already a secret fan. After *Talking Cure*, she gave up television and moved to France with her partner and three children. She now works as an English language teacher in Bordeaux and has recently acquired French nationality.

CHAPTER FORTY-ONE

The *Tavistock Gazette*, pantomimes, and books

Valerie Sinason

In 1996 Otto Kernberg published a hilarious and serious seminal paper on thirty ways of destroying the creativity of candidates in analytic trainings (Kernberg, 1996). These features included monolithic tendencies regarding theoretical approaches, isolation of candidates from the professional and scientific activities of the psychoanalytic society, and accentuation of the hierarchical relations among the faculty.

Twenty years earlier, from and due to Alexis Brook's and then Anton Obholzer's chairmanship, the Tavistock had largely succeeded in avoiding this. There were no beautiful paintings down all the corridors (but there soon were; see Garland, Chapter 29). There was no high-tech conference centre on the top floor. But the building shone with the pleasure of students and staff lucky enough to enter the Tavistock when it could be an institution that was not institutionalised, a true home for students, staff, and patients.

As a child psychotherapy trainee who began the clinical part of the training in 1976, I became slowly aware of the lack of a house journal to link the different parts that made up the Centre and share information and humour. I was sure it would aid the empowering atmosphere.

From the non-clinical staff there were fresh understandings of the culture that would be wonderful in print. Lofty, the iconic caretaker, loved describing rushing into a therapy room to remove a child from a windowsill while the therapist continued her interpretation of the child wishing to leave her. A secretary in the Adolescent Department would roar with laughter at typing up an elderly professional's case notes in which the interpretation was made that the patient could not bear how beautiful she was. "You don't need face creams if you have got this transference stuff going towards you," she laughed. John Scragg, the earlier porter, could regale you on his being asked to go to rooms where kids had piled furniture on top of each other to get to the light bulb and smash it, or help with the home cooking that used to exist. At night he felt the place was haunted.

I told my next-door neighbour, Susan Reid, a teacher on the course, of my wish which she immediately passed to Isca Wittenberg, who warmly supported the idea. Indeed, Mattie Harris, the director of the child psychotherapy training, told me she would personally reimburse the typing and other costs of a first issue as she felt it was so important, and she provided a major paper for the first issue, spring 1979. Alexis Brook, chair of the Professional Committee, sent a warm thank-you for the idea and provided a support meeting with names of staff who might be willing to help. He praised the quality of the first issue and provided encouraging support. There were, as he appreciatively wrote, "news items, gossip, scientific reports and satire, seriousness and fun, just what we need". There was no censorship.

I was a trainee. In hierarchical terms I was the bottom of the chain and yet the chair of the Clinic and the head of my training were both trusting my creativity and sense of balance. This was the opposite of the Kernberg situation!

Wonderfully, senior staff John Byng-Hall, Susan Lipshitz, Peter Reder,[1] Susan Zawada, and John Fader joined at the start, representing the Department for Children and Parents, the Adult Department, Adolescent Department, and Institute of Marital Studies. It was very important to have senior staff join, as it is hard to convey the terror the idea of the *Gazette* initially evoked in students and junior staff. In a reversal of usual hierarchy problems, it was the senior staff who lent themselves to trying to demystify the culture for everyone else. One trainee said she could not write in a journal that might be left inadvertently in the building and be seen by one of her patients. Another was more concerned her analyst would read what she had written. Some superb artwork from John Byng-Hall and Cecily Bentovim was nervously attacked for being sexual, as if that could not be allowed in the building! Indeed, it was important to have John Fader writing about the men's toilets and the men's staff toilets to free up thinking! The key problem he raised was junior male staff or even applicants for training finding themselves at the urinal next to the senior person who had just interviewed them! Having senior staff to defend editorial choices was important. However, the *Gazette* was embraced, and continued for more than fourteen years.

Where else could you have Mattie Harris, the director of the child therapy training, write about Bion, a personal friend? There were interviews with John Bowlby, Bowlby on Piaget, Bob Gosling interviewed, Gosling on Bion, John Byng-Hall on David Malan, Helene Dubinsky and Jean Magagna remembering Mrs Bick remembering Mrs Klein. There were interviews with Melanie Klein's housekeeper and family about the play "*Mrs Klein*".

The *Gazette* valued contributions from all staff. Unusual contributions came from loyal committed secretaries—such as Janice Uphill who was also a steam train driver, Dorothy Clark from the Adolescent Department who wrote recipes, Dorothy Southern and Marjorie Harborough granting interviews on their role as executive secretaries. Anne Belter, a ground floor telephonist wrote a poem about a profoundly disabled patient of mine who died.

Alexis Brook asked me to use my editorial contacts to create a concert for the Diamond Jubilee. After walking out of his office I bumped into Jon Stokes (see Chapter 39) and asked if he would contribute. It turned out Jon was a serious drummer and he offered some music and we then found out he was a brilliant comedy writer and actor. Our concert evening of comedy, opera, poetry, and song was to reactivate the talent of old and new staff including Arnon Bentovim who had last provided a concert twenty years earlier. Isca Wittenberg, Arnon Bentovim, and Anton Obholzer encouraged trainees to be creative and the comedy baton passed on to Jenny Sprince and Paul Pengelly (who joined the *Gazette*, and have written about the pantomimes in Chapter 42) and then to Brett Kahr.

From shows to public talks! The year 1983 marked an interview with D. M. Thomas about his bestseller *The White Hotel*, a novel about Freud. This was a wonderful coup for the *Gazette* as also was getting him to speak to a packed audience at the Tavistock, the success of which encouraged further cultural events such as an evening with Al Alvarez, and on another, Alexis inviting his brother Peter Brook to give a talk on his work. The freedom and confidence shown by the chair allowed creativity to flourish and further cultural links with the outside.

The *Gazette* continued and I returned when there was a gap in editors. In 1988, I wrote an editorial saying I was now great-great grandmother of the *Gazette* and thanked Anton Obholzer for his creative leadership and support. However, I did not want to carry on as a stopgap indefinitely. Anton reminded me that if the institution could not find a new editor then it meant it did not require the *Gazette*. I listened and withdrew after issue 22, and a further editor did appear!

Also in 1988, after being asked with Eileen Orford to find a way of encouraging writing at the Tavistock, I converted a personal request from Rosendale Press for a series of parenting books to a Tavistock-based series (*Understanding Your Child*, published by Jessica Kingsley, in ten volumes from babies to teenagers, including children with special needs[2]). It became very successful. With the plethora of workshop books and co-edited books, and the (so far) fifty-six volumes of the Tavistock series that appeared since then (see Waddell, Chapter 43), it is hard to remember that other than the "classics" of Freud, Klein, Bion, Bowlby, hardly any Tavistock books were published at this time.

Anton Obholzer's leadership position and attitude added to the intellectual and cultural flourishing. First, he asked staff not to be paranoid about the press and realise we could do more with newspaper help than a paper or chapter could.[3] He added—and this was extremely important—that if the press abused this sharing then colleagues should support their member who was misquoted. Departments were encouraged to pin press cuttings to the wall, whether positive or negative. I agreed to write a monthly problem page for *The Guardian* (which lasted for four years) in which I carefully quoted Tavistock specialist opinions. This included quotes from senior staff who would not have provided them for the general public without the clear backing of Anton. In the familiar large-group silence at the start of major clinic meetings Anton's humour always worked. "Alright—well, you have reminded yourselves what a silence is like so can we have some work now?"

There was the freedom to run workshops and start courses that did not require hierarchical or bureaucratic burdens. There was such a creative buzz about these developments. You could invite outside guests and not charge them an entrance fee. As a trainee I could also convene a "Mental Handicap" workshop. You could also raise research project ideas freely and be encouraged to follow them through. Whilst in the Adolescent Department I could set up a poetry group for unemployed young people, as well as examining the function of tattoos in teenagers.

In 1990 a Swedish colleague came for help with a case that changed my life. His patient, who had an intellectual disability, had been ritually abused. Others in the UK followed. Undertaking this work, and gaining a Department of Health grant for it, was another example of the Tavistock following and trying to understand new patient groups in a professional way through research, regardless of some negative response in the media. I fondly recall the launch of *Treating Survivors of Satanist Abuse*, published by Routledge in 1994 and with major Tavistock contributions from Professor Judith Trowell, Dr Arnon Bentovim, Dr Robert Hale, Professor Joan Bicknell, et al. There was a big launch party at the Tavistock with detectives from Scotland Yard, Department of Health officials, and Anton Obholzer presiding. Sadly, this subject, and the dissociative identity disorder that was at the heart of it, could not be held at the Portman without a protective grant and I finally left to set up my own Clinic for Dissociative Studies which is now twenty years old and which I retired from two years ago.

Despite all the turmoil that greets societally unwelcome subjects I was given for twenty years an internal Tavistock space in that golden era which I have carried to all my work since. I was allowed my observations. I was given a voice and through that hopefully helped to provide a voice for others.

Notes

1. Dr Reder was a senior registrar in child and adolescent psychiatry; senior in name but trainee in role. (Ed.)
2. Sold by Karnac https://karnacbooks.com/SeriesDetail.asp?SID=17
3. It was at around this time that the anonymous number "120" at the front entrance to the Clinic was replaced by the words "Tavistock Centre". Before that the Tavistock was effectively "ex-directory" (Ed.).

* * *

Valerie Sinason, PhD, is a poet, writer, child and adult psychotherapist and psychoanalyst. She has published more than fifteen books (solo and co-edited) including *Mental Handicap and the Human Condition: An Analytic Approach to Intellectual Disability*, and 189 papers and chapters. She is on the board of the International Society for the Study of Trauma and Dissociation (ISSTD) which gave her a lifetime achievement award in 2016. She is an honorary consultant psychotherapist to the Cape Town Child Guidance Clinic, a trustee of the Bushman Heritage Centre, and president of the Institute of Psychotherapy and Disability where she was also the first recipient of the Valerie Sinason Award in 2017.

CHAPTER FORTY-TWO

Tavistock pantomimes

Jenny Sprince and Paul Pengelly

The tradition of revue was well-established when we arrived at the Tavistock in, respectively, 1970 (Paul) and the mid-1980s (Jenny). It felt a privilege to be invited to contribute (and some did not need to be asked twice, the urge to perform having never quite been analysed out of them). There were a few members of the students' common room who had come into psychoanalytic work from professional theatre. We got together and decided we would be daring and put on the first ever Tavistock Christmas Pantomime. It turned out to be the pilot for a series of ever more ambitious shows (Pengelly & Sprince 2011).

Our first effort (1989) was written in traditional rhyming couplets and boasted a pantomime horse which described itself as a combined object. Both the rhymes and the theoretical interpretations were to prove a constant feature in the pantomimes that followed over the next six years. One child psychotherapist soprano claimed to have learned more theory from taking part in the pantos than from all the seminars and lectures she'd attended during her training.

A pattern emerged: Jenny and Paul wrote the scripts and most of the songs—set to well-known tunes, in the tradition of English ballad opera. Eileen Orford contributed her own additional and delightful lyrics. She and Paul starred, alongside Jeannie Milligan, our soubrette extraordinaire. Jenny directed, and the four of us recruited the supporting cast from every department and discipline within the Clinic. We discovered and showcased hidden talents at all levels of the psychoanalytic hierarchy, not forgetting the administrative and ancillary staff and the IMS (Institute of Marital Studies, now Tavistock Relationships). Jenny's rather basic musicianship was supplemented by that of other colleagues—most notably Brett Kahr in the final show. None of it would have been possible without Mike Shaw, long-term head porter, who kept us all sane with his quiet ability to find a solution to every panic about the practicalities of room availability, chairs, lighting, heating, piano hire, and general stage management.

Each show was put together in a couple of weekends before the performance, but the preparations—and the afterglow—permeated the building over the entire year. The process was at least as enjoyable as the product. Jokes and friendships were shared across departments, and serious conversations were embarked upon in lifts and corridors: around the theoretical underpinning of the Greek myths, the psychic significance of travesty, and the use of rhyming couplets as an aide memoire, to give a few examples.

Inspiration for the second pantomime (1990) came when a pair of shapely legs caught Paul's attention as they passed the table where we were sitting eating lunch together in the Tavistock canteen. We knew we'd found the ideal Principal Boy. And we were proud to educate the multinational population of the building in the glorious tradition of British pantomime cross-dressing. We persuaded Anton Obholzer to embrace the role of Widow Twankey—our most triumphant coup, and a performance that lives in the memory of all who were fortunate to witness it.

The third pantomime (1992) took the form of a group relations conference: the delegates attempted to tackle the conference task while battling gender issues, the demands of evidence-based performance indicators, and Bion's three basic assumptions—represented in person by concrete manifestations, who were themselves distracted by ongoing free market rivalry. The Conference Director finally recalled the primary task ("something about authority …" he mused) only just in time for the dénouement.

The fourth panto (1993) was more apocalyptic—reflecting increasingly troubled times within the NHS and the country as a whole. Noah's ark arrived in an unpleasantly flooded NW3, and the pantomime's existence was threatened by the Fates who introduced staff cuts and privatisation, while assorted deities impotently patched together competitive tenders.

An external consultation

This might well have been the end of the series, but there was one more to come, a couple of years later, after both of us had left the building. We were invited back by Anton, who wanted us to write a final show to help celebrate the Tavistock's seventy-fifth anniversary (1995). For the first time, we asked for payment for our services. We were now being outsourced and we knew, if we were to write something that would successfully meet the mood of our audience, that we would need to put in many extra hours to attune ourselves to current staff preoccupations. Anton readily agreed: he told us he regarded us as external consultants, and expected our pantomime to provide a transformative interpretation. It was a tall order, but we did our best—after all, the transformation scene has always been an essential ingredient of British pantomime. We held several focus group meetings with our cast, moving further and further towards paralysis and pessimism, until we arrived at our own understanding of what we were being told through our countertransference, and felt able to embody it in song, dance, and rhyming couplets.

The plot confronts the professional staff's response to the changes in NHS requirements through several contrasting groups: the professional committee, a pair of Tavi alumni, a selection of overworked but insightful administrative staff, past and present, and a number of bewildered ghosts of former Tavi luminaries—introjects who have somehow been extruded, through a collective failure to process the traumatic impact of managerial demands. Recapitulating the epic history of the institution from its origins, we managed—we hoped—to arrive at the conclusion that the psychoanalytic process could still enable the staff to challenge irrational resistance to change, while continuing to hold firmly to the rigour and integrity of their work. The introjected ghosts returned safely to their posts, committing to provide benign governance of the internal world, and we ended on a hopeful note: "There'll always be a Tavi" (sung to the familiar WW2 anthem).

We thought it was a success. When we played the video at a reunion party a few years later, the audience responded with a rueful mix of smiles and tears: we gather that the fight continues.

* * *

Jenny Sprince is a Tavistock-trained child psychotherapist and organisational consultant. From 1990 to 2011 she worked as external consultant to Thornby Hall, part of the Peper Harow Foundation (later Childhood First). She was co-founder and clinical director of Placement Support (https://placementsupport.co.uk/) from 2001 to 2019, and is co-founder and chair of APPCIOS (http://appcios.info/). She maintains a small private practice as a consultant and supervisor. Publications include "Towards an Integrated Network" (*Journal of Child Psychotherapy*, 2000); "Developing Containment" (*Journal of Child Psychotherapy*, 2002); "The Forever Family and the Ghosts of the Dispossessed" in *The Emotional Experience of Adoption—a Psychoanalytic Perspective*, edited by D. Hindle and G. Shulman (Routledge, 2008); "Working with Complex Cases" (*NICE Public Health Guideline 28*, 2011); "The Riddle of the Sphinx" in *Waiting To Be Found*, edited by Andrew Briggs (Karnac, 2012); "From Owning to Belonging" in *Towards Belonging: Negotiating New Relationships for Adopted Children and Those in Care*, edited by Andrew Briggs (Routledge, 2015); and with William Halton, "Oscillating Images: Perceptions of Couples in Organisations" in *Couple Dynamics*, edited by Aleksandra Novakovic (Routledge, 2016).

Paul Pengelly undertook the advanced social work clinical training at the Tavistock Clinic in 1970–1971 during his twelve years as a probation officer and supervisor in Middlesex Probation Service. He trained and worked as a couple psychoanalytic psychotherapist between 1978 and 1994 at the Institute of Marital Studies (now Tavistock Relationships), which at that time was housed in the Tavistock Centre. He was a principal adult psychotherapist at Bournewood Mental Health NHS Trust, Surrey, from 1995 to 2002 and continued in private practice until he retired in 2006. He co-wrote, with Douglas Woodhouse, *Anxiety and the Dynamics of Collaboration* (Aberdeen University Press, 1991) and, with Lynette Hughes, *Staff Supervision in a Turbulent Environment* (Jessica Kingsley, 1997).

CHAPTER FORTY-THREE

The Tavistock Clinic Series

Margot Waddell

In 1996, rather to my surprise, I found myself acting, along with Nicholas Temple (at the time chair of the Tavistock Professional Committee) as series editor of books that would reflect the depth and diversity of the work of the Clinic. Michael Rustin had put forward the original idea that I should do some research into which publisher would be best suited to entrust with such a series. I was already familiar with Duckworth in its heyday and, drawing on its psychological and cultural experience, we set out with the firm. I did not, however, expect to find myself first of all co-editor and then sole editor of the entire enterprise—one that now numbers fifty-six volumes.

I shall quote from the preface of our first publication (1997), *Multiple Voices: Narrative in Systemic Psychotherapy*, edited by John Byng-Hall and Renos Papadopoulos.

> The Clinic's philosophy has been one of influencing mental health work toward therapeutic and humane methods and has, as an aim, the dissemination of training, clinical expertise and research throughout Britain and the rest of the world. This major new book series is designed to make available the extensive experience that the work of the Clinic represents, covering all its departments, specialist workshops and research seminars. The Series seeks to be accessible to a wide audience by presenting new approaches and developments in a clear, readable style and at reasonable prices. It will enable the Clinic to describe many aspects both of its established clinical work and of current growing points and innovations in the practice, theory and research of experts.
>
> In this book members of the Systems Group of the Tavistock Clinic address various aspects of the narrative approach to psychotherapy. The recent increased interest in this perspective to psychotherapy has created a rather confused field with different meanings,

definitions and directions. This book offers a coherent approach based on clinical research and therapeutic work: the chapters address theoretical issues and clinical applications of a variety of contexts, including narratives in families with physical illness, fostering and adoption, divorce, bilingualism and refugees.

In those days, I had no notion of how timely Michael Rustin's suggestion would turn out to be; how bursting with thoughts and ideas about their ongoing work were the staff groups in all departments, and how significant it was that the publications of the huge range of the Clinic's passions and commitments needed to be represented.

   With Duckworth, we were to bring out some further key texts, two edited by David Bell, *Reason and Passion* and *Psychoanalysis and Culture*, each encompassing intense engagements with the psychoanalytic innovations of Melanie Klein in relation to Hanna Segal's legacy. There was also a groundbreaking book edited by Caroline Garland on *Understanding Trauma* (1998). Again I shall quote from the preface, for it locates the history of the Tavistock and its origins, now 100 years ago.

> The Clinic's philosophy has been one of influencing mental health work towards therapeutic and humane methods and has, as an aim, the dissemination of clinical expertise and research throughout Britain and the rest of the world.

> ...

> This book describes the work of the Unit for the Study of Trauma and its Aftermath in the Adult Department of the Tavistock Clinic. This challenging and innovative work is rooted in psychoanalysis, both clinically and theoretically. The thoughtful and detailed account given here shows how much can be done for traumatised individuals, but also the complex and long-standing nature of their problems.

> The book takes us back directly to the clinical experience of trauma which led to the founding of the Tavistock Clinic in 1920 by Crichton-Miller and his colleagues. These psychologically-informed physicians had had extensive experience of the treatments of traumatised soldiers in the First World War. The men had been psychologically damaged by their battlefield experience and showed many similar experiences to the patients described in this book. The founding of the Tavistock came out of the physicians' determination to provide psychological treatment for traumatised people, not only in war but in everyday life. The knowledge that the Clinic had gained from this work was then applied in the Second World War, when the staff of the Clinic had a major involvement in army psychiatry, which had meanwhile developed a humane and thoughtful way of dealing with the problems of battle trauma and war neurosis. In turn, this war work led to many advances in psychiatry and psychological treatment which have since been drawn on more generally

in the Tavistock. This strong reparative ambition or desire is at the heart of the ethos of the Clinic and continues to inform its clinical and theoretical development.

These pages revisit the whole field, but from the point of view of new psychoanalytic ideas that have been developed in recent years. The link between understanding trauma and the wider work of the Clinic is emphasised by Caroline Garland. She points out that the task of therapy is hard since the extent of human destructiveness has to be faced in both perpetrator and survivor. The place of this book in the Series is particularly fitting when we consider that the Clinic began in 1920, having to face the destructiveness of the war and its sacrifice of young lives.

The subsequent twenty years of publications, after Karnac Books took over the series, offers a rather extraordinary range of the volumes which, to my mind, so uniquely and movingly sum up the work of the Clinic. It is a story of which one can be very proud. It ranges from, most recently, *A for Adoption: An Exploration of the Adoption Experience for Families and Professionals* (by Alison Roy), the first of our books to have a remote launch, a wonderful event for which even Zoom managed to capture the celebratory spirit. In the interim, we have had a wide range of contributions, including *Looking into Later Life; Oedipus and the Couple; Organization in the Mind; The Anorexic Mind; The Groups Book; Adoption; Learning Disabilities*—and practically everything in between.

The fifty-six volumes, the last three published by Routledge, between them encapsulate the depth and breadth of the Clinic's work across disciplines, age groups, and theoretical outlooks. This is my personal story, now, mercifully, shared with my co-editors Jocelyn Catty and Kate Stratton, in encouraging authors and making these volumes available. But much more significantly, it is the Tavistock's ongoing story—one of dedication to work in the wider community and commitment to the endeavour, one of the capacity to think creatively through the pains of life's circumstances, at whatever age, in whatever setting. This is a proud and continuing task.

Tavistock Clinic Series

A for Adoption: An Exploration of the Adoption Experience for Families and Professionals, Alison Roy
Acquainted with the Night: Psychoanalysis and the Poetic Imagination, eds. Hamish Canham, Carole Satyamurti
Addictive States of Mind, eds. Marion Bower, Robert Hale, Heather Wood
Assessment in Child Psychotherapy, eds. Margaret Rustin, Emanuela Quagliata
Borderline Welfare: Feeling and Fear of Feeling in Modern Welfare, Andrew Cooper, Julian Lousada
Childhood Depression: A Place for Psychotherapy, ed. Judith Trowell, with Gillian Miles
Conjunctions: Social Work, Psychoanalysis, and Society, Andrew Cooper

Consultations in Dynamic Psychotherapy, Peter Hobson

Contemporary Developments in Adult and Young Adult Therapy: The Work of the Tavistock and Portman Clinics, ed. Alessandra Lemma

Couple Dynamics: Psychoanalytic Perspectives in Work with the Individual, the Couple, and the Group, ed. Aleksandra Novakovic

Creating New Families: Therapeutic Approaches to Fostering, Adoption and Kinship Care, eds. Jenny Kenrick, Caroline Lindsey, Lorraine Tollemache

Doing Things Differently: The Influence of Donald Meltzer on Psychoanalytic Theory and Practice, eds. Margaret Cohen, Alberto Hahn

Engaging with Complexity: Child and Adolescent Mental Health and Education, eds. Rita Harris, Sue Rendall, Sadegh Nashat

Facing It Out: Clinical Perspectives on Adolescent Disturbance, eds. Robin Anderson, Anna Dartington

Inside Lives: Psychoanalysis and the Growth of the Personality, Margot Waddell

Internal Landscapes and Foreign Bodies, Gianna Williams

Living on the Border: Psychotic Processes in the Individual, the Couple, and the Group, eds. David Bell, Aleksandra Novakovic

Looking into Later Life: A Psychoanalytic Approach to Depression and Dementia in Old Age, ed. Rachael Davenhill

Making Room for Madness in Mental Health: The Psychoanalytic Understanding of Psychotic Communication, Marcus Evans

Managing Vulnerability: The Underlying Dynamics of Systems of Care, Tim Dartington

Melanie Klein Revisited: Pioneer and Revolutionary in the Psychoanalysis of Young Children, Susan Sherwin-White

Mirror to Nature: Drama, Psychoanalysis and Society, Margaret Rustin, Michael Rustin

Multiple Voices, eds. Renos K. Papadopoulos, John Byng-Hall

New Discoveries in Child Psychotherapy: Findings from Qualitative Research, eds. Margaret Rustin, Michael Rustin

Oedipus and the Couple, ed. Francis Grier

On Adolescence: Inside Stories, Margot Waddell

Organization in the Mind: Psychoanalysis, Group Relations and Organizational Consultancy, David Armstrong, ed. Robert French

Psychoanalysis and Culture: A Kleinian Perspective, ed. David Bell

Psychotic States in Children, eds. Margaret Rustin, Maria Rhode, Hélène Dubinsky, Alex Dubinsky

Reason and Passion: A Celebration of the Work of Hanna Segal, ed. David Bell

Reflecting on Reality: Psychotherapists at Work in Primary Care, eds. Sue Blake, Dilys Daws, John Launer

Researching the Unconscious: Principles of Psychoanalytic Method, Michael Rustin

Sent Before My Time: A Child Psychotherapist's View of Life on a Neonatal Intensive Care Unit, Margaret Cohen

Sexuality and Gender Now: Moving Beyond Heteronormativity, eds. Leezah Hertzmann, Juliet Newbigin

Short-term Psychoanalytic Psychotherapy for Adolescents with Depression: A Treatment Manual, Jocelyn Catty, Simon Cregeen, Carol Hughes, Nick Midgley, Maria Rhode, Margaret Rustin

Sibling Matters: A Psychoanalytic, Developmental, and Systemic Approach, eds. Debbie Hindle, Susan Sherwin-White

Social Defences against Anxiety: Explorations in a Paradigm, eds. David Armstrong, Michael Rustin

Surviving Space: Papers on Infant Observation, ed. Andrew Briggs

Sustaining Depth and Meaning in School Leadership: Keeping Your Head, eds. Emil Jackson, Andrea Berkeley

Talking Cure: Mind and Method of the Tavistock Clinic, ed. David Taylor

The Anorexic Mind, Marilyn Lawrence

The Groups Book: Psychoanalytic Group Therapy: Principles and Practice, ed. Caroline Garland

The Learning Relationship: Psychoanalytic Thinking in Education, Biddy Youell

The Many Faces of Asperger's Syndrome, eds. Trudy Klauber, Maria Rhode

Therapeutic Approaches with Babies and Young Children in Care: Observation and Attention, Jenifer Wakelyn

Therapeutic Care for Refugees: No Place Like Home, ed. Renos K. Papadopoulos

Thinking Space: Promoting Thinking about Race, Culture and Diversity in Psychotherapy and Beyond, ed. Frank Lowe

Towards Belonging: Negotiating New Relationships for Adopted Children and Those in Care, ed. Andrew Briggs

Turning the Tide: The Psychoanalytic Approach of the Fitzjohn's Unit to Patients with Complex Needs, eds. Rael Meyerowitz, David Bell

Understanding Trauma: A Psychoanalytical Approach, ed. Caroline Garland

Unexpected Gains: Psychotherapy with People with Learning Disabilities, eds. David Simpson, Lynda Miller

Waiting To Be Found: Papers on Children in Care, ed. Andrew Briggs

What Can the Matter Be?: Therapeutic Interventions with Parents, Infants and Young Children, eds. Elizabeth Bradley, Louise Emanuel

Work Discussion: Learning from Reflective Practice in Work with Children and Families, eds. Jonathan Bradley, Margaret Rustin

Working Below the Surface: The Emotional Life of Contemporary Organizations, eds. Clare Huffington, William Halton, David Armstrong, Jane Pooley

Young Child Observation: A Development in the Theory and Method of Infant Observation, eds. Simonetta M. G. Adamo, Margaret Rustin

[Margot Waddell's biography appears on p. xiii]

CHAPTER FORTY-FOUR

Tavistock policy seminars: a contained and disruptive space

Andrew Cooper

S ince 2003 Tavistock Policy Seminars have been a regular feature of the Trust's public facing programme of events, introducing a fresh dimension to the wide-ranging and evolving project of our engagement with mental health and public policy processes. The seminars were initiated by the Trust's Professional Committee which wished to see the Tavistock engage more actively in these areas. Organised by a steering group of current and former staff members, seminars take place on certain Thursday evenings where, from 6 to 8 pm, the lecture theatre is set up "in the round" and two, or occasionally more, speakers present talks and a response on public policy related themes, followed by a break for (free at the point of need) drinks and snacks. The audience then return, and are invited to develop their thinking as a group. We regard the presentations as the hors d'oeuvre, while the discussion is the main course. Towards the end, speakers re-enter the group and offer reflections on what they have heard.

This model, which like other Tavistock reflective spaces has affinities with Quaker traditions, knowingly aims to disrupt a dominant model of both policy making and learning—namely a top–down, linear transmission model in which experts analyse problems, decide on a course of ameliorative action or education, and then implement it with a relatively passive population, professional domain, or body of learners. This has never been the Tavistock culture of learning which by contrast emphasises group-based "learning from experience" and the development of relationship-based understandings of complex human predicaments conceived as "psychodynamic systems". Attention to "unconscious processes" is part of this picture, but so is attention to the social and political context; human psychosocial processes are produced and reproduced within this matrix of complexity, and policy processes, analyses, and solutions are, in our view, no exception. We consider the experiential "intelligence" of those who "live" predicaments—whether they be "clinical", familial, social, or political—is a key source of potential for change and development.

The Policy Seminar space attempts to embody and facilitate attention to these multiple layers of meaning, causation, perspective, and possibility in relation to themes pertinent to contemporary public policy. Sometimes these themes have drawn on the work of the Trust itself, sometimes on public issues of immediate concern and relevance, and at other times on more theoretical and political preoccupations. Thus, the first seminar in the series responded to the social and professional upheaval created by the case of Victoria Climbié's murder and its fallout, while the second explored how applied complexity theory might be a stronger theoretical model for public policy analysis. The meaning of the English riots of 2011, journalistic practice and trauma, the social and professional dynamics surrounding work with asylum seekers, the lived experience of probation officers in the modern era, are among the many topics with which (at the time of writing) the sixty-six seminars have engaged. Most recently two full houses heard compelling presentations about the passions of Brexit; audiences of both leavers and remainers engaged in incisive, unsettling, revealing dialogue about the disruptions to identity and political alignment revealed and produced by the referendum. At the second of these one speaker delivered a sustained and challenging psycho-political "interpretation" asking "remainers" to engage with their own complicity in the outcome of the vote, a consequence in his view of their (our) political complacency towards the European project they aspired to so love.

Somewhere in all this work there is the germ of a new "method" for the psychoanalytically and systemically informed understanding of social and policy related processes. One early attempt to conceptualise this can be found in Cooper (2018). There are numerous publications arising from the seminar series (e.g., Abse, 2019[1]; Barnett, 2019; Rustin, 2004), but no systematically codified synthesis of outputs. One might ask, what then has been the impact or influence of the initiative? First, it has widened the Tavistock's "reach", or "footprint" in contemporary jargon, to audiences and constituencies it has not previously touched. Second, its participative form of discussion has influenced other organisations and individuals in their approach to conducting participatory explorations of difficult topics; and there is a resonance with current interest in, for example, citizens' assemblies as a route to thickening and deepening our forms of democratic engagement. But as with many Tavistock practices and trainings the influence is possibly more "molecular" than systemic, modifying people's assumptions, habits of thought, and practices through osmosis and local capillaries of transmission.

Over the years the Tavistock has touched untold thousands of citizens and professionals through its continuity and longevity. It has evolved and reproduced a particular culture of learning that is shared across disciplines, modes of clinical activity, education, and training, as well as these more socially engaged forms of activity. It may be a weakness of the Trust's endeavours that it does not more rigorously audit, research, evidence, and evaluate its work. On the other hand it knows the dangers of over-dependence on these linear forms of "self-knowledge" that obscure subtlety, complexity, and the importance of developmental processes in favour of the kind of static "proxy" world view that a business-driven "audit society" favours—a tension which has been one recurring preoccupation of the seminar series itself.

The audience dialogues at seminars are never recorded or streamed, because they operate under "Chatham House rules" in which individual contributions must not be publicly attributable. This boundary helps to free people to speak their minds, argue, contest, and voice dangerous thoughts without risk of repercussions. Freedom of thought is the root of creativity, and public policy needs more not less creativity in pursuit of public benefit. Freedom to speak safely is an aspect of the provision of "containment" so that creative disruptions can be tolerated in the service of generating new ideas, alternative practices, and social progress.

[Andrew Cooper's biography appears on p. 245]

The 66 seminars so far organised[2] are listed below.

	Title	Date	Speaker	Discussant
1	After Victoria Climbié: Can procedures make us work more effectively?	05.06.03	William Utting	Andrew Cooper
2	Facing complexity in public policy	03.07.03	Jake Chapman	Nick Temple
3	Rethinking audit and inspection: Engaging professionals in the improvement of services	16.10.03	Michael Rustin	David Bawden
4	Building a new professionalism in children's services	11.12.03	Ilan Katz	Barry Luckock
5	Primitive forces in society—How do we hold unaccompanied children in mind?	19.02.04	John Simmonds	Selam Kidane
6	W(h)ither treatments for personality disorder?	06.05.04	Kingsley Norton Fiona Warren	Phil Richardson
7	What is childcare for?	10.06.04	Lisa Harker	Louise Emanuel
8	Emotionally intelligent policy: a debate	28.10.04	Andrew Cooper Linda Hoyle	Lucy de Groot Tom Bentley
9	Adoption policy today—fantasy and reality	18.11.04	Charlotte Noyes	Jeffrey Coleman
10	Young people and sexual exploitation	20.01.05	Jenny Pearce Sue Jago	Joanna Phoenix

	Title	Date	Speaker	Discussant
11	Art, health and regeneration: from individual responsibility to community responsiveness	17.02.05	Frank Creber	Prue Chamberlayne Lynn Froggett
12	Not so sure start?	26.05.05	Norman Glass	Jane Roberts
13	Adolescents in distress: Britain on the slide?	30.06.05	Robert Goodman	Stephen Briggs
14	Borderline welfare	20.10.05	Andrew Cooper	Tom Bentley
15	Journalism and trauma	17.11.05	Barry Richards	
16	Children's NSF—the policy experience	16.02.06	Caroline Lindsey	Ricky Emanuel
17	Homelessness, dangerousness and the forensic dilemma	19.10.06	Christopher Scanlon John Adlam	Vickie Cooper
18	What's wrong with happiness?	15.03.07	Michael Rustin	Alessandra Lemma
19	Is the post-war Bevanite welfare state dead?	28.06.07	Andrew Cooper	Michael Rustin
20	Young people's voices—Stories from the care system	11.10.07	Julia Granville Caroline Lindsey	
21	Predictive policy: Can social policy join up with itself across the lifespan?	24.01.08	Naomi Eisenstadt	Sebastian Kraemer
22	Is dependency dead?	21.02.08	Tim Dartington	Angela Foster
23	Jewel in the crown or last days of the Raj?	24.04.08	John Launer	Stephen Amiel
24	Markets, meaning and madness	20.11.08	David Tuckett	Richard Strang
25	Public value and health service outcomes: Dialogue, measurement or contest	05.03.09	John Benington	Dione Hills
26	Policy and emotion	10.12.09	Paul Hoggett	
27	Sources of the self	21.01.10	Madeleine Bunting	Sebastian Kraemer
28	The psychology of spin	11.02.10	Jessica Evans	Ursula Murray
29	New ways of teaching and learning about mental health: The personality disorder knowledge understanding framework	11.03.10	Nick Benefield Heather Wood	Neil Gordon

	Title	Date	Speaker	Discussant
30	God is alive and hiding in Whitehall: The symbolic comforts of modern public policy	13.05.10	Andrew Cooper	John Simmonds
31	Safeguarding in the 21st century: Where to now?	25.11.10	Jane Barlow	
32	"The state we're getting into . . ."	16.12.10	Polly Toynbee	
33	Paired leadership in society	24.02.11	Tim Dartington	Olya Khaleelee
34	Inequality: the big argument	10.03.11	Richard Wilkinson	Kate Pickett
35	Social dreaming	24.03.11	Gordon Lawrence	Ruth Silver
36	"All that is solid melts into air"	09.06.11	David Bell	Andrew Cooper
37	Democratic leadership	10.10.11	David Armstrong Michael Rustin	
38	"You can only get it wrong": Adoption and the placement of children from minority ethnic backgrounds	01.12.11	John Simmonds Ravinder Barn	
39	The "English Riots" as a communication: Winnicott, the antisocial tendency, and public disorder	14.12.11	Adrian Ward	
40	The psychology of neoliberalism	01.03.12	Michael Rustin	
41	Welfare professions today: Reflections on research on contemporary probation officers and head teachers	15.03.12	David Forbes Simon Tucker	
42	Complexity, psychoanalysis and society—one day conference	18.05.12	Terry Marks-Tarlow Joseph Dodds Graham Shulman Margaret Lush Andrew Cooper	
43	What happened to the idea of unconscious defences against anxiety?	14.06.12	Andrew Cooper Angela Foster Tim Dartington	
44	Can a doctor in the House make a difference? The conflicts between political leadership and clinical judgement	11.10.12	Richard Taylor	

	Title	Date	Speaker	Discussant
45	Not in your genes: The gobsmacking implications of evidence from the human genome project	21.02.13	Oliver James	Andrew Cooper
46	Can the NHS learn? (from the Francis Report II)	21.03.13	Rob Senior	Jocelyn Cornwell
47	Life at the border: Young refugees and migrants surviving and thriving on the margins of modern Britain	27.06.13	Yesim Devici Heather Price	
48	Climate change—from care to action	10.10.13	Sally Weintrobe Anne Karpf	
49	Can the state be human?	07.11.13	Marc Stears	Jon Stokes
50	Early years and society	13.03.14	Zoe Williams	
51	Don't look back, we're going forward! Living without history in modern policy and practice	12.06.14	Tim Dartington Andrew Cooper	
52	After neoliberalism?	06.11.14	Jon Cruddas MP	Bernadette Wren Michael Rustin
53	Social defences against anxiety: Explorations in paradigm	20.11.14	David Armstrong and Michael Rustin	Liz Tutton William Halton Larry Hirschhorn
54	An empire of money	21.05.15	David Marquand	David Armstrong
54	Emotionally Intelligent Policy Making	21.01.16	Matthew Taylor	John Simmonds
55	"What's our state of mind? Borderline welfare ten years on"	*Day conference* 17.06.16	Andrew Cooper Julian Lousada	
56	"What happens when the rich get richer?" A showing of *The Divide* documentary film	07.07.16	Richard Wilkinson	
57	Exploring online health communities	22.09.16	Paul Hodgkin Ben Metz Bernadette Wren	
58	The emotional politics of child protection	17.11.16	Joanne Warner Sharon Shoesmith	

	Title	Date	Speaker	Discussant
59	Our present woes: What can be learned from the history of the Tavistock that is relevant today?	01.12.16	David Armstrong Michael Rustin	
60	The passions of Brexit I	10.01.19	Anthony Barnett Susanna Abse	
61	Reflective social work practice	28.03.19	Tom Stibbs Amanda Lees Sylvia Smith Anna Harvey Andrew Cooper	
62	The passions of Brexit II	30.01.20	Anthony Barnett Susanna Abse	
63	Organisational work and the continuing relevance of Isabel Menzies Lyth	12.03.20	Jennie McShannon Kay Trainor	
64	Contributions of system psychotherapy to contemporary mental health work	23.03.20	Sarah Helps Karen Partridge Wendy Lobatto	
65	"What do policymakers need to know about attachment, and why do they not yet know it?"	14.05.20	Pasco Fearon Graham Music	
66	Psychoanalytic psychotherapy in the NHS	25.06.20	Gail Lewis Katie Argent	

Notes

1. https://www.bpc.org.uk/sites/psychoanalytic-council.org/files/NA%2028%20Summer_2019_landscape_WEB.pdf
2. During the coronavirus lockdown some were postponed while others were held in a virtual space (Ed.)

Afterword

Soldiering on

Sebastian Kraemer

Although not all the pieces are here, there is a common thread running through this patchwork of writings and recollections. It is of the Tavistock's self-consciousness as an organisation reaching out to influence a wider society, but one in which it is not an easy fit. The Tavistock can even make fun of itself (Sprince & Pengelly, Chapter 42) though it was rarely driven to take its own medicine—namely external consultation—when in crisis. The nearest we get to that is in a group relations conference (Shapiro & Carr, 2012) an intense, living anthropology in which members' professional uniforms provide less than usual insulation from social uncertainty. Instead each has to find their own way as individuals in a group, which is our human evolutionary heritage. Such events are highly sensitive to the cultural environment, often reflecting prevailing social tensions with uncanny accuracy (Khaleelee & Miller, 1993). This is powerful learning for both consulting staff and members, but the rest of the Clinic tend to carry on regardless, dismissing participants' reports of enlightenment with a kind of indulgence, thus protecting the institution from any urgent internal pressure to change. And yet, at any time in the wider Tavistock represented here, someone will be learning from their experience of self with others.

In September 1920, the original staff of the Tavistock Square Clinic (at number 51) were a small band of physicians who felt it their Christian duty to give psychological help to people who could otherwise not afford it, an ambition to get beyond the private clinic to a community in need. Their mission was not directed at the spirit but at society; to promote "mental hygiene" there. They distanced themselves from the prevailing medical attitude to mental distress, which was dismissive and moralising—as it often still is—but in those days with an added dose of discriminatory genetics. Already before the First World War the Tavistock's founder, the general practitioner-turned-psychotherapist Hugh Crichton-Miller (1877–1959), had concocted his own blend of Freud, and related "new psychology", for his method: "hypnotic suggestion and waking suggestion, psycho-analysis, Persuasion à la Dubois, Vittoz' re-education, and what I designate as 'mind-drill'" (1912, p. 18). The Clinic also did medical investigations, to rule out or treat focal sepsis which they believed could be the cause of mental disorder.[1]

They also kept their distance from Freudian psychoanalysis, represented in Britain by the British Psychoanalytical Society,[2] founded the previous year. By this time the dreadful experiences of the Great War had generated new thinking about mental trauma and—perhaps typically British—revisions of psychoanalysis. The pioneering anthropologist and physician William H. R. Rivers (1864–1922) "saw the instinct of self-preservation, and not the sexual instinct, as the driving force behind war neuroses" (Myers, 1923, p. 169). The gap between the Tavistock and the Institute of Psychoanalysis was mutually maintained. Ernest Jones, its founder and director, forbade his colleagues to work there. Neither fish nor fowl, the Tavistock continued on its nonconformist path, soldiering on.

During that time the Clinic grew, adding trainings and lectures[3] which attracted many enthusiasts. It became too big for one person to "own". In 1933 one of Crichton-Miller's protégés, Jack Rawlings Rees (always known as JR) was elected medical director in his place. Rees made the Tavistock's governance more democratic and, in light of the very visible effects of the Great Depression,[4]

> raised new questions concerning the role of social factors in psychological illness. This organizational revolution brought to the front a younger generation of clinicians with a level of ability and a maverick quality that would otherwise have been lost. (Trist & Murray, 1990b, p. 2)

In a footnote, Trist and Murray name these clinicians: Rees himself, Henry Dicks, Ronald Hargreaves, A. T. M. (Tommy) Wilson, and Wilfred Bion, all of whom, they said, would have left the Tavistock without this change.

Hoping to gain London University's acceptance as a training organisation, the Clinic moved to bigger premises in Malet Place, but apart from a few courses, the Maudsley (an innovative mental hospital for voluntary patients which opened in 1923) monopolised academic and training accreditation, blocking most of JR's efforts. Because of the presence on the Clinic staff of so many active Presbyterians, Edward Mapother, the head of the Maudsley, mockingly dubbed the Tavistock "the parsons' clinic". The rivalry between the two centres was partly competition for precious US charitable money from the Rockefeller Foundation—which after the war did support the Tavistock (Armstrong & Rustin, Chapter 3)—but Mapother was also envious of the international popularity of the Clinic's courses which, "as a good Catholic" (Dicks, 1970, p. 62), he confessed to JR on his deathbed.

Despite this disappointment, Rees was generally a very effective networker, promoting a model of preventive psychiatry wherever he went. Now, as war approached, the British Army recalled the mental damage done in the previous war, summarised in the famous "shell shock" report (HMSO, 1922), and was keen not to enlist soldiers who would be likely to break down permanently, thus requiring a lifelong military pension. To forestall that, they needed psychological expertise. The Institute of Psychoanalysis offered the army its services,[5] but it was Rees—now a brigadier—whom they appointed as their consulting psychiatrist in 1938. Then in 1940 the "sharp and self-confident" young Tavistock psychiatrist Ronald Hargreaves by chance met General Sir Ronald Adam, just back from Dunkirk (Shephard, 2000, p. 188). By the following year Adam was responsible for all questions of medicine and morale in the army, and asked Hargreaves to help him create a modern technocratic army like the Wehrmacht, whose leaders had been "carefully hand-picked by 200 well-trained psychiatrists" (Shephard, 2000, p. 189). British army officers were, by contrast, still appointed on the basis of their class and public school education. Against enormous resistance from the old guard (including the prime minister, Winston Churchill) General Adam cleverly sidestepped efforts to undermine him and gathered together a group of experts—including Rees, Hargreaves, Dicks, Wilson, and Bion—to work out how to be more discriminating. Adding to this ("maverick") group of pre-war Tavistock clinicians, the War Office Selection Board (WOSB) project recruited Jock Sutherland, John Bowlby, Eric Trist, Isabel Menzies (then a student), and later Elliott Jaques, Harold Bridger, and Tom Main, all of whom had, or would soon have, psychoanalytic training or experience.

What these individuals devised in 1942 has become part of Tavistock mythology, which many people refer to without much detailed knowledge. Starting with the idea that some kind of psychological testing would be required, this group of psychiatrists and social scientists—who had themselves by now become army officers—devised the predicament of a "leaderless group".[6] Given a series of practical tasks, but without a leader to follow, a group of men competitively seeking officer training had to define for themselves what leadership actually is. To the multidisciplinary board of observers, "officer material" was evident from the way in which "the man with good contact identifies himself with the purpose of the group, namely to achieve a co-operative solution to the set problem" (Rees, 1945, p. 69; Stokes, Chapter 39). These pioneering social scientists had learned that an exploration of differences within a peer group can lead to emotional learning about one's own part in it. This has to include a sense of attentive concern—a maternal function, perhaps. "Authority then becomes a power within oneself to relate to others, rather than to control them. Individuals who had to direct fighting men at the front line were selected on the basis of their capacity to manage *themselves* in this role" (Kraemer, 2015, p. 147). What made WOSB acceptable to the army was the impression that their officers, and not the "trick-cyclists",[7] were doing the selecting,[8] although in truth it was the men who were selecting themselves.

Then, in the famous first Northfield experiment later that year, Wilfred Bion joined his former training analyst John Rickman at a military mental hospital near Birmingham, full of vulnerable soldiers deemed unfit for active service. Instead of treatment they were offered small (and later large) group discussions. "In these the same freedom was allowed as is permitted in any form of free association; it was not abused. These small groups were similar in organisation to the Leaderless Group Tests … though for a different purpose" (Bion, 1946, cited by Trist, 1985, p. 15). Bion's and Rickman's aim was to turn these men from patients into soldiers; the "enemy" was their own resistance to change. This required a firm conviction on the psychiatrists' part that intra-group exploration would be therapeutic, which it was, but only after several weeks of chaos. Within a month the men had decided to organise themselves into working groups (including a dancing class), using—in a phrase now hallowed by Tavistock use—their own authority (Armstrong & Rustin, Chapter 3). After the premature closure of Northfield, Bion and Rickman, no longer working together, rejoined the War Office Selection Boards for the rest of the war, developing further the then novel idea of a therapeutic community (Main, 1981), as did their successors in "Northfield II" (Harrison, 2000), and, after the war, in the Civil Resettlement Units (Curle & Trist, 1947). Forty years later Trist—paraphrasing Bion (1948)—wrote that these innovations in social psychology had brought "a new type of knowledge to humankind" (Trist, 1985, p. 26).[9]

Operation Phoenix

Like the *Seven Samurai*,[10] a small number of gifted and independently minded individuals had been recruited to work together on a singular task. "Our first experiment with group methods was on ourselves" (Trist & Murray, 1990b, p. 7). The Second World War had created a different Tavistock, risen from the ashes. In February 1946 Bion replaced J. R. Rees as chair of the Tavistock Planning Committee. While working part-time as a private psychotherapist (and still in analytic training, now with Melanie Klein), Bion directed several projects, including a group for interns who wanted to learn how to work in non-medical organisations, one for senior managers in industry, and another for patients. In the patient group, in which the social psychologist Eric Trist was his co-therapist, "Bion was detached, yet warm, utterly imperturbable and inexhaustibly patient. … He expressed himself in direct, concise language that everyone could understand. If a patient made an intervention before he did, so much the better; there was no need for him to make it" (Trist, 1985, pp. 30–31). "Always pay attention to how the group makes you feel," said Bion to Trist. As the time approached to become a foundation member of the National Health Service the Clinic was in crisis about who should stay and who should go. Bion set up a two-hour weekly therapeutic group for the whole Tavistock staff—pre-war and post-war, professional and non-professional—while resigning all his leadership roles. "This made plain to all that he had no stake in the future of the organisation and could be accepted as a disinterested party" (Trist, 1985, p. 37). Trist records the healing effect of this intervention, which "prevented the formation of organized factions" (1985, p. 38). These meetings lasted for a year, and then Bion left the Tavistock.

From the War Office Selection Boards came the new leaders of the reformed, NHS Tavistock. Jock Sutherland became the medical director and head of the Adult Department, where every consultant—almost all medical—did group therapy alongside individual analytic therapy.

Such an apparently efficient use of resources appealed to an NHS founded in an economy dependent almost entirely on borrowed money. Meanwhile John Bowlby was appointed deputy medical director and head of the Children's Department. He brought with him from pre-war experience in the London Child Guidance Clinic (Hopkins, Chapter 14) and then from WOSB[11] a respect for multiple points of view, reflecting the irreducible complexity of a child's life.

The Tavistock was the only NHS clinic offering outpatient psychotherapy, but it also wanted to reach out and intervene in society—like the new welfare state in which it was embedded—from cradle to grave: "co-operating closely with the local health authority in such fields as maternal and infant welfare, schoolchildren, young families resettling, war veterans and the like" (Dicks, 1970, p. 159). Following the preventive thread from before the war, the multidisciplinary "family clinic" model was much more sophisticated than the mental hygiene one it now replaced.

The non-clinical Tavistock Institute of Human Relations (TIHR) was led by A. T. M. (Tommy) Wilson who had been on the Clinic staff before the war, and in WOSB during it. His deputy was Eric Trist. Besides Bion and Bowlby, Trist is an unrecognised genius in his own right. As many of his colleagues attest, "Eric had the remarkable gift of bringing his exceptional intelligence into conversation with others in such a way that left the others feeling clearer and more intelligent rather than being in awe of him" (Shapiro & Krantz, Chapter 36). In 1947 he and Ken Bamforth, a Coal Board executive who had joined TIHR, were asked by the newly nationalised Coal Board (NCB) to look at working practices in Haighmoor mine in Yorkshire. The NCB had introduced a mechanised "longwall" system of mining. The researchers found that if the men were permitted to work as teams, each with his own authority to contribute to the task—as their fathers had done—their productivity and morale were enhanced; "It is difficult to see how these problems can be solved effectively without restoring responsible autonomy to primary groups throughout the system" (Trist & Bamforth, 1951). The NCB rejected their recommendation, preferring to maintain managerial command and control. Trist directed the very first Tavistock group relations conference, at Leicester University, in 1957.

These developments give a flavour of the Tavistock's vision in the decade after the war. A leitmotiv of subversive nonconformism—of doing things differently—appears throughout this book. It is based on the idea of *observation that includes the observer*, which requires a theoretical shift from objective to subjective (Rustin & Armstrong, Chapter 4). This was a new paradigm for looking at human relations, which reached far beyond a clinical one, ambitiously aiming to change society ("sociatry"). Unlike the pre-war Clinic the new Tavistock was staffed almost exclusively by people who had had their own psychoanalysis (and the clinicians were also qualified analysts), whose motto was "no research without therapy, no therapy without research" (Rickman, 1949). Although at the time they had many staff in common the Tavistock was not a community outpost of the Institute of Psychoanalysis. Being part of a socialist-inspired health service demanded a larger ethical frame, but of course there were many different ways of working in it.

A safe base from which to explore

Despite his pre-eminence as one of the greatest developmental psychologists of the twentieth century, John Bowlby was *a maverick in his own clinic*. In his child analytical training at the Institute of Psychoanalysis he had clashed with his supervisor, Melanie Klein, yet learned much from her, completing his trainings in both adult and child psychoanalysis before the war. In 1948 he appointed a psychoanalyst, Esther Bick, to start a Tavistock training in child psychotherapy and, at the same time, more or less invented family therapy from scratch (Rustin, Chapter 7; Helps, Barratt, & Daniel, Chapter 24). He published an account of this experiment, with a case history, in *Human Relations*, the new Tavistock Institute journal dedicated to social relationships in work-related settings, which had been founded with Kurt Lewin's support two years earlier (Armstrong & Rustin, Chapter 3). Having no literature on this kind of therapy, Bowlby cited the anthropologist Margaret Mead (1948) whom he had heard speaking of "the vicious circle of insecure parents creating insecure children, who grow up to create an insecure society which in its turn creates more insecure parents" (Bowlby, 1949, p. 297). His only other sources in this remarkable paper were his wartime colleagues John Rickman, Wilfred Bion, and Elliott Jaques, from whose work with groups "this technique stems directly" (p. 295). This is the only time that Bowlby cited Bion in any publication.[12] Decades later Bowlby told his supervisee Arturo Ezquerro that he regarded Bion

> as a creative man and a charismatic figure who had a significant influence on him during the war and in his early days at the Tavistock after the war. [He] felt that Bion had been significantly traumatised by witnessing the brutal death of his friends and comrades in the Front during the First World War. Bowlby was impressed by Bion's intellectual calibre but gradually lost interest in Bionian theorising, as he felt it was becoming too speculative. (Ezquerro, 2017, p. 32)

Bowlby was already captivated by the impact on mental health of early childhood separations and, thanks to his association in WOSB with Ronald Hargreaves (1908–1962)—now the head of the Mental Health Division of the World Health Organization—he was invited to travel for several months during 1950 to continental Europe and the USA to study child care and development. He read the literature and met many clinicians and scientists. His report *Maternal Care and Mental Health* (WHO, 1952) became—in its edited paperback version *Child Care and the Growth of Love* (1953)—a best-seller. Bowlby was a social reformer as well as a scientist. Knowing the greater impact on learning of case discussion over lectures, he led a 1954 study group recommending weekly groups for health visitors and others in child welfare (Bowlby, 1954).

But what was to preoccupy Bowlby for the rest of his life began as a revision of psychoanalysis, and ended as attachment theory. In contrast to Mrs Klein's view of the primacy of a child's inner life,[13] he wanted to show that what actually happens to children and their parents and caregivers makes a fundamental difference, both in clinical practice and in social policy.

His heroic effort to critique psychoanalysis with "objective" science led him away from its practice into a paradigm shift in developmental psychology, namely the description of a third imperative for survival in most living things. Besides needing to eat and to reproduce, we also need protection, a drive independent of the other two. Rather as the pre-war Tavistock had done—but with an entirely different aim—Bowlby doggedly steered a path between prevailing reductionist science and clinical psychoanalysis (Rustin, Chapter 7), modifying the object relations theory in which he had been trained to accommodate detailed child observations from Mary Ainsworth and James Robertson and "evolution theory, ethology, control theory, and cognitive psychology" (Bowlby, 1988a, p. 120). Towards the end of his life, noting how little impact his discoveries had had on the real world (as opposed to the scientific one) he mused:

> Man and woman power devoted to the production of material goods counts a plus in all our economic indices. Man and woman power devoted to the production of happy, healthy, and self-reliant children in their own homes does not count at all. We have created a topsy-turvy world. (Bowlby, 1988a, p. 22)

After their encounters in the 1940s, Bowlby and Bion—the two giants of the modern Tavistock—moved in quite opposite directions, barely acknowledging each other's courage and brilliance; a curious polarity.

Multidisciplinary reflections

During the 1950s Bowlby changed the name of his department to the Department for Children and Parents, by implication including fathers for the first time in child mental health services, but it was more than a decade after his death before family systems therapists had their own profession in the Clinic (Helps, Barratt, & Daniel, Chapter 24). Until Bowlby's and Jock Sutherland's retirements the prevailing analytic stance of the Clinic's leadership was an "independent" one, but with the creation of child psychotherapy as an NHS discipline in its own right there was a brilliant flowering of psychoanalytical work on a different line, with foundations in literature and in post-Kleinian developments, represented in several chapters in this book. Tavistock child psychotherapists had a major impact on the thinking and work of the Clinic, and through their teaching and writing, on child mental health practice around the world. Gianna Williams's long-standing collaboration in Italy (Chapter 18) is just one example of a global spread of Tavistock teaching in many European countries, the Americas, Russia, the Near and Far East, Africa, and the Antipodes—places to which colleagues return again and again, their words and texts translated when need be.

While the roles of psychologists in the Tavistock have expanded fruitfully since the early days (Lyon & Dowling, Chapter 31), its founders and leaders were physicians.[14] The first employed trainees in the NHS Tavistock were psychiatrists, and many still are. Yet because they now mostly start their training having completed higher clinical diplomas, they do not enlist on scholarly courses (nor do they pay fees), and therefore feature less prominently in Trust training prospectuses. Until the 1980s there were shared core theoretical trainings for psychiatrists and psychotherapists (Rustin, Chapter 10). What remains common for all is group relations, work discussion, and related experience, but professional trainings are nowadays more tightly regulated, and distinct. Yet in almost every clinical or study team will be found a cross-section of disciplines whose capacity to work together depends on a fundamental respect for difference. In most public services this notion is a platitude, with no thought given to the serious obstacles—indeed sabotage (Obholzer, Chapter 1)—to achieving it. There is no protocol for "working with contradictions" (Waddell, Preface); as the wartime pioneers discovered, it is an ethical obligation to notice where others stand in relation to oneself.

Significantly, there is no chapter on psychiatrists here. The Tavistock was never a "mental hospital" yet it remains true that wherever there is mental disorder there is anxiety about danger and madness, which often calls for a doctor in the house. In the outside world, the courts (Trowell, Chapter 34) still expect psychiatrists to have the most authority, and some of the most impressive "instrumental" research from the Tavistock on serious mental disorders and sexual abuse has been led by practising psychiatrists—Peter Hobson, Matthew Patrick, Israel Kolvin, Judith Trowell (Chapter 34), and David Taylor (Chapter 26)—and published in conventional scientific journals (which our rivals at the Maudsley Hospital would have to acknowledge as valid).[15] The pre-war Tavistock's failure to secure a robust university link was redressed towards the end of the century by the appointment here of several psychiatrist-professors; in the Adult Department, Peter Hobson; in the Child and Family Department, Issy Kolvin, succeeded by Alan Stein. Judith Trowell's chair at the University of Worcester was based on her extensive Tavistock research. There were also several non-medical professorial chairs; Phil Richardson in psychology, Margaret Yelloly, succeeded by Andrew Cooper, in social work (Chapter 32), and Maria Rhode in child psychotherapy (Chapter 17). A great deal of negotiation with a number of universities was required to take these momentous steps, which was part of a blossoming of creativity in the Trust, with new clinical and consulting outreach projects, academic courses and research, and an enhanced national and international reputation.

Yet, still, the paradigm shifts in human science discovered by the Tavistock remain poorly understood; its vaulting ambitions frustrated. Anton Obholzer's 1997 speech (Chapter 1) could have been delivered now, almost a quarter of a century later. The need for workers in any service or industry to find, and use, their own authority has never been greater. One consequence of better staff conversations is a dawning realisation that their work is not sustainable under current circumstances. The ethos reflected in much of this book is subversive, and may not be welcome in an overregulated world; but it is needed.

The Tavistock's tradition of egalitarianism is at odds with increasingly evident wealth inequality. The damage this causes is now well documented, but too easily ignored by governments: "If health has stopped improving it is a sign that society has stopped improving" (Marmot, Allen, Boyce, Goldblatt, & Morrison, 2020, p. 5). Every index of psychological and social harm is made worse by the steep slope of inequality, on which no one—even the least deprived—can be healthily comfortable (Wilkinson & Pickett, 2019). The construction of this historical book in 2020 has been overtaken by a historic political crisis, in which the governing class's capricious disdain for poverty and ethnicity is now fully exposed. This is not a society in balance with itself, or with nature (Weintrobe, 2013). Marmot and colleagues' report of a recent, and unprecedented, rise in infant mortality in more disadvantaged families (2020, p. 37) is the tip of an iceberg of human devastation. Bowlby's lament above becomes ever more urgent, the more we know of the intergenerational transmission of insecurity that attachment research reveals.

There is more to do. "We can't solve problems by using the same kind of thinking we used when we created them" (Albert Einstein).

Acknowledgements

I am grateful to Margot Waddell and Anton Obholzer for encouraging critical comments.

[Sebastian Kraemer's biography appears on p. 150]

Notes

1. Not such a far-fetched idea, given new scientific thinking about depression (Canli, 2014).
2. The Institute of Psychoanalysis, the training body of the British Psychoanalytical Society, was founded in 1924.
3. Most famously by C. G. Jung (1935), some of which were attended by the young Tavistock psychotherapist Wilfred Bion. Tavistock staff were less keen on Freud, rejecting both his sexual theory and the transference. Jung's lectures and the discussions that followed, including Bion's penetrating questions, were transcribed and circulated but not published until after Jung's death in 1961.
4. Such as the highest rates of male suicide ever recorded in England and Wales (just over 30 men per 100,000) (Thomas & Gunnell, 2010).
5. The founder, and still president, of the Institute of Psychoanalysis Ernest Jones "later complained that advertising men had more influence on the running of the war" (Shephard, 2000, p. 168).
6. "Histories of science, especially when written by those within the discipline, often select heroes and promote the notion of a 'lone genius revealing the secrets of nature single-handedly in his … basement laboratory', and the history of Human Relations, limited though it is, has done likewise with regards to the Leaderless Group test. Most historiographical accounts of the Leaderless Group tests attribute it to Wilfred R. Bion, one of the most notorious members of the Tavistock group. However, archival sources indicate that in fact, Bion had sidelined this work and its revival and use in WOSBs was the result of a lowly MTO [Military Testing Officer]. The unpublished manuscript account of the WOSBs states: 'At No. 4 Board, Garston … the military testing officer's group of candidates was given a practical problem and left to its own devices in solving it. This development

was largely independent of Bion's work with the leaderless group method with which he had begun to experiment quite early on, but which he did not consider ready yet for general adoption' ("The Development of a Testing Programme and the Setting Up of the New Boards", in *Unpublished WOSBs Write-Up MSS*, p. 32", White, 2015, p. 102).

7. Slang for psychiatrist.

8. Alice White shows how the selection procedure was understood differently by army and psychological staff. "These practical tests offered the perfect object for collaboration; ostensibly military, involving assault courses and demonstrations of physical aptitude; psychological staff adapted them so that their 'real' purpose was to highlight psychological qualities" (White, 2015, p. 103).

9. In an echo of the name taken by the seventeenth-century founders of the Royal Society, the war-time gathering of inspired individuals called themselves "the invisible college" (Dicks, 1970, p. 107). [The Invisible College 1645–1662. *Nature, 142*: 67–68 (1938).]

10. The 1954 film by Akira Kurosawa.

11. Bowlby did the only formal follow-up of WOSB. It showed that the dropout rate of officers selected fell from 45% to 15% under the new procedure, but was never published. This major piece of work was supervised by Eric Trist, whom Bowlby regarded as one of the most brilliant men he had ever met. Trist is also gratefully acknowledged in his WHO monograph *Maternal Care and Mental Health* (Bowlby, 1951).

12. There are no citations of Bowlby's work in Bion's publications.

13. … as recollected by Bowlby. In a talk given by Melanie Klein at the London Institute of Education in May 1939—around the time she was supervising his child analytic work—Mrs Klein speaks simply about the real events in an infant's life: "Again and again the baby will wish to see his mother, or to hear her voice or even her footsteps" (published for the first time in Klein, 2020, p. 45). (See also Rustin, Chapter 7.)

14. It was not until near the end of the century that the Tavistock's constitution was changed to permit a non-medical professional (Margaret Rustin) to be elected chair of its Professional Committee.

15. There is also a continuation of systematic research in child and adolescent mental health led by psychiatrists Drs Eilis Kennedy and Rob Senior (see Rustin & Armstrong, Chapter 4).

"the more peoples there are in the world who stand in some particular relationship with one another, the more world there is to form between them, and the larger and richer that world will be"

—Hannah Arendt

References

Abse, S. (2019). Brexit—trauma, identity and the core complex. *New Associations, 28*: 7–11.

Abse, S., Casey, P., Hewison, D., & Meier, R. (2016). *What Works in Relationship Support: An Evidence Review*. London: Tavistock Centre for Couple Relationships. http://tavistockrelationships.ac.uk/images/uploads/20150608EvidenceReview2015pdf-min.pdf

Adamo, S. M. G., & Rustin, M. E. (Eds.) (2014). *Young Child Observation: A Development in the Theory and Method of Infant Observation*. London: Karnac.

Adamo, S. M. G., & Williams, G. P. (1991). *Working with Disruptive Adolescents*. Naples, Italy: Napoli Instituto per gli Studi Filosofici.

Adorno, T., & Horkheimer, M. (1997). *The Dialectic of Enlightenment*. London: Verso. First published as: Dialektik der Aufklarung, New York: Social Studies Association, 1944.

Afuape, T., & Hughes, G. (Eds.) (2016). *Liberation Practices: Towards Emotional Wellbeing through Dialogue*. London: Routledge.

Ainsworth, M. (1983). A sketch of a career. In: A. O'Connoll & N. Russo (Eds.), *Models of Achievement: Reflections of Eminent Women in Psychology (Vol. 2)* (pp. 200–219). New York: Columbia University Press. Reprinted 2013 as: Mary D. Salter Ainsworth: an autobiographical sketch, *Attachment & Human Development, 15*(5–6): 448–459. https://doi.org/10.1080/14616734.2013.852411.

Altschuler, J. (1997). *Working with Chronic Illness: A Family Approach*. London: Macmillan.

Altschuler, J. (2016). *Migration, Illness and Health Care*. London: Palgrave.

Alvarez, A. (1992). *Live Company: Psychoanalytic Psychotherapy with Autistic, Borderline, Deprived and Abused Children*. London: Routledge.

Alvarez, A., and Reid, S. (Eds.) (1999). *Autism and Personality: Findings from the Tavistock Autism Workshop*. London: Routledge.

Amias, D., Hughes, G., & Barratt, S., (2014). Multi-layered systemic and narrative interventions with refugees and asylum seekers in a community child and adolescent mental health service. *Human Systems: The Journal of Therapy, Consultation & Training, 25*(1): 20–30.

Anderson, R., & Dartington, A. (Eds.) (1998). *Facing It Out: Clinical Perspectives on Adolescent Disturbance (Tavistock Clinic Series)*. London: Routledge.

Ariès, P. (1960). *Centuries of Childhood: A Social History of Family Life*. R. Baldick (Trans.). London: Pimlico, 1996.

Armstrong, D. (2005). *Organization in the Mind: Psychoanalysis, Group Relations and Organizational Consultancy (Tavistock Clinic Series)*. London: Karnac.

Armstrong, D. (2012). Terms of engagement: looking backwards and forwards at the Tavistock enterprise. *Organisational and Social Dynamics, 12*(1): 106–121.

Armstrong, D. (2017). "Psychoanalytic study" and the ethical imagination: the making, finding and losing of a tradition. *Organisational and Social Dynamics, 17*(2): 222–234.

Armstrong, D., & Rustin, M. J. (2012). What happened to democratic leadership? *Soundings, 50* (Spring): 59–71.

Armstrong, D., & Rustin, M. J. (Eds.) (2015). *Social Defences Against Anxiety: Explorations in a Paradigm (Tavistock Clinic Series)*. London: Karnac.

Astor, J. (1995). *Michael Fordham: Innovations in Analytical Psychology*. London: Routledge.

Auden, W. H. (1939). In Memory of Sigmund Freud. In: *Another Time*, 1940. New York: Random House.

Babüroğlu, O. (1988). The vortical environment. *Human Relations, 41*(3): 181–210.

Balfour, A. (2014). Developing therapeutic couple work in dementia care—the living together with dementia project. *Psychoanalytic Psychotherapy, 28*(3): 304–320.

Balfour, A. (2020). The fragile thread of connection: Living as a couple with dementia. In: S. Evans, J. Garner, & R. Darnley-Smith (Eds.), *Psychodynamic Approaches to the Experience of Dementia*. London: Routledge.

Balfour, F., Clulow, C., & Dearnley, B. (1986). The outcome of maritally focused psychotherapy offered as a possible model for marital psychotherapy outcome studies. *British Journal of Psychotherapy, 3*(2): 133–143.

Balfour, A., Clulow, C., & Thompson, K. (Eds.) (2018). *Engaging Couples: New Directions in Therapeutic Work with Families* (pp. 15–28). London: Routledge.

Balfour, A., & Lanman, M. (2012). An evaluation of time-limited psychodynamic psychotherapy for couples: a pilot study. *Psychology and Psychotherapy: Theory, Research and Practice, 85*(3): 292–309.

Balfour, A., Morgan, M., & Vincent, C. (Eds.) (2012). *How Couple Relationships Shape Our World: Clinical Practice, Research, and Policy Perspectives*. London: Karnac.

Balfour, A., & Salter, L. (2018). Living together with dementia. In: A. Balfour, C. Clulow, & K. Thompson (Eds.), *Engaging Couples: New Directions in Therapeutic Work with Families* (pp. 189–202). London: Routledge.

Balint. E. (1993). Unconscious communication between husbands and wives. In: S. Ruszczynski (Ed.), *Psychotherapy with Couples: Theory and Practice at the Tavistock Institute of Marital Studies* (pp. 30–43). London: Karnac.

Balint, E., Courtenay, M., Elder, A., Hull, S., & Julian, P. (1993). *The Doctor, the Patient and the Group: Balint Revisited*. London: Routledge.

Balint, E., & Norell, J. (Eds.) (1973). *Six Minutes for the Patient: Interactions in General Practice Consultation*. London: Tavistock.

Balint, M. (1957). *The Doctor, His Patient and the Illness*. London: Churchill Livingstone.

Balint, M., & Balint, E. (1961). *Psychotherapeutic Techniques in Medicine (Mind and Medicine Monographs 1)*. London: Tavistock.

Balint, M., Balint, E., Gosling, R., & Hildebrand, P. (1966). *A Study of Doctors (Mind and Medicine Monographs 13)*. London: Tavistock.

Balint, M., Hunt, J., Joyce, D., Marinker, M., & Woodcock, J. (1970). *Treatment or Diagnosis: A Study of Repeat Prescriptions in General Practice (Mind and Medicine Monographs 20)*. London: Tavistock.

Bambrough, S., Crichton, N., & Webb, S. (2019). Better outcomes and better justice: The Family Drug and Alcohol Court. In: A. Foster (Ed.), *Mothers Accused and Abused: Addressing Complex Psychological Needs* (pp. 125–137). Abingdon, UK: Routledge.

Bannister, K., Lyons, A. P., Robb, J., Shooter, A., & Stephens, J. (1955). *Social Casework in Marital Problems: The Development of a Psychodynamic Approach. A Study by a Group of Caseworkers*. London: Tavistock.

Bannister, K., & Pincus, L. (1965). *Shared Phantasy in Marital Problems: Therapy in a Four-person Relationship*. London: Institute of Marital Studies.

Banton, R., Clifford, P., Frosh, S., Lousada, J., & Rosenthall, J. (1985). *The Politics of Mental Health*. London: Macmillan.

Barnes, D., & Hall, J. (2008). *Survey of the Current Provision of Psychological Therapy Services in Primary Care in the UK*. Chichester, UK: Artemis Trust.

Barnes, E. (Ed.) (1968). *Psychosocial Nursing Studies from the Cassel Hospital*. London: Tavistock.

Barnes, E., Griffiths, P., Ord, J., & Wells, D. (Eds.) (1998). *Face to Face with Distress: The Professional Use of Self in Psychosocial Care*. Oxford: Butterworth Heinemann.

Barnett, A. (2019). The passions of Brexit. *New Associations, 28*: 1–5.

Barratt, S., & Lobatto, W. (Eds.) (2016). *The Systemic Thinking and Practice Series: Surviving and Thriving in Care and Beyond: Personal and Professional Perspectives*. London: Karnac.

Bateson, G., Jackson, D. D., Haley, J., & Weakland, J. H. (1956). Toward a theory of schizophrenia. *Behavioral Science, 1*: 251–264.

Bateson, G., Jackson, D. D., Haley, J., & Weakland, J. H. (1963). A note on the double bind—1962. *Family Process, 2*(1): 154–161.

Bell, D. (1997). *Reason and Passion: A Celebration of the Work of Hanna Segal (Tavistock Clinic Series)*. London: Routledge.

Bell, D. (1999). *Psychoanalysis and Culture: A Kleinian Perspective (Tavistock Clinic Series)*. London: Karnac.

Bell, D. (2003). *Paranoia*. Cambridge: Icon.

Bell, D., & Novakovic, A. (Eds.) (2013). *Living on the Border: Psychotic Processes and the Individual, the Couple and the Group (Tavistock Clinic Series)*. London: Routledge.

Belson, P. (2004). To get our agenda on to other people's agenda. In: H. Curtis & M. Sanderson (Eds.), *The Unsung Sixties: Memoirs of Social Innovation* (pp. 357–365). London: Whiting & Birch.

Benjamin, A., Chahal, P., Mulley, S., & Reay, A. (2018). Working with couple violence. In: A. Balfour, C. Clulow, & K. Thompson (Eds.), *Engaging Couples: New Directions in Therapeutic Work with Families* (pp. 150–163). London: Routledge.

Berenstein, I. (2012). "Vínculo" as a relationship between others. *Psychoanalytic Quarterly, 81*(3): 565–577.

Bergman, A. (1999). *Ours, Yours, Mine: Mutuality and the Emergence of the Separate Self*. Northvale, NJ: Jason Aronson.

Bergman, A. (2004). *The Power of the Relationship: A Film Portrait of Dr Anni Bergman*. New York: Base One Productions.

Bettelheim, B. (1967). *The Empty Fortress: Infantile Autism and the Birth of the Self*. New York: Basic Books.

Bion, F. (1994). The days of our lives. In: C. Mawson & F. Bion (Eds.), *The Complete Works of W. R. Bion, Vol. XV* (pp. 91–111). London: Karnac, 2014.

Bion, W. R. (1946). The leaderless group project. *Bulletin of the Menninger Clinic, 10*: 77–81.

Bion, W. R. (1948). Psychiatry at a time of crisis. *British Journal of Medical Psychology, 21*(2): 81–89.

Bion, W. R. (1961). *Experiences in Groups*. London: Tavistock.

Bion, W. R. (1962). *Learning from Experience*. London: Heinemann.

Bion, W. R. (1982). *The Long Weekend, 1897–1919: Part of a Life*. Abingdon, UK: Fleetwood.

Bion, W. R., & Rickman, J. (1943). Intragroup tensions in therapy: their study as the task of the group. *The Lancet, 2*: 678–681. Reprinted in "Pre-view" in Bion, W. R. (1961). *Experiences in Groups* (pp. 11–26). London: Tavistock.

Black, D., McFadyen, A., & Broster, G. (1990). Development of a psychiatric liaison service. *Archive of Disease in Childhood, 65*: 1373–1375.

Boston, M., & Szur, R. (1983). *Psychotherapy with Severely Deprived Children*. London: Routledge.

Bott, E. (1957). *Family and Social Network*. London: Tavistock.

Bott, E. (1976). Hospital and society. *British Journal of Medical Psychology, 49*: 97–140.

Bourdieu, P. (1980). *The Logic of Practice*. Stanford, CA: Stanford University Press.

Bourne, S. (1968). The psychological effects of stillbirths on women and their doctors. *Journal of the Royal College of General Practitioners, 16*: 103–112.

Bourne, S., (1981). *Under the Doctor: Studies in the Psychological Problems of Physiotherapists, Patients and Doctors*. Amersham, UK: Avebury.

Bourne, S., & Lewis, E. (1984). Pregnancy after stillbirth or neonatal death: psychological risks and management. *The Lancet, 2*(8393): 31–33.

Bower, M. (2004). *Psychoanalytic Theory for Social Work Practice: Thinking under Fire*. London: Routledge.

Bower, M., & Solomon, R. (Eds.) (2017). *What Social Workers Need to Know: A Psychoanalytic Approach*. London: Routledge.

Bowlby, J. (1939). Substitute homes. *Mother and Child*, April 3–7, p. 6, cited by S. van Dijken, *John Bowlby: His Early Life*, 1998, p. 94.

Bowlby, J. (1944a). Forty-four juvenile thieves: their characters and home-life. *International Journal of Psychoanalysis, 25*: 19–53.

Bowlby, J. (1944b). Forty-four juvenile thieves: their characters and home-life (II). *International Journal of Psychoanalysis, 25*: 107–128.

Bowlby, J. (1949). The study and reduction of group tensions in the family. *Human Relations, 2*: 123–128. Reprinted in E. Trist & H. Murray (Eds.), *The Social Engagement of Social Science: A Tavistock Anthology, Vol. 1: The Socio-Psychological Perspective* (pp. 291–298). Philadelphia, PA: University of Pennsylvania Press, 1990.

Bowlby, J. (1951). *Maternal Care and Mental Health*. Geneva: World Health Organization.

Bowlby, J. (1953). *Child Care and the Growth of Love*. London: Pelican.

Bowlby, J. (1954). Preventive mental health in the maternity and child welfare service. Report by a study group From the Public Health Department, London County Council, and the Tavistock Clinic. *The Medical Officer, 92*: 303–307.

Bowlby, J. (1969). *Attachment and Loss, Vol. 1: Attachment*. London: Penguin, 1984.

Bowlby, J. (1973). *Attachment and Loss, Vol. 2: Separation: Anxiety and Anger*. London: Hogarth.

Bowlby, J. (1980). *Attachment and Loss, Vol. 3: Loss: Sadness and Depression*. London: Hogarth.

Bowlby, J. (1987). A historical perspective on child guidance. *Child Guidance Trust: Newsletter, 3* (June): 1–2.

Bowlby, J. (1988a). *A Secure Base: Clinical Applications of Attachment Theory*. London: Routledge.

Bowlby, J. (1988b). On knowing what you are not supposed to know and feeling what you are not supposed to feel. In: *A Secure Base: Clinical Applications of Attachment Theory* (pp. 99–118). London: Routledge.

Bowlby, J., Miller, E., & Winnicott, D. W. (1939). Evacuation of small children [letter]. *British Medical Journal, 2*: 1202.

Bowlby, J., & Robertson, J. (1953). A two-year-old goes to hospital. *Proceedings of the Royal Society of Medicine, 46*(6): 425–427.

Bowlby, J., Robertson, J., & Rosenbluth, D. (1952). A two year old goes to hospital. *Psychoanalytic Study of the Child, 7*(1): 82–94.

Box, S. J. (1979). The elucidation of a family myth. *Journal of Family Therapy, 1*(1): 75–86.

BPS Division of Clinical Psychology (2018). *Power Threat Meaning Framework*. Leicester, UK: British Psychological Society. https://bps.org.uk/power-threat-meaning-framework

Bradford, L. P., Gibb, J. R., & Benne, K. D. (Eds.) (1964). *T-Group Theory and Laboratory Method: Innovations in Re-education*. New York: Wiley.

Brandon, S., Lindsay, M., Lovell-Davis, J., & Kraemer, S. (2009). "What is wrong with emotional upset?" 50 years on from the Platt Report. *Archives of Disease in Childhood, 94*: 173–177.

Bravesmith, A. (2004). Brief therapy in primary care: the setting, the discipline and the borderline patient. *British Journal of Psychotherapy, 21*(1): 37–48.

Bridger, H. (1990). The discovery of the therapeutic community: The Northfield Experiments. In: E. Trist & H. Murray (Eds.), *The Social Engagement of Social Science: A Tavistock Anthology, Vol. 1: The Socio-Psychological Perspective* (pp. 68–87). London: Free Association.

Briggs, A. (2002). *Surviving Space: Papers on Infant Observation*. London: Karnac.

Briggs, S. (2008). *Working with Adolescents and Young Adults: A Contemporary Psychodynamic Approach*. London: Macmillan International Higher Education.

Briggs, S., & Lyon, L. (2012). Time-limited psychodynamic psychotherapy for adolescents and young adults. In: A. Lemma (Ed.), *Contemporary Developments in Adult and Young Adult Therapy: The Work of the Tavistock and Portman Clinics, Vol. 1 (Tavistock Clinic Series)*. London: Karnac.

Britton, R. (2005). Re-enactment as an unwitting professional response to family dynamics. In: M. Bower (Ed.), *Psychoanalytic Theory for Social Work Practice: Thinking under Fire* (pp. 169–180). Abingdon, UK: Routledge.

Brook, A. (1966). Emotional problems in general practice. *Journal of the College of General Practitioners*, *11*: 184–194.

Brook, A. (1967). An experiment in general practitioner/psychiatrist co-operation. *Journal of the Royal College of General Practitioners*, *13*: 127–131.

Brook, A. (1978). An aspect of community mental health: consultative work with general practice teams. *Health Trends*, *10*(2): 37–40.

Brook, A. (1994). Be honest about referrals [letter]. *British Medical Journal*, *308*: 340.

Brook, A., Elder, A., & Zalidis, S. (1998). Psychological aspects of eye disorders. *Journal of the Royal Society of Medicine*, *91*: 270–272.

Brook, A., & Temperley, J. (1976). The contribution of a psychotherapist to general practice. *Journal of the Royal College of General Practitioners*, *26*: 86–94.

Bruggen, P., Byng-Hall, J., & Pitt-Aitkens, T. (1973). The reason for admission as a focus of work for an adolescent unit. *British Journal of Psychiatry*, *122*: 319–329.

Burck, C., Barratt, S., & Kavner, E. (2013). *Positions and Polarities in Contemporary Systemic Practice: The Legacy of David Campbell*. London: Routledge.

Burck, C., & Daniel, G. (1995). *Gender and Family Therapy*. London: Karnac.

Burck, C., & Daniel, G. (2010). *Mirrors and Reflections: Processes of Systemic Supervision*. London: Karnac.

Burck, C., & Hughes, G. (2018). Challenges and impossibilities of "standing alongside" in an intolerable context: learning from refugees and volunteers in the Calais camp. *Clinical Child Psychology and Psychiatry*, *23*(2): 223–237.

Butler-Sloss, E. (1988). *Report of the Inquiry into Child Abuse in Cleveland 1987, Cm 412*. London: Her Majesty's Stationery Office.

Byng-Hall, J. (1973). Family myths used as defence in conjoint family therapy. *British Journal of Medical Psychology*, *46*: 239–250.

Byng-Hall, J. (2002). Telling one's own story: from farmer to family therapist, and my story: why I became a family therapist. In: J. Hills (Ed.), *Rescripting Family Experiences—The Therapeutic Influence of John Byng-Hall*. London: Whurr.

Campbell, David (1995). *Learning Consultation: A Systemic Framework*. London: Karnac.

Campbell, David (2000). *The Socially Constructed Organization*. London: Karnac.

Campbell, David, & Draper, R. (1985). *Applications of Systemic Family Therapy: The Milan Approach.* London: Grune & Stratton.

Campbell, David, & Huffington, C. (Eds.) (2008). *Organizations Connected: A Handbook of Systemic Consultation.* London: Karnac.

Campbell, Donald, & Hale, R. (2017). *Working in the Dark: Understanding the Pre-suicide State of Mind.* Abingdon, UK: Routledge.

Canli, T. (2014). Reconceptualizing major depressive disorder as an infectious disease. *Biology of Mood and Anxiety Disorders,* 4: 10.

Carr, W. (1985). *The Priestlike Task: Model for Developing and Training the Church's Ministry.* London: SPCK.

Carr, W. (1994). *Brief Encounters: Pastoral Ministry through Baptisms, Weddings and Funerals.* London: SPCK.

Carr, W. (2000). Some reflections on spirituality, religion and mental health. *Mental Health, Religion & Culture,* 3(1): 1–12.

Carrington, A., Rock, B., & Stern, J. (2012). Psychoanalytic thinking in primary care: the Tavistock Psychotherapy Consultation model. *Psychoanalytic Psychotherapy,* 26(2): 102–120.

Casey, P., Cowan, P. A., Cowan, C. P., Draper, L., Mwamba, N., & Hewison, D. (2017). Parents as partners: a UK trial of a US couples-based parenting intervention for at-risk low-income families. *Family Process,* 56(3): 589–606.

Cattan, S., Conti, G., Farquharson, C., & Ginja, R. (2019). *The Health Effects of Sure Start.* London: The Institute for Fiscal Studies.

Cleavely, E. (1993). Relationships: interaction, defences, and transformation. In: S. Ruszczynski (Ed.), *Psychotherapy with Couples: Theory and Practice at the Tavistock Institute of Marital Studies* (pp. 55–69). London: Karnac.

Clulow, C. (1982). *To Have and to Hold: Marriage, The First Baby and Preparing Couples for Parenthood.* Aberdeen, UK: Aberdeen University Press.

Clulow, C. (1985). *Marital Therapy: An Inside View.* Aberdeen, UK: Aberdeen University Press.

Clulow, C. (1990). *Marriage: Disillusion and Hope. Papers Celebrating Forty Years of the Tavistock Institute of Marital Studies* (pp. 23–32). London: The Tavistock Institute of Marital Studies & Karnac.

Clulow, C. (Ed.) (1993). *Rethinking Marriage: Public and Private Perspectives.* London: Karnac.

Clulow, C. (Ed.) (1995). *Women, Men and Marriage.* London: Sheldon.

Clulow, C. (Ed.) (1996). *Partners Becoming Parents.* London: Sheldon.

Clulow, C. (Ed.) (2001). *Adult Attachment and Couple Psychotherapy: The "Secure Base" in Practice and Research.* London: Brunner-Routledge.

Clulow, C. (Ed.) (2009). *Sex, Attachment and Couple Psychotherapy: Psychoanalytic Perspectives.* London: Karnac.

Clulow, C., & Donaghy, M. (2010). Developing the couple perspective in parenting support: evaluation of a service initiative for vulnerable families. *Journal of Family Therapy,* 32(2): 142–168.

Clulow, C., & Mattinson, J. (1989). *Marriage Inside Out: Understanding Problems of Intimacy*. London: Penguin, 1995.

Clulow, C., Nyberg, V., & Hertzmann, E. (2018). Couple psychoanalysis in the United Kingdom: past, present and future. *Psychoanalytic Inquiry*, 38(5): 364–377.

Clulow, C., Shmueli, A., Vincent, C., & Evans, C. (2002). Is empirical research compatible with clinical practice? *British Journal of Psychotherapy*, 19(1): 33–44.

Clulow, C., & Vincent, C. (1987). *In the Child's Best Interests? Divorce Court Welfare and the Search for a Settlement*. London: Sweet & Maxwell.

Clyne, M. (1961). *Night Calls: A Study in General Practice (Mind and Medicine Monographs 2)*. London: Tavistock.

Coates, S., Friedman, R., & Wolfe, S. (1991). The aetiology of boyhood gender identity disorder: a model for integrating temperament, development and psychodynamics. *Psychoanalytic Dialogues*, 1: 481–523.

Coates, S., & Spector Person, E. (1985). Extreme boyhood femininity: isolated behaviour or pervasive disorder? *Journal of the American Academy of Child and Adolescent Psychiatry*, 24: 702–709.

Cohen, M. (2003). *Sent Before My Time: A Child Psychotherapist's View of Life on a Neonatal Intensive Care Unit (Tavistock Clinic Series)*. London: Karnac.

Cohen, S. (2001). *States of Denial: Knowing about Atrocities and Suffering*. Cambridge: Polity.

Cohen-Kettenis, P. T., & van Goozen, S. H. M. (1997). Sex reassignment of adolescent transsexuals: a follow-up study. *Journal of the American Academy of Child and Adolescent Psychiatry*, 36: 263–271.

Colman, A., & Bexton, W. (Eds.) (1975). *Group Relations Reader I*. Washington, DC: A. K. Rice Institute.

Colman, W. (1989). *On Call: The Work of a Telephone Helpline for Child Abuse*. Aberdeen, UK: Aberdeen University Press.

Colman, W. (1993). Marriage as a psychological container. In: S. Ruszczynski (Ed.), *Psychotherapy with Couples: Theory and Practice at the Tavistock Institute of Marital Studies* (pp. 70–96). London: Karnac.

Cooper, A. (2005). Surface and depth in the Victoria Climbié Inquiry Report. *Child & Family Social Work*, 10: 1–9.

Cooper, A. (2018). *Conjunctions: Social Work, Psychoanalysis, and Society (Tavistock Clinic Series)*. London: Karnac.

Cooper, A., & Lousada, J. (2005). *Borderline Welfare: Feeling and Fear of Feeling in Modern Welfare (Tavistock Clinic Series)*. London: Karnac.

Courtenay, M. (1968). *Sexual Discord in Marriage: A Field for Brief Psychotherapy (Mind and Medicine Monographs 16)*. London: Tavistock.

Cowan, P., & Pape Cowan, C. (2009). Couple relationships: a missing link between adult attachment and children's outcomes. *Attachment and Human Development*, 11(1): 1–4.

Cregeen, S., Hughes, C., Midgley, N., Rhode, M., & Rustin M. E. (2017). *Short-term Psychoanalytic Psychotherapy for Adolescents with Depression: A Treatment Manual*. London: Karnac.

Crichton-Miller, H. (1912). The limits of legitimate psychotherapy [paper read to the Psycho-Medical Society, London, 25 January 1912]. *Transactions of the Psycho-Medical Society*, 3(1): 18–24.

Cullington-Roberts, D. (2004). The psychotherapist's miscarriage and pregnancy as an obstacle to containment. *Psychoanalytic Psychotherapy*, 18(1): 99–110.

Curle, A., & Trist, E. (1947). Transitional communities and social reconnection: a follow-up study of the civil resettlement of British prisoners of war, Part 2. *Human Relations*, *1*(2): 240–290.

Daniel, G. (2019). *Family Dramas: Intimacy, Power and Systems in Shakespeare's Tragedies*. Abingdon, UK: Routledge.

Dartington, A. (1995). Very brief psychodynamic counselling with young people. *Psychodynamic Counselling*, *1*(2): 253–261.

Dartington, A. (2010). My unfaithful brain: a journey into Alzheimer's disease. In: T. Dartington, *Managing Vulnerability: The Underlying Dynamics of Systems of Care (Tavistock Clinic Series)* (pp. 154–165). London: Karnac. Previously published in: R. Davenhill (Ed.), *Looking into Later Life: A Psychoanalytic Approach to Depression and Dementia in Old Age (Tavistock Clinic Series)*, London: Karnac, 2007.

Dartington, A. (2019). Where angels fear to tread: idealism, despondency and inhibition of thought in hospital nursing. In: A. Obholzer & V. Z. Roberts (Eds.), *The Unconscious at Work: A Tavistock Approach to Making Sense of Organisational Life (Second Edition)* (pp. 99–108). London: Routledge.

Dartington, T. (2010). *Managing Vulnerability: The Underlying Dynamics of Systems of Care (Tavistock Clinic Series)*. London: Karnac.

Davanloo, H. (2001). *Intensive Short-Term Dynamic Psychotherapy: Selected Papers of Habib Davanloo*. Chichester, UK: Wiley.

Daws, D. (1985). Two papers on work in a baby clinic: (i) Standing next to the weighing scales. *Journal of Child Psychotherapy*, *11*(2): 77–85.

Daws, D. (1989). *Through the Night: Helping Parents and Sleepless Infants*. London: Free Association. Republished as Daws, D. with Sutton, S., *Parent–Infant Psychotherapy for Sleep Problems: Through the Night*. London: Routledge, 2020.

Daws, D. (2005). A child psychotherapist in the baby clinic of a general practice: standing by the weighing scales thirty years on. In: J. Launer, S. Blake, & D. Daws (Eds.), *Reflecting on Reality: Psychotherapists at Work in Primary Care*. London: Karnac.

Daws, D., & Boston, M. (Eds.) (1997). *The Child Psychotherapist and Problems of Young People*. London: Wildwood.

Daws, D., & de Rementeria, A. (2015). *Finding Your Way With Your Baby: The Emotional Life of Parents and Babies*. London: Routledge.

Di Ceglie, D. (1998). Management and therapeutic aims with children and adolescents with gender identity disorders and their families. In: D. Di Ceglie & D. Freedman (Eds.), *A Stranger in My Own Body: Atypical Gender Identity Development and Mental Health* (pp. 185–197). London: Karnac.

Di Ceglie, D. (2000). Gender identity disorder in young people. *Advances in Psychiatric Treatment*, *6*: 458–466.

Di Ceglie, D. (2009). Engaging young people with atypical gender identity development in therapeutic work: a developmental approach. *Journal of Child Psychotherapy*, *35*(1): 3–12.

Di Ceglie, D. (2014). Care for gender-dysphoric children. In: B. P. C. Kreukels, T. D. Steensma, & A. L. C. de Vries (Eds.), *Gender Dysphoria and Disorders of Sex Development: Progress in Care and Knowledge* (pp. 151–169). New York: Springer.

Di Ceglie, D. (2018). The use of metaphors in understanding atypical gender identity development and its psychosocial impact. *Journal of Child Psychotherapy, 44*(1): 5–28.

Di Ceglie, D., & Coates, T. E. (2006). An experience of group work with parents of children and adolescents with gender identity disorder. *Clinical Child Psychology and Psychiatry, 11*: 387–396.

Diamond, M., & Sigmundson, H. K. (1997). Management of intersexuality. *Archives of Paediatric & Adolescent Medicine, 151*: 1046–1050.

Dicks, H. V. (1967). *Marital Tensions: Clinical Studies Towards a Theory of Marital Interaction*. London: Routledge & Kegan Paul.

Dicks, H. V. (1970). *50 Years of the Tavistock Clinic*. London: Routledge & Kegan Paul.

Dowling, E., & Elliott, D. (2012). *Understanding Children's Needs When Parents Separate*. Abingdon, UK: Routledge.

Dowling, E., & Gorell Barnes, G. (2000). *Working with Children and Parents through Separation and Divorce*. London: Macmillan.

Dowling, E., & Osborne, E. (1985). *The Family and The School: A Joint Systems Approach to Problems with Children (Second Edition)*. London: Karnac, 2003.

Dufton, K. (2004). Somebody else's baby: evidence of broken rules and broken promises? *Psychoanalytic Psychotherapy, 18*(1): 111–124.

Dugmore, P., Partridge, K., Sethi, I., & Krupa-Flasinska, M. (2018). Systemic supervision in statutory social work in the UK: systemic rucksacks and bells that ring. *European Journal of Social Work, 21*(3): 400–414.

Duschinsky, R., & White, K. (2019). *Trauma and Loss: Key Texts from the John Bowlby Archive*. London: Routledge.

Elder, A. (2005). Psychotherapy in primary care. *Psychiatry, 4*: 24–28.

Elder, A. (2009a). The GP surgery as a secure base? Patterns of attachment in primary care. *Psychodynamic Practice, 15*(1): 57–71.

Elder, A. (2009b). Building on the work of Alexis Brook: further thoughts about brief psychotherapy in primary care. *Psychoanalytic Psychotherapy, 23*(4): 307–320.

Elder, A., & Holmes, J. (2002). *Mental Health in Primary Care: A New Approach*. Oxford: Oxford University Press.

Elder, A., & Samuel, O. (Eds.) (1987). *While I'm Here, Doctor: Study of Doctor–Patient Relationships*. London: Tavistock.

Emery, F. E. (1970). *Freedom and Justice within Walls: The Bristol Prison Experiment*. London: Tavistock.

Emery, F. E., & Trist, E. L. (1965). The causal texture of organisational human relations. *Human Relations, 18*(1): 21–32.

Emery, F. E., & Trist, E. L. (1973). *Towards a Social Ecology*. London: Plenum.

Erikson, E. H. (1964). *Insight and Responsibility: Lectures on the Ethical Implications of Psychoanalytical Insight*. New York: W. W. Norton.

Erikson, E. H. (1968). Insight and Freedom. T. B. Davie Memorial Lecture. Cape Town, South Africa: University of Cape Town.

Erikson, E. H. (1969). *Gandhi's Truth: On the Origins of Militant Nonviolence*. New York: W. W. Norton.

Ezquerro, A. (2017). *Encounters with John Bowlby: Tales of Attachment*. Abingdon, UK: Routledge.

Ezriel, H. (1952). Notes on psychoanalytic group therapy: II. Interpretation and research. *Psychiatry, 15*: 119–126.

Fallon, P., Bluglass, R., Edwards, B., & Daniels, G. (1999). *Report of the Committee of Inquiry into the Personality Disorder Unit, Ashworth Special Hospital, Cm 4194-ii*. London: The Stationery Office.

Fisher, J. (1999). *The Uninvited Guest: Emerging from Narcissism Towards Marriage*. London: Karnac.

Fisher, J., & Crandell, L. (2001). Patterns of relating in the couple. In: C. Clulow (Ed.), *Adult Attachment and Couple Psychotherapy: The "Secure Base" in Practice and Research* (pp. 15–27). London: Brunner-Routledge.

Fivaz-Depeursinge, E., Cairo, S., Scaiola, C. L., & Favez, N. (2012). Nine-month-olds' triangular interactive strategies with their parents' couple in low-coordination families: a descriptive study. *Infant Mental Health Journal, 33*(1): 10–21.

Fonagy, P., Rost, F., Carlyle, J., McPherson, S., Thomas, R., Fearon, P., Goldberg, D., & Taylor, D. (2015). Pragmatic randomized controlled trial of long-term psychoanalytic psychotherapy for treatment-resistant depression: the Tavistock Adult Depression Study (TADS). *World Psychiatry, 14*: 312–321.

Foster, J. (2016). *Building Effective Social Work Teams*. London: Routledge.

Fraiberg, S. (1980). Ghosts in the nursery: a psychoanalytic approach to the problem of impaired infant-mother relationships. In: S. Fraiberg (Ed.), *Clinical Studies in Infant Mental Health*. London: Tavistock.

Freud, A. (1973). *The Writings of Anna Freud. Vol. 3: Infants Without Families Reports on the Hampstead Nurseries*. New York: International Universities Press.

Freud, S. (1930a). *Civilization and Its Discontents*. S. E., *21*: 57–145. London: Hogarth.

Friedman, L. (1962). *Virgin Wives: A Study of Unconsummated Marriages (Mind and Medicine Monographs 5)*. London: Tavistock.

Frosh, S., Phoenix, A., & Pattman, R. (2002). *Young Masculinities*. London: Palgrave.

Garland, C. (1980). *Children and Day Nurseries*. London: Wiley/Blackwell.

Garland, C. (Ed.) (1998). *Understanding Trauma (Second Enlarged Edition) (Tavistock Clinic Series)*. London: Routledge, 2017.

Garland, C. (Ed.) (2010). *The Groups Book: Psychoanalytic Group Therapy, Principles and Practice (Tavistock Clinic Series)*. London: Karnac.

Gibb, E. (2004). Reliving abandonment in the face of the therapist's pregnancy. *Psychoanalytic Psychotherapy, 18*(1): 67–85.

Giddens, A. (1984). *The Constitution of Society: Outline of the Theory of Structuration*. Cambridge: Polity.

Gledhill, C. (1987). Sir Harry Platt, MD, MS, FRCS 1886–1986 [obituary]. *British Medical Journal, 294*(6564).

Goffman, E. (1969). The insanity of place. *Psychiatry, 32*(4): 357–387.

Goodyer, I. M., Reynolds, S., Barrett, B., Byford, S., Dubicka, B., Hill, J., Holland, F., Kelvin, R., Midgley, N., Roberts, C., Senior, R., Target, M., Widmer, B., Wilkinson, P., & Fonagy, P. (2017). Cognitive behavioural therapy and short-term psychoanalytical psychotherapy versus a brief psychosocial intervention in adolescents with unipolar major depressive disorder (IMPACT): a multicentre, pragmatic, observer-blind, randomised controlled superiority trial. *The Lancet Psychiatry, 4*(2): 109–119.

Gorell Barnes, G., Thompson, P., Daniel, G., & Burchardt, N. (1997). *Growing Up in Stepfamilies*. Oxford: Oxford University Press.

Gosling, R. (1996). Enid Balint. *British Psycho-Analytical Society Bulletin, 32*(1a).

Gosling, R., Miller, D., Woodhouse, D., & Turquet, P. (1967). *The Use of Small Groups in Training*. London: Karnac, 2004.

Gould, L. J., Stapley, L. F., & Stein, M. (Eds.) (2001). *The Systems Psychodynamics of Organizations*. London: Karnac.

Graham, H., & Sher, M. (1976). Social work in general practice. *Journal of the Royal College of General Practitioners, 26*: 95–105.

Green, R. (1968). Childhood cross-gender identification. *Journal of Nervous and Mental Diseases, 147*: 500–509.

Green, R. (1971). Diagnosis and treatment of gender identity disorders during childhood. *Archives of Sexual Behaviour, 1*: 167–174.

Green, R. (1974). *Sexual Identity Conflict in Children and Adults*. New York: Basic Books.

Grier, F. (Ed.) (2005). *Oedipus and the Couple*. London: Karnac.

Griffiths, P. (forthcoming). Contemporary nursing experience viewed through a Menzian lens.

Guthrie, L., & Mattinson, J. (1971). *Brief Casework with a Marital Problem*. London: Institute of Marital Studies.

Gutting, G. (Ed.) (2001). *Cambridge Companion to Foucault*. Cambridge: Cambridge University Press.

Gutting, G., & Oksala, J. (2019). Michel Foucault. *Stanford Encyclopedia of Philosophy*. https://plato.stanford.edu/archives/spr2019/entries/foucault/

Haag, G. (1991). Nature de quelques identifications dans l'image du corps (hypothèses). *Journal de la Psychanalyse de l'Enfant, 4*: 73–92.

Hale, R., & Dhar, R. (2008). Flying a kite: observations on dual and triple diagnosis. *Criminal Behaviour and Mental Health, 18*: 145–152. Reprinted in: M. Bower, R. Hale, & H. Wood (Eds.), *Addictive States of Mind (Tavistock Clinic Series)* (ch. 6). London: Karnac, 2012.

Hale, R., & Hudson, L. (1999). Doctors in trouble. In: J. Firth-Cozens & R. L. Payne (Eds.), *Stress in Health Professionals: Psychological and Organisational Causes and Interventions* (pp. 219–230). Chichester, UK: Wiley.

Hall, G. S. (1904). *Adolescence: Its Psychology and Its Relations to Physiology, Anthropology, Sociology, Sex, Crime, Religion, and Education* (2 vols.). New York: Appleton.

Halton, W. (2015). Obsessional-punitive defences in care systems: Menzies Lyth revisited. In: D. Armstrong & M. Rustin (Eds.), *Social Defences against Anxiety: Explorations in a Paradigm* (pp. 27–38). London: Karnac.

Halton, W., & Sprince, J. (2016). Oscillating images: perceptions of couples in organisations. In: A. Novakovic (Ed.), *Couple Dynamics: Psychoanalytic Perspectives in Work with the Individual, the Couple, and the Group (Tavistock Clinic Series)*. London: Karnac.

Hard, E., Rock, B., & Stern, J. (2015). Paradigms, politics and pragmatics: psychotherapy in primary care in City and Hackney—a new model for the NHS. Part 2: operational model, practice and outcomes. *Psychoanalytic Psychotherapy, 29*(2): 1–22.

Hare, R. D., & Neumann, C. S. (2009). Psychopathy. In: P. H. Blaney & T. Millon (Eds.), *Oxford Textbook of Psychopathology* (pp. 622–650). Oxford: Oxford University Press.

Harris, M., Bick, E., & Williams, M. H. (2018). *The Tavistock Model: Papers on Child Development and Psychoanalytic Training*. London: Harris Meltzer Trust.

Harrison, T. (2000). *Bion, Rickman, Foulkes and the Northfield Experiments: Advancing on a Different Front*. London: Jessica Kingsley.

Harrison, T. (2018). Social fields, battle fields and Northfield: the legacy of the "Northfield Experiments". *Group Analysis, 51*(4): 442–454.

Healy, W. (1915). *The Individual Delinquent: A Text-Book of Diagnosis and Prognosis for All Concerned in Understanding Offenders*. Boston, MA: Little, Brown. https://archive.org/details/individualdelin02healgoog/page/n442

Helps, S. (2015). Working as an expert witness within the family courts—the performance of giving evidence. *Context, 139*: 2–4.

Helps, S. (2016a). How some systemic practices might help young women with autistic spectrum conditions, and their families. *Context, 144*: 24–26.

Helps, S. (2016b). Systemic psychotherapy with families where someone has an autism spectrum condition. *NeuroRehabilitation, 38*(3): 223–230.

Helps, S. (2017). The ethics of researching one's own practice. *Journal of Family Therapy, 39*(3): 348–365.

Helps, S. (2018). Telling and not telling: sharing stories in therapeutic spaces from the other side of the room. In: L. Turner, N. Short, A. Grant, & T. Adams (Eds.), *International Perspectives on Autoethnographic Research and Practice* (pp. 55–63). Abingdon, UK: Routledge.

Henry [Williams], G. (1981). Psychic pain and psychic damage. In: S. J. Box, B. Copley, J. Magagna, & E. Moustaki (Eds.), *Psychotherapy with Families: An Analytic Approach*. London: Routledge.

Herbst, P. G. (1976). *Alternatives to Hierarchies*. Leiden, The Netherlands: Martinus Nijhoff.

Hernandez Halton, I. (2004). Two is too much: the impact of a therapist's successive pregnancies on a female patient. *Psychoanalytic Psychotherapy, 18*(1): 86–98.

Hertzmann, L., Target, M., Hewison, D., Casey, P., Fearon, P., & Lassri, D. (2016). Mentalization-based therapy for parents in entrenched conflict: a random allocation feasibility study. *Psychotherapy, 53*(4): 388–401.

Hetherington, R., Baistow, K., Katz, I., Mesie, J., & Trowell, J. (2002). *The Welfare of Children with Mentally Ill Parents: Learning from Inter-Country Comparisons*. Chichester, UK: Wiley.

Hewison, D., Casey, P., & Mwamba, N. (2016). The effectiveness of couple therapy: clinical outcomes in a naturalistic United Kingdom setting. *Psychotherapy, 53*(4): 377.

Hewison, D., Clulow, C., & Drake, H. (2014). *Couple Therapy for Depression: A Clinician's Guide to Integrative Practice*. Oxford: Oxford University Press.

Hildebrand, D. (2018). John Dewey. *Stanford Encyclopedia of Philosophy*. https://plato.stanford.edu/entries/dewey/#InquKnowTrut

Hingley-Jones, H., Parkinson, C., & Allain, L. (Eds.) (2017). *Observation in Health and Social Care: Applications for Learning, Research and Practice with Children and Adults*. London: Jessica Kingsley.

Hinshelwood, R. D., & Skogstad, W. (2000). *Observing Organisations: Anxiety, Defence and Culture in Health Care*. London: Routledge.

HMSO (1922). *Report of the War Office Committee of Enquiry Into "Shell-Shock"*. Reprinted by Imperial War Museum, London, 2014.

HMSO (1992). *The Report of the Inquiry into the Removal of Children from Orkney in February 1991*. Edinburgh, UK: HMSO.

Hobson, R. P. (2002). *The Cradle of Thought: Exploring the Origins of Thinking*. London: Pan Macmillan.

Hobson, R. P., Patrick, M. P., Crandell, L., & García-Pérez, R. (2005). Personal relatedness and attachment in infants of mothers with borderline personality disorder. *Development and Psychopathology*, *17*(2): 329–347.

Hobson, R. P., Patrick, M. P., Hobson, J., Crandell, L., Bronfman, E., & Lyons-Ruth, K. (2009). How mothers with borderline personality disorder relate to their year-old infants. *British Journal of Psychiatry*, *195*(4): 325–330.

Hobson, R. P., Patrick, M. P., & Valentine, J. D. (1998). Objectivity in psychoanalytic judgements. *British Journal of Psychiatry*, *173*: 172–177.

Hodges, S. (2002). *Counselling Adults with Learning Disabilities*. London: Palgrave.

Holmes, J. (1993). *John Bowlby and Attachment Theory*. London: Routledge.

Home Office (1979). *Marriage Matters*. London: HMSO.

Hopkins, J. (1992). Infant–parent psychotherapy. *Journal of Child Psychotherapy*, *18*: 5–18.

Hopkins, J. (2015). *An Independent Mind: Collected Papers of Juliet Hopkins*. A. Horne & M. Lanyado (Eds.). London: Routledge.

Hopkins, S. (2004). Pregnancy: an unthinkable reality. *Psychoanalytic Psychotherapy*, *18*(1): 44–66.

Houzel, D., & Rhode, M. (Eds.) (2006). *Invisible Boundaries: Psychosis and Autism in Children and Adolescents*. London: Routledge.

Huffington, C., Armstrong, D., Halton, W., Hoyle, L., & Pooley, J. (Eds.) (2004). *Working Below the Surface: The Emotional Life of Contemporary Organisations*. London: Karnac.

Hughes, L., & Pengelly, P. (1997). *Staff Supervision in a Turbulent Environment*. London: Jessica Kingsley.

Hyatt Williams, A. (1998). Foreword. In: R. Anderson & A. Dartington (Eds.), *Facing It Out: Clinical Perspectives on Adolescent Disturbance*. London: Routledge.

Ishikawa, K. (1985). *What Is Total Quality Control? The Japanese Way*. Englewood Cliffs, NJ: Prentice Hall.

Jaques, E. (1951). *Glacier Metal: The Changing Culture of a Factory*. London: Tavistock.

Jaques, E. (1953). On the dynamics of social structure: a contribution to the psychoanalytical study of social phenomena deriving from the view of Melanie Klein. *Human Relations*, *6*: 3–24.

Jaques, E. (1955). Social systems as a defence against persecutory and depressive anxiety. In: M. Klein, P. Heimann, & R. E. Money-Kyrle (Eds.), *New Directions in Psychoanalysis* (pp. 478–498). London: Tavistock.

Jordan, S. (2019). *The Uses and Abuses of Humour in Social Work*. London: Routledge.

Jung, C. G. (1935). *Analytical Psychology: Its Theory and Practice (The Tavistock Lectures)*. London: Routledge & Kegan Paul, 1968.

Kahr, B. (2017). "How to Cure Family Disturbance": Enid Balint and the creation of couple psychoanalysis. Twenty-first Enid Balint Memorial Lecture 2016. *Couple and Family Psychoanalysis*, *7*: 1–25.

Karen, R. (1998). *Becoming Attached*. Oxford: Oxford University Press.

Keats, J. (1817). [Letter]. http://mason.gmu.edu/~rnanian/Keats-NegativeCapability.html

Kennedy, H. (1996). Memories of Anna Freud. *American Imago, 53*(3): 205–208.

Keogh, T., & Palacios, E. (Eds.) (2019). *Interpretation in Couple and Family Psychoanalysis: Cross Cultural Perspectives*. London: Routledge.

Kernberg, O. F. (1996). Thirty methods to destroy the creativity of psychoanalytic candidates. *International Journal of Psychoanalysis, 77*: 1031–1040.

Khaleelee, O., & Miller, E. (1993). Beyond the small group; society as an intelligible field of study. In: M. Pines (Ed.), *Bion and Group Psychotherapy* (pp. 354–385). London: Routledge & Kegan Paul.

Khan, S. (2018). Retirement—preparation, prevention, and potential. A review of the thinking behind and development of the "Couple 50+ MOT Programme" at Tavistock Relationships. *Couple and Family Psychoanalysis, 8*(2): 163–174.

King, P., & Steiner, R. (Eds.) (1991). *The Freud-Klein Controversies 1941–45*. London: Routledge.

Kjeldmand, D. (2006). *The Doctor, the Task and the Group: Balint Groups as a Means of Developing New Understanding in the Physician-Patient Relationship*. Uppsala, Sweden: Uppsala University Press.

Klein, M. (1930). The importance of symbol formation in the development of the ego. In: *The Writings of Melanie Klein—Vol. 1* (pp. 219–232). London: Hogarth, 1975.

Klein, M. (1932). The psychoanalysis of children. *The Writings of Melanie Klein—Vol. 2*. London: Karnac, 1975.

Klein, M. (2020). Sadness and loss in the emotional life of a young child. In: J. Milton (Ed.), *Essential Readings from the Melanie Klein Archives* (pp. 44–56). London: Routledge.

Klein, S. (1980). Autistic phenomena in neurotic patients. *International Journal of Psychoanalysis, 61*: 395–401.

Kolaitis, G., Giannakopoulos, G., Tomaras, V., Christogiorgos, S., Pomini, V., Layiou-Lignos, E., Tzavara, C., Rhode, M., Miles, G., Joffe, I., Trowell, J., & Tsiantis, J. (2014). Self-esteem and social adjustment in depressed youths: a randomized trial comparing psychodynamic psychotherapy and family therapy. *Psychotherapy and Psychosomatics, 83*(4): 249–251.

Kraemer, S. (1983). Who will have my tummy ache if I give it up? *Family Systems Medicine, 1*: 51–59.

Kraemer, S. (2015). Anxiety at the front line. In: D. Armstrong & M. Rustin (Eds.), *Social Defences against Anxiety: Explorations in a Paradigm*. London: Karnac.

Kraemer, S. (2016). The view from the bridge: bringing a third position to child health. In: S. Campbell, R. Catchpole, & D. Morley (Eds.), *Critical Issues in Child & Adolescent Mental Health*. London: Palgrave Macmillan.

Kraemer, S. (2018). Stop running and start thinking. *Child and Adolescent Mental Health, 23*(4): 381–383.

Kraemer, S. (2019). Deliberate self-poisoning by teenagers. *Archives of Disease in Childhood, 104*(8): 728–729.

Kraemer, S., Graham, H., Senior, R., Dickie, S., Bard, I., & Chan, M. (2018). A richer system: a reflecting team in primary care. *Context, 160*: 22–25.

Kraemer, S., & Roberts, J. (Eds.) (1996). *The Politics of Attachment: Towards a Secure Society*. London: Free Association.

Kraemer, S., Steele H., & Holmes, J. (Eds.) (2007). A tribute to the legacy of John Bowlby at the centenary of his birth. *Attachment & Human Development, 9*(4): 303–306.

Krantz, J. (2019). Leadership, betrayal, and institutional integrity. *Organisational and Social Dynamics, 19*(1): 112–120.

Krause, I. B. (2019). Intercultural therapy and neoliberalism. In: B. Ababio & R. Littlewood (Eds.), *Intercultural Therapy, Challenges, Insights and Developments* (pp. 10–23). London: Routledge.

Kuhn, T. S. (1962). *The Structure of Scientific Revolutions.* London: Chicago University Press

Laing, R. D. (1960). *The Divided Self: An Existential Study in Sanity and Madness.* London: Tavistock.

Laing, R. D. (1961). *The Self and Others.* London: Tavistock.

Lane, C., & Nicholls, C. (2018). Looking both ways: the role of the administrator in the Fitzjohn's Unit. In: R. Meyerowitz & D. Bell (Eds.), *Turning the Tide: The Psychoanalytic Approach of the Fitzjohn's Unit to Patients with Complex Needs (Tavistock Clinic Series)* (pp. 37–44). London: Karnac.

Lanman, M., & Grier, F. (2001). A psychoanalytic approach to brief marital psychotherapy. In: F. Grier (Ed.), *Brief Encounters with Couples: Some Analytical Perspectives* (pp. 113–133). London: Karnac.

Lanman, M., Grier, F., & Evans, C. (2003). Objectivity in psychoanalytic assessment of couple relationships. *British Journal of Psychiatry, 182*: 255–260.

Launer, J. (2007). Moving on from Balint: embracing clinical supervision. *British Journal of General Practice, 57*(536): 182–183.

Lawrence, M. (2008). *The Anorexic Mind (Tavistock Clinic Series).* London: Karnac.

Lawrence, M., Mondadori, R., Simpson, A., & Williams, G. (2004). Editorial. *Psychoanalytic Psychotherapy, 18*(4): 361.

Lawrence, W. G. (1988). *Social Dreaming @ Work.* London: Karnac.

Layard, R. (2005a). Mental health: Britain's biggest social problem? Paper presented at the *No.10 Strategy Unit Seminar on Mental Health,* January 20.

Layard, R. (2005b). *Happiness: Lessons from a New Science.* London: Allen Lane.

Layard, R., & Clark, D. M. (2014). *Thrive: The Power of Psychological Therapy.* London: Penguin.

Legg, C. (2019). Pragmatism. *Stanford Encyclopedia of Philosophy.* https://plato.stanford.edu/entries/pragmatism/

Lemma, A., Target, M., & Fonagy, P. (2011). *Brief Dynamic Interpersonal Therapy: A Clinician's Guide.* Oxford: Oxford University Press.

Lewin, K. (1920). Die Sozialisierung des Taylorsystems: eine grundsätzliche Untersuchung zur Arbeits- und Berufspsychologie. *Praktischer Sozialismus: Schriftenreihe, Heft 4.*

Lewin, K. (1939). Experiments in social space. Reflection. *Journal of the Society for Organisational Learning, 1*(1): 7–13. https://academia.edu/29645335/Experiments_in_Social_Space_1939

Lewin, K. (1947). Frontiers in group dynamics: concept, method and reality in social science; social equilibria and social change. *Human Relations, 1*(1): 5–41.

Lewin, K. (1952). *Field Theory in Social Research.* London: Tavistock.

Lewis, E. (1976). The management of stillbirth: coping with an unreality. *The Lancet, 2*(7986): 619–620.

Lightwood, R., Brimblecombe, F., Reinhold, J., Burnard, E., & Davis, J. (1957). A London trial of home care for sick children. *The Lancet, 269*(6963): 313–317.

Likierman, M. (2001). *Melanie Klein: Her Work in Context*. London: Continuum.

Lindsay, M. (2017). I sit in the diabetic clinic. *Archives of Disease in Childhood: Education & Practice, 102*: 282–284.

Long, J., & Trowell, J. (2001). Individual brief psychotherapy with sexually abused girls: what can we learn from the process notes? *Psychoanalytic Psychotherapy, 15*(1): 39–59.

Lowe, F. (Ed.) (2014). *Thinking Space: Promoting Thinking about Race, Culture and Diversity in Psychotherapy and Beyond (Tavistock Clinic Series)*. London: Karnac.

Lucas, R. (1998). [Book reviews] *R. D. Laing—His Life and Legacy*: J. Clay (1997). *R. D. Laing. The Divided Self: An Existential Study in Sanity and Madness*. London: Sceptre; Z. Kotowicz (1997). *R. D. Laing and the Paths of Anti-Psychiatry*. London and New York: Routledge; A. Laing (1997). *R. D. Laing: A Life*. London: Harper Collins; B. Mullan (1995). *Mad to be Normal: Conversations with R. D. Laing*. London: Free Association. *International Journal of Psychoanalysis, 79*: 1229–1239.

Luff, M. C., & Garrod, M. (1935). The After-results of psychotherapy in 500 adult cases. *British Medical Journal, 2*; 54–59. https://www.bmj.com/content/bmj/2/3888/54.full.pdf

MacCarthy, D. (1954). Remembering your childhood. *The Lancet, 264* (6838): 595–596.

MacCarthy, D., Lindsay, M., & Morris, I. (1962). Children in hospital with mothers. *The Lancet, 1* (7230): 603–608.

Mahler, M. S. (1961). On sadness and grief in infancy and childhood—loss and restoration of the symbiotic love object. *Psychoanalytic Study of the Child, 16*: 332–351.

Mahler, M. S. (1968). *On Human Symbiosis and the Vicissitudes of Individuation*. New York: International Universities Press.

Main, T. (1961). New developments in the psychiatrist's role. In: J. Johns (Ed.), *The Ailment and Other Psychoanalytic Essays* (pp. 66–76). London: Free Association, 1989.

Main, T. (1981). The concept of the therapeutic community. In: J. Johns (Ed.), *The Ailment and Other Psychoanalytic Essays* (pp. 123–141). London: Free Association, 1989.

Mainprice, J. (1974). *Marital Interaction and Some Illnesses in Children*. London: Institute of Marital Studies.

Malan, D. H. (1963). *A Study of Brief Psychotherapy*. London: Tavistock.

Malan, D. H. (1976a). *The Frontier of Brief Psychotherapy*. New York: Plenum.

Malan, D. H. (1976b). *Toward the Validation of Dynamic Psychotherapy: A Replication*. New York: Plenum.

Malan, D. H. (1979). *Individual Psychotherapy and the Science of Psychodynamics (Second Edition)*. London: Butterworth-Heinemann, 1995.

Malan, D. H. (1997). *Anorexia, Murder, and Suicide*. London: CRC Press.

Malan, D. H., & Coughlin Della Selva, P. (2006). *Lives Transformed: A Revolutionary Method of Dynamic Psychotherapy*. London: Karnac.

Malan, D. H., & Osimo, F. (1992). *Psychodynamics, Training and Outcome in Brief Psychotherapy*. London: Butterworth-Heinemann.

Marmot, M., Allen, J., Boyce, T., Goldblatt, P., & Morrison, J. (2020). *Health Equity in England: The Marmot Review 10 Years On*. London: Institute of Health Equity. http://instituteofhealthequity.org/the-marmot-review-10-years-on

Marshall, G. (1990). *In Praise of Sociology*. London: Hyman Unwin.

Martin, F. E. (1977). Some implications from the theory and practice of family therapy for individual therapy (and vice versa). *British Journal of Medical Psychology, 50*: 53–64.

Martin, F. E., & Knight, J. (1962). Joint interviews as part of intake procedure in a child psychiatric clinic. *Journal of Child Psychology and Psychiatry, 3*: 17–26.

Mattinson, J. (1973). Marriage and mental handicap. In: F. De La Cruz & G. Laveck (Eds.), *Human Sexuality and the Mentally Retarded* (pp. 169–185). New York: Brunner/Mazel.

Mattinson, J. (1975). *The Reflection Process in Casework Supervision (Second edition)*. London: Tavistock Marital Studies Institute, 1992.

Mattinson, J. (1988). *Work, Love and Marriage: The Impact of Unemployment*. London: Duckworth.

Mattinson, J., & Sinclair, I. (1979). *Mate and Stalemate: Working with Marital Problems in a Social Services Department*. Oxford: Blackwell.

McCann, D., & Polek, E. (2020). The feasibility and effectiveness of a time-limited psychodynamic couple-focused therapy for adoptive parents: preliminary evidence from the Adopting Together project. *Adoption & Fostering, 44*(1): 75–91.

McDougall, J. (1985). *Theatres of the Mind: Illusion and Truth on the Psychoanalytic Stage*. New York: Basic Books.

McDougall, J. (1989). *Theatres of the Body*. New York: W. W. Norton.

McQuown, N. A. (Ed.) (1971). *The Natural History of an Interview*. University of Chicago Library. Microfilm collection of manuscripts on cultural anthropology, no 95 series xv. https://lib.uchicago.edu/mca/mca-15-098.pdf

McWhinney, I. (1998). The physician as healer: the legacy of Michael Balint. *Proceedings of 11th International Balint Congress edited by John Salinsky*. London: The Balint Society. https://balintinternational.com/wp-content/uploads/2019/11/Proceedings-book-Porto-2019.pdf

Mead, M. (1948). The individual and society. *Proceedings of the International Congress on Mental Health, 4*: 121–127.

Meltzer, D. (1975). Adhesive identification. *Contemporary Psychoanalysis, 11*(3): 289–310.

Meltzer, D., Bremner, J., Hoxter, S., Weddell, D., & Wittenberg, I. (1975). *Explorations in Autism: A Psycho-Analytical Study*. London: Harris Meltzer Trust, 2018.

Meltzer, D., & Sabatini Scolmati, A. (1986). Psychotic illnesses in early childhood: ten years on from Explorations in Autism. In: D. Meltzer, with M. Albergamo, E. Cohen, A. Greco, M. Harris, S. Maiello, G. Milana, D. Petrelli, M. Rhode, A. Sabatini Scolmati, & F. Scotti, *Studies in Extended Metapsychology: Clinical Applications of Bion's Ideas* (pp. 122–135). Strath Tay, UK: Clunie.

Menzies, I. E. P. (1960). A case-study in the functioning of social systems as a defence against anxiety: a report on a study of the nursing service of a general hospital. *Human Relations, 13*(2): 95–121. Reprinted in Menzies-Lyth, I. (1988). *Containing Anxiety in Institutions: Selected Essays. Vol. 1* (pp. 43–97). London: Free Association.

Meyerowitz, R., & Bell, D. (Eds.) (2018). *Turning the Tide: The Psychoanalytic Approach of the Fitzjohn's Unit to Patients with Complex Needs (Tavistock Clinic Series)*. London: Karnac.

Miller, E. J. (1990a). Experiential learning in groups I: The development of the Leicester model. In: E. Trist & H. Murray (Eds.), *The Social Engagement of Social Science: A Tavistock Anthology, Vol. 1: The Socio-Psychological Perspective* (pp. 165–185). Philadelphia, PA: University of Pennsylvania Press.

Miller, E. J. (1990b). Experiential learning in groups II: Recent developments in dissemination and application. In: E. Trist & H. Murray (Eds.), *The Social Engagement of Social Science: A Tavistock Anthology, Vol. 1: The Socio-Psychological Perspective* (pp. 199–220). Philadelphia, PA: University of Pennsylvania Press.

Miller, E. J. (1993). *From Dependency to Autonomy: Studies in Organisation and Change*. London: Free Association.

Miller, E. J., & Gwynne, G. V. (1972). *A Life Apart: A Pilot Study of Residential Institutions for the Physically Handicapped and the Young Chronic Sick*. London: Tavistock.

Miller, E. J., & Lawrence, G. (1993). A Church of England diocese. In: E. J. Miller (Ed.), *From Dependency to Autonomy* (pp. 102–119). London: Free Association.

Miller, E. J., & Rice, A. K. (1967). *Systems of Organisation*. London: Tavistock.

Miller, L., Rustin, M. E., Rustin, M. J., & Shuttleworth, J. (Eds.) (1989). *Closely Observed Infants*. London: Duckworth.

Ministry of Health, Central Health Services Council (1959). *The Welfare of Children in Hospital Report of the Committee (The Platt Report)*. London: HMSO.

Ministry of Justice (2018). New and forthcoming research and analysis for the family justice system. In: *Family Justice Research Bulletin 7* (p. 11).

Minuchin, S. (1974). *Families and Family Therapy*. London: Tavistock.

Minuchin, S., & Fishman, C. (1979). The psychosomatic family in child psychiatry. *Journal of the American Academy of Child Psychiatry, 18*: 76–90.

Money, J. (1994). The concept of gender identity disorder in childhood and adolescence after 39 years. *Journal of Sex and Marital Therapy, 20*: 163–177.

Moore, E. C. (1961). *American Pragmatism: Peirce, James and Dewey*. New York: Columbia University Press.

Morgan, M. (2001). First contacts: The therapist's "couple state of mind" as a factor in the containment of couples seen for initial consultations. In: F. Grier (Ed.), *Brief Encounters with Couples: Some Analytical Perspectives* (pp. 17–32). London: Karnac.

Morgan, M. (2005). On being able to be a couple: the importance of a "creative couple" in psychic life. In: F. Grier (Ed.), *Oedipus and the Couple* (pp. 9–30). London: Karnac.

Morgan, M. (2019a). *A Couple State of Mind: Psychoanalysis of Couples and the Tavistock Relationships Model*. Abingdon, UK: Routledge.

Morgan, M. (2019b). A psychoanalytic understanding of the couple relationship: past, present and future. In: M. Morgan (Ed.), *A Couple State of Mind: Couple Psychoanalysis and the Tavistock Relationships Model* (pp. 1–13). Abingdon, UK: Routledge.

Morra, P. (2015). Bereavement and triangular relationships in a case of a child suffering from anorexia. *Journal of Child Psychotherapy, 41*(3): 242–254.

Morra, P. (2018). Il pensiero disincarnato delle anoressiche. *Richard e Piggle, 26*(4): 398–414.

Murray, J., Hallal, P. C., Mielke, G. I., Raine, A., Wehrmeister, F. C., Anselmi, L., & Barros, F. (2016). Low resting heart rate is associated with violence in late adolescence: a prospective birth cohort study in Brazil. *International Journal of Epidemiology*, *45*(2): 491–500.

Music, G. (2017). *Nurturing Natures: Attachment and Children's Emotional, Sociocultural and Brain Development (Second Edition)*. Abingdon, UK: Routledge.

Music, G. (2019). *Nurturing Children: From Trauma to Growth Using Attachment Theory, Psychoanalysis and Neurobiology*. Abingdon, UK: Routledge.

Myers, C. S. (1923). The influence of the late W. H. R. Rivers. In: *W. H. R. Rivers: Psychology and Politics and Other Essays* (pp. 149–181). London: Kegan Paul, Trench, Trubner. https://archive.org/details/in.ernet.dli.2015.218424/page/n9

Nathans, S., & Schaefer, M. (Eds.) (2017). *Couples on the Couch: Psychoanalytic Couple Therapy and the Tavistock Model*. Abingdon, UK: Routledge.

Nease, D. E., Lichtenstein, A., Pinho-Costa, L., & Hoedebecke, K. (2018). Balint 2.0: a virtual Balint group for doctors around the world. *The International Journal of Psychiatry in Medicine*, *53*(3): 115–125. https://doi.org/10.1177/0091217418765036

Obholzer, A. (2019). Managing social anxieties in public sector organisations. In: A. Obholzer & V. Z. Roberts (Eds.), *The Unconscious at Work: A Tavistock Approach to Making Sense of Organisational Life (Second Edition)* (pp. 174–183). London: Routledge.

Obholzer, A., & Roberts, V. Z. (2019). *The Unconscious at Work: A Tavistock Approach to Making Sense of Organisational Life (Second Edition)*. London: Routledge.

Ogden, T. H. (1984). Instinct, phantasy and psychological deep structure: a reinterpretation of aspects of the work of Melanie Klein. *Contemporary Psychoanalysis*, *20*(4): 500–525.

Oliver-Bellasis, E. (1998). "Is anyone there?" The work of the Young People's Counselling Service. In: R. Anderson & A. Dartington (Eds.), *Facing It Out: Clinical Perspectives on Adolescent Disturbance (Tavistock Clinic Series)* (pp. 113–126). London: Duckworth.

O'Reilly, J. (2000). The practice as a patient: working as a psychotherapist in general practice. *Psychoanalytic Psychotherapy*, *14*(3): 253–266.

Pailthorpe, G. W. (1932). *What We Put in Prison*. London: Williams and Norgate.

Papadopoulos, R., & Byng-Hall, J. (1997). *Multiple Voices: Narrative in Systemic Family Psychotherapy (Tavistock Clinic Series)*. London: Duckworth.

Parkes, C. M., Stevenson-Hinde, J., & Marris, P. (Eds.) (1993). *Attachment Across the Life Cycle*. London: Routledge.

Partridge, K., Dugmore, P., Mahaffey, H., Chidgey, M., & Owen, J. (2019). "Step by step, side by side": the quest to create relational artistry through systemic practice within children's social care. *Journal of Family Therapy*, *41*(3): 321–342.

Patrick, M., Hobson, P., Castle, D., Howard, R., & Maughan, B. (1994). Personality disorder and the mental representation of early social experience. *Development and Psychopathology*, *6*: 375–388.

Pengelly, P., & Sprince, J. (Eds.) (2011). *Five Tavistock Pantomimes*. APPCIOS/Psychodynamic Thinking. https://psychodynamicthinking.info/group/five-tavistock-pantomimes

Phillipson, H. (1955). *The Object Relations Technique*. London: Tavistock.

Pichon-Rivière, E. (1980). *La Teoría del Vínculo*. Buenos Aires: Paidós.

REFERENCES 361

Pietroni, M., & Vespe, A. (2000). *Understanding Counselling in Primary Care: Voices from the Inner City*. London: Churchill Livingstone.

Pincus, L. (1960). *Marriage: Studies in Emotional Conflict and Growth*. London: Institute of Marital Studies, 1973.

Pines, M. (Ed.) (1985). *Bion and Group Psychotherapy*. London: Routledge & Kegan Paul.

Raitt, S. (2004). Early British psychoanalysis and the medico-psychological clinic. *History Workshop Journal, 58*: 63–85.

Rapoport, R., & Rapoport, R. N. (1969). The dual career family: a variant pattern and social change. *Human Relations, 22*(1): 3–28.

Rees, J. R. (1945). *The Shaping of Psychiatry by War*. New York: W. W. Norton.

Reid, S. (Ed.) (1997). *Developments in Infant Observation: The Tavistock Model*. London: Routledge, (pp. 19–32).

Rendall, S., & Stuart, M. (2005). *Excluded from School: Systemic Practice for Mental Health and Education Professionals*. Hove, UK: Routledge.

Renton, T. (1990). Remarks on an anniversary. In: C. Clulow (Ed.), *Marriage: Disillusion and Hope. Papers Celebrating Forty Years of the Tavistock Institute of Marital Studies* (pp. 10, 11). London: The Tavistock Institute of Marital Studies & Karnac.

Rhode, M. (2012). Infant observation as an early intervention. In: C. Urwin & J. Sternberg (Eds.), *Infant Observation and Research: Emotional Processes in Everyday Lives* (pp. 104–114). Hove, UK: Routledge.

Rhode, M. (2018). Object relations approaches to autism. *International Journal of Psychoanalysis, 99*(3): 702–724.

Rhode, M. (2020). Notes on "Dick". In: J. Milton (Ed.), *Essential Readings from the Melanie Klein Archives: Original Papers and Critical Reflections*. London: Routledge.

Rhode, M., & Klauber, T. (Eds.) (2004). *The Many Faces of Asperger's Syndrome (Tavistock Clinic Series)*. London: Routledge.

Rice, A. K. (1958). *Productivity and Social Organization: The Ahmedabad Experiment*. New York: Garland, 1987.

Rice, A. K. (1963). *The Enterprise and Its Environment: A System Theory of Management Organisation*. London: Routledge/Taylor & Francis, 2001.

Rice, A. K. (1965). *Learning for Leadership: Interpersonal and Intergroup Relations*. London: Karnac, 1999.

Rice, A. K., & Miller, E. J. (1967). *Systems of Organization: The Control of Task and Sentient Boundaries*. London: Routledge/Taylor & Francis, 2001.

Rickman, J. (1949). The technique of interviewing in anthropology and psychoanalysis. In: P. King (Ed.), *No Ordinary Psychoanalyst: The Exceptional Contributions of John Rickman* (pp. 148–156). London: Karnac, 2003.

Rioch, M. (1975). Group relations: rationale and technique. In: A. Colman & W. Bexton (Eds.), *Group Relations Reader*. Washington, DC: A. K. Rice Institute.

Rivers, W. H. R. (1918). The repression of war experience. *Proceedings of the Royal Society of Medicine, 11*: 1–20. Also published in *The Lancet*, February 2, 1918, pp. 173–177. https://bl.uk/collection-items/w-h-r-rivers-on-the-treatment-of-shell-shock-from-the-lancet

Robertson, J. (1952). *A Two-Year-Old Goes to Hospital [Film]*. Ipswich, UK: Concord Media. https://concordmedia.org.uk/categories/robertson-films/

Robertson, J. (1958a). *Going to Hospital with Mother [Film]*. Ipswich, UK: Concord Media https://concordmedia.org.uk/products/going-to-hospital-with-mother-51/

Robertson, J. (1958b). *Young Children in Hospital*. London: Tavistock.

Robertson, J. (1959). Going to hospital with mother: a documentary film. *Proceedings of the Royal Society of Medicine, 52*(5): 381–384.

Robertson, J. (1962). *Hospitals and Children: A Parent's Eye View: A Review of Letters from Parents to* The Observer *and the* BBC. London: Gollancz.

Robertson, J., & Bowlby, J. (1952). Recent trends in the care of deprived children in the UK. *Bulletin of the World Federation for Mental Health, 4*(3): 131–139.

Robertson, J., & Robertson, J. (1969). *Young Children in Brief Separation—"John, 17 months, for 9 days in a residential nursery" [Film]*. Ipswich, UK: Concord Media. https://concordmedia.org.uk/products/young-children-in-brief-separation-john-17-months-for-9-days-in-a-residential-nursery-24/

Robertson, J., & Robertson, J. (1971). Young children in brief separation: a fresh look. *Psychoanalytic Study of the Child, 26*: 264–315.

Robertson, J., & Robertson, J. (1989). *Separation and the Very Young*. London: Free Association.

Robertson, Joyce. (2011). A Parent's view. Early days: 1945, 1954, postscript 2009. *Celebration of a Transformation*. Stockport: Action for Sick Children, p. 25 http://kodomoryoyoshien.jp/_src/79/celebration20of20a20transformation3f.pdf

Robertson, Joyce, & Freud, A. (1956). A mother's observations on the tonsillectomy of her four-year-old daughter. *Psychoanalytic Study of the Child, 11*(1): 410–327.

Rock, B., & Carrington, A. (2011). Addressing complexity in primary care. *Healthcare Counselling and Psychotherapy Journal, 11*: 35–39.

Rock, B., & Carrington, A. (2012). Complexity in primary care. In: A. Lemma (Ed.), *Contemporary Developments in Adult and Young Adult Therapy: The Work of the Tavistock and Portman Clinics, Vol. 1 (Tavistock Clinic Series)* (pp. 111–133). London: Karnac.

Rosenfeld, D. (2014). *The Body Speaks: Body Image Delusions and Hypochondria*. London: Karnac.

Rost, F., Luyten, P., Fearon, P., & Fonagy, P. (2019). Personality and outcome in individuals with treatment-resistant depression—Exploring differential treatment effects in the Tavistock Adult Depression Study (TADS). *Journal of Consulting and Clinical Psychology, 87*(5): 433–445.

Royal College of General Practitioners Working Party (1972). *The Future General Practitioner: Learning and Teaching*. London: *British Medical Journal*.

Royal College of Psychiatrists (1998). Gender identity disorders in children and adolescents—Guidance for management. Council report CR63. London: Royal College of Psychiatrists.

Royal College of Psychiatrists in partnership with Royal College of General Practitioners (2008). *Psychological Therapies in Psychiatry and Primary Care: College Report 151*. London: Royal College of Psychiatrists.

Rustin, M. E. (1991). The strength of the clinical practitioners' workshop as a new model in clinical research. In: R. Szur & S. Miller (Eds.), *Extending Horizons: Psychoanalytic Psychotherapy with Children, Adolescents and Families*. London: Karnac.

Rustin, M. E. (1999). The training of child psychotherapists at the Tavistock Clinic: Philosophy and practice. *Psychoanalytic Enquiry*, *19*(2): 125–141.

Rustin, M. E. (2005). A conceptual analysis of critical moments in Victoria Climbié's life. *Child & Family Social Work*, *10*(1): 11–19.

Rustin, M. E. (2008). Some historical and theoretical observations. In: M. E. Rustin & J. Bradley (Eds.), *Work Discussion: Learning from Reflective Practice in Work with Children and Families* (pp. 3–21). London: Karnac.

Rustin, M. E., & Bradley, J. (2008). *Work Discussion: Learning from Reflective Practice in Work with Children and Families (Tavistock Clinic Series)*. London: Karnac.

Rustin, M. E., Rhode, M., Dubinsky, H., & Dubinsky, A. (Eds.) (1997). *Psychotic States in Children (Tavistock Clinic Series)*. London: Karnac.

Rustin, M. E., & Rustin, M. J. (2016). *Reading Klein*. Abingdon, UK: Routledge.

Rustin, M. E., & Rustin, M. J. (Eds.) (2019). *New Discoveries in Child Psychotherapy: Findings from Qualitative Research (Tavistock Clinic Series)*. London: Routledge.

Rustin, M. J. (2003). Learning about emotions: The Tavistock approach. *European Journal of Psychotherapy, Counselling and Health*, *6*(3): 187–208.

Rustin, M. J. (2004). Rethinking audit and inspection. *Soundings*, *64*: 86–107.

Rustin, M. J. (2019). *Researching the Unconscious: Principles of Psychoanalytic Method*. London: Routledge.

Rustin, M. J., & Armstrong, D. (2019). Psychoanalysis, social science and the Tavistock tradition. *Psychoanalysis Culture and Society*, *24*(4): 473–492.

Ruszczynski, S. (Ed.) (1993). *Psychotherapy with Couples: Theory and Practice at the Tavistock Institute of Marital Studies*. London: Karnac.

Ruszczynski, S. (2005). Reflective space in the intimate couple relationship: the "marital triangle". In: F. Grier (Ed.), *Oedipus and the Couple* (pp. 31–47). London: Karnac.

Ruszczynski, S., & Fisher, J. (Eds.) (1995). *Intrusiveness and Intimacy in the Couple*. London: Karnac.

Sadowski, H., Trowell, J., Kolvin, I. T., Weeramanthri, T., Berelowitz, M., & Gilbert, L. H. (2003). Sexually abused girls: patterns of psychopathology and exploration of risk factors. *European Child & Adolescent Psychiatry*, *12*: 221–230.

Salinsky, J., & Sackin, P. (2000). *What Are You Feeling, Doctor? Identifying and Avoiding Defensive Patterns in the Consultation*. Oxford: Radcliffe Medical Press.

Salzberger-Wittenberg, I. (1970). *Psycho-Analytic Insight and Relationships: A Kleinian Approach*. London: Routledge & Kegan Paul.

Salzberger-Wittenberg, I. (1997). Beginnings: the family, the observer and the infant observation group. In: S. Reid (Ed.), *Developments in Infant Observation: The Tavistock Model* (pp. 19–32). London: Routledge.

Salzberger-Wittenberg, I. (1999). What is psychoanalytic about the Tavistock model of studying infants? Does it contribute to psychoanalytic knowledge? *International Journal of Infant Observation and Its Applications*, *2* (3): 4–15.

Salzberger-Wittenberg, I. (2013). *Experiencing Endings and Beginnings*. London: Karnac.

Scharff, D. E., & Palacios, E. (Eds.) (2017). *Family and Couple Psychoanalysis: A Global Perspective*. London: Karnac.

Scharff, D. E., & Savege Scharff, J. (Eds.) (2014). *Psychoanalytic Couple Therapy: Foundations of Theory and Practice*. London: Karnac.

Scharff, D. E., & Vorchheimer, M. (Eds.) (2017). *Clinical Dialogues on Psychoanalysis with Families and Couples*. London: Karnac.

Searle, L., Lyon, L., Young, L., Wiseman, M., & Foster-Davis, B. (2011). The Young People's Consultation Service: an evaluation of a consultation model of very brief psychotherapy. *British Journal of Psychotherapy, 27*: 56–78.

Searles, H. F. (1955). The informational value of the supervisor's emotional experience. In: H. F. Searles, *Collected Papers on Schizophrenia and Related Subjects* (pp. 157–176). London: Karnac, 1986.

Selvini Palazzoli, M., Boscolo, L., Cecchin, G., & Prata, G. (1980). Hypothesising-circularity-neutrality: three guidelines for the conductor of the session. *Family Process, 26*(4): 405–413.

Senn, M. J. E. (2007). Interview with John Bowlby, October 19, 1977. Published online in *Beyond the Couch*, 2. http://archive.is/f0GrH [manuscript in National Library of Medicine, Washington, DC].

Shapiro, E. (1997). *The Inner World in the Outer World: Psychoanalytic Perspectives*. New Haven, CT: Yale University Press.

Shapiro, E. (2020). *Finding a Place to Stand: Developing Self-Reflective Institutions, Leaders and Citizens*. Bicester, UK: Phoenix.

Shapiro, E., & Carr, A. W. (1991). *Lost in Familiar Places: Creating New Connections between the Individual and Society*. New Haven, CT: Yale University Press.

Shapiro, E., & Carr, W. (2012). An introduction to Tavistock-style group relations conference learning. *Organisational and Social Dynamics, 12*(1): 70–80.

Sharifi, P., & Jayyusi, S. (2004). Personal communication.

Shephard, B. (2000). *A War of Nerves: Soldiers and Psychiatrists 1914–1994*. London: Jonathan Cape. Paperback published by Pimlico, London, 2002 *[from which the page references in the text are taken]*.

Sher, M. (2012). *The Dynamics of Change: Tavistock Approaches to Improving Social Systems*. London: Karnac.

Shmueli, A. (2018). Working with the fractured container. In: A. Balfour, C. Clulow, & K. Thompson (Eds.), *Engaging Couples: New Directions in Therapeutic Work with Families* (pp. 169–182). London: Routledge.

Shorer, Y., Biderman, A., Levy, A., Rabin, S., Karni, A., Maoz, B., & Matalon, A. (2011). Family physicians leaving their clinic—the Balint group as an opportunity to say good-bye. *Annals of Family Medicine, 9*(6): 549–551.

Shuttleworth, A. (1999). Finding new clinical pathways in the changing world of district child psychotherapy. *Journal of Child Psychotherapy, 25*(1): 29–49.

Shuttleworth, A. (2002). Turning towards a bio-psycho-social way of thinking. *European Journal of Psychotherapy, Counselling and Health, 22*(1): 3–30.

Sinason, V. (1992). *Mental Handicap and the Human Condition: New Approaches from the Tavistock*. Revised edition. London: Free Association, 2010.

Sinason, V. (1994). *Treating Survivors of Satanist Abuse*. London: Routledge.

Singh, R., & Dutta, S. (2010). *"Race" and Culture: Tools Techniques and Trainings: a Manual for Professionals*. London: Karnac.

Skrine, R. (Ed.) (1987). *Psychosexual Training and the Doctor/Patient Relationship. Institute of Psychosexual Medicine Digests*. London: Montana.

Skuse, D., Mandy, W., Steer, C. D., Miller, L. L., Goodman, R., Lawrence, K., Emond, A. M., & Golding, J. (2009). Social communication competence and functional adaptation in a general population of children: Preliminary evidence for sex-by-verbal IQ differential risk. *Journal of the American Academy of Child & Adolescent Psychiatry*, 48: 128–137.

Smith, C. W. L., Gross, V. S., Graham, H. G., & Reilly, J. (1983). The health care meeting: eight years of collaborative work in general practice. *Group Analysis*, 16(1): 52–66.

Smith, J. D. (2013). A base for a new beginning: benign regression in a GP practice. *Psychoanalytic Psychotherapy*, 27(1): 3–20.

Smith, J. D. (2019). Emotional play and resonating to the shape of the valued self with fellow-feeling: therapeutic conversations in brief dynamic therapy. *Psychodynamic Practice*, 25(3): 223–242.

Snodgrass, J. (1984). William Healy (1869–1963): pioneer child psychiatrist and criminologist. *Journal of the History of the Behavioural Sciences*, 20(4): 332–339.

Soreanu, R. (2019). *Michael Balint: Early Interventions, Early Groups. Proceedings of 21st International Balint Congress* (pp. 57–61), Associação Portuguesa de Grupos Balint. https://balintinternational. com/wp-content/uploads/2019/11/Proceedings-book-Porto-2019.pdf

Spillius, E. (2007). Anthropology and psychoanalysis: a personal concordance. In: *Encounters with Melanie Klein: Selected Papers of Elizabeth Spillius* (pp. 7–24). London: Routledge.

Sprince, J. (2008). The network around adoption: the forever family and the ghosts of the dispossessed. In: D. Hindle & G. Shulman (Eds.), *The Emotional Experience of Adoption: A Psychoanalytic Perspective*. Abingdon, UK: Routledge.

Sprince, J. (2012). The riddle of the Sphinx. In: A. Briggs (Ed.), *Waiting To Be Found: Papers on Children in Care (Tavistock Clinic Series)*. London: Karnac.

Sprince, J. (2015). From owning to belonging. In: A. Briggs (Ed.),*Towards Belonging: Negotiating New Relationships for Adopted Children and Those in Care (Tavistock Clinic Series)* (pp. 105–132). London: Karnac

Stanford, R. (1992). *A Study of Police and Social Worker Joint Investigations of Cases of Suspected Child Abuse*. Doctoral dissertation, Brunel University, London.

Steiner, J. (1993). *Psychic Retreats: Pathological Organizations in Psychotic, Neurotic and Borderline Patients*. London: Routledge.

Steiner, J. (2004). Foreword. *Psychoanalytic Psychotherapy*, 18(1): 1–4.

Steiner, J. (2011). *Seeing and Being Seen*. Hove, UK: Routledge.

Steiner, J. (Ed.) (2017). *Lectures on Technique by Melanie Klein*. Abingdon, UK: Routledge.

Steiner, J. (2020). *Illusion, Disillusion, and Irony in Psychoanalysis*. Abingdon, UK: Routledge.

Stern, J., Hard, E., & Rock, B. (2015). Paradigms, politics and pragmatics: psychotherapy in primary care in City and Hackney—a new model for the NHS. Part 1: the historical, political and economic drivers behind the creation of the service. *Psychoanalytic Psychotherapy*, 29(2): 117–138.

Stewart, H. (1996). *Michael Balint: Object Relations Pure and Applied*. London: Routledge.

Stewart, J. (2013). *Child Guidance in Britain, 1918–1955. Studies for the Society for the Social History of Medicine, No. 12*. London: Routledge, 2016.

Stokes, J. (1999). Why do we work. In: D. Taylor (Ed.), *Talking Cure: Mind and Method of the Tavistock Clinic (Tavistock Clinic Series)*. London: Karnac, 2017.

Stokes, J. (2017). Using emotion as intelligence. In: E. Schein & J. Ogawa (Eds.), *Organizational Therapy* (pp. 23–49). San Jose, CA: Process Consultation.

Stokes, J. (2018). Executive & leadership coaching. In: E. Cox, T. Bachkirova, & D. A. Clutterbuck (Eds.), *The Complete Handbook of Coaching (Third Edition)*. London: Sage.

Stokes, J. (2019a). Institutional chaos and personal stress. In: A. Obholzer & V. Roberts (Eds.), *The Unconscious at Work: A Tavistock Approach to Making Sense of Organisational Life (Second Edition)* (pp. 136–143). London: Routledge.

Stokes, J. (2019b). The unconscious at work: teams, groups and organisations. In: A. Obholzer & V. Roberts (Eds.), *The Unconscious at Work: A Tavistock Approach to Making Sense of Organisational Life (Second Edition)* (pp. 28–36). London: Routledge.

Stokes, J., & Dopson, S. (2020). *From Ego to Eco, Leadership for the Fourth Industrial Revolution*. Oxford: Saïd Business School.

Stoller, R. J. (1968). *Sex and Gender (Vol. 1)*. New York: Science House.

Stoller, R. J. (1975). *Presentations of Gender*. New Haven, CT: Yale University Press.

Stoller, R. J. (1992). Gender identity development and prognosis: A summary. In: C. Chiland & J. G. Young (Eds.), *New Approaches to Mental Health from Birth to Adolescence* (pp. 78–87). New Haven, CT: Yale University Press.

Sutherland, J. D. (1985). Bion revisited: group dynamics and group psychotherapy. In: M. Pines (Ed.), *Bion and Group Psychotherapy* (pp. 47–86). London: Routledge & Kegan Paul.

Swann, G. (2015). Breaking down barriers: developing an approach to include fathers in children's social care. Professional doctorate thesis, Tavistock and Portman NHS Foundation Trust. http://repository.tavistockandportman.ac.uk/1125/

Target, M., Hertzmann, L., Midgley, N., Casey, P., & Lassri, D. (2017). Parents' experience of child contact within entrenched conflict families following separation and divorce: a qualitative study. *Psychoanalytic Psychotherapy*, 31(2): 218–246.

Taylor, D. (Ed.) (1999). *Talking Cure: Mind and Method of the Tavistock Clinic (Tavistock Clinic Series)*. London: Karnac, 2017.

Taylor, D., Carlyle, J. A., McPherson, S., Rost, F., Thomas, R., & Fonagy, P. (2012). Tavistock Adult Depression Study (TADS): a randomised controlled trial of psychoanalytic psychotherapy for treatment-resistant/treatment-refractory forms of depression. *BMC Psychiatry*, 11: 12 –60.

Thomas, J. (1990). "And mother came too" [letter]. *The Tablet* [details unknown].

Thomas, K., & Gunnell, D. (2010). Suicide In England and Wales 1861–2007: a time trends analysis. *International Journal of Epidemiology*, 39: 1464–1475.

Thorpe, C., & Trowell, J. (Eds.) (2007). *Re-rooted Lives: Interdisciplinary Work within the Family Justice System*. Bristol, UK: Jordan.

Tizard, B. (2009). Looking back: The making and breaking of attachment theory. *The Psychologist*, 22: 902–903.

Toulmin, S. (1990). *Cosmopolis: The Hidden Agenda of Modernity*. Chicago, IL: Chicago University Press.

Toulmin, S. (2001). *Return to Reason*. Cambridge, MA: Harvard University Press.

Trist, E. L. (1985). Working with Bion in the 1940s, the group decade. In: M. Pines (Ed.), *Bion and Group Psychotherapy* (pp. 1–46). London: Routledge & Kegan Paul.

Trist, E. L., & Bamforth, K. W. (1951). Some social and psychological consequences of the Longwall Method of coal-getting: an examination of the psychological situation and defences of a work group in relation to the social structure and technological content of the work system. *Human Relations*, 4(1): 3–38.

Trist, E. L., Higgin, G. W., Murray, H., & Pollock, A. B. (1963). *Organisational Choice: Capabilities of Groups at the Coal Face Under Changing Technologies: The Loss, Transformation and Rediscovery of a Work Tradition*. London: Tavistock.

Trist, E. L., & Murray, H. (Eds.) (1990a). *The Social Engagement of Social Science: A Tavistock Anthology, Vol. 1: The Socio-Psychological Perspective*. London: Free Association.

Trist, E. L., & Murray, H. (1990b). Historical Overview. In: E. L. Trist & H. Murray (Eds.), *The Social Engagement of Social Science: A Tavistock Anthology, Vol. 1: The Socio-Psychological Perspective* (pp. 1–43). London: Free Association.

Trist, E. L., & Murray, H. (Eds.) (1993). *The Social Engagement of Social Science: A Tavistock Anthology, Vol. 2: The Socio-Technical Perspective*. Philadelphia, PA: University of Pennsylvania Press.

Trist, E. L., & Murray, H. (Eds.) (1997). *The Social Engagement of Social Science: A Tavistock Anthology, Vol. 3: The Socio-Ecological Perspective*. Philadelphia, PA: University of Pennsylvania Press.

Trist, E. L., & Sofer, C. (1959). *Exploration in Group Relations*. Leicester, UK: University of Leicester Press.

Trowell, J. (1982). Possible effects of emergency caesarian section on the mother–child relationship. *Early Human Development*, 7(1): 41–51.

Trowell, J. (1983). Emergency caesarian section: a research study of the mother/child relationship of a group of women admitted expecting a normal vaginal delivery. *Child Abuse & Neglect*, 7(4): 387–394.

Trowell, J. (1996). The Monroe Young Family Centre. In: M. Bower & J. Trowell (Eds.), *The Emotional Needs of Young Children and Their Families*. London: Routledge.

Trowell, J., Davids, Z., Miles, G., Shmueli, A., & Paton, A. (2008). Developing healthy mental health professionals: what can we learn from trainees? *Infant Observation*, 11(3): 333–343.

Trowell, J., & Etchegoyen, A. (Eds.) (2002). *The Importance of Fathers: A Psychoanalytic Re-evaluation*. Hove, UK: Routledge.

Trowell, J., Joffe, I., Campbell, J., Clemente, C., Almqvist, F., Soininen, M., Koskenranta-Aalto, U., Weintraub, S., Kolaitis, G., Tomaras, V., Anastasopoulos, D., Grayson, K., Barnes, J., & Tsiantis, J. (2007). Childhood depression: a place for psychotherapy: an outcome study comparing individual psychodynamic psychotherapy and family therapy. *European Child & Adolescent Psychiatry*, 16: 157–167.

Trowell, J., Kolvin, I., Weeramanthri, T., Sadowski, H., Berelowitz, M., Glaser, D., & Leitch, I. (2002). Psychotherapy for sexually-abused girls: psychopathological outcome findings and patterns of change. *British Journal of Psychiatry, 180*: 234–247.

Trowell, J., & Miles, G. (1991). The place of an introduction to young child observation in social work training. In: *CCETSW Guidelines on the Teaching of Child Care in the Diploma of Social Work*. London: Central Council for Education and Training in Social Work.

Trowell, J., & Miles, G. (2004). The contribution of observation training to professional development in social work. *Journal of Social Work Practice, 18*(1): 49–60.

Trowell, J., & Miles, G. (Eds.) (2011). *Childhood Depression: A Place for Psychotherapy (Tavistock Clinic Series)*. London: Karnac.

Trowell, J., Paton, A., Davids, Z., & Miles, G. (1998). The importance of observational training: an evaluative study. *Infant Observation, 2*(1): 101–111.

Trowell, J., Ugarte, B., Kolvin, I., Berelowitz, M., Sadowski, H., & Le Couteur, A. (1999). Behavioural psychopathology of child sexual abuse in schoolgirls referred to a tertiary centre: a North London study. *European Child & Adolescent Psychiatry, 8*: 107–116.

Tsiantis, J., & Trowell, J. (Eds.) (2018). *Assessing Change in Psychoanalytic Psychotherapy of Children and Adolescents*. Abingdon, UK: Routledge.

Tunnadine, D., & Green, R. (1978). *Unwanted Pregnancy: Accident or Illness?* Oxford: Oxford University Press.

Tustin, F. (1980). Autistic objects. *International Review of Psycho-Analysis, 7*: 27–40.

Tustin, F. (1984). Autistic shapes. *International Review of Psycho-Analysis, 11*: 279–290.

Tustin, F. (1991). Revised understandings of psychogenic autism. *International Journal of Psychoanalysis, 72*: 585–592.

Tustin, F. (1994). The perpetuation of an error. *Journal of Child Psychotherapy, 20*: 3–23.

Van der Horst, F., & Van der Veer, R. (2009). Separation and divergence: the untold story of James Robertson's and John Bowlby's theoretical dispute on mother–child separation. *Journal of the History of the Behavioral Sciences, 45*: 236–252.

Van Dijken, S. (1998). *John Bowlby: His Early Life—A Biographical Journey into the Roots of Attachment Theory*. London: Free Association.

Vetere, A., & Dowling, E. (Eds.) (2017). *Narrative Therapies with Children and Their Families: A Practitioners Guide to Concepts and Approaches (Second Edition)*. London: Brunner/Routledge.

Waddell, M. (2002). *Inside Lives: Psychoanalysis and the Growth of the Personality*. London: Karnac.

Waddell, M. (2005). *Understanding 12–14-Year-Olds*. London: Jessica Kingsley.

Waddell, M. (2006). Infant observation in Britain: the Tavistock approach. *International Journal of Psychoanalysis, 87*(4): 1103–1120.

Waddell, M. (2018). *On Adolescence: Inside Stories*. Abingdon, UK: Routledge.

Wakelyn, J. (2019). *Therapeutic Approaches with Babies and Young Children in Care: Observation and Attention (Tavistock Clinic Series)*. Abingdon, UK: Routledge.

Watson, R. (2019). Jointly created authority: a conversation analysis of how power is managed by parents and systemic psychotherapists in children's social care. *Journal of Family Therapy, 41*(3): 357–383.

Weintrobe, S. (Ed.) (2013). *Engaging with Climate Change: Psychoanalytic and Interdisciplinary Perspectives*. Hove, UK: Routledge.

White, A. (2015). *From the Science of Selection to Psychologising Civvy Street: The Tavistock Group, 1939–1948*. Doctor of philosophy (PhD) thesis, University of Kent. https://kar.kent.ac.uk/55057/

Whyte, N. (2004). Introduction. *Psychoanalytical Psychotherapy, 18*(1): 5–14.

Wiener, J., & Sher, M. (1998). *Counselling and Psychotherapy in Primary Health Care*. London: Macmillan.

Wilkinson, R., & Pickett, K. (2019). *The Inner Level: How More Equal Societies Reduce Stress, Restore Sanity and Improve Everyone's Well-being*. London: Penguin.

Williams, G. (1997a). *Internal Landscapes and Foreign Bodies: Eating Disorders and Other Pathologies*. London: Karnac.

Williams, G. (1997b). Reflections on some dynamics of eating disorders: "no entry" defences and foreign bodies. *International Journal of Psychoanalysis, 78*: 927–941.

Williams, G., Williams, P., Desmarais, J. H., & Ravenscroft, K. (Eds.) (2004). *The Generosity of Acceptance: Exploring Feeding Difficulties in Children, Vol. 2*. London: Karnac.

Williams, G., Williams, P., Ravenscroft, K., & Desmarais, J. H. (Eds.) (2003). *The Generosity of Acceptance: Exploring Eating Disorders in Adolescents, Vol. 1*. London: Karnac.

Williams, G. P. (1998). Una famiglia in fuga dalla pena depressiva. In: S. M. G. Adamo & G. P. Williams (Eds.), *Il Lavoro con Adolescenti Difficili: Nuovi Approcci dalla Tavistock* (pp. 161–177). Naples, Italy: Idelson Gnocchi Editori.

Williams, M. H. (Ed.) (1987). *The Philosophy of the Tavistock Child Psychotherapy Training: The Collected Papers of Martha Harris and Esther Bick*. Strath Tay, UK: Clunie.

Wilmott, S. (in press). On working intermittently over the long term with difficult to refer patients: struggling with complexity in primary care.

Wilson, A. T. M. (1947). The development of a scientific basis in family casework. *Social Work, 4*: 62–69.

Wilson, A. T. M. (1949). Some reflections and suggestions on the prevention and treatment of marital problems. *Human Relations, 2*: 233–252.

Wilson, A. T. M., Doyle, M., & Kelnar, J. (1947). Group techniques in a transitional community. *The Lancet, 1*(6457): 735–738.

Wilson, A. T. M., Trist, E. L., & Curle, A. (1952). Transitional communities: a study of the civil resettlement of British prisoners of war. In: G. E. Swanson, T. M. Newcomb, & E. L. Hartley (Eds.), *Readings in Social Psychology* (pp. 561–579). New York: Henry Holt.

Winnicott, D. W. (1963). The mentally ill in your caseload. In: *The Maturational Processes and the Facilitating Environment: Studies in the Theory of Emotional Development* (pp. 217–229). London: Hogarth, 1965.

Winnicott, D. W. (1971). The use of an object and relating through identifications. In: *Playing and Reality* (pp. 101–121). London: Tavistock.

Winnicott, D. W. (1987). *The Spontaneous Gesture: Selected Letters of D. W. Winnicott*. F. R. Rodman (Ed.). London: Karnac, 1999.

Wittenberg, I., Williams, G., & Osborne, E. (1993). *The Emotional Experience of Learning and Teaching*. London: Karnac.

Woodhouse, D., & Pengelly, P. (1991). *Anxiety and the Dynamics of Collaboration*. Aberdeen, UK: Aberdeen University Press.

Wrong, D. (1961). The oversocialized conception of man in modern sociology. *American Sociological Review, 26*(2): 183–193.

Yakeley, J., Schoenberg, P., Morris, R., Sturgeon, D., & Majid, S. (2011). Psychodynamic approaches to teaching medical students about the doctor–patient relationship: randomised controlled trial. *The Psychiatrist, 135*: 308–313.

Yelloly, M., Loughlin, B., Rolph, K., Stanford, R., & Trowell, J. (1994). Shared learning in child protection: an evaluation. *Paediatric Nursing, 6*: 7–9.

Young, L., & Lowe, F. (2018). The Young People's Consultation Services: a model of engagement. In: A. Lemma (Ed.), *Contemporary Developments in Adult and Young Adult Therapy: The Work of the Tavistock and Portman Clinics* (ch. 4). London: Karnac.

Zucker, K. J., & Bradley, S. J. (1995). *Gender Identity Disorder and Psychosexual Problems in Children and Adolescents*. New York: Plenum.

Index

AAIMH *see* Australian Association for Infant Mental
     Health
Abse, S., 179, 320
ACPs *see* advanced clinical practitioners
action research, 19
Adamo, S. M. G., 37
adhesive identification, 152
Adolescent Department, 155–157, 159, 165–167,
     169, 171–172, 181, 189, 210, 238, 243, 300,
     303, 304, 306
    adolescent disturbance, 171–172
    psychotherapy training, 170
    staff group, 170
Adorno, T., 31
Adult Attachment Interview, 32, 33
Adult Department, 77, 78, 87, 98, 156, 157, 166, 169,
     170, 178, 189, 199, 200, 201, 209, 213, 299,
     300, 304
    Anton's progress, 224–226
    art and literature, 223–224
    Borderline Workshop, 216, 222
    collaborative care, 213
    Community Unit, 88
    Fitzjohn's Unit, 229
    Gentleman's Club, The, 219
    group as treatment, 220–222
    group at work, 219–226, 236
    groupings in department, 220
    Groups Waiting List, 221

    Groups Workshop for trainees, 222
    Interdisciplinary Training in Adult
       Psychotherapy, 215
    local commissioning of services, 217
    and nursing, 249–250
    psychoanalytic theory and clinical work, 215
    qualifying course in psychotherapy, 216
    reputation, 214
    shared event with, 96
    structure, 220
    Tavistock Trauma Service, 223
    Trauma Unit, 222
    trauma workshop, 222–223
    Welfare Settlement, 213
advanced clinical practitioners (ACPs), 252
AHPs *see* allied health care professionals
AIMH *see* Association for Infant Mental Health
Ainsworth, M., 50
    and her work, xvii, 32, 50, 58, 59, 262, 335,
AKRI *see* A. K. Rice Institute
A. K. Rice Institute (AKRI), 278–280
Allain, L., 245
Allen, J., 336
allied health care professionals (AHPs), 249
Altschuler, J., 237
    and Tavi, 214, 235, 300
Alvarez, A., 38, 42, 151
Amias, D., 192
Anderson, R., 243

371

Anna Freud Centre, 33
Anna Freud Clinic, 139
Anselmi, L., 269
anxiety
    managing social, 266–267
    protective mechanisms against, 267–268
APP see Association for Psychoanalytic Psychotherapy
APPCIOS see Association for Psychodynamic Practice
        and Counselling in Organisational Settings
Arendt, H., 339
Ariès, P., 171
Armstrong, D., 16, 18, 20, 21, 23, 24, 26, 33, 35, 96,
        100, 143, 219, 220, 238, 247
Association for Infant Mental Health (AIMH), 93
Association for Psychoanalytic Psychotherapy (APP),
        89, 93, 211
Association for Psychodynamic Practice and
        Counselling in Organisational Settings
        (APPCIOS), 282
Association of Child Psychotherapists, 68
Astor, J., 14
attachment see also Adult Attachment Interview
    concept of, 53
    and families, 188–189
    and gender identity, 161
    and medical care, 91–92
    research, 31–33, 337
    theory, 33, 67, 69, 178, 334
Auden, W. H.
    In Memory of Sigmund Freud, 11, 12, 13
Australian Association for Infant Mental Health
        (AAIMH), 114
autism, 151–153 see also psychoanalytic approaches
        to autism
    Lifespan, 191
    study of, 42
autonomic countertransference, 265, 268–270
    autonomic system, 269
    clinical vignette, 272–274
    countertransference, 265
    defences against madness and badness, 265–268
    displacement, 268
    dual diagnosis, 270
    early traumatic experiences, 271
    eroticisation, 268
    Fallon Inquiry, 269
    feared scenario, 270–272
    Hare Psychopathy Checklist, 274, 275
    intellectualisation, 268
    managing social anxieties, 266–267
    object constancy, 271

Portman Clinic, 265
prodromal psychotic state, 271
projection, 268
protective mechanisms against anxieties, 267–268
psychic survival mechanism, 271
psychopathy, 271, 273
revulsion, 273
supervision group, 274–275
autonomic system, 269 see also autonomic
        countertransference
Aylesbury Prison, 266

Babüroğlu, O., 36
Baistow, K., 261, 263
Balfour, A., 38, 179, 180, 181
Balfour, F., 178
Balint, E., 93
Balint, M., 91
Balint groups, 73, 177
    case discussion, 75
    College of GPs, 73
    cornerstone of family medicine, 82
    developments and change, 80
    The Doctor, His Patient and the Illness, 75–76
    Family Discussion Bureau, 74
    general practitioner training scheme, 76
    Israeli Balint group, 81–82
    Leaders' Workshop, 78
    mind and medicine monographs, 83–84
    multidisciplinary organisational, 82–83
    origins of, 74–75
    research project, 78–80
    six minutes group, 78–79
    training-cum-research seminars, 75
    wider influence, 77–78
Bambrough, S., 244
Bamforth, K. W., 21, 295, 333
Bannister, K., 176, 177, 184
Banton, R., 218
BAP see British Association for Psychotherapy
Bard, I., 89
Barnes, D., 89
Barnes, E., 248
Barnett, A., 320
Barratt, S., 24, 190–191, 192, 193, 194–195
        see also family therapy
Barrett, B., 40
Barros, F., 269
basic assumption(s), 23, 310
    groups, xii, xvi
Bateson, G., 188

Bell, D., 230
Belson, P., 58
Benjamin, A., 180
Benne, K. D., 51
Berelowitz, M., 40, 261, 262, 263
Berenstein, I., 185
Bettelheim, B., 153
Bexton, W., 279
Bick, E., 37, 68, 170
Biderman, A., 81
Billen, 214
Bion, F., 289
Bion, W. R., 16–17, 20, 21, 25, 39, 147, 149, 171, 221,
        332, 337
    and John Bowlby, 334, 335
    container–contained concept, 70, 290
    and groups, xvi, xvii, 209
    and C. G. Jung, 337
    Leaderless Group test, 337–338
    leadership, 290
    mentor of, 71
    narcissism to social-ism, 221
    Northfield Experiments, 16–18, 331–332
    and Operation Phoenix, xii, 18, 332
    psychoanalytic approaches to autism, 152
    and training, xiv, 23
boarding school, xiv, 49, 289
    therapeutic community, 281–282
Borderline Workshop, 210, 216, 222
Boscolo, L., 189
Boston, M., 38
Bott, E., 21, 35
Bourdieu, P., 25
Bourne, S., 77, 107
Bower, M., 245
Bowlby, J., 25, 49, 50, 52, 53, 59–60, 67, 69, 110,
        124, 125, 144, 149 170, 193, 334, 335, 338
        see also Separation Research Unit
    approach of, 70–71, 188
    Association of Child Psychotherapists, 68
    attachment research, 31–33, 50
    boarding school, 289
    and Esther Bick, 68, 96
    clinical thinking, 69
    Department for Children and Parents, 335
    impact on child psychotherapists, 70–71
    and Edward Glover, 32
    and Melanie Klein, 32, 71, 334, 338
    and Freda MacQueen, 149
    object relations theory, 18, 24
    Operation Phoenix, xii

pre-war child guidance model, 67
and James Robertson, 51–54
theory of container and contained, 70
Boyce, T., 336
BPAS see British Psychoanalytical Society
BPC see British Psychoanalytic Council
Bradford, L. P., 51
Bradley, J., 37, 96
Bravesmith, A., 89
Bremner, J., 42, 151
Brent Consultation Service, 165
Bridger, H., 16, 17, 26
Brief Psychotherapy Workshop, 199 see also
        psychotherapy, brief
    Davanloo's technique, 200–201
    First International Experiential Dynamic
        Therapy Conference, 201
    myth of superficiality, 200
    reorientation in thinking and therapeutic
        reflexes, 202
    triangle of conflict, 199
    triangle of persons, 199
Briggs, A., 37
Briggs, S., 238
British Association for Psychotherapy (BAP), 215
British Psychoanalytical Society (BPAS), 32
British Psychoanalytic Council (BPC), 184, 213
Britton, R., 147, 260
Bronfman, E., 33
Brook, A., 85, 109
    early influences, 87–88
    as innovator, 86–87
    practice as secure base, 91–92
    primary care mental health services, 90–91
    psychotherapeutic listening, 86
    reasons for referral to psychiatrist, 90
    Tavistock "clinic workers", 88
    Tavistock approach, 89–90
    Tavistock community unit, 88–89
Bruggen, P., 189
Burck, C., 24, 190, 193
Butler-Sloss, E., 257
Byford, S., 40
Byng-Hall, J., 97, 144, 188, 189, 236

Cairo, S., 148
CAISS see Camden Adolescent Intensive Support
        Service
Camden Adolescent Intensive Support Service
        (CAISS), 250
Camden's pupil referral unit, 235

CAMHS *see* Child and Adolescent Mental Health Services
Campbell, D., 190, 238
Canonbury Child Guidance Clinic *see* Child Guidance Training Centre
Care Quality Commission (CQC), 240
Carlyle, J., 41, 215, 238
Carr, A. W., 143, 279, 280, 286, 287, 329
Carrington, A., 90, 216
case discussion seminar, 75
Casey, P., 179, 180
Castle, D., 33
Cattan, S., 9
Cavill, Ines, 214, 299
CBT *see* cognitive behavioural therapy
Cecchin, G., 189
CGTC *see* Child Guidance Training Centre
Chahal, P., 180
Chan, M., 89
Chatham House rules, 321
Chidgey, M., 193
Child and Adolescent Mental Health Services (CAMHS), 119, 192, 234, 250
Child and Family Department, 118, 123, 127, 133, 139, 144, 190, 191, 210, 234, 249, 250, 299, 300, 336
Child Guidance Training Centre (CGTC), 95, 113, 123, 143, 241
    change in hierarchy, 124
    child guidance staff training, 125
    Day Unit, 131–133
        1968, 126
        1970s and early 80s, 138–140
    medical model, 124
    multifactor theory of delinquency, 123
    narcissism of minor difference, 127
    personal experience, 127–128
    post-war period, 125
    threat to close, 126–127
Childhood Depression Study, 40, 261–262
child protection and courts, 257
    child abuse assessment team, 258
    childhood sexual awareness, 260
    containment, 259–260
    Family Division, 257
    Leaving Care Act, 257–258
    multidisciplinary working, 259
    Orkney child abuse scandal, 260
    physical abuse, 257
    psychoanalytic understanding of violence and sexuality, 260–261

    research, 261–262
    sexual abuse referrals, 258
    unconscious processes, 259
child psychotherapy training, 96–97 *see also* psychotherapy, child
children in substitute care, 58–59
Children, Young Adult and Families Department (CYAF), 250
Clark, D. M., 41
Cleavely, E., 184
Clifford, P., 218
clinical social work, 241, 244 *see also* social work and Tavistock
Clulow, C., 177, 178, 179, 180, 181, 183, 185
Coates, S., 161
COFAP *see* Committee on Couple and Family Psychoanalysis
cognitive behavioural therapy (CBT), 40, 205, 235, 237, 239
    trauma-focused, 223
collaborative care, 213
College of GPs[2], 73, 84 *see also* Balint groups
Colman, A., 279
Colman, W., 178, 184
commissioners, 8
Committee on Couple and Family Psychoanalysis (COFAP), 185
community mental health, 31, 38, 68, 95, 100, 135, 213–214, 235
Community Unit, 88, 90
container–contained, 70, 290
Conti, G., 9
Cooper, A., 23, 24, 218, 245–246, 320
Coughlin Della Selva, P., 201
countertransference, 37, 75, 118, 177, 259, 265, 268, 310 *see also* autonomic countertransference; transference
couple psychoanalysis, 183–185 *see also* Tavistock Relationships
Courtenay, M., 93
Cowan, C. P., 180
Cowan, P. A., 180
CQC *see* Care Quality Commission
Crandell, L., 33, 178
Cregeen, S., 40
Crichton, N., 244
Crichton-Miller, H., 330
Cullington-Roberts, D., 211
Curle, A., 176, 332
CYAF *see* Children, Young Adult and Families Department

D58, 211, 216, 253
Daniel, G., 190, 191–192, 195 *see also* family therapy
Dartington, A., 243, 248, 254
    and Tavi, 155, 247
Dartington, T., 21, 254
Davanloo, H.,
    work of, 200–201
Davids, Z., 263
Daws, D., 88, 109–115 *see also* parent–infant
    psychotherapy
Day Unit *see* Child Guidance Training Centre
DC&P *see* Department for Children and Parents
Dearnley, B., 178
Department for Children and Parents (DC&P), 126,
    335
Department for Work & Pensions (DWP), 180
Department of Education and Training (DET), 254
Department of Health and Social Care (DHSC), 180
depression, 41, 206, 337 *see also* Childhood Depression
    Study; International Study of Childhood
    Depression; Tavistock Adult Depression
    Study
    adolescent, 40
    in adults, 45, 238
    in children, 262
    in couples, 180
    Meltzer, 152
    post-natal, 109, 114
Dermod MacCarthy Medal, 60
Desmarais, J. H., 38
DET *see* Department of Education and Training
detachment, 50
Dhar, R., 270
DHSC *see* Department of Health and Social Care
Diamond, M., 162
Di Ceglie, D., 38
Dickie, S., 89
Dicks, H. V., 19, 20, 31, 148, 169, 170, 175, 177, 181,
    188, 330, 338
dismantling, 152
Disorder of Sex Development (DSD), 162–163 *see also*
    gender identity issues
displacement, 268
DIT *see* Dynamic Interpersonal Therapy
Doctor, His Patient and the Illness, The, 75–76 *see also*
    Balint groups
Donaghy, M., 179
Dopson, S., 292
double bind theory, 188 *see also* family therapy
double dissonance, 16
Dowling, E., 234, 235, 240

Drake, H., 180
Draper, L., 180
Drysdale, 132
DSD *see* Disorder of Sex Development
Dual Career Family, The, 35
dual diagnosis, 270
Dubicka, B., 40
Dufton, K., 211
Dugmore, P., 192, 193
Duschinsky, R., 149, 193
DWP *see* Department for Work & Pensions
Dynamic Interpersonal Therapy (DIT), 235

early traumatic experiences, 271
Eating Disorders Workshop (ED Workshop), 155–158
    course for eating disorders, 157
    family therapy assessments, 156
    Thanatophilia, 157
Educational Psychology training, 236
ED Workshop *see* Eating Disorders Workshop
EFPP *see* European Federation for Psychoanalytic
    Psychotherapy
Elder, A., 74, 85, 91, 92, 93
Elementary Education Act, 132
Elmhirst, S. I., 262
EMDR *see* eye-movement desensitisation and
    reprocessing
Emery, F. E., 21, 34, 36, 294
Emond, A. M., 153
ENB *see* English National Board for Nursing
English National Board for Nursing (ENB), 249
eroticisation, 268
Erikson, E. H., xi, xvi, xix
Etchegoyen, A., 263
European Federation for Psychoanalytic
    Psychotherapy (EFPP), 185
Evans, C., 179
experiential learning, 39, 189, 279
eye-movement desensitisation and reprocessing
    (EMDR), 223
Ezquerro, A., 334

*Facing It Out: Clinical Perspectives on Adolescent
    Disturbance*, 171–172
Fairbairn's concept of the "internal saboteur", 17
Fallon Inquiry, 269
Family Discussion Bureau (FDB), 74, 175 *see also*
    Tavistock Relationships
Family Division, 257
Family Drug and Alcohol Court Service (FDAC), 250
family medicine, 82

Family Nurse Partnership (FNP), 44, 250
family therapy, 187
    Barratt, S., 190–191, 194–195
    Daniel, G., 191–192, 195
    double bind theory, 188
    first fifty years, 187–190
    Hall's reorientation, 189
    Helps, S., 192–193, 193–194
    Milan group of family therapists, 189–190
    programme, 144
    researchers, 188
Farquharson, C., 9
Favez, N., 148
FDAC *see* Family Drug and Alcohol Court Service
FDB *see* Family Discussion Bureau
Fearon, P., 41, 179, 180, 215, 238
field theory, 19
Fisher, J., 178, 185
Fishman, C., 145, 189
Fitzjohn's Unit, 229–230
Fivaz-Depeursinge, E., 148
FNP *see* Family Nurse Partnership
Fonagy, P., 40, 41, 215, 235, 238
Forward Psychiatry, 171
Foster, J., 243
Foucault, M., 31
Fourth Industrial Revolution, 291 *see also* leadership
Fraiberg, S., 70
Freud, A., 48, 54 *see also* Hampstead Wartime
    Nurseries
    and the Robertsons, 49, 54
Freud, S., 127 *see also* Auden, W. H.
    concept of unconscious resistance, 17
Friedman, L., 144
Friedman, R., 161
Frosh, S., 218, 236

García-Pérez, R., 33
Garland, C., 38, 39, 222, 227, 236, 314
    and Tavi, 214, 235, 238, 300, 315
Gazette, 303–306
gender dysphoria, 162 *see also* gender identity issues
Gender Identity Development Service (GIDS), 164,
    234, 235, 244, 250
gender identity issues, 159–164
    literature on transsexualism, 160
    Mermaids, 163
    service for children and adolescents, 161
Gentleman's Club, The, 219
Gibb, E., 211

Gibb, J. R., 51
Giddens, A., 22
GIDS *see* Gender Identity Development Service
Ginja, R., 9
Glaser, D., 40, 261, 262, 263
Gloucester House, 131
    case history, 136–137
    CGTC Day Unit in 1970s and early 80s, 138–140
    charitable donors, 140
    current endeavour, 135–136
    Day Unit provision, 131
    Elementary Education Act, 132
    history, 132–134
    Mulberry Bush Day Unit, 132–133
    personal reminiscence, 134–135
    staff members, 140
Goldberg, D., 41, 215, 238
Goldblatt, P., 336
Golding, J., 153
Goodman, R., 153
Goodyer, I. M., 40
Gorell Barnes, G., 235
Gosling, R., 37, 77, 80
Gould, L. J., 279
Graham, H., 88, 89
Graham, H. G., 88
Great Person theory of leadership, 290 *see also*
    leadership
Green, P., 91
Green, R., 161
Grier, F., 178, 179, 185
Griffiths, P., 248, 254
Gross, V. S., 88
group relations, 37, 39, 45, 237, 278–279
    conference, 23, 215, 329 *see also* Leicester
    conferences
    principles of, 17
    and religion, 285–286
Group Relations Programme, 285
Groups Waiting List, 221
Groups Workshop, 235–236
    for trainees, 222
Gunnell, D., 337
Guthrie, L., 177
Gutting, G., 31
Gwynne, G. V., 21

Hale, R., 38, 267, 270, 275–276
Haley, J., 188
Hall, J., 89

Hallal, P. C., 269
Halton, W., 21, 23, 26, 35, 238
Hampstead Wartime Nurseries, 47–48
Hard, E., 90
Hare, R. D., 274
Hare Psychopathy Checklist, 274, 275
Harris, M., 37
    and Tavi, xiv, 12, 38, 68, 96, 101, 158, 304
Harrison, T., 16, 26, 332
Healy, W., 123
Helps, S., 192–194 see also family therapy
Herbst, P. G., 21
Hernandez Halton, I., 211
Herrick, D., 285–286
Hertzmann, E., 178
Hertzmann, L., 179, 180
Hetherington, R., 261, 263
Hewison, D., 179, 180
Higgin, G. W., 21
Hildebrand, D., 30
Hill, J., 40
Hingley-Jones, H., 245
Hinshelwood, R. D., 247
Hobson, J., 33
Hobson, P., 33
Hobson, R. P., 33, 42, 179
Hodges, S., 235
Hoedebecke, K., 80
Holgate, B., 301
Holland, F., 40
Holmes, J., 31, 32, 91, 92
Hopkins, J., 38, 112, 128–129, 211
Horkheimer, M., 31
Howard, R., 33
Hoxter, S., 42, 151
Hoyle, L., 21, 23, 35, 238
Hudson, L., 267
Huffington, C., 21, 23, 35, 190, 238
Hughes, C., 40
Hughes, G., 192, 193
Hughes, L., 179
Hull, S., 93
human
    sexuality, 260
    technologies, 36
Human Relations, 20, 334

IAPT see Improved Access to Psychological
    Therapies
IBF see International Balint Federation

IEDP see intensive experiential dynamic
    psychotherapy
ILEA see Inner London Education Authority
IMP see Institute of Medical Psychology
IMPACT Study, 40
Improving Access to Psychological Therapies (IAPT),
    40, 86, 180, 192
IMS see Institute of Marital Studies
Independent Psychoanalytic Child and Adolescent
    Psychotherapy Association (IPCAPA), 129
Individual Psychotherapy Workshop (IPW), 155
infant observation, 37, 96, 117–119
Inner London Education Authority (ILEA), 133, 140
Institute for Psychoanalytic Teaching and Research
    (IPTAR), 280
Institute of Marital Studies (IMS), 177 see Tavistock
    Relationships
Institute of Medical Psychology (IMP), 62 see also
    Tavistock Institute of Medical Psychology
    donations, 62–63
    leaders of, 63
Institute of Psychoanalysis, 68, 337
intellectualisation, 268
intensive experiential dynamic psychotherapy (IEDP),
    199, 201
intensive short-term dynamic psychotherapy
    (ISTDP), 200
Interdisciplinary Training in Adult Psychotherapy, 215
internal working model, 32
International Association of Couple and Family
    Psychoanalysis, 185
International Balint Federation (IBF), 80, 93
International Experiential Dynamic Therapy
    Conference, 201 see also experiential
    learning; intensive experiential dynamic
    psychotherapy
International Psychoanalytical Association (IPA), 185
International Society for the Psychoanalytic Study of
    Organizations (ISPSO), 280
International Society for the Study of Trauma and
    Dissociation (ISSTD), 306
International Study of Childhood Depression, 237
invisible college, 338
IPA see International Psychoanalytical Association
IPCAPA see Independent Psychoanalytic Child and
    Adolescent Psychotherapy Association
IPTAR see Institute for Psychoanalytic Teaching and
    Research
IPW see Individual Psychotherapy Workshop
Ishikawa, K., 26

ISPSO *see* International Society for the Psychoanalytic
    Study of Organizations
Israeli Balint group, 81–82 *see also* Balint groups
ISSTD *see* International Society for the Study of
    Trauma and Dissociation
ISTDP *see* intensive short-term dynamic psychotherapy

Jackson, D. D., 188
James Spence Medal, 60
Jaques, E., 21, 35
Jayyusi, S., 91
Johns, M., 141
Jordan, S., 243
Jowell, T., 9
Julian, P., 93
Jung, C. G., 337

Kahr, B., 66, 176
    and Tavi, 305, 309
Karen, R., 54
Karni, A., 81
Katz, I., 261, 263
Kavner, E., 24
Keats, J., 12
Kelvin, R., 40
Kennedy, H., 48
Keogh, T., 185
Kernberg, O. F., 303
Khaleelee, O., 329
Khan, S., 180
King, P., 32
Kjeldmand, D., 81
Klein, M., 151, 160 *see also Mrs Klein*
Klein, S., 153
Kleinian child analysis, 151
Knight, J., 149, 193
Kolvin, I., 40, 261, 262, 263
Kraemer, S., 32, 33, 51, 89, 110, 145, 147, 148,
    150, 331
Krantz, J., 279, 280
Krause, I. B., 193
Krupa-Flasinska, M., 192
Kuhn, T. S., 30

Lanman, M., 178, 179
Lassri, D., 179, 180
Launer, J., 84
Lawrence, K., 153
Lawrence, M., 39
Layard, R., 41

leadership, 289, 331
    from ego to eco, 294
    being accountable, 292
    co-creating structure, 294
    collective intelligence, 294
    developing narrative, 293
    enabling sense of purpose, 293
    Fourth Industrial Revolution, 291
    Great Person theory of leadership, 290
    leadership 4.0, 295
    leading in glass box, 292
    leaning into uncertainty, 293
    living in radical uncertainty, 293–294
    nudging the context, 294
    pluralise participation, 295
    required qualities, 291–292
    shaping context, 293
    shaping conversation, 294
    understanding, 290–291
    working with enemy, 292
    working with plurality, 292–293
Leaving Care Act, 257–258
Legg, C., 30
Leicester conferences, 12, 23
Leitch, I., 40, 261, 262, 263
Leith-Ross, S., 66
    and TIMP, 61, 62
Lemma, A., 235
Levy, A., 81
Lewin, K., 19, 34, 35
Lichtenstein, A., 80
Likierman, M., 39
Lindsay, M., 55, 60
Lobatto, W., 193
LOGIC *see* longitudinal outcomes of gender identity
    in children
London Child Guidance Clinic *see* Child Guidance
    Training Centre
Long, J., 263
longitudinal outcomes of gender identity in children
    (LOGIC), 43
Loughlin, B., 261, 263
Lousada, J., 23, 24, 218, 245
Lowe, F., 168, 243
Lowenfeld, Margaret, 68, 71
Lucas, R., 188
Luyten, P., 41
Lyon, L., 238, 240
Lyons, A. P., 176
Lyons-Ruth, K., 33

MacCarthy, D., 54, 55
MacQueen, F., 149
Mahaffey, H., 193
Main, T., 87, 138, 332
Mainprice, J., 177
Majid, S., 81
Malan, D. H., 38, 89, 200, 201
MALT *see* multi agency liaison team
Mandy, W., 153
Maoz, B., 81
Marmot, M., 336
Marris, P., 33
Martin, F. E., 149, 193
Matalon, A., 81
matrix, 25
Mattinson, J., 147, 177, 178, 184
Maughan, B., 33
McCann, D., 180
McDougall, J., 161
McPherson, S., 41, 215, 238
McQuown, N. A., 188
McWhinney, I., 81
MDT *see* multidisciplinary team
Mead, M., 334
medically unexplained symptoms (MUS), 144
medical model, 124
medical psychology, 62
Meier, R., 179
Meltzer, D., 42, 151, 152
    adhesive identification, 152
    dismantling, 152
    theoretical formulations, 151
mental health improvement, 3
    challenge, change, and sabotage, 3–9
    fundamental problem, 3
    illness rates in care in community, 5
    projective identification, 4
    psychiatrists, 4
    staff development systems, 7
    working with mentally ill, 6–7
Mentalization for Offending Adult Males (MOAM), 45
Menzies, I. E. P., 21, 35
    study, 22, 247, 252, 266–267
Mermaids, 163 *see also* gender identity issues
Mesie, J., 261, 263
Midgley, N., 40
Mielke, G. I., 269
Milan group of family therapists, 189–190 *see also*
        family therapy
Miles, G., 40, 242, 263

Military Testing Officer (MTO), 337
Miller, D., 37, 77
Miller, E., 49, 329
Miller, E. J., 21, 25, 36, 38, 39, 217, 278
Miller, L., 37, 119–120
Miller, L. L., 153
Milligan, Jeannie, 243, 309
Mind and Medicine Monographs, 83–84
minimum sufficient network, 145, 149
Minuchin, S., 145, 189
MOAM *see* Mentalization for Offending Adult Males
Money, J., 161
Moore, E. C., 30
Morgan, M., 178, 181, 184, 185, 186
Morris, I., 55
Morris, R., 81
Morrison, J., 336
MOSAIC, 153, 250
Mother Care for Children in Hospital, 57
mothers get together as pressure group, 57–58
Mrs Klein, 304
MTO *see* Military Testing Officer
Mulberry Bush Day Unit, 132–133
Mulley, S., 180
multi-agency liaison team (MALT), 250
multidisciplinary team (MDT), 146
multifactor theory of delinquency, 123
Murray, H., 17, 19, 20, 21, 31, 176, 277, 295, 332
Murray, J., 269
MUS *see* medically unexplained symptoms
Music, G., 33
Mwamba, N., 180
Myers, C. S., 330

Nathans, S., 185
National Association for the Welfare of Children in
        Hospital (NAWCH), 57, 58, 59
National Health Service (NHS), xi–xii, xvii, xix, 8,
        20, 24, 26, 32, 34, 39, 40, 45, 56, 68, 78, 95,
        97–100, 148, 149, 201, 206, 211, 216–217,
        234, 310, 333, 335
    and Community Care Act, 213
National Institute for Clinical Excellence (NICE),
        40, 41
National Institute for Health and Care Excellence
        (NICE), 239
National Institute for Health Research (NIHR), 43
Nationalised Coal Board (NCB), 333
National Workforce Skills Development Unit
        (NWSDU), 251

NAWCH *see* National Association for the Welfare of Children in Hospital

NCB *see* Nationalised Coal Board

NDUs *see* nursing development units

Nease, D. E., 80

Neumann, C. S., 274

NHS *see* National Health Service

NICE *see* National Institute for Clinical Excellence; National Institute for Health and Care Excellence

Nicholson, N., 140

NIHR *see* National Institute for Health Research

Northfield Experiments, 16, 26, 34, 270, 331 *see also* Tavistock initiative

nursing at Tavistock Clinic, 247, 253 *see also* Tavistock Clinic

    core nursing skills of engagement, 251

    Isabel Menzies' study of nursing, 247

    nursing practice development, 250–251

    nursing presence, 247–248

    skill recognition, 251

    strategic influence, 251–253

    training and conferences, 252

    training development for nurses, 248–250

nursing development units (NDUs), 252

NWSDU *see* National Workforce Skills Development Unit

Nyberg, V., 178

Obholzer, A., 12, 21, 23, 35, 217, 266–267, 296, 336

    "Anton's Progress", 224–226

    institutional observation, 26

    and Tavi, xi, xiii, 9, 14, 26, 65, 169, 170, 211, 215, 216, 222, 243, 281, 282, 299, 300, 303, 305, 306, 310

object

    constancy, 271

    relations, 18, 32, 234, 335

Observation Course, 97

occupational health, 4

Ogden, T. H., 268

Oksala, J., 31

Operation Phoenix, xii, xvi, 19, 31, 295, 332

Ord, J., 248

Orford, Eileen, 305, 309

Orkney child abuse scandal, 260 *see also* child protection and courts

Osborne, E., 96, 234

Osimo, F., 200

Owen, J., 193

paediatrics, 143

    core aspects of psychiatry training, 144–145

    family therapy programme, 144

    MDT, 145

    mental health in, 148–149

    Mental Health Team, 147

    minimum sufficient network, 145, 149

    participant anthropology, 145–146

    problematic cases, 146–147

    qualification, 144–145

    suicidal self-poisoning, 147, 149

    system around sick child, 145–146

Pailthorpe, G. W., 266

Palacios, E., 185

pantomimes, 178, 214, 309

    external consultation, 310–311

Papadopoulos, R., 97, 144, 236

Pape Cowan, C., 180

parent–infant psychotherapy, 109

    as dramatic and moving, 111

    health visitors, 113–114

    infant mental health, 114

    sleep problems, 110–111

    spreading the work, 113

    Standing by the Weighing Scales, 110

    trainings for work with under-fives, 113

    transitional object, 112

Parkes, C. M., 33

Parkinson, C., 245

Partridge, K., 192, 193

Patient and Public Involvement (PPI), 251

Paton, A., 263

Patrick, M., 33

Patrick, M. P., 33, 179

Pattman, R., 236

Pengelly, P., 178, 179, 247, 309, 311

Peper Harow Community, 282

personalised programmes for children (PPC), 43

Phoenix, A., 236

PHP *see* Practitioner Health Programme

Pichon-Rivière, E., 185

Pickett, K., 337

Pietroni, M., 89

Pincus, L., 177, 184

Pinho-Costa, L., 80

Pitt-Aitkens, T., 189

Placement Support, 283

Platt Report, 56–57 *see also* Robertson, J.

Polek, E., 180

Policy Seminars, 319–325
    Chatham House rules, 321
    psychodynamic systems, 319
Pollock, A. B., 21
Pooley, J., 21, 23, 35, 238
Portman Clinic, 238, 265
post-war civilian resettlement programme, 17–18 see
        also Tavistock initiative
Power Threat Meaning Framework, 239
PPC see personalised programmes for children
PPI see Patient and Public Involvement
practice-based conception of knowledge, 30
Practitioner Health Programme (PHP), 82, 93
Prata, G., 189
pre-war child guidance model, 67
primary sclerosing cholangitis (PSC), 44
projection, 268
projective identification, 4, 184, 268
PRUs see Pupil referral units
PSC see primary sclerosing cholangitis
psychiatrists, 4
    reasons for referral to, 90
psychiatry, 265
psychic survival mechanism, 271 see also autonomic
        countertransference
psychoanalytic approaches to autism, 151
    adhesive identification, 152
    autistic anxieties, 153
    Bion, 152
    dismantling, 152
    Kleinian child analysis, 151
    Meltzer's theoretical formulations, 151
    Tustin, 153
Psycho-Analytic Insights and Relationships, 215
Psychoanalytic Psychotherapy, 157, 211
psychoanalytic thinking
    courses, 283
    in organisational settings, 281–283
    Peper Harow Community, 282
    Placement Support, 283
psychology discipline, 233
    Camden's pupil referral unit, 235
    Community Psychology approach, 235
    consultancy and wider organization, 238–239
    Consulting to Individuals, Groups and
        Organisations, 236
    current picture, 239
    discipline strategy, 239
    Educational Psychology training, 236
    Educational Therapy, 234

    forms of assessment, 234
    Groups Workshop, 235–236
    innovations in clinical work, 234–236
    Power Threat Meaning Framework, 239
    publications by psychologists, 239
    research, 237
    Rorschach method, 234
    "Shared-Talk" project, 234
    Systemic Family Therapy training, 236
    Tavistock Consultancy Service, 238
    training, 236–237
psychopathy, 269, 270, 271, 273 see also autonomic
        countertransference; Hare Psychopathy
        Checklist
psychotherapeutic listening, 86
psychotherapy, 34, 61, 63, 86–89, 165, 167, 213, 281
    brief, 199–200, 209
    child, 43, 62, 68, 70, 96–97, 109, 113, 117, 125,
        126, 135, 137, 138, 144, 151, 165–166, 261,
        262, 283, 335
    couple, 65, 176, 178, 180, 184, 185
    group, 235
    individual, 229
    and nursing, 249–250, 253
    psychoanalytic, 41, 166, 206, 207, 213, 216,
        217, 235
    systemic, 190, 192, 235
publications on reactions to deaths, 105, 106
    doctors in stillbirth, 106
    Dr Emanuel Lewis's advent, 106–107
    mourning stillbirth, 105
Pupil referral units (PRUs), 140

Qualifying Course in Psychodynamic Psychotherapy
        see D58

Rabin, S., 81
Raine, A., 269
randomised controlled trial (RCT), 205
Ravenscroft, K., 38
RCPsych see Royal College of Psychiatrists
RCT see randomised controlled trial
reactions to deaths, publications on, 105
Reay, A., 180
Rees, J. R., 331
Reid, S., 37, 38, 42, 151
    and Tavi, 304
Reilly, J., 88
Rendall, S., 236
Renton, T., 176

research at Tavistock, 29
    attachment theory, 32
    current, 43
    developments in organisational theory, 36
    Dual Career Family, The, 35
    group relations and conferences, 39
    human technologies, 36
    infant observation, 37
    intergenerational trauma study, 44
    internal working model, 32
    knowledge and understanding, 29–30
    knowledge generation, 36
    learning from emotional experience, 36–38
    longitudinal outcomes of gender identity, 43
    mentalization for offending adult males, 44
    Michael Balint's group work with GPs, 38
    personalised programmes for children, 43
    practical institutional design, 31–33
    practice-based conception of knowledge, 30
    psychoanalytic supervision, 37
    psychological intervention in PSC wellbeing
        study, 44
    research collaborations, 44
    research doctorates, 42
    science and social purpose, 30
    single institutional study, 35
    Strange Situation Test, 32
    studies of outcomes of psychotherapies, 39–42
    systematic research, 33
    Tavistock's professional doctoral research
        programmes, 42–43
    therapeutic innovations, 38–39
    TIHR's research programme, 33–36
    unconscious defences against anxiety, 35
    work discussion, 37
research doctorates, 42
revulsion, 273
Reynolds, S., 40
Rhode, M., 38, 40, 45, 153–154
Rice, A. K., 21, 36, 39, 278
Rickman, J., 147, 149, 333
Rivers, W. H. R., 226, 330
Robb, J., 176
Roberts, C., 40
Roberts, J., 33
Robertson, J., 43, 47, 49, 50, 51, 52, 53, 55, 56, 57,
        58, 59, 60
    children in substitute care, 58–59
    contribution to improvement of child care, 59
    feeling control, 51–54

Mother Care for Children in Hospital, 57
    mothers get together as pressure group, 57–58
    Platt Report, 56–57
    in practice, 54–56
    psychological processes, 53
    relationship with Spence, 60
    Separation Research Unit, 48–51
Robertson, Joyce, 43, 48, 50, 51, 52, 53, 54, 55, 56,
        57, 58, 59
    and Hampstead Wartime Nurseries, 47–48
Roberts, V. Z., 12, 21, 23, 35, 296
Rock, B., 90, 216
Rolph, K., 261, 263
Rorschach method, 234
Rosenbluth, D., 52
Rosenthall, J., 218
Rost, F., 41, 215, 238
Royal College of Psychiatrists (RCPsych), 263
Rustin, M. E., 23, 24, 26, 37, 38, 40, 43, 96, 147
    and Tavi, 45, 113, 117, 149, 212, 214, 299, 338
Rustin, M. J., 16, 20, 21, 22, 23, 24, 25, 26, 30, 35, 37,
        43, 247, 296, 320
    and Tavi, 313, 321, 322, 323, 324, 325
Ruszczynski, S., 178, 185, 184

Sabatini Scolmati, A., 152
Sackin, P., 74, 79
Sadowski, H., 40, 261, 262, 263
Salinsky, J., 74, 79
Salter, L., 180
Salzberger-Wittenberg, I., 37, 215 see also
        Wittenberg, I.
Samuel, O., 74, 93
Savege Scharff, J., 185
Scaiola, C. L., 148
Schaefer, M., 185
Scharff, D. E., 185
Schoenberg, P., 81
Searles, H. F., 184
Selvini Palazzoli, M., 189
SEMH see social, emotional, and mental health
Senior, R., 40, 89
separation effect on children, 47 see also Robertson, J
Separation Research Unit, 48–51 see also Bowlby, J.;
        Robertson, J.
    Ainsworth, 50
    child's behaviour on returning home from
        hospital, 50
    detachment, 50
    first-hand observations, 50

medical and nursing staff, 49
    stages of protest, despair, and denial, 51
    studies about separation, 49
service for under-fives in child and family department, 117–119
Sethi, I., 192
Shapiro, E., 143, 279, 329
Sharifi, P., 91
Shaw, Mike, 309
Shephard, B., 331
Sher, M., 21, 88, 89
Shmueli, A., 180, 263
Shooter, A., 176
Shorer, Y., 81
short-term psychoanalytic psychotherapy (STPP), 40
Shuttleworth, A., 45
Shuttleworth, J., 37
Sigmundson, H. K., 162
Sinason, V., 306
single institutional study, 35
six minutes group, 78–79 see also Balint groups
Skogstad, W., 247
Skrine, R. (Ed.), 77
Skuse, D., 153
SLaM see South London and Maudsley hospitals
Smith, C. W. L., 88
Snodgrass, J., 123
Social Dreaming, 39
social, emotional, and mental health (SEMH), 137
social work and Tavistock, 241–245
    clinical social work, 241, 244
    management and leadership, 242–243
    poor self-esteem, 242
    "relationship based" social work, 245
    student body, 243
    Thinking Spaces, 243
    Trust's Gender Identity Development Service, 244
social workers, 241
socio-psychological dialogue, 22
socio-technical thinking, 277
SOE see Special Operations Executive
Sofer, C., 21, 39
Solomon, M., 235
Solomon, R., 245
Soreanu, R., 74
South London and Maudsley hospitals (SLaM), 249
Special Operations Executive (SOE), 202
Spector Person, E., 161
Sprince, J., 179, 309, 311
Stanford, R., 261, 263

Stapley, L. F., 279
Steele H., 32
Steer, C. D., 153
Steiner, J., 23, 38, 211, 212
Steiner, R., 32
Stein, M., 279
Stephens, J., 176
Stern, J., 90
Stevenson-Hinde, J., 33
stillbirth, mourning, 105–106
Stokes, J., 290, 292, 295–296, 331
Stoller, R. J., 160
STPP see short-term psychoanalytic psychotherapy
Strange Situation Test, 32, 33, 262
Stuart, M., 236
study of autism, 42 see also autism
Sturgeon, D., 81
subversive nonconformism, 333
suicidal self-poisoning, 147, 149
Swann, G., 243
systemic family therapy, 187 see also family therapy; psychotherapy, systemic
Szur, R., 38

TADS see Tavistock Adult Depression Study
Talking Cure (BBC), 150, 214, 227, 237, 299, 300
TAP see Team Around the Practice
Target, M., 40, 179, 180, 235
TAU see treatment-as-usual
Tavistock, 329 see Tavistock Institute of Medical Psychology; Tavistock Relationships
    and academic social sciences, 16
    clinic, 24–26
    Clinic for Functional Nervous Disorders, 61, 62
    Clinic Series, 313–317
    clinic workers, 88
    Consultancy Service, 238
    double dissonance, 16
    field theory, 19
    Functional Nervous Disorders, 63
    Gazette, 303–306
    group, 16
    initiatives during Second World War, 16–18
    internal saboteur, 17
    leadership, 331
    Mulberry Bush Day Unit, 132–133
    multidisciplinary reflections, 335–337
    NHS review of Tavistock's activity, 98
    Operation Phoenix, 19, 332–333
    orientation, 15

pantomimes, 178–179, 309–311
partnerships with senior local professionals, 99
Policy Seminars, 319–325
post-war ambition, 95
project after war, 18–23
psychoanalysis, social science, and, 15–27
publications from, 21
safe base, 334–335
socio-psychological dialogue, 22
socio-technical perspective, 20
Square Clinic, 63, 330
staff groups, 98–99
tradition, 184
tradition of egalitarianism, 336
Trauma Service, 223
turbulent environment, 23
TV programme, 299–300
to understand social practices, 21
Tavistock Adolescent Department, 155
Tavistock Adult Depression Study (TADS), 41,
    205–207, 215, 238
    depression, 206
    outcome findings, 205–206
    semi-structured interviews, 207
Tavistock Centre, 11, 95
    conferences in, 11–12
    Consulting to Institutions workshop, 12–13
    Leicester conferences, 12, 23
    Obholzer, 12
    societal pressures, 13
Tavistock Centre for Couple Relationships (TCCR),
    179 see also Tavistock Relationships
Tavistock Clinic, 175 see also nursing at Tavistock
    Clinic
    applications of psychoanalytic thinking, 281–283
    child psychotherapy training, 96
    core of, 97–98
    efforts to make links with London University, 98
    Observation Course, 97
    study groups, 96
    training and counselling provided in, 97
    training expansion, 99–101
    trainings within, 96
Tavistock Clinic Adult Department, 209
    Borderline Workshop, 210
    D58, 211
    patient assessment, 210–211
Tavistock Clinic and TIHR, 15
    Jaques' study, 21
    Menzies' study, 22

recruitment and training, 22
research studies, 21
Tavistock Community Unit see Community Unit
Tavistock Consulting, 19, 22, 24, 31, 238, 290
Tavistock initiative, 16
    Bion's own initiatives, 17
    Northfield Experiments, 16
    object relations theory, 18
    post-war civilian resettlement, 17–18
Tavistock Institute of Human Relations (TIHR), 15,
    333
Tavistock Institute of Medical Psychology (TIMP),
    61–66
Tavistock legacy in America, 277
    group relations, 278–279
    socio-technical perspective, 277–278
Tavistock Relationships (TR), 175–181
    collaborative projects, 184–185
    couple psychoanalysis, 183–185
    Denning Report of 1947, 176
    foundations, 176–177
    integration of elements, 181
    post-Kleinian perspective on internal world of
        couple, 178
    psychoanalytic clinical services, 180
    randomised control trial, 179–180
    research, 178, 179
    roots, 176
    social policy context, 176
    talking therapy to couples, 176
    Tavistock Pantomimes, 178–179
    training in couple psychoanalytic psychotherapy,
        184
    training the trainers consultative programmes,
        179
    transitions, 177–178
Taylor, D., 41, 207–208, 214, 215, 238
Taylor, H., 217
TCCR see Tavistock Centre for Couple Relationships
Team Around the Practice (TAP), 90, 93, 251
Temperley, J., 88, 89
tf-CBT see cognitive behavioural therapy
T-Groups (training groups), 39
Thanatophilia, 157
theory of container and contained, 70
Thinking Spaces, 243
Thomas, J., 57
Thomas, K., 337
Thomas, R., 41, 215, 238
Thompson, K., 181

Thorpe, C., 263
TIHR *see* Tavistock Institute of Human Relations
Tizard, B., 289
TR *see* Tavistock Relationships
training
    -cum-research seminars, 75
    expansion, 95–101
    the trainers, 179
transference, 37, 118, 200, 202, 259, 303, 337 *see also*
    countertransference
    negative, 118
    Workshop, 237
transitional object, 112
transsexualism, 160, 162, 163 *see also* gender identity
    issues
treatment-as-usual (TAU), 41
triangle of conflict, 199
triangle of persons, 199
Trist, E. L., 16, 17, 19, 20, 21, 31, 36, 39, 176, 277, 294,
    295, 332, 333
Trotter, W, 71
Trowell, J., 38, 40, 242, 261, 262–263
Tsiantis, J., 263
turbulent environment, 23
Turquet, P., 37, 77
Tustin, F., 152, 153

UCH *see* University College Hospital
UCLA *see* University of California at Los Angeles
UEL *see* University of East London
Under Fives Counselling Service, 113–114 *see also*
    service for under-fives in child and family
    department
University College Hospital (UCH), 93
University of California at Los Angeles (UCLA), 277
University of East London (UEL), 98, 157

Valentine, J. D., 179
Vespe, A., 89
Video-feedback Intervention to promote Positive
    Parenting (VIPP), 44, 239
Vincent, C., 178
VIPP *see* Video-feedback Intervention to promote
    Positive Parenting
Vorchheimer, M., 185

Waddell, M., 37, 336
    and Tavistock, 156, 212, 214, 337

War Office Selection Board (WOSB), 17, 331
wartime psychiatrists, 32
Watson, R., 193
WEA *see* Workers' Educational Association
Weakland, J. H., 188
Webb, S., 244
Weddell, D., 42, 151
Weeramanthri, T., 40, 261, 262, 263
Wehrmeister, F. C., 269
Weintrobe, S., 337
Welfare Settlement, 213
Wells, D., 248
White, A., 34, 338
White, K., 149, 193
Whyte, N., 38, 211
Widmer, B., 40
Wiener, J., 89
Wilkinson, P., 40
Wilkinson, R., 337
Williams, G., 38, 96, 155–158
Williams, M. H., 37
Williams, P., 38
Wilmott, S., 89
Wilson, A. T. M., 176
Winnicott, D. W., 49, 60, 112
Wittenberg, I., 42, 96, 151 *see also*
    Salzberger-Wittenberg, I.
    and Tavi, 155, 158, 170, 212, 304, 305
Wolfe, S., 161
Woodhouse, D., 37, 77, 178, 247
work discussion, 25, 37, 96
work groups, xii, xvi
Workers' Educational Association (WEA), 47
WOSB *see* War Office Selection Board

Yakeley, J., 81
Yelloly, M., 261, 263
young child observation, 37
Young, L., 168
Young People's Consultation Service *see* Young People's
    Counselling Service
Young People's Counselling Service (YPCS), 165–168,
    171
YPCS *see* Young People's Counselling Service

Zalidis, S., 85